Living Every
Second

TRACY EDWARDS

Living Every Second

CORONET BOOKS
Hodder & Stoughton

First published in Great Britain in 2001
First published in paperback in 2001
by Hodder and Stoughton
A division of Hodder Headline

A Coronet paperback

4 6 8 10 9 7 5

A CIP catalogue record for this title
is available from the British Library

ISBN 0 340 77043 0

Typeset in Bembo by Hewer Text Ltd, Edinburgh
Printed and bound in Great Britain by
Clays Ltd, St Ives plc

Hodder and Stoughton
A division of Hodder Headline
338 Euston Road
London NW1 3BH

For my daughter Mackenna

If I took every wonderful moment of my life; every achievement; every beautiful sunrise on an angry sea; every moonlit night on a silvery ocean; every moment of laughter; every triumph, and put them all together, they would be shadows to the joy and love I feel when I look at you.

ACKNOWLEDGEMENTS

I would like to offer sincere and heartfelt thanks to the following people, without whom this book would not have been written:

Mark Lucas – I was told that you were the best agent in Britain but what they didn't tell me was that you would be a dear friend, patient confidante and a damp shoulder! You have been all this to me and more.

Mike Robotham – you put up with me, got the words out of my head and made my life sound interesting!

Everyone at Lucas Alexander Whitley, with special thanks to Araminta for not letting me give up.

Everyone at Hodder who has worked so tirelessly and enthusiastically on this book. You gave my confidence back to me!

Claire Higgs who ran my life so efficiently for me, enabling me to write.

Ildiko Sarkadi who looked after Mackenna and remained calm when I was tearing my hair out!

Aisha Quirini who stepped into the breech and now runs my life! You are your mother's daughter.

Thank you to:

My wonderful family. Mum, Trevor, Gregor, Kerry, Kaia, Aunty Edna, Uncle Arthur, Aunty May, Uncle Alec, Janie and family. Sometimes I don't know how you put up with me, but you all do and are always there for me.

Mackenna's father – you gave me the greatest gift of all. She has your sweetness of nature already. Long may it last!

Fiona Brook, I'm sorry we wasted so much time. You have taught me that true friendship never ends. I am so happy to be a part of your life again. Thank you for your friendship, support, making me laugh, for being Mack's godmother and watching her come into the world. (Sorry about grinding your knuckles!)

Howard Gibbons for making *Maiden* happen and for always being there. You really are marvellous!

Suzy Mayhew, your friendship has been one of the most important things in my life and I know Mack will have in you a wonderful godmother.

Colin Moynihan for support during *Maiden* when no-one else was there and for agreeing to be Mack's wonderful godfather.

The crew of *Maiden* for taking that first precious step across the abyss and for just being absolutely fantastic!

The shore team of *Maiden* and everyone who helped make it happen.

The crew of *Royal & SunAlliance* for being the best female sailing team in the world. The dangers were many but you didn't falter.

The shore team of RSA and everyone who helped make it happen.

The sub sponsors of the Jules Verne Trophy and in particular: Freud Communications, Clarins, Fujifilm, Henri Lloyd, Computacenter, BT, Speedo, Vauxhall.

James Hayes and everyone at BBC Documentaries who believed nothing was impossible and made the documentary with integrity and enthusiasm.

The race committees and organisers who work so hard and often with little thanks, to make the races and challenges happen.

42nd Squadron at RAF Kinloss for the drop in the Southern Ocean (and the song).

Mike Noel-Smith for helping me pull my team together. And the Noel-Smith family for giving up so much, for believing that we could do it and for friendship.

To everyone at TEAM for joining up.

Anna and Paul Stevens and all my friends in Wales for laughter through the tears and support during the bad times.

Damian Foxall who stood me on my feet again.

Mike Corns and Jaynie Boys who believed in me and got me started.

All my skippers who have not only put up with me but who took the time and trouble to teach me and encourage me.

Andy Miller for getting us the *Royal & SunAlliance* sponsorship and for continued friendship.

Felix Dennis for friendship and great advice!

Mike Rees for believing in us. I'm sorry you were misled by certain people who shall remain nameless but I know what is true and will always be thankful to you.

All the wonderful and completely mad friends I have made in the sailing world whether racing or cruising. We had some good times and we had some great times!

All my friends in Reading who have always been there and now help me in the transition to motherhood and beyond!

Ali Ghandour and everyone at Royal Jordanian Airlines for sponsoring *Maiden* and for so much more.

Martin Booth, for pushing back the boundaries, for friendship and support.

Mike Jones and everyone at *Royal & SunAlliance* for sponsoring us and supporting us.

And finally I would like to say thank you to the wonderful man who changed my life. His Majesty King Hussein I of Jordan, I miss you so much, as do we all. I wish Mack could have known you. You made the world a better place.

So many people in my life have helped me, inspired me, offered me friendship and support and a boot up the backside when I needed it. I have been so lucky. I would like to thank all of you and if through lack of space I have omitted you here, please forgive me and know that my thanks go out to you. You know who you are!

I would like to say a very special thank you indeed to The Royal Bank of Scotland. In today's fast and furious world of banking, where most people feel as if they are treated as numbers and not individuals, The Royal Bank of Scotland holds on to its values and cares about its customers. The fact that they treated the Jules Verne Challenge as they would any business made it possible for us to get to the start line.

PANGBOURNE, BERKSHIRE
6 AUGUST 1998

A CCORDING to the ultrasound I have an all-female crew on board. They can't be 100 per cent certain, of course, but the images were pretty clear. A girl. I'm glad.

I still can't quite believe this is happening to me. It is so unexpected and so wonderful.

I felt quite anxious about the ultrasound. I lay on the table at St Margaret's Hospital in Windsor and unbuttoned my top. Fiona, my best friend and an expectant godmother, sat beside the table smiling at me reassuringly. She had already been through this twice herself and knew what to expect. I was so glad to have her there.

'Sorry we don't warm this up,' the operator said, as she squeezed a splodge of gel on to my stomach.

'How many weeks?'

'Twenty.'

'Is it your first?'

I nodded.

The sonar device felt cool on my stomach as it smeared through the gel. I suddenly had this waking nightmare about there being nothing inside me. No baby. Maybe it's simply indigestion, or water retention. I've stopped eating Brie and drinking coffee for no reason. How embarrassing!

'Someone's awake,' she said, glancing at the screen.

It took me a few seconds to single out the grainy image from the black screen. Then it rapidly fell into place. 'Oh, my God. It's a baby. Will you look at that!' I couldn't hold back my tears. Even Fiona began crying although she later denied it, claiming something had lodged in her eye. Yeah right!

'Can you see the curve of the spine? And the little heart beating.'

'It's moving,' I said incredulously. 'I can see it moving.'

She smiled. 'See its little hand up there, near its cheek? Maybe it's waving at us.'

By then I was incapable of intelligent speech. I watched the screen, wide-eyed, and realised that TV would never be the same again.

The photographs of the ultrasound are now sitting on the kitchen table. I keep looking at them and grinning. Worse still, I can actually see how easily I could become one of those baby bores, only I'm starting four months early.

For years I have listened to women go on about babies and thought: Oh, my God why don't they get a life? Haven't they got anything else to talk about?

Pregnant friends used to say, 'You get this overwhelming feeling of love for something that is not even a person yet.'

And I'd think: How weird. I even went so far as to imagine they were simply trying to make themselves feel better, or convince themselves they were going to love this thing inside them.

I was perhaps the ultimate cynic when it came to children. I used to try to stop myself saying things like, 'I love children but I could never manage a whole one.' It would come out of my mouth automatically and mothers would just as automatically clutch their offspring a little closer.

I admit I was wrong. This *is* something that takes over your life. It's like flipping a switch. Suddenly, every thought is prefaced or punctuated by the bump in front of you.

In the past five months I have learned more about the subject than the sum total of my previous thirty-six years. Admittedly, this is due to my having subconsciously managed to avoid babies and children for all this time. Now I find myself actually looking into prams or staring at children. What planet do they come from? Do they come in peace?

I now have a shelf of well-thumbed pregnancy books and a collection of videos. Like everything else in my life, I'm approaching this with wholehearted determination and enthusiasm. I'm not going to be ambushed. I'll be ready.

Who am I kidding?

I can't shake off this feeling of how unnatural it all seems, to have something growing inside of me, taking what it needs. In one of my videos the narrator says the only other living thing which can take over a body so completely is cancer. There's a comforting thought.

I've always trusted my body until now. Now it's deserting me. That's why I oscillate between delirious joy and absolute terror. It's not that I ever question whether I want this baby or not. Instead I worry about whether I'm going to be a good mother. Not many people around me have children. How will I know what to do? I think I've held two babies in my entire life. Both of them at arm's reach. 'Oh God, it's crying. Want it back?'

The most terrifying part for me is going to be straight after the birth. The labour doesn't frighten me at all. I'm quite looking forward to it. That's the competitor in me. It's like an endurance test that I have to pass.

The first hour of being a mother fills me with so much terror that if I think about it too much I start to lose it. I know it's a selfish fear. I hate being embarrassed in front of other people. This has always been one of my big horrors in life – having people laugh at me, or see that I don't know what I'm doing.

That's why I'm going to have to ban everyone from the room for that first hour. I'll be so unsure of myself that I don't want people to see me.

For the moment, I'm trying not to think about it. Instead I worry about refined sugars, artificial additives, processed meats, mayonnaise and nicotine withdrawal. Oh, and I'm also trying to buy a house and sell this one, as well as run a company. I must be mad.

I haven't mentioned 'the father'. It's not something I want to talk about except to make known that he isn't here and I'm not upset. We had a wonderful six-month relationship. Both of us hoped it would go further but it wasn't meant to be. We made the decision to break up before I discovered I was pregnant.

I came home from a holiday and had an inkling. Normally I'm as regular as clockwork – bang on the dot, 11 a.m. today. Only it wasn't today, or the next day.

I sent Claire, my indestructible PA, out to get a pregnancy test. I couldn't quite believe this was happening. 'Do I want to be pregnant?' I asked myself. 'The timing is lousy . . .'

The first test was inconclusive, which is quite unusual. Normally they are very accurate. Claire and I stared at the test strip and both agreed that only one line was showing.

So I tried again the next day. No mistake. The second line came up. Claire was leaping around the office, bursting with excitement. Her infectiousness was catching. I felt ecstatic, I mean completely and utterly full of joy. Then a split second later, I thought: Oh, my God. What have I done?

That was the start of a rollercoaster ride of emotions that lasted two months. One minute I was up, and the next down. Six or seven times a day I changed my mind about how I felt about the baby. A lot of that came down to not knowing how people were going to take it.

Single parenthood is fairly acceptable these days, but I'm actually quite old-fashioned about such things and I kept judging myself.

I swore Claire to secrecy. I didn't want to tell anyone until I had decided exactly how I felt about it. Two weeks later, I broke the news to my brother Trevor, my cousin Gregor and his partner Kerry. I didn't tell Mum for a bit longer. First I wanted to inform the father and find out what he planned to do. I knew people were going to ask about him and I wanted to have all the answers.

In a perfect world children would grow up with two loving parents. Unfortunately, we don't live in a perfect world. If given the choice, of course I'd like my daughter to have a father. I don't want her growing up with the influence of only one person in her life. I know what that's like. It happened to me when I was very young. That's why I feel trapped between my need for independence and my need to provide my daughter with a whole family. It feels like a lesson of some kind. A reminder that we can't change nature.

The most precious thing I own is a tape recording of my father's voice. He's reciting my times tables for me, so that I can learn them parrot fashion. 'One times two is two. Two times two is four. Three times two is six . . .'

That's how I know my tables today – although I still have to go through the whole table to get to the number I need. I was never much good at maths.

I have very few pictures of Dad because he was always behind the camera. It's the same with the cine-camera footage from my childhood. The grainy black and white images, flecked with age, show me playing in the garden and at the beach. I'm such a little madam, tossing my pigtails and smiling coyly at the camera.

As the footage continues, details change. Children grow up, their clothes are different, rooms are redecorated and more candles appear on the birthday cakes. Although Dad is never visible, he's always there. A hidden heart to the family.

I only have to see the way I respond to him to know this is true. He was the centre of my world.

I've been thinking a lot about this lately. I've been researching my family tree and going back over the photo albums. Perhaps this is natural.

In many ways this book is part of the same process. I used to think I'd wait until I was old and grey before writing my autobiography. But now it seems important to write things down in case I forget them. If Dad had known what was going to happen to him, would he have left more than just the tape?

But I'm getting ahead of myself. I should take you back to the very beginning; to 5 September 1962, and the corridor of Battle Hospital in Reading where Mrs Patricia Edwards awaited her own arrival. She, too, carried an all-female crew.

ONE

I CAME into the world feet first in the midst of the Cuban Missile Crisis – the closest the world has ever come to nuclear war. As Khrushchev and Kennedy huffed and puffed, my mother did the same on a trolley outside the delivery suite.

She has a vivid memory of looking down and seeing me coming, 'Oh, my God, it's happening! It's happening!'

The nurse kept telling her, 'Hang on, Mrs Edwards, hang on.'

'I can't hang on.'

I kept coming, feet to the fore, sending nurses and doctors into a whirl.

Of course, Dad had disappeared off to the pub. In those days there was none of that touchy-feely stuff about fathers being present for the birth. He had a pint in one hand and a cigar in the other – celebrating with Uncle Arthur and Uncle Alec, my Mum's brothers.

Something must have gone wrong in the delivery suite. Perhaps the cord was wrapped around my neck, or I wasn't breathing properly. The midwife whisked me away. I was transferred to another hospital and Mum spent two days fearing the worst. None of the doctors would tell her what had happened. Those were the days when mothers didn't need to know such details.

I've heard this story countless times from Mum. I used to make all the right noises, without really understanding what the fuss was about. Now I appreciate what she went through. The thought of it brings me out in a cold sweat.

After two days in intensive care, I was brought back to her. As she tells the story, I was everything a first-born baby should be – lots of dark hair, huge dark eyes and a pleasant temperament. Boy, was that to change!

So much snow fell that year that all the cine-camera footage shows the village of Purley, Berkshire as a winter wonderland. Our car is half buried in the driveway and there are snowmen on every street corner. Mum has an amazing bouffant hairdo, bobby socks and dresses that are cinched at the waist. She truly is beautiful.

Patricia Bint was a dancer when she met my father. She had performed all over the world, ballet and modern, at venues from India to Italy and beyond.

Anthony Herbert Edwards, nine years her senior, was a radio engineer, who had started his own electronics company. He also ran an electrical shop in Reading with his older brother Roy. He was very handsome with dark hair and a gentle manner.

Mum and Dad met on the car rallying circuit when both of them were competing. Mum also raced in karts and rode her brother's Triumph Tiger motorcycle. She always joked that the first present my father gave her was a spare tyre for her car. And they say romance is dead?

When I hear people talking about my dad, he seems like a completely different person to the one I remember. My uncles tell stories of his sense of humour and his rallying exploits. The man I knew was so quiet and gentle he seemed capable of becoming invisible – just like in the cine reels. Although he was full of love and affection, he didn't know how to show it. A lot of men of his era were uncomfortable with hugs and kisses.

We lived in an old converted coach house in Purley, that my parents spent four years renovating. The stables were underneath, with exposed beams and damp cobblestone floors. It's strange how a child's mind views the world. My earliest memory is of feeding the horses and using stiff brushes to groom their coats. My cousin Gregor has precisely the same memory, just as vivid as mine. Unfortunately, it simply didn't happen. The horses were long gone by the time we arrived, or perhaps they were an invisible presence.

My brother Trevor arrived three years after me and I never let him forget it. I was always louder and more aggressive. It wasn't jealousy, I loved him desperately and I would push his pram around the garden, doting on him. But we were like chalk and cheese. In spite of that, or maybe because of it, we were always very close. I was loud, outgoing and full of myself. Trevor was thoughtful, quiet and gentle. Everyone used to call him 'the professor'.

Purley was a lovely little village, surrounded by countryside that seemed to start at our back door. Uncle Arthur and Auntie Edna had built their own bungalow almost next door to the coach house and my cousins Gregor and Graeme would come and play with us. Late on summer evenings, we'd still be running wild in the fields and not get home until after dark. I ran the four of us like a troop commander – organising the games and making up the rules. We were the 'Fantastic Four' – saving the world on a daily basis. I was the Invisible Girl, Graeme the Rubber Man, Trevor the Human Torch and Gregor the Thing.

Although our heroes came from comic books and cartoons, we didn't watch much television. Dad believed that children should make their own entertainment. As a result we began staging our own reviews, writing sketches and songs for an open-air performance in the back garden. The entire village was invited – much to Mum's dismay. At fifteen minutes' notice, I'd be asking her to do squash and biscuits for everyone.

We also put on jousting tournaments and fought on broomstick horses. Elaborate helmets were constructed to be worn by the knights. One memorable example was a copper coal bucket with a mauve plastic bottle of bubble bath in the shape of a dolphin stuck on the top with a peacock feather coming out of the hole.

'I shall be the Earl of Godolphin,' I announced, as I slipped the helmet over my head.

'But you have to be Lady Guinevere,' declared Trevor. 'She's a girl.'

'I'm not going to be Lady Guinevere. I want to be a knight.'

'Girls can't be knights,' argued Gregor.

'Yes, they can.'

'They can't.'

'I don't care.'

A feminist at the age of seven, I settled the argument in a joust. I won, of course – as I normally did. I hated losing.

All proceeds from our performances were given to Mother Teresa in Calcutta. The coins were sealed in an envelope and posted to a far-off place where children didn't complain about eating broccoli and Brussels sprouts, because they had precious little to eat at all.

We were Roman Catholics and I was brought up with an unquestioning belief in God. Although we didn't go to church every week, there was Sunday School and bedside prayers every night.

'A prayer is not a wish list,' my mum would say. 'It's not a, "Dear God, I want a new bike and an A in my maths test tomorrow". You can't ask God to change things. Instead, you ask him for the courage so that *you* can change them.'

It's a lesson that I've never forgotten.

Mum was always thinking up new and exciting ways for us to spend our time. She had a wonderful sense of fun and adventure. Housework could always wait: perfect days were for picnics by the river or expeditions to Windsor Safari Park. We were never alone. All my friends sussed out very quickly that my family had fun. That's why our car was always full of other people's children on weekends.

All the women in my family have been strong characters. None more so than my grandmother, Jean Foy-Hooks, who is like a rock that anchored my family and weathered every storm. When I started doing my family tree I discovered she had been christened Jane and not Jean. She also lied about her age. No wonder it took so long to find her birth certificate.

She is the most enduring memory from my childhood because I saw her almost every day after school and at weekends. She was quite a small woman, with snow-white hair. Her fringe was yellowed by nicotine from the cigarette hanging out of her mouth. She would shut one eye to keep the smoke out as she chatted away and the ash grew longer. The corners of her mouth were stained with brown spittle from eating Victory Vs – a stronger version of Fisherman's Friends. One of those things could blow the top of my head off, but Grandma ate them constantly. And each time she kissed me, it left a stain on my cheek.

I never saw her wear anything other than her spotless white nurse's uniform, starched to within an inch of its life. She swore like a trooper, but in a very ladylike way. I know that sounds impossible, but somehow she managed it. At the same time, she invented a whole early life for herself, which I never doubted.

Grandma talked of her mother as being a great lady. There were wonderful stories of garden parties, county fairs and summer holidays at the beach – all told in a lilting Scottish accent.

It wasn't until years later, when I began researching my family tree, that I discovered the truth. In reality, my grandmother was one of seven children, each born at a different address. Three of them died soon after birth. Her father swept out mines for a living (putting him lower down the food chain than even the miners) and her mother worked in a rubber coat factory.

I went up to Markinch with Trevor not long ago to see where my grandmother was born. The countryside is bare and bleak, scarred by the mines and years of neglect. I didn't have an address for the house. I doubt if it still exists.

The village must have been a flourishing place before the mine closed down and ripped out its heart. Now it seemed grimy and unloved. Windows were boarded up and coal dust was etched into the brickwork.

I don't know why my grandma felt she had to lie about her past. Perhaps she was embarrassed by the poverty. She moved away from Scotland and came down to Reading to do nursing. That's where she met my grandfather, George Frederick Bint, who was a jockey's valet in Newmarket. It seemed to be almost a marriage of convenience, according to Mum. She couldn't remember any real love or affection between her parents. Instead, they seemed to be good friends.

George spent a lot of the time away at various race meetings, where he gambled too much. Grandma fought hard to make sure that Alec, Arthur and Mum had things that she didn't have. She ran her own nursing home in Reading in a big old house with dozens of rooms and hiding places. Everywhere smelt of polish.

The larder was an Aladdin's cave, cram-packed with jams, biscuits and jars of sweets. In the sitting room was a cupboard about the size of a phone box. This became our Tardis in *Dr Who* games.

'I'm Dr Who.'

'You can't be. You're a girl,' declared Trevor. 'You have to be his assistant.'

'Dr Who can so be a girl.'

'No he can't!'

'Yes he can! He transforms!'

Of course I won again. Poor Trevor, it's a wonder he ever played with me.

Grandma kept the house spotlessly. She polished the brass front of the steps every single day of her life. These are my strongest memories of her, along with the image of Christmas mornings, when the table in the sitting room would be weighed down with presents.

I didn't realise then just how lucky we were. Most of the presents were from Grandma. Perhaps she was trying to make up for the empty Christmas mornings of her youth.

Dad's family was from Wales and was dominated by train drivers and miners. There was, however, a master mariner among them – my great-grandfather, Lewis Williams who was from Merthyr Tydfil in the valleys. He probably sailed on the coal ships coming out of Newport and Swansea at the turn of the century.

My grandfather Lewis John Edwards was a fighter pilot in the First World War and a radio engineer afterwards. He put the first radio system into a public place in Britain, at Battle Hospital in Reading. This led to the first hospital radio station.

Dad was born above the electrical shop in Reading. The building is still there, only now it's a computer store.

The old stables under the coach house were turned into Dad's office and workshop. He disappeared down there each morning and built speakers for stereos and public address systems. This was before the Japanese and Germans had discovered the electronics market and people still bought British.

Each new advance in technology brought great delight to my father, because of the pleasure it could give to others. We were the first family in Purley to have a colour TV set and Dad would invite neighbours around to marvel at it – not out of boastfulness, but because he wanted to share his enjoyment. Another of his great loves was listening to sport on the radio and the house was constantly awash with singing from the terraces at Twickenham or polite applause from Lords.

The other abiding sound of my early childhood was classical music. Dad had built himself a highly sensitive stereo system and would play the music at full volume while sitting in his black leather armchair with his eyes closed and his head resting back.

Trevor and I once made the mistake of running across the sitting room and causing the needle to jump. We never did it again.

Each weekend, Dad held impromptu classical music appreciation sessions. Trevor, Gregor, Graeme and I would be forced to sit still for what seemed like hours but was probably only twenty minutes. I was bored rigid yet my love of classical music is one of the most precious gifts my father gave me. All these years later, if I want to feel truly close to him, I put Rachmaninov's *Lentamente* from *Vocalise* Op.34 Nr. 14 on the stereo. I close my eyes and I'm back there, in that sitting room, listening to the music and watching Dad, with his eyes closed and his fingers lightly tapping.

It was in that same room, on 20 July 1969, that we watched Neil Armstrong step on to the moon. Trevor and I were squeezed on either side of Dad in his leather armchair.

'I want you both to remember this,' he said. 'History is being made at this moment.'

One afternoon at Grandma's house, Dad pulled out a tape recorder – his latest gadget. I must have been about seven and Trevor, five. The conversation is etched into my mind because I've heard it so often.

'What's that?' I ask him.

'It records the noises that you're making.'

'What noises?'

'Well, right now it's picking up the sound of you eating that banana.'

'Oh Daddy,' I say, laughing.

Then Grandma starts singing 'Away in a Manger,' which is hilarious because she forgets the words and just makes them up as she goes along.

Trevor tries to ask something, but Dad can't understand him. Until he was six or seven years old, Trevor had speech problems and I used to translate for him. Mum made a real effort, but other people just pretended they understood what he said. Not surprisingly, Trevor would get frustrated, throwing tantrums and banging his head against the wall.

On the tape, Dad is encouraging him to speak more clearly and the three of us are talking. I've heard this tape countless times and I never get tired of listening to Dad's voice. It's all that I have left of him – a voice from across the years – and it's better than any photograph or silent home movie.

I can hear him now. 'Four twos are eight, five twos are ten, six twos are twelve . . .'

Our neighbour was Richard Cole, the road manager of Led Zeppelin. At the age of eight, I was convinced that I'd die if he didn't marry me.

He wore leather jackets and had long hair, with a beard. He also rode a chopper motorbike that sounded like a 747 when it took off. Richard's house was a playground, full of pool tables and pinball machines with the money slots taken out. The walls were decorated with gold and platinum records.

His parties were legendary. They went on for days. Music rattled the window frames and people arrived at odd hours. The village should have been scandalised by having a wild rocker in its midst – what with the drugs and the orgies – but nobody batted an eyelid.

Trevor and I were always round at Richard's house, sitting on his motorbike or playing with his latest games. He had a dog called Mot (I didn't know what the word meant at that stage) and it smelt of Richard's aftershave. I was always following it around and hugging it, burying my face in its fur.

Our jousting tournaments in the back garden were open to visitors. One afternoon we entertained all of Led Zeppelin there, with Jimmy Page playing Lady Guinevere and Robert Plant as Sir Lancelot. I giggled at how silly adults could be as I fell more in love with Richard.

At school that year I made a stuffed cat with a long tail which stopped winter draughts from coming beneath the door. It was a patchwork cat, with buttons for eyes and one ear that had gone slightly askew.

Having lavished so much care and attention on the project, I decided to give it to Richard as a Christmas present.

There was a party going on when I arrived. I could hear the thump of the music as I shuffled nervously at the door. I clutched the stuffed cat beneath my arm, its tail almost dragging on the ground.

I realised immediately that I shouldn't be there.

The door opened. It was Mary, Richard's sweet and gorgeous girlfriend.

'Hello, Tracy.' She gave me a lovely smile.

'Oh . . . look . . . um . . . I'm sorry . . . I . . . I was going to give this to Richard. But I'll come back.'

'No, no, come in. He's upstairs.'

The place was heaving. A guy with dreadlocks and no shirt was balancing a champagne bottle on his forehead and walking on his knees. There were hot, sweating bodies everywhere and strange-smelling cigarettes. An eight-year-old walking through, holding a stuffed cat didn't raise an eyebrow.

Mary took me up the stairs, chatting to me about school and horses. Richard was in the bedroom, with a dozen or so people, mellowing out.

This is a really bad idea, I thought. I don't want to be here.

'Look what Tracy made for you for Christmas,' announced Mary.

The room stopped.

Mary nudged me forwards and I held out my poor stuffed cat, with its wonky ear and elongated tail. Richard accepted my gift with enormous grace. Then he held it aloft, showing everybody. I thought I might die of embarrassment.

Dad took me sailing for the first time that summer. He had a mate called David Merry who used to sail out of Hayling Island.

We arrived in the morning and spent an hour getting the boat ready. I was quite excited, although a little nervous. Despite the swimming lessons, I wasn't confident in the water. Trevor was too young to be scared. He looked like a junior Michelin Man in his life-vest.

I had never thought of Dad as a sailor, but apparently he went a lot before we were born. He cast off and we motored away from the dock. As the mainsail rose, so did the noise of flapping canvas and the groaning of ropes on the winches.

The yacht was only 25 feet long and the seas were calm. We set off for the Isle of Wight and within minutes Trevor and I were as sick as dogs. He had just eaten a Tyne & Brand steak and kidney pie which made great burly.

I hung over the side, with Dad's hand gripping the back of my life-vest so I didn't fall overboard. This is death, I thought. Forget the humiliation of stuffed cats and rock stars – I'd rather die of embarrassment any day than go through this.

By the time we reached the Isle of Wight I had decided to live there for the rest of my life.

'I don't want to go back. Just leave me here,' I pleaded. 'I'll be fine by myself.'

Of course that didn't happen. I was forced back on to the boat where I died all over again. I vowed never to step on to another boat as long as I lived.

What short memories people have!

TWO

I COULDN'T decide whether I wanted to be a ballerina or a showjumping star. My ballet lessons had started at the age of three. Mum was teaching at the Phyllis Kedge School of Dancing, her old alma mater in Reading. Mrs Kedge was still there, cajoling another generation to pirouette and plié.

Every year I entered the Sunshine Dancing Competition, a highlight of the dancing calendar. Even now I cringe when reminded of how I dressed up as Peter Rabbit and sang 'Why do I do it?' or performed a Norwegian traditional dance in full Scandinavian costume.

Horses were my other great love, along with Donny Osmond. Dad always said that my perfect Christmas gift would be Donny Osmond riding a horse. Instead, I had to make do with posters on my bedroom wall.

I had weekly riding lessons at a local stables. I made Trevor come too, although he hated it. He has never really been a strong advocate of going near anything that bites and kicks for no apparent reason. In every picture we have of the two of us on ponies, I look supremely happy and Trevor appears to have been glued to the saddle as a form of torture.

We both went to Highlands Primary School – a happy place, full of all our friends. I loved school then. It was a natural extension of my perfect life. People often wear rose-tinted glasses when looking back on their childhoods, but mine truly did seem to be like a breakfast cereal commercial.

I don't know if Trevor felt the same way. He was sent to St Andrews, a nearby private boys' school, at the age of eight. Apparently the doctors thought he might start talking properly if he was dragged away from Mum's apron strings. I think he found it very difficult at first. People couldn't understand what he was saying and he missed home dreadfully. He began as a day student and didn't start boarding until he turned twelve.

I had dreams of being an actress or a prima ballerina and decided I wanted to go to an arts school. At the age of ten I began auditioning for various stage schools, including Arts Educational at Tring in Hertfordshire.

Although it rarely showed, Mum was fighting a constant battle with Multiple Sclerosis. She'd been diagnosed before she became pregnant with me. Back then her symptoms were very minor. She had pins and needles in her hands and occasionally felt dizzy or tired. At first the doctors didn't know what to make of this. MS was still relatively unknown. After dozens of tests and various theories, the sad truth became known. My earliest memory of her illness was when a nurse showed me how to inject Mum in case she couldn't do it. She had bruises all over her legs from the needles and it upset me because I knew it must have been painful.

She never tried to hide her illness from Trevor or me. Instead, when she lost her balance she'd make a joke about looking drunk. This was her way of making us feel better.

Grandma became ill that winter. For all her strength and apparent invincibility, she couldn't hold back the clock. In the end they had to sell the old people's home because she couldn't carry on. They bought her a bungalow in Purley, close to the rest of the family.

But it wasn't for Grandma. She spent her whole life looking after other people and was too independent to let others do the same for her. She went downhill pretty fast from there – becoming old and frail.

Up early one morning, I couldn't find Mum in the kitchen and went looking for her. She was in the bedroom, putting on her tights.

'I have some bad news,' she said. 'I'm afraid that Grandma died last night.'

It didn't come as a shock. I guess we'd been forewarned. But as I watched Mum calmly get dressed and brush her hair, I marvelled at how quiet and composed she seemed. Every movement was studied and correct – like the dancer she was, she moved through a perfectly choreographed routine. This is how she held herself together.

I don't remember Grandma's funeral, although it was the first time I heard someone request no flowers; instead she wanted the money to go to charity. Funny the things you remember.

About nine months later, I woke in the middle of the night. My feet were on my pillow and my head towards the end of the bed. As I sorted myself out and slid back beneath the blankets, I heard Mum screaming. I sat up and listened.

My bedroom was across the hall and Trevor's room was next to mine. I could hear Mum saying Edna's name – obviously talking to Auntie Edna.

What had happened? I knew it was terrible. She was shouting, 'Hurry up. Hurry up.'

I sat on the edge of my bed, staring at the thin strip of light beneath the door. The darkness of my room was impenetrable. I didn't know what had happened, but I knew it was something important.

I could hear it in Mum's voice, muffled and broken by sobs. Something awful was unfolding in front of me, but I couldn't open the door. We weren't allowed to leave our rooms at night – that was a family rule. We had to stay there until Mum or Dad came to get us up in the morning.

I didn't hear anything for a long while. Then I heard Mum

crying. I still wouldn't move. I couldn't. Instead, I hugged my knees and rocked back and forth on my bed.

My life was changing and I didn't know why. Willing myself to be brave, I padded across the floor. Grasping the door handle, I opened it a crack. Auntie Edna was standing outside. She motioned for me to get back inside my room. She didn't mean to snap. I could see she was upset. So was I. I just wanted to know what was happening.

I closed the door and waited. There were more voices – people I didn't recognise; heavy footsteps on the stairs; tyres crunching on the gravel outside.

I don't know how long I waited. It seemed like hours. Finally the door opened and Mum came into my room. She was silhouetted against the light, so I couldn't see her face at first. She sat on the bed and took my hands. She looked so incredibly composed.

'Something really bad has happened,' she said, brushing hair from my eyes. 'There is no easy way to tell you. Daddy has had a heart attack. The ambulance couldn't get here in time. He has died.'

I knew what 'died' meant. She didn't have to explain that to me. Strangely, I felt absolutely no emotion at all. It was as though I lost a father quite regularly; or perhaps those hours in the darkness had given me time to comprehend that something terrible had happened.

Daddy wouldn't be there in the morning, sitting at the kitchen table, eating toast and drinking his cup of tea. The rational part of me understood this, but emotionally it hadn't registered.

'Do you want to go and say goodbye?' said Mum.

I nodded.

She led me by the hand to their bedroom. I am glad she did that. My father lay on the bed, dressed in his pyjamas.

They've made an awful mistake, I thought. He's just asleep. He looked so peaceful that I didn't want to wake him. I gave him a kiss on the cheek and it was cool. Not cold, just cooler than normal.

Then I came back out and went into the sitting room. There were lots of people there, mainly relatives – Uncle Arthur, Auntie Edna, Uncle Alec and Auntie May. The ambulance arrived to take Dad's body and they closed the door so I wouldn't see anything.

I was ten years old and didn't understand the protocol or process of grieving.

'Would anyone like an omelette,' I announced, as if that would make everything all right.

'Perhaps some more tea, instead,' suggested Edna.

When the ambulance had gone, Mum came back to the sitting room. I sat on her lap, leaning my head against her shoulder.

'Now Daddy's gone, I'm going to look after you,' I told her.

'Thank you, dear,' she whispered, squeezing my hand.

My father's death was unexpected to everyone except perhaps himself. In the aftermath we discovered that he'd been given two warnings from his doctor about his heart condition. He hadn't told Mum. Nor had he cut down on butter or stopped smoking and drinking.

Dad went through two packs of Senior Service untipped every day. To make matters worse, his family had a history of heart disease. Very few of the men survived past forty-five. Trevor, be warned!

Throughout all of that night's drama, Trevor had slept soundly. Mum told him the next morning, but he had no concept of what had happened. For days he kept asking, 'When is Daddy coming home?'

At the funeral in Purley the priest asked us to choose a spot in the cemetery for Dad's ashes. We decided on a place beneath a tree by a stone wall.

Mum didn't want us to wear black to the service so I wore a mauve dress with tiny white flowers on it. We sat in the front row in the church as they carried the coffin inside. For the first time Mum's perfect veneer of calmness cracked. Her shoulders crumpled forward and she dissolved into a flood of tears. As the coffin went past, she reached out, calling 'Tony'. It broke my heart.

I didn't appreciate how young she was then and how much in love she'd been with my father. They were soul mates. She was thirty-seven years old, widowed with two young children. Nothing would ever be the same.

I can't remember missing my dad, although I miss him desperately now. The impact of losing someone takes a long while to affect me. It's as though I convince myself that they're on a holiday, or simply away. This is easier because I have a lot of friends I don't see for months, or even years at a time. It's a legacy of sailing and knowing people all around the world.

Several months after Dad's death, I came home from school to find a note that Mum had pinned to the front door. 'Welcome home, Tring school girl.'

I'd been accepted into Arts Educational – the boarding school that specialised in drama and dance. I looked around to find Dad. I knew he'd be so proud. Then I realised that he wasn't there. Dad's business had been quite successful and as long as it continued to flourish our family was reasonably well off. For the time being, at least, we had enough money to send me to Arts Educational.

And so, on a Monday morning in early September 1974, Mum drove me through the school gates. She had helped me pack my suitcase and given me a diary with a tiny brass lock on the front. Her other gift was the tape of Dad's voice reciting the times tables.

My first entry in the diary reads:

Monday evening. I was shown around the school today. It's very beautiful. Lessons don't start for another two days. I'm lonely this evening and my heart is longing and hoping. I want to go home . . .

Things got worse. I cried through Tuesday and described the place as 'a prison walled in by hate and envy'. I've always been good at over-dramatising events. I should have been training to be an actress, not a dancer! The other girls were all taller and slimmer – more like ballerinas than I would ever be. I didn't fit in.

Surely my heart would break if I didn't see Mum. I had to get away. On Wednesday, I managed to get through dancing and drama in the morning without crying. At teatime I ran away. Still in my school uniform, I raced down the long, long drive, beneath the trees. The large stone gates opened out into the village of Tring. Just to the left of them was a pub. I called Mum from the pay-phone inside.

She was just about to leave for the theatre where she was performing in a local rep production. I screamed hysterically, 'I want to come home! I want to come home!'

'No, Tracy,' she said firmly.

'Please, please . . .' I sobbed.

'No. I am not coming to get you. This is what you wanted. You can't suddenly change your mind.'

I pleaded and cried until my money had almost run out. 'What am I going to do?' I asked.

'You'll go back to school and tell the house mistress what you've done.'

'I'll die here.'

'No you won't.'

Much later, Mum told me that saying no to me was the hardest thing she had ever done.

I trudged up the long drive to school, with the weight of the world on my shoulders. My diary tells the rest of the story.

Thursday – 'More misery. More hatred. God get me out.'

Friday – 'I didn't cry today.'

Saturday – 'I enjoyed myself. I didn't cry all day.'

Monday – 'The food was lovely today: boiled eggs and warm rolls for breakfast. Ballet is boring. Mummy sent me a letter and some books.'

The school was a beautiful old stately home, once the home of the Rothschilds, and loaned to Charles II for his secret liaisons with

Nell Gwyn. The rooms were all of the same opulent splendour with a magnificent ballroom and dining room where most of our dancing lessons were held. The top floor had been the servants' quarters and was now dormitories. Students weren't allowed to use the grand staircase – back stairs only – but we soon discovered all the secret passageways and hiding places.

My life was now run by two matrons, Mrs Hughes and Mrs O'Doherty. They were both Irish and the latter of them, better known as 'Dot', had no roof to her mouth, which made her almost impossible to understand.

It was a fairly strict school, with no television, homework each Saturday and only two visits home every term. Of a Sunday – our only day off – about six of us had to get up early to go to mass. We were the only Roman Catholics at the school. Our compensation was to get back to school just as the Protestant girls were filing down to church in the village. For the next hour we could secretly raid the breakfast room, pinching boiled eggs and freshly baked rolls.

Most of us were half starved. Being dancers, we weren't allowed to put on weight. This meant that tuck-boxes were banned, along with all chocolates and biscuits. With Gestapo-like glee, Mrs Hughes and Dot would even confiscate our Easter eggs, allowing us the occasional nibble and polishing the rest off themselves.

Not long ago I saw a TV show where the comedienne Caroline Quentin took a look at her old school – Arts Educational. She was a year above me and, as far as I know, is the only student who actually made it on to TV or into films. Caroline was describing the starvation regime. She summoned the camera closer and knelt on the dormitory floor.

'But we still found ways of hiding our tuck,' she said, picking up a loose floorboard. It was the same hiding place that I'd used for my sweets.

I made two great friends at the school – Anita Jones and Niki-Sue May. We had a talent for creating chaos, usually with me at the front. Although I had ambitions of being a celebrated ballet dancer,

I knew quite early that it wasn't going to happen. I had a lot of feeling and expression in my dancing, but no technique. That was me all over – it came from my heart and not my head. I didn't have the discipline and work ethic to improve.

Most chorus lines average about five foot six inches tall. Anyone significantly taller or shorter has to dance on her own and therefore must be exceptionally good. I knew that wasn't to be. Apart from my lack of application, my legs were too short and I felt chubbier than the other girls. Instead, I tried to concentrate on drama and singing.

My classmates had nicknamed me 'The Edwards Kid' and whenever I walked into a room they began singing the Milky Bar Kid song: 'The Edwards Kid is strong and tough but only the best is good enough . . .'

At home Mum struggled to keep the electronics business going. She and Dad's secretary Ann Guy tried to convince suppliers and customers that they could still rely on the company. Unfortunately, they were women in a man's world. For two years the money slowly leaked away until eventually, Mum had no choice but to sell up.

Being a young widow, there was a general expectation in the family that she'd remarry, probably sooner rather than later, because of Trevor and me. We needed a father, and she needed a companion.

In a roundabout way I was responsible for her meeting Peter Gascoigne. During the summer holidays I pestered her about going pony trekking in Wales. The fact that we had precious little money didn't enter my head. Twelve-year-olds just expect it to be available. Trevor still hated riding, but I convinced him to come along. Together we managed to wear down Mum's resolve.

She dropped us at the trekking school and then drove back towards Pangbourne. Her car broke down on the M4 near the Severn Bridge and a young man stopped to help her. A year later she married him, and Peter Gascoigne became my stepfather.

In the beginning I thought Peter was lovely. He had a raffish

charm and a playboy's love of spending money. I wrote him letters
from school and was thrilled when he told me that we were all
going to live in Wales. I had read a James Herriot novel and I
imagined us in an idyllic world of horses and friendly farming
people. I quickly forgot about being an actress. Now I wanted to be
a vet.

Peter was the somewhat wayward son of a wealthy industrialist.
He had been educated at all the best schools, but never quite settled
into a career or followed the path mapped out for him by his
family. After marrying my mother Peter had virtually no contact
with his family. Whatever the reason, I can't remember visiting
Peter's family more than half a dozen times during those years.

Moving to Wales meant leaving boarding school, but that wasn't
a sacrifice when set against my dreams of horse-riding and growing
up on a farm. Trevor stayed at St Andrews because his school fees
were being paid by the Masons. Later he went on to Pangbourne
College and I saw him only during the school holidays.

I don't remember that first day we arrived in Llanmadoc on the
Gower Peninsula, but the scenery is still etched in my mind. I can
conjure it up by closing my eyes – the limestone cliffs, rolling
plateau and steep-sided valleys. The river estuary was destined to
become the first Area of Outstanding Natural Beauty to be
declared in Britain.

The peninsula is dotted with tiny villages made of rough pinkish
stone and lichen-covered slate. A century of coal dust still blackens
the chimneys. Village life revolved around the seasons and pub
opening times – both as regular as the tides that covered and
uncovered the miles of sea-grasses in the estuary.

I spent most of that summer living in a caravan on a farm in
Llangennith. I thought I'd died and gone to heaven. Here I was
surrounded by animals. There were places to explore, horses to ride
and friends to meet.

Shortly after my thirteenth birthday I fell madly in love with the
brown eyes of David Beynon, a local boy. The most romantic thing
we ever did was to pretend that the stream at the bottom of the

village was the Amazon and explore it together. Even then, we were never alone. A whole gang of us spent the summer together.

David's younger brother Nicky resented my arrival. My English accent made me automatically different no matter how muddy my jeans or tangled my hair.

A few weeks before the holidays ended, Nicky persuaded David to start ignoring me. This was a very subtle way of being dumped and it took me a few days to realise that I was being cold-shouldered. It was my first broken heart and an elementary lesson in the strange ways of men. Suddenly, they seemed to come from another planet. They still do.

THREE

THE school bus stopped at every village through the valley. It was a clunking old Bedford double-decker, with vinyl seats and metal rivets in the floors. The rear window could be pushed outwards on a hinge 'in case of emergency' but the boys who sat along the back seat would open it at any time.

Shuffling nervously in my new school shoes, I waited at the bus stop. The only sounds I could hear were the baaing of sheep and the thumping of my heart. I wore a knee-length navy skirt, a white shirt, navy and maroon tie and maroon jumper. I clutched my black plastic sports bag to my chest.

Nobody sat next to me on the bus until we reached the village of Bury Green. A girl called Kathie Davies, whom I had met during the summer, slumped alongside me. She made some comment about hating new school years.

Thank God, Kathie befriended me. Otherwise, I wouldn't have known where to go, or what to do when we finally reached Gowerton Lower School.

As a thirteen-year-old, privately educated English schoolgirl, in a Welsh comprehensive school, the culture shock couldn't have been greater. Each time I opened my mouth, I drew attention to myself. A lot of Welsh kids had inherited their parents' prejudices when it came to the English. Others simply didn't like anyone who seemed different.

It seems strange to be writing about people who are now my friends, but they made my life hell when I first met them.

Sarah was probably the most beautiful girl I had ever seen. She was sophisticated and seemingly grown-up. She wore make-up and had her hair styled. Puberty had arrived in a rush for Sarah, while the rest of us were still contemplating ponies and football games on the beach.

Sarah was under the impression that I fancied her boyfriend Alan. All summer I'd hung out with the boys in my village, riding, exploring and swimming. I wore scruffy clothes, normally muddy at the knees, and never washed my hair or took it out of pigtails. It didn't even occur to me that someone could see me as a threat. The truth is I found boys eminently more interesting than girls. I didn't want to discuss make-up and hairstyles. I preferred talking about motorbikes and rugby and Swansea City's promotion up through the leagues with John Toshack. Clearly, I didn't understand the politics of hanging out with other people's boyfriends.

As one of the most popular girls in the lower school, Sarah could make my life hell and she began this by setting an example of teasing and abuse that others followed.

One afternoon as I stepped off the school bus, a group of boys yelled at me from the top back window. As I turned, cans and apple cores rained down on me. I was too shocked to dodge them, or shout any protest. Instead, as the bus drove off, I sat on the grass verge and cried. That night I wrote in my diary: 'I am not going to last here. I am so unhappy.'

From that day onwards I started imitating a Welsh accent faster than you can say, 'Complete coward!' It didn't do me any good. When Sarah discovered that Micky was bullying me they teamed up and became partners in crime. In the caravan one night, while Mum and Peter were in the pub, I woke to the sound of rocks and bottles hitting the roof.

'Come out, come out wherever you are!' shouted Sarah. 'Come on, Moonie, I want to flatten your face.'

Micky was with her. He egged her on, calling me names and shaking the caravan on its springs. I cowered beneath the blankets, pretending that nobody was inside. I had never had anyone want to fight me before. This was a whole new experience. What had I done to them? Why were they picking on me?

Mum had raised me as a Christian and taught me that fighting didn't solve problems, but that message had obviously never been delivered to Sarah and Micky. They had grown up in the Welsh valleys – a totally different planet to quiet, middle-class Purley. These kids were bred to be tough.

Another rock crashed into the caravan. I cringed and curled up into a ball.

'Come on, she's not home,' said Micky.

'I bet she's hiding.'

'I'm not breaking in there.'

I could hear the disappointment in Sarah's voice. 'See you tomorrow, Moonie,' she laughed menacingly. I shuddered.

This became the pattern over the following months. I lived in fear of being caught alone by Sarah. At the same time, I grew harder.

Mum and Peter spent a lot of time going back and forth to Purley, arranging to sell the coach house. Although I was meant to stay at people's houses, I often chose to sleep in the caravan. Mum thought she could trust me, but she couldn't. I was given an inch of freedom and I took a mile.

Teaming up with the usual gang, I drifted between various houses and the grand-sounding 'Youth Club' in the village hall (there wasn't a ping-pong table in sight). The nearest cinema was sixteen miles away and the buses stopped running at 6 p.m. None of us had transport.

Age didn't seem to matter. There weren't enough of us to have a peer group of the same age, so we all hung out together, whether aged eleven or eighteen. This is what happens in isolated rural communities.

The older kids bought cider from the King's Head or the Brit and we sat around drinking and smoking. It made me feel grown up and, perhaps more importantly, accepted. On Monday morning I'd be back at Gowerton Lower School and the bullying would start again.

Sarah and Micky had grown bored; perhaps I was too easy a target. We ended up being friends. Soon afterwards, however, I made the stupid mistake of defending Kathie Davies against a group of girls who were bullying her. Suddenly, her life became a lot better and mine turned to crap.

The twins were the daughters of a local policeman. The school-yard equivalent of the Kray brothers, they struck terror in people's hearts. Since they were much older than me, I still don't know why they wasted their time on terrorising such a minnow. I probably seemed like great sport because I was so frightened. I almost wet myself each time I saw them walking towards me in the play-ground.

Keeping my head down, I began praying, 'Oh, please God, don't let me die.'

The twins grabbed hold of me by the collar and shoved me up against the chainlink fencing around the tennis court. They took turns punching me in the stomach. Fighting for breath, I kept telling myself: Please don't wet yourself, Tracy. Please don't throw up.

A crowd of kids gathered around. No one was silly enough to interrupt or go for help. We were all frightened of the twins.

After two attacks like this, I didn't want to go back to school. Every morning, I'd get dressed and catch the bus as expected but I wouldn't always arrive at Gowerton Comprehensive. Instead, I got off at Llandimore where I waited outside Carol Bowen's house until her parents had gone to work.

Carol was a classmate who'd been mitching for years, along with the likes of Christine Owen and Lyndon Williams. We'd spend the day together, either watching TV or going down to the marsh on Lyndon's Yamaha 50 motorbike. I wasn't nervous about missing school. I didn't care that it was wrong. I just wanted to avoid the bullying.

A year after arriving in Wales we found a house to buy — a derelict farmhouse nestled on a hillside above Llanmadoc, with beautiful views over the village and estuary beyond. Mum and Peter had sold the coach house. This was the only money they had between them.

The farmhouse had four stone walls and what can loosely be described as a roof. The previous owner, an old woman, had kept loads of cats and dogs in the kitchen. Rather than clearing up the mess, she simply put new layers of newspaper over the top. This all had to be cleaned before we moved in.

Trevor and I shared a bedroom in the attic. The only way to reach it was via a stepladder from the kitchen: it was like sleeping in an indoor tree house. Trevor was only home during the holidays. I missed him desperately and wrote to him every week. I didn't tell him about my troubles at school. I knew he couldn't help me.

Having sold the Coach House Mum and Peter were around more often. Even so, it was too late to save me from my troubles at school. I had moved from lower to upper at Gowerton and quickly learned how to use the school timetable to keep me out of trouble with the twins and the headmistress. I knew which lessons I could miss without the roll being called and what classes put me anywhere near the twins. By balancing all of these factors, I could avoid being suspended and protect myself from physical harm.

Occasionally, letters were sent home to Mum but I normally managed to intercept them. Our mailbox was down on the road and the drive up to the house was about half a mile long. I met the postman at the gate, grabbed the letters and sorted through them, taking what I needed and leaving the rest.

Then I'd catch the school bus and get off at Llandimore. By now our gang of 'mitchers' had grown to include Lorraine Hughes, Susan Elliot and Jo Gooding. We seemed to be drawn together because none of us fitted in at school. And, without exception, we thought we knew it all.

We had an improvised rota system that depended upon whose parents were home at what hours. At times, we'd go to the beach or the marsh or hang out with the boys, who were an equally motley and unlikely bunch. I can remember them still – Alan Watkins, Gareth Bowen, Lyndon Williams, Brian Davies, John Alexander, Rolf Mindt, Chris Howells, Doggo, Zombie and Diddy. We were all different ages and personalities, but stuck together. More than once, they saved me from a beating merely by being there.

Things were pretty bad at home. I had grown to dislike Peter more and more. He was a liar – a fact that shocked me at first. I didn't expect adults to lie to me. He was also a hopeless dreamer. He hadn't worked a single day at a proper job since we arrived in Wales. Meanwhile, Mum paid the bills from the proceeds of the Coach House. She had two jobs – at a dress shop and a local pub.

Peter came up with an idea of creating the first red deer farm in Wales. The cottage had nine acres of land and he set about repairing fences and buying animals. All these weird and wonderful creatures began turning up – llamas, peacocks, goats, wallabies and a wild boar. Unfortunately, Peter didn't get planning permission for any of this, so the day he opened the park, Swansea City Council closed it down.

The list of planning permission breaches was longer than my arm. He didn't have car parking facilities, toilets, veterinary certificates, public liability insurance . . . etc . . . etc . . . All Peter had done was buy some animals, stick up a fence and call it a 'wildlife park'.

This summed him up perfectly. He could never see anything through. Peter regarded himself as a planner, but he was only good in outline, never in the fine detail.

His other problem was alcohol. He seemed to spend most of his time in the pub, telling people about his grand plans. As the drink flowed he would tell stories about his past. I once heard him relating how difficult it was to land a jumbo jet in a crosswind. My God, he's really lost it, I thought. He soon became a figure of fun in the village. But although he spent Mum's money on ridiculous follies, Peter treated her pretty well. I thought he was taking us for a ride, but she couldn't see it.

I didn't try to hide the fact that I disliked him. On the contrary, I was openly hostile. This created a power struggle between us, with Mum caught in the middle.

The harder I fought against Peter's control, the more heavy-handed he became. But he was very careful never to hit me in Mum's presence, or within earshot. His threats were always muttered under his breath.

I had never mentioned the bullying at school to Mum. I don't know why. I guess I figured she had enough on her plate. We couldn't go back to Reading and there was no choice of schools here.

After a while, I stopped talking to her completely. I think she struggled to understand what had happened. Why had I inexplicably turned from being the perfect daughter into a feral child who ran wild in the village, getting home late, and sometimes not at all?

When I did venture back to the cottage, I had blazing rows with Peter. It must have been terrible for Mum to see two people she loved at each other's throats. She didn't know how to react or reach out to me. When she did, I pushed her away. Already I was hardening up. 'Get tough to survive,' I told myself. That meant blanking my emotions. I couldn't go home crying. Bullies prey on weakness. It had to be an all-or-nothing transformation.

The nastier and more aggressive I became, the easier my life became. The final proof of this came in my second year. I was mitching two and three days a week – hiding from the twins and their gang. I'd been caught and put on report. This meant that teachers would take a special note of my presence in class. And as the pressure began building I did something really really stupid. I went to see the deputy headmistress, Mrs Borthwick.

She was in her office, just before home-time. For weeks I'd been thinking about what to do, weighing up my options. I still couldn't see any way out. I wanted her to understand why I couldn't go to school. I was so naïve.

'Please don't tell them that I told you,' I pleaded. 'You don't understand what they'll do to me.'

Mrs Borthwick nodded thoughtfully. She had chalk dust on the front of her dress and dandruff on the shoulders. I don't know what I expected her to do. In truth, I knew she couldn't stop them. At the time I was so desperate, I clutched at straws.

'I'll have to think about this, Tracy,' she said sympathetically. 'But you must start coming to school. Running away isn't the answer.'

I slid off a chair and edged out of her office, checking the coast was clear. The last thing I needed was somebody seeing me in conference with the deputy headmistress.

What happened next was unforgivable and nearly caused my death. I know that sounds melodramatic but I'm convinced of it.

I went back into the cloakroom to pick up my bag. The twins were there, along with Suzy Mayhew and a girl called Denise, who were also in the gang. They were the four toughest, most feared girls in the school.

A couple of my friends were nearby, but they scarpered pretty quickly when I came in. They didn't want to be associated with someone being bullied as much as I was. Quite sensible, too.

I grabbed my coat and turned to walk out. Mrs Borthwick appeared. 'Oh, Tracy, I'm glad I caught up with you.' She held on to my arm. 'Right, you lot,' she said, turning to the girls. 'Tracy tells me that you have made her life here a misery. That you're bullying her. And it's going to stop now.'

I looked at their faces. My God, I'm dead!

'From now on, I want you to be civil to each other. If I hear any more reports of bullying, I'll be sending letters home to your parents.'

Letters? Do you think these girls care about letters?

It couldn't possibly be worse. Thankfully, I managed to reach the school bus before the mob caught me. I was safe for the time being.

The following day, I convinced my teacher to let me out of class early so I could run down to the bus. Quickly I lay under one of the seats so that they couldn't find me. I could hear them outside as they peered through the windows. My friends from Llangennith sat around me, hiding me as the bus pulled away.

I ran this gauntlet every day for a week but knew that it couldn't go on. Finally, I stopped going to school completely.

A group of us used to hang about at 'the swings', a field up behind the school. We fixed up pulleys and flying foxes and spent our time smoking and wandering into town. We ate beans and chips at Belli's, a local café, and hung out at the bus station. The aim was to look 'really hard'. Shoplifting became a way of life and even though I knew it was wrong I did it anyway. The long slippery slope beckoned and I was building up speed as I fell.

About a month later, I made my next truly big mistake. I went to an eighteenth-birthday dance in Langrove. My date Billy wasn't really my boyfriend. He and I were both into horses and would go riding together.

This was my first big dance. Mum didn't want me to go because I was only fourteen. There had been a spate of birthdays over the previous few months – normally at dreadful venues like run-down hotels and village halls. I had pestered her about going to them, and she refused. This time she agreed because she liked Billy and there was a bus going from the village that would bring us home.

I bought brand new clothes for the big event – a mauve velvet jacket, with matching satin skirt, a blue blouse with wide collar and a pair of brown boots with six-inch heels. I could barely walk in them. I topped this off with enough blue mascara and eyeliner to audition for *The Rocky Horror Show*.

The bus picked us up from outside the Britannia Inn. A lot of my friends from the village were going, all of them equally dressed up. Billy sat with the boys down the back, while the girls chatted excitedly at the front. At the Langrove Hotel we piled off the bus and into the events room. It was dark, hot and noisy, with sweaty bodies dancing to the latest seventies sounds. All of us were drinking alcohol, underage or otherwise, and trying to look tough and cool.

Everything went perfectly until I spied the twins and Suzy. Suddenly, I felt sick. Billy told me not to worry. I think he saw himself as a knight in shining armour. All evening Sheila and Suzy were eyeing me up, or nudging me in the back on the dance floor, muttering obscenities. I tried to put on a brave face. Didn't they have better things to do with their time? One of them spat in my hair.

'I've got to get out of here, Billy,' I said.

'I'll walk with you.'

Teetering in my boots, I pushed through the crowd into the darkness of the carpark. I don't know what I planned to do. Walk home, perhaps. It was fifteen miles. I knew I couldn't stay there.

Halfway out of the carpark, I realised my mistake. Suzy had followed me.

I said to Billy, 'Go inside now. Get help.'

'No, I'll stay here and look after you.'

'Please Billy, I'm in serious trouble. Get help.'

He didn't move.

I turned to face Suzy, feeling terrified. I raised my hands. 'Look, Suzy, can't we just . . .'

She grabbed my wrists and bent them back until I fell to my knees. Then she drove her knee into my face. I tasted the blood streaming from my nose.

She began kicking me in the stomach and head. I screamed for help, begging Billy to get someone, anyone. Suzy didn't let up. As I lay on my stomach, she seized my hair and smashed my face into the gravel. Over and over she smacked it down. At one point, my head came up, and I saw a car stop. Someone looked out of the window. 'Help me,' I pleaded. It drove around us.

I wasn't fighting back. I didn't know how. Billy spent the entire time running up and down on the spot as Suzy took my face and ground it against the asphalt as if trying to remove all features. I spat blood on to the gravel and felt it smash down again.

The manager of the hotel eventually dragged her off me. My face had been ripped to pieces and my new clothes ruined. I had saved up to buy them. Inside the hotel the manager gave me a glass of water. My eyes had started to swell.

'Do you want me to call your parents?' he asked.

'No.'

'I think someone should come and fetch you.'

One of the girls offered to look after me on the bus. I sat down in the seat, feeling a mess of pain. My eyes had almost closed and I could barely see. Suddenly, I felt another arm around me. It was Suzy.

'What's the matter, love? Had a bit of a problem, have we, love? You're not crying, are you? Oh, dear, what happened to your face? Not so pretty is it? Then again, it could be worse, eh?'

Nobody said a word for the next hour as Suzy kept up the verbal assault, intimidating me into silence.

I didn't go to school for a long time after the attack. I didn't want to leave the house until my face returned to normal. Mum asked me about the injuries, but I didn't name names. I knew to keep my mouth shut.

Yet something strange happened on my first day back at school. The twins made some crack about me and Suzy – normally the quiet member of the trio – told them to back off. It shocked me a little. I wasn't used to someone defending me, especially one of the opposition.

A few days later, Suzy turned up at the swings while I was mitching school. She asked me a few questions and I answered nervously. It was as though the anger had gone out of her and chemically something had changed between us.

Then one day she asked me if I wanted to go to the youth club in Killay that night. 'Ah, well . . . OK.'

From being so terrified of her, I suddenly started to relax when she was around. Suzy seemed to be moving away from the twins, closer to me and my group of friends. It's strange when you consider what she did to me. Within three months of the dance we had become almost inseparable.

Although I didn't try to rationalise it until much later, I knew that Suzy wasn't evil. A culture of violence seemed to exist for quite a few of the children I grew up alongside. When we did eventually get around to talking about the incident I was humbled by Suzy's honesty and angry with myself for judging her. She said she was jealous of my friendship with some of her friends. She didn't know how to express herself and had lashed out. Suzy hated herself for what she had done to me and although I forgave her it took a long time before she forgave herself.

I didn't know Suzy's story then, but I knew that something must have happened to her. Much later I learned the truth, but that's not my story to tell.

The uncertainty and anxiety of adolescence bonded a group of us together. I made friends in those days who are still with me now – people like Jo Gooding and Suzy. We relied on each other and had different rules and values from those of our parents and teachers.

Life at home was hardly inspiring with Trevor away at Pangbourne College and Peter squandering Mum's money. I spent as much time as possible away, often lying about sleeping over at someone else's house.

We had a sort of clubhouse in an old caravan in Llanmadoc. It was in the yard of a house and the mother who lived there was quite relaxed about the cider and cigarettes. The older teenagers did the buying – I was too young to get into the pubs.

At the age of fourteen I started mucking about with boys. Casual sex was almost incidental and contraception an afterthought. Boyfriends and girlfriends were passed around irreverently within the group. None of us understood that this was unusual or wrong. A quick coupling in a barn or back lane was normal.

Somehow, the older girls found ways of getting into Swansea – they didn't want to hang around with labourers and farmers. This left the younger girls behind, who were often easily impressed by guys a few years older. We tended to get into teasing relationships, without fully understanding our sexuality and its effect on boys. There was always the danger of lighting a fuse and then hanging around for the fireworks to go off.

I wasn't naïve enough to think it was love. I knew it wasn't. Yet I had an overwhelming need to be with another human being. I craved affection and having someone hold me. It wasn't the sexual act – it was the physical closeness that I took comfort from.

A month was considered a long-term relationship in our world. We chopped and changed, fought and made up. I was probably the worst. Part of the attraction was the chase. For me the first kiss was always the best one. It's not even the kiss. It's that moment, just before you think someone is going to kiss you, when your heart is pounding so loudly that you swear they must be able to hear it.

That sweet moment of anticipation is the finest point of any relationship. After that it was all downhill.

Home had, by now, become a war zone. I would answer Peter back and openly show my hatred. At first he became quite heavy-handed and tried to stop me going out. Then he started to embarrass me in front of my friends, or would threaten to beat up my boyfriends.

I don't know what he could have done differently. Perhaps nothing. I hated the fact that he wasn't my father. He wasn't fit to take his place. I can't blame Peter for being angry with me. He could see that I was hurting Mum. My life was careering off the rails. I didn't care about school, or Mum, or my own responsibilities.

In Peter's defence I'll admit that he didn't hit me first. He caught me taking £5 from Mum's purse and sneaking out of the house. He called me a tramp and I told him to drop dead.

He blocked the doorway, almost daring me to get past him. We were face to face, screaming at each other. Spittle flew from his lips. A red mist descended and I hurled myself at him with fists flying.

This was a full-on fight, with no quarter given. I punched and kicked and wrapped my fingers around his throat. Instead of behaving like a grown-up and a stepfather, Peter hit back. To him I was an adversary, not a child being bullied at school and struggling to fit in.

The intensity of the fight was frightening, but I refused to back down. Perhaps all is fair in such a fight, but Peter should have known better. I turned to Mum: surely she'd side with me? But she chose neither side. My selfishness and self-absorption blinded me to this. She should have chosen me. She should have loved *me* the most.

Peter's favourite tactic to get under my skin was to tell me I could do something and then change his mind. Of course, he'd deny this when I pleaded with Mum to intervene. During one of these arguments I got so angry that I picked up a china plate that hung on the wall. I had given it to Mum for Mother's Day (I bought it in the village shop). 'To the best Mum in the world,' it said. I held the plate above my head. I could see the hurt in Mum's eyes.

'Please don't throw that,' she said.

I hurled it to the floor where it shattered.

I couldn't look at Mum. I didn't want to see the pain. Perhaps she didn't love me any more. Her child had turned into a selfish, petulant creature from hell.

A few days later, I went down to the village shop and bought her another plate. Without any ceremony, I hung it on the wall and went out again.

The thirteen-year-old girl who arrived in Wales from boarding school was a totally different person from the fifteen-year-old about to sit her O-levels. I had become self-seeking and petulant. I was horrible to people whom I didn't like and hurt those I loved. When Peter beat the crap out of me I would flee to Suzy's house.

Her mother Val was one of the most impressive women I had ever met and would brook no nonsense from people like my stepfather: or the police for that matter.

When Peter came knocking on the door, she would swing it open and fill the entire frame.

'Yeah, what do you want?'

'Is Tracy Edwards here, please?'

'No.'

'Listen, Val, I know she's here,' he'd say, wearily.

'Maybe she is, but she's not going with you.' Then she'd slam the door.

I ended up virtually living with Suzy for a while. Her family became my family: they seemed to understand what I was going through. But Mum always convinced me to come home in the end. Deep down – in a place that I didn't show the world – I still loved her.

My problems paled into insignificance compared to those of some of my friends. One of them was, however, prove to exaggerating and was a bit of a drama queen.

One of them called me one evening, just after dusk. 'Can you come and get me?' she asked. Her voice was incredibly calm – almost dead inside.

'What's wrong?'

'He beat me up really badly this time. I have to get out of the house before he gets back. I've cleaned it all up, but I can't stay.'

I didn't hesitate in saying yes, I couldn't take the chance that she might not be exaggerating but I had no idea of how to reach her. She lived about four miles away.

Then I remembered Zombie's grandfather's van. Zombie lived at the bottom of our drive, on the outskirts of the village. He would secretly 'borrow' his grandpa's van and we'd go driving on the farm tracks and back lanes. Zombie wasn't old enough to have a licence. None of us were. But most of the farming kids had learned to drive at an early age.

Zombie had given me the spare set of keys of the van, for safe keeping. As I retrieved them from my hiding place, I was already planning to borrow the van for just long enough to rescue my friend and bring her back.

In darkness, I trudged down the long drive to the gate. I knew every rock and blade of grass by now; I'd come home late so often.

The van wasn't there. Damn! I thought of her mopping blood off the kitchen floor. I couldn't let her down.

Opposite I noticed two cars at a house that belonged to Randolph Jenkins, a town councillor and upstanding member of the community. He didn't particularly like our family or, to be exact, me. He saw me as a tearaway and troublemaker – a bad influence on local youth. He was right.

I looked closely at the two cars . . . and I just wondered. Then I walked up and tried the van's key in the door of the Cortina. It worked! As I slid the key into the ignition, I told myself that if the car started I would take it. I could get to her and back within half an hour.

Fate? Blind-arsed luck? Take your pick.

The engine rumbled to life and I put it into gear. I didn't turn the headlights on until I got away from the house and on to the road. Leaning forward to see over the steering wheel I drove extra carefully until I reached the village. I parked in the Greyhound car park, just next door to my friend's house.

As she opened the door, I quickly surveyed the damage. Her bottom lip had been split and she had bruises on her right cheek.

'Come on, let's go,' I said quickly. 'I have to get this car back.'

At the moment, Randolph Jenkins walked past the kitchen window. Behind him was Seth Bowen, the village constable. Randolph had obviously seen me take the car and followed me.

Seth was a lovely man, approaching retirement, with a down-to-earth attitude towards small-town policing. When he caught kids riding motorbikes without helmets, he'd give them a clip round the ear rather than clog up the courts.

As they reached the front door, we legged it out the back. I burst straight through the back hedge and across the car park.

My friend shouted, 'Follow me!' and headed towards the common. I didn't hear her. All I could think was: How the hell am I going to get home?

Suddenly, I heard Seth call out, 'Tracy Edwards, I know it's you.'

My heart pounded. How do I get out of this one? Oh, Tracy, you've really done it now.

I had to get home. If I could beat Seth there, I could claim to have been in all night and insist that Randolph had been mistaken. I ran around the house and doubled back inside through the front door. My friend's brother was watching TV. I begged him to take me home on his motorbike.

At that moment Seth came back into the house. I tried to run past him and he literally picked me up by my collar. My legs flailed beneath me.

'Settle down, settle down.'

'Please, please let me go. Oh God, I'm so sorry.'

Randolph arrived and started abusing me. 'I want her charged. I want the book thrown at her.'

Seth tried to calm him down. 'It's OK. Leave this to me,' he said.

'No, I want her charged. She's a bloody thief.'

Seth carried me down to the police station about four doors away. He handcuffed me to the radiator because I kept trying to run. I knew I'd really overstepped the mark this time.

I could hear Seth trying to convince Randolph not to press charges: 'Look, she is just a kid. You've got the car back. It's not damaged.'

'I'm not having it. I want that girl charged.'

Then he called my mother.

'Oh, please God not that,' I whispered, slumping against the radiator.

When Peter and Mum turned up I couldn't look at them. I had never been so embarrassed. All of those lectures from Peter about screwing up my life now came back to haunt me. But I couldn't show him that I was sorry. So I put on my tough, I–don't–care act. Poor Mum had to see this.

'I'm sorry, but he's pressing charges,' Seth told them.

'I'll talk to him,' said Peter, playing the stern father. It made no difference. Randolph wouldn't budge.

We drove home in silence from the police station. I can't be sure, but I think Mum shed a few quiet tears in the front seat. As we walked in the door, I spied Trevor. He was home for school holidays.

'Well, your sister has finally done it,' said Peter bitterly. 'She's humiliated the family completely. The final straw.'

I went upstairs and stayed there for a long time.

A week later I appeared in court. Mum made me wear my school uniform and put my hair in pigtails.

'For goodness sake, Tracy, at least try and look sorry.'

She didn't understand. I couldn't back down. I had to be this way to survive the bullying. I had become part of what was going on around me. Even more so, I overcompensated and launched pre-emptive strikes. There was no romance in being a rebel. I didn't see myself as an outlaw.

As the court clerk called my name I stood alongside my solicitor. I felt anxious and alone.

The magistrate asked me why I had taken the car. I couldn't tell the truth about my friend and her father's alleged brutality. I'd promised to protect her. I shook my head in silence.

'Surely there must have been a reason, young lady,' urged the magistrate.

I shrugged and shuffled my feet.

The more he asked, the more defiant I became. Without an excuse, I came across as a petulant joy-rider, who should have known better.

In passing sentence the magistrate made a reference to my 'not looking very sorry'. Then he came down harshly, giving me two years' probation, a £150 fine and six points on my licence when eventually I obtained it.

Boldly I strode out of court, feeling angry at the world. I

couldn't pinpoint exactly why. Circumstances, I guess. Something burned inside me – a need to prove myself, a determination to overcome adversity – but instead of using this positively, I had let it become twisted and abhorrent.

The stain of what I'd done didn't wash off easily. I had to live in the village where everybody knew. Stealing a car far outweighed the normal indiscretions of the village youth. The two hardest things to bear were not being able to tell people why and the general sense of disappointment. A lot of people liked me in the village and, more importantly, they loved Mum.

Initially, I thought, how could you possibly be disappointed? I'm just living up to what you think of me. Then I realised that people didn't think that at all. Some of them saw something in me that I couldn't see; or that I didn't even know was there.

In many ways, if I hadn't been able to draw upon my idyllic childhood, I might not have pulled through these times. The principles and morals that Mum and Dad had taken such care to instil in me were buried deep inside me. I might have forgotten them for the moment, but they were still there. When I hear experts say that the first seven years of your life are the most important, I agree with them entirely. This is when a child develops their character and learns the difference between right and wrong.

A part of me knew I'd screwed up big-time. I hated myself for that because I don't like to lose.

All these years later, I still can't explain why I ran so far off the rails. Perhaps I was given too much freedom when I was too young. Maybe I never got over Dad's death. Whatever the reason, I hurt my mother more than she will ever admit.

FOUR

THE highlight of the local calendar was the village panto-mime. This was my chance to redeem myself. I was cast as Cinderella and by the time I discovered that Randolph Jenkins was to play one of the Ugly Sisters it was too late to back out. There was a forced truce between us during rehearsals.

Cathy Luporini directed the production with military precision, while Mum choreographed the dances. We practised in the village hall after school, bopping away to 'Boogie Nights' and trying to stay warm.

Apart from being Cinderella I was also in the dance chorus with Lorraine Hughes, and Susan Elliott. For all of us, it was a huge excuse to show off.

Not surprisingly, I'd been grounded after the court case. Mum escorted me home after each rehearsal, before going back to the Brit to start work. I still managed to sneak out occasionally and one night Mum caught me necking with Anthony Watkins behind the school hall. Busted!

Cinderella was sold out. On opening night the cast gathered in the kitchen of the hall to get dressed. We were all nervous. You would have thought we were about to perform in the West End. In reality, we were sixteen miles from the nearest entertainment, in a place where sheep outnumbered people. Believe me – this made the panto a big deal. It was so cold in the hall that every breath looked like a speech bubble. The audience stayed wrapped in thick coats and the standing ovation had a lot to do with staying warm. We accepted it graciously.

For that one evening, village politics and disagreements were forgotten. Even Randolph and I managed to congratulate each other. I have to admit he made a great Ugly Sister.

After the performance, the audience put the chairs away while the cast got changed. Once the hall had been locked, we hurried through the cold, across the road to the Brit where Tony and Beryl put on a lavish spread for audience and performers. Everyone drank too much, laughed too much and relived the highlights of the show.

The teenager hiding inside me came out for one performance only. I wasn't so bad after all. Just misunderstood.

My O-level exams were approaching and I barely gave them a second thought. Any ambition to become a vet had disappeared when I discovered it was a five-year course. I had never managed to stick at anything for more than a few months.

Three weeks before the exams a school prefect caught me smoking on the bus. She promised not to report me so I went mitching for the day, heading down to the swings. At lunchtime Suzy came looking for me.

'Daniels is after you,' she said.

'What for?'

She shrugged. A summons from the headmaster couldn't be good news. I went back to school and prepared for the worst. I should have been more nervous, but a part of me didn't care what happened.

'I'm giving you a two-day suspension for smoking and a two-day suspension for missing school,' he said.

Not bad, I thought. He'd let me off pretty lightly. It was still pretty ludicrous to punish someone for missing school by suspending them. Of course, letters would be sent home. I'd have to intercept then before they reached Mum.

Just as I was walking out of the headmaster's office, my drama teacher arrived.

'Oh, Miss Edwards. Just the person I want to see. Drinking on the school drama trip. What do you have to say for yourself?'

Milford Haven the week before.

If all of these misdemeanours had happened separately I might have survived, but added together they looked even worse.

'I've had enough of you,' said Daniels, his voice shaking. 'You're a disgrace to this school and to your family. I'm expelling you.'

I was fifteen years old and my formal education had ended. I didn't bother trying to hide the letter from Mum. I didn't want to go back to school.

She cried, of course. She sat in the kitchen with her elbows on the table and her head in her hands. I would have preferred her to shout or scream at me but the fight had gone out of her. I dumped my schoolbag, changed out of my uniform and walked past her as I left.

By next morning she had marshalled herself for one last battle. She marched me down to the school and into Daniels's office. Then she begged for me to be allowed to return to do my O levels.

It didn't matter to me. Already, I had my immediate future all figured out. I'd get a job in a local factory that put the piping on the back of gas ovens. I'd buy a motorbike and go to all the parties.

Daniels let me sit my exams but wouldn't allow me back into school, I spent the next few weeks studying at home, with Mum watching me like a hawk so I couldn't slip away. On the first day of exams it was like a school reunion, as I waved to friends and chatted afterwards. I wrote the essays and answered the questions, with one eye on the clock. Soon I'd never have to sit in a classroom again or run the gauntlet of the bullies. Surprisingly, my results weren't that bad considering my level of apathy. I didn't give then a second look.

*   *   *

During the summer I ran away. I had started dating Chris Howells, the son of an important old Gower family. His father, Edward Rees, owned a large house in Llangennith, along with the caravan site and most of the beach. Chris was one of five children. He had long hair, flared jeans, an earring and a leather jacket. Peter, of course, hated him.

Chris had a motorbike, which was another huge attraction. That was the summer that Lyndon Williams first let me ride his new Kawasaki 250 S1. Everybody seemed to have a motorbike and, when I turned sixteen, I bought a little Yamaha 50 from Sput, a friend, for £50. I knew his young brother had died on the bike. I was even wearing the same helmet.

Chris was my first serious boyfriend, and I thought of us as renegades – almost like Bonnie and Clyde. We met at school and there were lots of stops and starts before we finally got together. He was quite shy, particularly with girls, but among guys he was outgoing and a natural leader. We were part of the same gang of friends and I would do the ironing and cleaning for his wonderful Mum, Angela, to earn a bit of pocket money.

At the start of the summer I had a barbecue at the house for all my friends. It had taken a long time to convince Mum and Peter to let me arrange the night. I was trying to be very grown up. They arranged to go out, giving me the house until 11 p.m. I made dips and salads, and set up tables outside on the terrace.

At half-past ten Peter arrived home. He walked on to the terrace and declared: 'Right, you've had your fun. You've eaten my food. You've drunk my booze, now get your skates on and fuck off out of here.'

He was drunk, of course, but that didn't make things any better. Mum was inside and didn't hear him.

I lost the plot completely. It was so humiliating. I had tried to be responsible. For once I had done the right thing. All my friends left, except for Jo. Peter was supposed to give her a lift home. She was in the sitting room when I exploded and began laying into Peter. He hit me back and Jo watched in shock as the punches flew.

I was screaming, 'But you said we could stay up . . . but you said . . .' I could hear the childishness in my voice and it made me even angrier. I hated my weakness. I had let him get to me.

Peter was a big man, tall and well built. He was also incredibly fit and didn't muck about when he swung his punches. I was trying to scratch out his eyes when Mum came into the room screaming at us to stop. It was my fault, of course. She hadn't seen Peter hit me. She hadn't heard how he talked to my friends.

I was sent to my room. 'Why do you provoke him?' she asked me later. 'You know better than that.'

I tried to explain to her what happened.

'I didn't hear him say that,' she said, defending him.

'You weren't there.'

'Can't you just be adult about it?'

'He's the bloody adult, tell *him* to grow up.'

Early the next morning Mum left to spend a few days in Reading. Peter took her to the train station and as they bounced down the driveway in the Land Rover, I began packing my bag. I simply couldn't stay under the same roof with Peter any longer.

Sound travelled a long way up the valley. I could hear the Land Rover stop as Peter got out to open the gate. The church bells were ringing in the village and I heard the voices of people talking in the High Street.

By the time the Land Rover reached the station I had called Chris and asked him to come and pick me up. I didn't take much – just a few T-shirts, a pair of jeans and some shorts. I tossed them into a holdall and then fished my old sleeping bag out of the cupboard. I purposely didn't leave a note or take enough stuff to make it obvious I was running away. Peter wouldn't even start looking for me until Mum was due back.

Chris rode over the hill on farm tracks rather than taking the road. The bike bounced and skidded over rocks as I held on to my bag and to his waist.

For the next few days we stayed at his house. His mum, Angela, didn't realise I'd run away until Peter called. She had no great love for Peter and she covered for me.

By then, Chris and I had grabbed some camping gear and headed up on to the top of Harding Down, a hill overlooking Llangennith. We pitched our two small tents in a depression in the ancient ruins of a Viking burial mound. There was just enough room for our sleeping bags, a torch and a few basic supplies. We arranged to arrive at a friend's house, or Chris's parents, just as dinner or lunch was being served. Or when the rain pelted down and turned the hill tracks into waterfalls.

Chris had money every now and then. We didn't need much. Romance provided most of the comforts and we revelled in the freedom of doing as we pleased on long, hot, lazy days. I wanted that summer to last for ever.

I called Mum and told her that we were camping. She seemed OK about it. I think she was relieved that Peter and I were apart.

Lyn and Mike Bosley were good friends and they ran virtually an open house in Llangennith, with friends dossing on the floor or staying for meals. Lyn worked in the oven factory and managed to get me a job there. I had to lie about my age.

The factory was on an industrial estate in Crofty, almost on the estuary towards Swansea. Each morning we caught the bus and arrived at a big warehouse. Workers had a card to clock in and out each day. This should have been a surefire giveaway that the job was boring and mechanical. We sat in front of a board with nails placed on it. Then we picked up pipes from different boxes and began placing them in a set design before securing them with plastic ties. These would eventually become the backs of ovens.

It took only seconds to assemble each one but quickly I learned that you didn't do them too fast because it made everyone else look bad. Twice I was told to slow down by a woman who had wrists as solid as axe handles.

In other parts of the factory they were probably making the rest of the ovens, but I never bothered finding out. I left after four weeks, when my first pay packet arrived.

Towards the end of the summer, Chris and I moved our tents down to the beach, pitching camp at the caravan site. This became the social centre for all our friends, who rocked up on their motorbikes and slept over in the caravans for hire.

One morning Tom Edwards, the local policeman, came down to tell me that Mum wanted me to come home. 'She's worried about you. She can't see the tent any more,' he explained. Being able to see our hilltop camp had been reassuring.

'Summer's nearly over,' said Tom, plucking a dandelion and scattering the seeds with his large fingers. 'I know things aren't very good at home, but your mum needs you. Things aren't so good for her either.'

Tom was a lovely gentle man and I knew that he was right. Maybe it was time to go home.

Packing a few things in my holdall, I left the camp-ground and had Chris drop me at the house. As I walked through the front door, Peter looked up from an armchair and said, 'What the hell are you doing here?'

I spun on my heels and walked out again. Later that day, I called Mum from a phone box and arranged to meet her in the pub. I told her what had happened when I tried to go home, but I don't think she believed me. Peter was a very clever man. He didn't want me in the house. Life was much more peaceful without me.

'I think I'll just stay at the caravan site for a bit longer,' I said.

Mum didn't try to change my mind. She wasn't worried about where I lived, as long as I was happy. She did, however, want me to go to secretarial college.

'You need to have a safety net,' she said. 'Something you can fall back on.'

'But I don't want to be a secretary.'

'I know, but it's a good skill to have.'

I still wasn't sure.

'Look if you never do anything for me, just do this one thing. Please.'

In September I enrolled at Tyoch College in Sketty, just outside Swansea. The bus trip every day took fifty minutes and the bus dropped me at the bottom of the hill that led up to the college. I lasted about two months before I couldn't stand it any more – not even for Mum. All that Pitman's shorthand, typing and letter writing – I was useless at it.

Although it's a part of my life that I've tried to blank out, I remember moving back home during that time. Things had calmed down quite a bit, but Peter and Mum were having problems. Money and drinking were at the core. After Swansea City Council turned down his application for a wildlife park, Peter seemed to lose interest. He still saw himself as a Gerald Durrell figure, but now he had a whole lot of animals running around which he had to keep fed and watered.

Peter loved animals. It was people he couldn't handle. When he wasn't drinking at the pub, he carved the antlers of our red deer, creating heads for walking-sticks in the shapes of dolphins and wolves. They were truly beautiful pieces and showed a rare, hidden depth to Peter.

I started work at the King's Head at Llangennith, owned by Chris's uncle, George Rees. Chris and I virtually ran the restaurant, serving typical pub meals to the tourists who swelled the village each summer.

George was a great character. He spent half his year playing piano on the cruise ships in the Mediterranean and in Greek bars. He even had an apartment in Athens that was like a second home. He'd arrive home each winter, full of stories of exotic places and strange sights. Listening to his adventures, I was swept up with the idea of going backpacking around Europe. Mum thought it was a great plan. I think she wanted to separate me from my friends and get me out of Wales. Perhaps I would find myself, or at least lose some of my anger.

George had been working at Zea Marina, a quaint little quay around the corner from Piraeus, the main port in Athens. It was full of rich boats and sailors, he said. There were often jobs to be had in the restaurants and bars, or I could try olive picking in season. Another option was becoming a nanny. I bought a copy of the

Lady magazine and scanned the classified columns. A Greek family was looking for an English nanny for their two young children. I applied for the job, lying shamelessly in my résumé about my extensive experience.

The ploy worked: they agreed to hire me for six months. I had to get myself to Greece and they would pick me up from the airport. I then made the very naïve mistake of mentioning in a letter that Chris was also coming with me to Athens. Boyfriends and nannies were not a good combination and the family telephoned the day before we left saying that somebody else had been hired.

Chris and I were committed. Our tickets had been booked and paid for. There was no turning back.

I was sixteen years old and had visions of island-hopping on ferries and eating wonderful food in outdoor cafés. I'd learn the language and the wonderful history.

On the morning of our flight, I visited Dad's grave to say goodbye. I told him about my big adventure and knew that he'd approve. Then Chris and I were driven to the airport where both our mothers cried buckets of tears.

We waved goodbye and set off. It was 29 February 1980.

FIVE

WITH £100 between us, we had grand dreams of staying in Greece for a year. The plane arrived late on a balmy night in Athens. I walked out of the airport and smelt a world that seemed alien and frightening.

There were no friendly bobbies offering directions. Instead, the police had machine-guns and arrogant expressions. Taxi drivers began chasing us, tugging at our bags. Chris told them to get lost, but they didn't understand.

We didn't know where to go, or whom to ask about accommodation. Eventually, the tourist police arranged a taxi and gave us the name of a cheap *pensione*. The driver reeked of garlic and had the radio tuned to a soccer game with the volume turned up full blast. Every so often, he screamed and hammered his fists on the wheel.

The streets were buzzing. Pedestrians spilled from footpaths and music filtered from outdoor cafés. I found it intimidating rather than exciting.

Turning left and right through a maze of narrow streets, the taxi pulled up outside a lone building in a street of rubble and debris. The block looked almost bombed out, or condemned. The driver charged us too much money and said he didn't have change.

An old woman with no teeth took us to a room. She moved so slowly up the creaking stairs I thought the sun would come up before we arrived. She pushed open the door and then disappeared surprisingly quickly. The room was cold, damp and rotten. The only window had been boarded up and the toilet wouldn't flush. Wires hung from the ceiling through broken holes in the plaster.

I sat down on the sagging mattress and started crying.

'I want to go home. I don't like this place.'

'It'll be better in the morning,' said Chris, trying to reassure me.

'No it won't.'

'Come on. We can't stay here.'

We locked our bags in the room and went looking for somewhere else to stay. It was already 2 a.m. and most places were shutting for the night. A few blocks away we found the Imperial Hotel. At £3.50 a night – it was well beyond our budget, but we had little choice.

I stayed in the room and had a shower while Chris went back to get our bags from the *pensione*. The old woman refused to give him a refund, but we were relieved to be out of there. In the morning we'd sort everything out and reappraise our budget.

I lay in bed and wrote my diary, lying about how much we spent on the hotel. I often did that in my diaries – wrote about how I wanted things to be rather than how they really were. I don't think I was trying to fool anybody. Perhaps I was trying to wish things into being.

That night I wrote:

This hotel is lovely and when I look out my window I can see the Acropolis on the hill opposite. I can't wait to see it by day. The noise of the traffic is very loud, car horns blare out, but there is a nice atmosphere here.

The manager of the hotel is nice and speaks good English. I rang Mum and told her where I am. She sounded happy about it. Christopher has gone to get us something to eat from up the road. Church bells are ringing outside. It sounds lovely. I'm OK

now. I was upset at first but now everything is falling into place.
I feel happy, homesick and eager.

The next morning, after a good night's sleep, I found a totally different city.

The area of Plaka, in the old section of Athens, was an oasis in a huge sprawling metropolis. It was full of narrow cobbled lanes, stairways and overhanging shops. This is where the hippies, back-packers and artists congregated. It was an explosion of tie-dyed tops, flared jeans with colourful patches, long hair, beads and bandannas.

People from all over the world were in Plaka. It was a stopping-off point before you headed off to the islands, or a last port of call before travelling overland to India or crossing the Mediterranean to Egypt. We had arrived at a crossroads and the streets were full of promise and adventure. People played guitars on street corners and swapped stories in the outdoor cafés.

Chris and I set out in the general direction of the Acropolis. The streets grew steeper and narrower. Following a cobbled lane we came across an American who was similarly lost. Together we found our way through the rows of tiny, whitewashed houses, with colourful flower boxes on their windowsills.

When we finally reached the Acropolis it took my breath away. It was everything I had imagined it would be. You could almost see the ancient Greeks walking through the temple of Athena. Below us, Athens seemed massive and immovable, having survived thou-sands of years. I walked around taking pictures and marvelling at the immense scale and beauty.

After visiting the amphitheatre and museum we walked back to Plaka and bought kebabs at eighteen pence each. Chris had become very good at asking for things by miming and he understood the money better than I did.

We had heard about the Irish Pub in Plaka that had a notice-board advertising accommodation and jobs. Through this we found a hostel in Niki Street which had two spaces left on the roof. We paid a week in advance and kept our bags downstairs in a storeroom while we slept under the stars, listening to the car horns and buzz of the streets.

I could see the Acropolis lit up by spotlights. At school I had done classical studies which had featured Greek and Roman history. It had been one of my favourite subjects and one of the few things I did well at. The teacher, Byron Davies, was my favourite among the staff. Like all good teachers, he brought the subject to life.

Working out our finances, we found we had enough money to last two months living on 100 drachmas a day. If we didn't find work in that time we'd have to go home.

Living on kebabs and coffee, we spent each day visiting shops, bars and restaurants asking for jobs. I learned my way around the city and wore out a pair of shoes. There seemed to be a severe unemployment problem in Athens and nobody was willing to hire foreigners and get them work permits. Some of the café owners went deaf very quickly or looked at me as though I had insulted them.

Each day I scanned the newspapers and noticeboards. It was the wrong time of year for fruit picking, and that would mean moving into the countryside. We tried to cut down to three kebabs a day and no drinks, only water. This meant spending only 40 drachmas. The man at the kebab shop now knew us and before Chris arrived he would have the kebabs ready – one without onions.

When I wasn't looking for work, I visited the markets because there was so much to see. Apart from the colourful stalls and gesticulating Greeks, you could turn a corner and unexpectedly come across another ruined temple.

Chris and I found a cheap trip to Aegina, the nearest island to Athens. The ferry trip took an hour and then we hired bikes and rode around part of the island, visiting the temple of Apollo, which was still being excavated. After lunch we bought postcards and watched the horse cart rides.

Back in Athens, Chris came down with a shocking flu and I

spent virtually the last of our money on medicine. He lay in bed at the hostel, drifting in and out of sleep. The other backpackers were convinced it was some weird British disease and expected Chris to leave in a coffin.

That night I counted our money. We had just enough to stay another two weeks. I'd sold some clothes, which was enough to buy presents and souvenirs for everyone at home.

The next morning, Chris's fever broke and I managed to find work. A girl at the hostel was leaving her job washing dishes at an Italian pizza restaurant. It was 3,000 drachmas for a six-day week, working from 6 p.m. to 1 a.m. I liked the idea that I had the daylight hours when I could explore.

On the Sunday before I started work, Chris and I went out to celebrate. We treated ourselves for the first time in three weeks, eating chicken and chips at a restaurant followed by *crème caramel* and coffees. We scraped through paying the bill with about two drachmas to spare.

The next day I arrived at Tavern Erato. The owner, Angelo, was a huge man with balding head, beautiful deep brown eyes and a bear-like grip. His laugh started as a deep rumble and could rattle the light fittings.

Angelo took me under his wing and I became virtually part of his family. He could speak a little bit of English, whereas the manager Dimitri and his wife Kiri Anita could speak none at all. The two waiters, Yorgos and Santos, were both completely mad.

I fell in love with the Greeks and their language. They express themselves with their whole bodies and put so much passion into even the most mundane conversations. My efforts to learn the language had mixed results. The Greek word for bread is *pesomi* and the word for penis is *pesemi*. At the baker's one day I ordered two hundred *pesemis* and wondered why the staff couldn't stop laughing.

Our cook at the restaurant looked like a Greek pirate with a bushy black moustache and weatherbeaten face. Once he had worked on a big square-rigger and – according to the stories – he'd been hit on the head by a piece of rigging. As a result he suffered from unexpected blackouts. A doctor had told him that whenever this happened, he had to train himself to stand absolutely still to avoid being hurt.

Consequently, amid the nightly pandemonium of pizza trays coming in and out, orders being shouted and dough spinning in the air, the chef would suddenly lose the plot completely and stand like a statue, holding a knife in one hand. We carried on around him for five or ten minutes until he snapped out of it and began chopping ingredients again.

His other eccentricity involved talking to the contents of the fridge. I think this started out as an attempt to improve his English. He would open the fridge door and go, 'Hello, chicken. Hello, spaghetti. Hello, tomato sauce.'

Soon I started working two shifts every day, with Sunday off. Chris and I would get to Piraeus early and catch a hydrofoil to one of the islands. We'd hire bikes and explore. On a windswept voyage back, we made love on the top deck of the ferry while the rest of the passengers sheltered inside.

Chris's uncle, George Rees had arrived back in Athens and was playing piano at a bar called the Landfall in Zea Marina, not far from Piraeus. Often we'd go down there for Sunday lunch and George would insist on paying. The Landfall was full of expats and yachties. One of them, Phyllis, looked 500 years old and was English to her deck shoes.

I loved my new lifestyle. Even riding the subway and learning the bus routes was an adventure. Chris, however, didn't have the same passion. He seemed to be biding his time until we went home again. He was on the outside looking in while I embraced everything about the new country and its culture. Chris found it harder to get work and he quickly lost heart. There were fewer jobs for men. Soon he spent most of his time at the Irish pub and in the outdoor cafés. I was supporting both of us. Of an evening he'd arrive at the restaurant quite late and sit in the kitchen until I finished work.

Our airline tickets were only open for a year. I wanted the time to pass more slowly, but Chris couldn't wait to get home. Inevitably, we were drifting apart.

We flew home early in 1981 and broke up soon afterwards. Chris went back to Wales while I stayed with Auntie Edna and Uncle Arthur in Reading. I got a job behind the bar at the George in Pangbourne and tried to decide what to do with my life.

Mum and Peter were still in Wales but things were not good. I went down to see them a couple of times but she didn't seem happy. She had grown to hate Wales and I couldn't see her staying with Peter for much longer. She deserved better. We had reached a truce of some sort.

Mum was happy that I'd enjoyed my travels and I think she hoped that I might go back. I seemed to be calmer.

Mum had done a lot of travelling as a dancer and she loved hearing stories about other countries and recalling her own adventures. We had found something in common.

Through all these years Mum had dealt with her MS in the same tough, determined way that she has handled every other hardship in her life. It amazed me then as it does now.

She also drew on her unquestioning belief in God and paid scant attention to the doctors who gave her only a limited time before the illness put her in a wheelchair. Mum listened to every word and then set about proving them wrong. She refused to go quietly, or to concede an inch.

Nine months after getting back to England, I still couldn't decide what to do with my life. For a while I contemplated going to drama school. I sent off a few applications but most were turned down. I did get one or two auditions but my heart wasn't really in them.

Still working in the pub, I moved into a house in Pangbourne with some friends. On a miserable November morning, I woke to find we'd run out of tea bags, there was no milk and it was raining cats and dogs.

'I want to go back to Greece,' I announced to the empty fridge. 'There is nothing for me here.'

I arrived back in Athens on 12 November 1981, on a £30 Magic Bus that took four days to drive from London. Nobody ever remembered to change money on the Magic Bus, which meant we were permanently hungry. Even those who packed sandwiches had eaten them on the ferry to Calais.

Thanks to George I landed a job at the Landfall, working behind the bar for a real sleaze of a boss. A lot of the sailors and crews from the yachts and charter boats drifted in and out. Each night was like a big pub crawl, starting off at the Landfall and ending up at a nightclub called Tramps.

The lifestyle of the charter crews was free and easy. They were at sea for weeks on end, but once on shore they were determined to party. They were full of stories about amazing places they had visited and people they had met. Many of them followed the sun to Bermuda and Antigua in the winter, or found other jobs until the next season began.

By Christmas I had a Greek boyfriend, Pavlos, the owner of Tramps, and my own flat at Zea Marina. I decided to take a short holiday home for New Year's Eve. Braving the Magic Bus back to England, I left Athens on 28 December. Pavlos took me down to the bus station after a farewell party at Tramps. I told him I loved him and immediately wished I'd kept quiet. Why do I always spoil things by falling in love?

I sat next to a Greek girl, Sandy, and we knew each other's life stories by the time we reached Yugoslavia. I fell asleep and woke at five in the morning. Deep snow covered the countryside, creating wonderful scenery, but slowing us down. We were all trying to get home for New Year's Eve.

Dozing again, I woke at 9.30 at the Italian border. We had been stuck there for two hours but were finally being waved through. All day we drove through Italy, wiping circles in the misted windows to glimpse the snow-covered countryside. Sandy must have thought I was a walking problem page, as I told her about all my hang-ups.

We started skidding in the snow thirty miles from France and had to stop for an hour to put chains on the coach. In the interim we had a snowball fight and finished up with wet clothes as we clambered back on board. This wasn't particularly wise, considering I only had shorts, a T-shirt, sandals and a light jacket.

Halfway across the Alps the road disappeared in a snowdrift. A blizzard created an almost perfect white-out and I found myself praying like mad that we'd get out safely. I had never been frightened of snow before, but the temperature had plummeted and we couldn't go forward or back.

Four hours later a snowplough reached us. It couldn't turn around and had to reverse for miles down the mountains, while the coach followed, edging forwards at a few miles an hour.

Finally we reached the French border at 1.30 a.m. and had to change coaches and drivers.

On 31 December I woke in Paris and saw the Eiffel Tower from the window of the bus. I woke Sandy because she'd never seen it. There were only ten of us left on board the bus, so we had room to stretch out at last. We arrived at Calais at three in the afternoon and had to wait nearly two hours for a ferry to Dover. I had a cup of English tea and a scone during the crossing.

The bus arrived in London at 7 p.m. – nearly four days after leaving Athens. I could still make Reading for New Year's Eve. I said goodbye to Sandy – my new lifelong friend – and got a lift to Paddington station. I had just enough money for the train ticket. 'I'm going home,' I told the ticket collector excitedly – as if he cared.

At Reading station, I phoned Auntie Edna, who came to collect me with Graeme and Trevor. It was fantastic to see them all and I felt almost like the prodigal daughter. At midnight we hugged and kissed. Then we played charades and I laughed until it hurt.

'So where do you call home?' asked Trevor, as we stacked glasses in the sink.

'It will always be here,' I answered, giving him a hug. At the same time, I realised that I now had two homes. A part of me belonged in Greece.

SIX

MIKE Corns leaned on the bar and watched me working. He was in his mid-thirties, stocky and very handsome. He was tanned, of course, like all the sailors. We'd chatted a few times before and I knew that Mike skippered *Kovalam* a classic 120-foot motor yacht.

'I've just lost my stewardess,' he said. 'She's run off with her boyfriend and I have a charter in two days. Would you like the job?'

I looked at him dubiously. 'What would I have to do?'

'Same as you do now – you pour drinks, you serve food. The big difference is it's sunnier and you get to swim every day.'

'But I don't know the first thing about boats.'

'That doesn't matter. If my cook likes you, you're on. If she doesn't – forget it.'

The following morning I took a taxi to Flisfos, a marina further along the coast. Luxury motor yachts were moored stern-to along the dock, their hulls gleaming white beneath a forest of masts. Some of them were expensive playthings for the rich, while others were owned by companies and businessmen who offered them for luxury charters.

I found *Kovalam* and stood on the pontoon, wondering what to

do next. Yachts don't have doorbells. Did I just go on board? Why
was there a basket full of shoes on the pontoon?

I stood there for a while until Robert, the engineer, came out on
the aft deck with a can of resin. He looked like a mad professor
with his shock of blond hair and big pebble glasses that gave him a
permanently startled look. His beautiful white uniform was covered in oil and hung from his skinny frame. Later I discovered that
Mike Corns affectionately called him 'the disagreeable lad'.

'Can I help you?' he asked

'I'm looking for Mike.'

'Come aboard. Are you here about the stewardess's job? You
have to go and see Jaynie.' He showed me along the side passage to
the saloon.

Jaynie Foster wore a white uniform – a cross-over skirt and shirt
– and stood in the middle of the biggest pile of laundry I had ever
seen in my life. Sheets, towels, uniforms, napkins and tablecloths
were spilling from the varnished table.

Usually I didn't care what people thought of me, but Jaynie
looked so stunning that I instantly wanted her to like me. This was
an entirely new concept.

Another face appeared from behind the pile of washing. Sue had
long, curly strawberry blonde hair and a face covered in freckles.
She was the senior stewardess on board.

'Oh, good excuse for a cup of tea,' said Jaynie, tossing a towel to
one side. She put the kettle on and we sat on the foredeck for the
interview.

Jaynie proved to be eccentric in the nicest possible way. She had
a wicked sense of humour and the spontaneity of a true romantic.
She never wore shoes on board, which drove Mike crazy. Since
they were sleeping together, Jaynie shrugged off his complaints.

The interview was more like morning tea with a friend than a
grilling on qualifications. My only reservation was about seasickness. Memories of my maiden voyage with Dad were still vivid.
Ugh! Surely, I must have outgrown it by now.

Kovalam was due to sail the next day on a two-week charter. I had just enough time to pack a bag, lock up my flat, hand in my notice at the Landfall and get back to the boat by evening. The yacht had accommodation for twelve guests and seven crew. The guests had beautiful cabins, fitted in teak and brass. The crew – depending on their place is the pecking order – lived in the equivalent of shoeboxes.

My quarters were in a horrible hole in the foredeck, reached via a hatchway and narrow set of stairs. It was a horrible, wet and smelly place, where the anchor chain came up into the boat. I had to take my bunk apart each time we weighed anchor and coil the chain into the locker.

Jaynie shared the captain's cabin with Mike, while Sue, who was dating Vasco, the first mate, also had a cabin. This meant that I had to share with Robert and Howie the deckhand.

Vasco looked like a pirate with blond hair and a Walter Raleigh beard. I hated him almost instantly because he was such a chauvinist.

On my first morning Sue showed me the ropes and reminded me in a subtle way that I was the lowest-ranking individual on board. I began cleaning cabins, packing away provisions and preparing for the charter passengers to arrive.

Our guests were a Swiss financier and his family. They were friends of *Kovalam*'s owner but very laid back and relaxed about the shipboard routines. In the evening they arrived and we did a short sail to a quiet bay and moored for the night.

I woke at six the next morning and helped Sue and Jaynie serve breakfast, before cleaning the heads (toilets) and cabins. Mid-morning we set off for one of the islands. Within twenty minutes my breakfast was a distant memory. I leaned over the rail and heaved my heart out. Why, oh why, did I agree to this? What could have possibly possessed me? I contemplated throwing myself overboard, or pleading with Mike to drop me on the nearest rock.

All I can remember of that entire trip is my seasickness. Thankfully, a lot of the time we were moored in quiet bays and coves and I'd be OK. But as soon as we hit open water, I felt sick again. I'd be cleaning the heads and throwing up into them at the same time. Mercifully, everybody made allowances for me, except for Mike who refused to let me take any pills.

'The only way to overcome it is to get used to it,' he said gruffly, as he shoved a bowl of mashed potato towards me. 'Keep eating, keep drinking and keep working.'

My favourite place on *Kovalam* was up on the boat deck in an alcove where there was a sheltered seating area, protected from the spray and wind. I would lie down breathing in the fresh air and trying to will the contents of my stomach to stay put. To a degree Mike was right about seasickness. I did get used to the motion of the boat until eventually it took a large swell to make me sick. I started to enjoy myself – not so much the work, but the surround-ings. We were roaming the Greek islands, following the sun and the breeze. Each day brought new sights and a sense of expectation.

Being a stewardess is a thankless job. It's a cross between being a waitress and a chambermaid, but you're also expected to help with the sailing and help look after the yacht.

Sometimes the charters were back-to-back and hard work. We had a day to drop off, do the laundry, stock the galley, clean the boat, and pick up the next guests. Jaynie and I would spend hours going to supermarkets and speciality shops. Ours was a strange relationship. We became really good friends – and were destined to remain so – but Jaynie also became the first person, apart from my mother, who really influenced me. She was like a mentor and I worshipped her in a sort of schoolgirl way.

I envied her confidence and worldliness. Regardless of whether we were entertaining crown princes or a newly minted, double-glazing millionaire, Jaynie treated them all the same. She didn't envy them. She loved her life and each day was an adventure.

Most of the guests were wealthy businessmen and industrialists, with a sprinkling of European blue-bloods and politicians. The Duke and Duchess of Valdorano were memorable. They were used to having staff and knew that politeness and civility won respect.

This lesson hadn't been learned by some of the Americans, who treated the crew as servants and were forever complaining that the ice-cubes weren't square enough or their hair-drier didn't fit the sockets.

The Greek islands were still unspoiled in those days. There were thousands of pristine bays, with brilliant blue water and blindingly white sand. During that first season, *Kovalam* sailed through the Corinth Canal to Corfu, Rhodes, Lesbos and Kos. We picked up and dropped off in Flisfos. As soon as the gangplank touched the dock I'd be out of there, off to see Pavlos for a night before taking a taxi back to the boat the next day.

At the end of the season *Kovalam* went to Malta for the winter to do a refit. Most of us agreed to stay on and help. We rented a flat for three months and spent our days sanding, painting, varnishing and scrubbing.

I hated the work at the boatyard and Malta proved to be wet, cold and miserable. It virtually shut down in winter when the last tourists had gone. There were no places to go out or eat.

For the first time since I left Wales, I felt lonely. People were coming and going, but nobody stayed long enough to touch me or make me feel better. I missed Jaynie desperately. She had left to live in Africa and had been replaced by an English girl called Jay, whom I hated instantly. To be fair to her, I would probably have disliked anyone who took Jaynie's place. It was like a re-run of the stepfather situation – only this time I had a new 'stepmother'. Poor Mike was caught in the middle and must have wondered what he'd done to deserve so much hostility.

There were tensions within the rest of the crew as well. Sue and Vasco eventually left and were replaced by Brindley and Caroline. Caroline was more my own age and we got on really well. I didn't miss Jaynie so much any more and, together, we made Jay's life a misery.

I'd finished with Pavlos during the summer when I discovered that he'd been screwing around while I was at sea. No surprises there, then. Unfortunately, this made me feel even lonelier. Malta was about to go down in my diary as a complete disaster when suddenly I met Doug Sayers and fell madly in love.

I didn't have flings. I had full-on relationships. I dived in feet first, without ever testing the temperature of the water, or the depth. One problem with this approach has to do with longevity. Most relationships take years to run their course. Somehow I managed to squeeze them into two months.

We had finished the refit and *Kovalam* had gone stern-to in Valletta. Moored next to us was a boat called *Welsh Conquest*, the smallest of three charter yachts (the others being *Welsh Liberty* and *Welsh Dragon*) all owned by the same businessman. His crews were fairly inexperienced, picked up from docks and marinas.

Doug was a deckhand on *Welsh Conquest*. He was medium height and handsome with a shock of black curly hair and the most gorgeous crooked smile I had ever seen. I fell head over heels, hook line and sinker . . . etc . . . etc . . .

For two months in Valletta we were inseparable. I had never had a relationship that was so intense. We were infatuated with each other and, although only nineteen, I couldn't imagine life without Doug.

I wanted *Welsh Conquest* to offer me a job. Then I prayed that one of our deckhands would leave so Doug could join *Kovalam*. We knew that both boats were doing summer charters around the Med, but that might mean not seeing each other for weeks or months. The chances of us being in the same port at the same time were remote.

When I finally had to say goodbye to Doug I didn't stop crying for two days. I almost didn't leave. For a moment, I contemplated diving off the stern and swimming back to the dock. I had never felt so miserable.

Doug gave me a tape of the Pink Floyd's *Wish You Were Here*, which I played so often that the others threatened to throw me overboard. He also gave me a postcard from the soundtrack showing a person diving into the water. I pinned it above my bunk in the fo'c'sle and made sure it was the first and last thing I saw when I woke up and went to sleep.

Kovalam went back to cruising the Greek islands and *Welsh Conquest* went to the South of France. The summer charters had a sameness about them, but Trevor came out to crew on the boat during his school holidays.

He'd been away at boarding school through most of my troubles in Wales and couldn't really understand what had happened and why I had rebelled. Even so, he never judged me. He remained my absolute best friend, with all the qualities that I lacked, such as calmness, intelligence and logic. Everybody loved Trevor and I was very proud of him.

Boat bums and navvies are always drifting between yachts and countries. It's almost impossible to keep a relationship going, but I tried my best with Doug. It took a lot of patience, stamina and loose change. At times I stood for hours at a phone box at the end of a marina, trying to get a call through to the South of France. I had to hope Doug was on board the yacht, or that somebody could find him.

In the middle of the season I had six days between charters and I pleaded with Mike to let me go to France. At last he agreed, as long as I promised to be back in time for our next charter. I called Doug and told him I was coming. He promised to get back to me with the details of where *Welsh Liberty* would be moored. He'd moved boats during the summer.

I flew from Athens to Nice on one of the epic journeys of my life. Doug hadn't managed to get a message to me so I had no idea where to find *Welsh Liberty*. Having checked out Nice, I took a train to Cannes.

There were two large marinas in the town. I checked out the first and then started walking along the seafront, carrying my small holdall over my shoulder. It was quite a long way on a hot day. A car pulled up alongside me and the driver asked if I was lost.

'How far is the marina?'

'About a mile. Do you want a lift?'

Normally, I'd never accept a lift from a stranger, but he seemed like a nice young man in a smart car.

I hesitated.

'I won't bite,' he laughed.

I tossed my bag on the back seat and climbed in. At the marina, he very helpfully talked to the harbour master and we discovered that *Welsh Liberty* had left that morning to sail to Monte Carlo.

'You'll need to catch a train,' he said. 'If you go direct it will only take a couple of hours.'

I felt relieved to know exactly where I was going. It was now late afternoon and I'd be with Doug by dinnertime.

'Do you want a lift to the station?' the Frenchman asked.

'Thanks.'

I bought a ticket and he put me on the right platform. As I stood there, waiting for the train, he came back.

'I'm sorry. You're on the wrong platform. I made a mistake.'

'Are you sure?'

'*Oui, oui*. This way. Come with me. It's on the other side.'

I knew he was wrong, yet he sounded so convincing.

'Hurry now. The train is coming.'

I grabbed my bag.

'We'll drive around. It's quicker.'

I jumped in the front and held my bag. It had everything in it – my passport, money, airline ticket, address book . . .

We turned into a dark enclosed alley. Cars parked on either side made it even narrower. He stopped. 'This is it?'

'What?'

'This is the station.'

Suddenly I knew what was going to happen. I reached for the handle and leaned against the door. As it opened, he shoved me hard and grabbed for my bag. At the same time he put his foot on the accelerator.

Somehow, I managed to do a U-turn in mid-air and grab hold of the seat, with my legs dragging on the ground through the open door. We each had hold of my bag. While still moving, he let go of the steering wheel and began punching me, trying to force me to let go. It must have looked like the Keystone Cops.

He crashed into a row of parked cars and swerved across to hit another. This gave me the chance to throw myself into the passenger seat. Before I realised it I was back in the car, strangling him. I had my hands at his throat, screaming, 'You bastard, you bastard.' I ripped the chain from around his neck. His eyeballs were on stalks.

'I'm sorry, I'm sorry,' he said. 'I don't know why I did it.'

I wanted to rip his head off, but the pleading in his voice got through to me. I believed him. I don't think he set out to rob me.

A crowd had now gathered to watch. Nobody offered to help me. I let go of his throat and slammed the car door as I left. I didn't get his licence plate as he drove off.

The knees of my white dungarees had been ripped out and my knees were bleeding, staining all the way down to my trouser cuffs. Without realising, I had been so frightened that I wet myself. The dungarees were plastered to my thighs. I also had tufts of hair hanging out where he had grabbed hold of my head and punched me in the face. I sat in the middle of the road and burst into tears. Meanwhile, the crowd watched as though the whole scene had been improvised street theatre.

Some time later, I walked back to the station and tried to clean myself up in the toilets. I waited an hour for the next train to Monte Carlo. During the journey other passengers tried hard not to stare at me. I'm sure they couldn't decide if I had just killed someone, or crawled out of a car wreck.

I arrived at about 10 p.m. The station is at the top of the town and I had a long walk to the marina. As I trudged down the hill, a man in a doorway asked if I needed help. I screamed at him so loudly to get lost that he ran inside and bolted the door.

By now I was dying to go to the loo. I couldn't go into a café – my dungarees were stained with mud, blood and urine. Instead I found a quiet, dark bush and crouched behind it. Pain shot through me. I'd sat on a cactus and turned my tender rump into a pincushion. Surely, life couldn't get any worse.

I was wrong. I reached the marina to discover no sign of *Welsh Liberty*. I recognised another boat and woke one of the crew.

'Oh, they're in Villefranche,' he said. 'Back up the coast. Are you OK?'

'Yeah, just fine.'

I didn't know whether to laugh or cry. It was too late to get a train. Instead I caught a taxi, which cost me £50. I reached Villefranche at two in the morning. *Welsh Liberty* was anchored offshore and due to leave on a charter in a few hours.

By now I had reached the end of my tether. I had been beaten, almost robbed, bloodied, pricked and misled. The path of true love might not be smooth, but it should be a bloody sight less rocky than this.

Walking down to the docks, I found where the dinghies were tied up. I stole one and began rowing across the moonlit bay towards the distant silhouette of what I hoped was *Welsh Liberty*. An hour later, I reached the ladder and hauled myself on board. The dinghy drifted away. One of the fishermen would find it in the morning and tow it back.

Everybody on board was asleep. I found the fo'c'sle and crawled down, bumping into one of the girls I had met in Malta.

'My God, where have you been?' she asked.

'You don't want to know. Where's Doug?'

She pointed to his bunk and I crawled in next to him.

'You were supposed to be here about twelve hours ago,' he whispered sleepily.

I could still smell the Frenchman's aftershave on my hands even though I'd washed them three times. It made me want to vomit.

Doug and I had a wonderful four days. He and the crew of *Welsh Liberty* really looked after me. I flew back to Athens in time for the next charter and made a promise that I'd never spend so long away from Doug again. Maybe next season we could crew together.

I resumed my phone-box vigils at Flisfos each time we ended a charter. It still took hours to reach Doug, or sometimes I failed completely. A month or so later I managed to get through to him. Straight away I recognised a change in his voice. Fear lurched in my stomach.

'Is anything wrong?' I asked.

'No.'

I could tell he was lying. We were soul mates. We were going to finish up on the same boat. He'd be skipper and I'd be cook. We'd get married and have kids and live happily ever after.

'You sound a bit down,' I said.

'No, everything's fine.' His voice was cold and flat.

The conversation went on like this until I said, 'Look Doug, what is it? What's happening?'

I didn't want to ask the question because I didn't want to hear the answer.

'I'm seeing someone else,' he said.

My world collapsed. I don't remember putting the phone down. I burst into tears and left it hanging there, with the line open.

I couldn't be consoled. For weeks afterwards I was prone to crying for the slightest reason and for years afterwards I still thought about Doug. Occasionally, I still do. He's married now and has a couple of children.

For a long while I carried on writing to his mother because she was my link with him. I had never met her, but we'd spoken on the phone. I thought that one day Doug might ask about me or come looking and she would always have an address. I also listened out for his name and kept track of where he was working. Everybody always does on boats.

Maybe we'd bump into each other in some distant port, I thought. Who knows what might happen?

SEVEN

A T the end of my second summer in the Mediterranean, I left *Kovalam* in Majorca. My love for boats, sailing and the sea had grown stronger with each new voyage.

Boat bumming wasn't a 'career' in my mother's definition of the word, but it was a nice way to spend the time until I found what I really wanted to do. I didn't have an ambition. I didn't see myself as being particularly driven or the sort of person who measured success in terms of money, prestige or responsibility. Having a good time was a more important priority. So much so, that it had become my guiding principle.

Most boat bums dream of skippering a yacht, or making enough money to own one. As a stewardess, I had no career ambitions at all. *Kovalam* was a floating 'gin palace' in the eyes of most professional sailors. I was a glorified waitress, not a real sailor.

I had listened to the stories of these real yachties in the bars and tavernas on the islands. They talked of sailing in 'God's great cathedral' (the Atlantic) at night, under clear skies when the water turned to glass, reflecting the stars, and the only sounds were the flapping of canvas and creak of the ropes. They also spoke about how quickly the sea could turn nasty and break a person's body and spirit.

As I listened, I realised how little I knew about sailing. Most people come into yachting through junior sailing clubs or weekend regattas. They move up through the ranks of bigger boats and challenges, but most prefer to stay amateur. Very few venture too far offshore.

Professional sailors, however, tend to fall into the way of life. They are a breed all of their own and I could see it in their eyes and weathered faces. A part of me wanted to be just like them.

In Majorca I hung around for a while hoping in vain that I might get a boat to the Caribbean. Apart from crossing the Atlantic, I could spend a season in the West Indies doing charters. Each day, I went down to the docks and found out which boats were looking for crew. But the answer was always the same. I didn't have the sailing experience and they couldn't afford to take passengers.

Eventually, I gave up and headed home to England. A few weeks later, I read a crew-finder classified in one of the yachting magazines:

Cook/deckhand wanted for yacht transfer from Sri Lanka to the Seychelles and charter season in the Indian Ocean. Call Chris.

The telephone number was in Cornwall and I arranged to meet Chris at a local yacht club. He turned out to be a short, weedy man, with sandy hair and a goatee. His eyes seemed to spend a little too long looking me up and down rather than focusing on my face.

'We pick up the boat in Sri Lanka, sail to the Maldives and then to the Seychelles,' he said. 'We'll charter there for the season. We'll pick up most of the crew locally, but I need a cook.'

'I can do that,' I said, blagging my way through the interview.

The boat was called *Passat*, a newly built, 70-foot wooden schooner owned by a German company.

'I can pay you US$200 a week when we start doing charters,' said Chris. 'For the transfer it's a flat fee of US$1,000. We leave in a fortnight.' He sounded quite relieved to have found someone.

The first indication that the trip wouldn't be plain sailing emerged when we arrived in Sri Lanka. There was no boat. The German skipper, his wife and two sons had sailed to the Maldives – a leg that we were supposed to do.

Chris sent a 'please explain' telegram to the owners in Germany. He also asked about the promised funds that hadn't been wired. I had no money at all and Chris had a few hundred dollars.

We spent a month waiting for new instructions. In the meantime, there was nothing else to do but lie by the pool and look around the island.

In the early 1980s Sri Lanka was a very peaceful place, as well as being beautiful. What a shame it has so many problems nowadays. We hired a taxi for two weeks for next to nothing and drove from the south to the north. The journey to Kandy was a mind-boggling experience of exotic colours, strange smells and beautiful people. We stopped to ride elephants, visited jewellery workshops and stayed in small guesthouses along the way. Kandy was like an E.M. Forster novel. I could have stayed for ever if it hadn't been for Chris, who spoiled my enjoyment of everything. He had all the courage and fortitude of a mouse when dealing with authority.

Once we had exhausted the sightseeing possibilities and our funds, instructions and money finally arrived. We were to fly to the Maldives, pick up the boat and then proceed to the Seychelles as planned.

Male, the capital island of the Maldives, lay 400 miles south-west of Sri Lanka. It is one of a string of islands that total only about a hundred square miles of land and rise no more than two yards above sea level.

We arrived mid-morning and as I stepped off the plane the heat sucked the moisture out of my skin. Breathing became an effort and I was convinced that my lungs were being scorched. By midday it was unbearable. All I could do was lie in a bed beneath a fan and keep completely still. There was no relief from the humidity. My clothes stuck to my skin and perspiration dripped from rat-tails of hair on my forehead.

This was long before the Maldives became a popular holiday destination. Most people had never heard of it. Only one hotel in town had air conditioning and I arrived to discover that everybody else was packed in there, huddling around the humming boxes, drinking warm soft drinks.

Male was flat, sandy and baked, with a stinking market and a
climate that could desiccate coconuts in the trees. The little
harbour was dotted with Arab dhows and most of the locals made
their living from fishing. Racks of salted fish lined the waterfront.

This was my first experience of a Muslim country and it didn't
seem particularly welcoming. The men would click their tongues
as I walked past, looking me up and down. As a Western woman –
even though modestly dressed – I was regarded as a slut. Some of
the younger men grabbed their crotches and thrust their hips at me.
The older men would leer with rotten teeth. Don't these people
have dentists? I hated the place and hated the people. The entire
island seemed like a lump of concrete from an unfinished building;
it was as if a tropical cyclone had flattened every feature.

The *Passat* was off cruising and we had to wait three days until it
arrived back. The German skipper and his family seemed reluctant to
hand it over. Again the lines of communication had broken down.
While we waited for a cable from the owners, we decided to go
cruising around the islands. There were over 2,000 to choose from.

On the positive side, I discovered that only the main island
sucked. The rest of the Maldives were beautiful – fringed by coral
reefs, turquoise lagoons, white sand and dotted with coconut
palms. These were fairytale islands that conjured up images of
Robinson Crusoe and *The Swiss Family Robinson*.

There were a couple of scuba-diving operations on the islands and
a handful of hotels – mostly run by Germans. Chris and I found
Ahmed and Mohammed, two locals, who agreed to help crew *Passat*
on the voyage to the Seychelles. We also met a British couple, Peter
and Barbara, from Guernsey. Peter was a fisherman rather than a
sailor, but as a man of the sea he was a good addition to the crew.
Barbara flew to the Seychelles and would meet us there.

I had to stock up for the voyage, which took five seconds
because there was nothing to buy in Male. Scouring the markets, I
managed to gather a few fresh bits and pieces to add to the cans of
German sausages, sauerkraut and beans already on board.

Two thousand miles lay ahead of us – a short hop across the

Indian Ocean, but the longest voyage I had ever taken. I had never been out of sight of land for more than four days. Now I had two weeks to look forward to. I had absolutely no idea what to expect, but I was excited, nervous and full of anticipation.

On the second day, methane from the sewage system began leaking into the yacht. It came up through the shower and the sink, creating an awful stench, making me dry-retch whenever I went below. My silver jewellery, rings and necklaces went black, along with all the brass fittings in the galley and washrooms.

'I'm going to have to pump this stuff out of the boat,' said Chris, who then beetled down below and pumped out the tanks.

He came up a little later. 'I don't know whether we should turn back or not,' he said.

'Why?'

'Well, because we haven't got any fresh water.'

'Yes, we have, I watched them fill up the tanks myself.'

'Yes, but I've just pumped them out by mistake.'

Peter and I looked at each other in disbelief.

Chris disappeared again, this time determined to discharge the sewage and get rid of the smell.

He came up again. 'We can't go back any more.'

'Why not?'

'Because we haven't got any diesel.'

Peter said: 'I definitely saw them put the diesel on board.'

'I've accidentally pumped it out,' said Chris.

This sailing lark is a bit strange, I thought. We had no wind, no water and no fuel. The dregs of diesel could run the generator every so often, but we couldn't run the engine. The breeze barely rippled the surface and was coming from the wrong direction.

Thank God I had Peter on board, otherwise I might have thrown Chris overboard. We kept each other sane and pretty much ignored Chris from then on. Poor Mohammed and Ahmed had difficulty understanding how anybody could have been stupid enough to discharge all our water and fuel. They weren't the only ones. At least we had plenty of food and surely the wind would pick up soon.

A week later we'd crawled only 500 miles from the Maldives. I had thrown away most of our fresh food, which had rotted in the freezers because we didn't have enough fuel to power them. This left us with cans of German food. I'll never look at pickled red cabbage again.

For a few days we lived on nothing but baked beans and could probably have powered the sails ourselves if we could have harnessed the gas. Mohammed and Ahmed started fishing with string and a sailing needle bent into a hook. They caught two huge tuna and I ate my first sushi. They salted and dried the rest because we didn't have the fuel to use the oven.

Fresh water didn't prove to be a problem. There were squalls every night and we rigged up a catchment system using the sails to collect water. The sails weren't proving much good for anything else.

On watch together one night, Peter and I decided to take a peek at the captain's log. Among the entries, Chris had written: 'I hope the satellite navigation doesn't give out.'

Brilliant! Along with being a first-class plonker, Chris was worried about navigating without the sat nav. What on earth was I doing?

Peter and I laughed about it, trying to hide our disquiet. Our leisurely two-week hop across the Indian Ocean had stretched to three weeks and we were still nearly 1,000 miles from the Seychelles.

The next day, while Peter had the wheel, I noticed a wall of black appear behind us, slightly off to port. It was marching towards us across the water.

'What do you suppose that is?' I asked.

'It looks weird.'

'But very impressive.'

Peter ran down to get Chris. 'You better come up and have a look at this.'

Chris poked his head out of the companionway hatch and went pale.

'What should we do?' I asked.

'Oh, it's a squall. Um, well, just make sure you keep the wind behind you.'

He disappeared again.

Peter looked at me and said, 'No, no, no.' He went back down, grabbed Chris and said, 'I want you to tell us what we do.'

'I'm sure there won't be much wind in it. It'll be fine.'

The black ugly wall marched closer. The waves had kicked up and white caps looked like teeth. Chris disappeared again and locked himself in his cabin.

'It's going to kill us,' I muttered.

Peter had had enough. He swung below, broke down the door to Chris's cabin and dragged him squealing and complaining on deck. Then he lashed his wrists to the binnacle.

'Now, what do we do?'

The sun had disappeared and the temperature suddenly plunged. Gusts of wind filled the sails, forcing us to heel over and then spring back.

'Take all the sails down,' screamed Chris.

We rushed about on deck, dragging down the main and head-sail. The wind tore at my T-shirt and *Passat* was now pitching and sliding into troughs. My heart was pounding. This was my first really big squall. It was almost as though it was chasing us. There is a whole ocean out there and it is coming for us.

I didn't have time to be truly frightened. I didn't know if I should be because I didn't know what was coming. Afterwards, I told myself that next time I'd remember to be scared witless. The rest of the trip passed in almost complete silence for Chris. He locked himself in his cabin and rarely surfaced except for meals. It took a month to reach the Seychelles. By then we had been mentioned in dispatches as missing at sea and Barbara, Peter's wife, had started to panic. With no fuel to run the generator, we had to limit our use of the radio.

My first glimpse of Mahé, the main island, took my breath away. The mountains plunged into the water, creating a dramatic back-drop to the rocky bays and crystal clear water. What a relief to see land.

Beautiful white-painted buildings and palm trees dotted the shore. There were hardly any boats on the water as we entered the harbour in Victoria. We eased alongside the dock to clear customs and immigration. Chris was a little nervous because he hadn't sailed *Passat* on to a quay without engines. Peter eventually did it for him.

After clearing the paperwork, we used our last dregs of fuel to motor to a mooring in the middle of the bay.

'Right, Mohammed, get the anchor out,' said Chris.

Mohammed opened the front hatch and grabbed the anchor.

'Toss it over,' yelled Chris.

I heard the splash and the sound of the anchor chain rattling over the deck. Mohammed sat watching more and more of the chain play out, until finally it disappeared completely over the side of the boat. It hadn't been attached to the boat.

'De anchor is going over de side,' he said.

'Good,' answered Chris.

'No, de anchor is gone.'

'Gone where.'

'Over de side.'

Peter and I had watched this comedy of errors in complete silence but now started laughing. That was enough for me. As soon as we reached the dock and tied up, I grabbed my bags and told Chris what I thought of his seamanship and his job.

'I want my money and I want to be flown home.'

'What about the charters?'

'You have got to be joking.'

Chris had no money. He promised to wire the owners. In the meantime, Barbara picked Peter and me up from the dock. We all went to the Coral Reef Hotel and spent a wonderful few days eating like pigs and relaxing. Peter paid for my share.

A few days later, I went down to the harbour to find *Passat* hauled up on to the slipway. Mohammed and Ahmed were still living on board, waiting to be paid. Chris had arranged for work to be done. I wondered if the locals were going to be so obliging if he didn't pay them.

Two days later, as I sat in the garden forecourt of the Coral Reef

Hotel, I read in the local paper that *Passat* had been impounded. The story didn't give a reason, but unpaid bills are my bet. I went back down to the dock and found hundreds of people all staring at the boat. Compared to anything else in the harbour *Passat* was the height of luxury. The guys were still living on board because they had nowhere else to stay.

Peter and Barbara were going home. They had been so generous that I couldn't accept their offer of an airfare. I was determined to stay in the Seychelles until I was paid. Chris owed me over US$2,000.

Peter and Barbara introduced me to a local schoolteacher Rodney Payet, who offered me somewhere to stay. I ended up living with his wonderful family along the coast at Pointe Larue. He also found accommodation for Mohammed and Ahmed with local families. We spent two months on the island, pestering Chris for money. He never did get the funds. Perhaps the company went bust. Mum sent me enough to tide me over until my visa ran out. Then I went to the British High Commission and asked them to get me home. I repaid the fare afterwards.

Although the entire episode had been a nightmare, I loved my time in the Seychelles, living with Rodney's family and going places that tourists don't get to see. Now I was even more determined to sail. No other lifestyle could match it.

After a month at home, I flew to Majorca and spent the summer doing day work on various boats. Of a morning, I'd go down to the marina, have a coffee and pastry in a café and then walk the docks, asking people for work.

I knew some of the boats and crews, but you lose any inhibition about meeting people. You are all part of the same small world. Most of the time I was really lucky. Apart from being a stewardess, I learned to sand and varnish – my least favourite job. I also did some secretarial work, typing up inventories and letters for Billy Porter, a living legend in sailing circles, who maintains to this day that I am the worst secretary he has ever had.

A lot of people in Palma that summer were to become part of my life in the years to follow. They were of different nationalities, on different boats. For the first time in my life, I felt as though I fitted right in. I belonged with these people. Apart from Billy Porter, who had probably sailed with Noah, I also met King Kong, the largest, loudest and most colourful Antiguan ever to grace foreign shores. He was the first person I'd ever met from the Caribbean and I remember thinking that if they were all like him then I had to get to Antigua fast.

Among the other yachties, I met Paul Standbridge and Arthur Radford, whom I was destined to sail alongside. They were modern-day 'pirates' who plundered good times rather than gold.

As the weather grew colder and the tourists thinned, I decided once again that I wanted to go to the Caribbean. There were plenty of boats going over, but I faced the same old problem of not having enough sailing experience.

One afternoon, I walked past *Southern Star*. The skipper John Pearson was sitting on the aft deck with his girlfriend Brownie, an American and the cook on board.

'Are you going over to the Caribbean?' I asked.

'How much experience have you got?'

'Not a lot,' I said, very truthfully.

John invited me on board for a drink. 'We're looking for a fun crew,' he said. 'We don't have a real timetable, so it's going to be very relaxed.'

My heart skipped.

'Does that mean I can come?'

'Well, we're actually looking for a couple. The only cabin left is a double.'

'I am a couple,' I said. 'I'll just go and get the other half.'

In the bar a few nights earlier I had met this Dutch guy, Marcel, who was contemplating going to the Caribbean. I found him at the same bar, sitting on the same stool. 'You're coming to the Caribbean,' I said, almost dragging him out the door. 'We're a couple, OK? This is the only way we're going to get there.'

Back on the boat, John sussed straight away that we weren't

together, but he didn't say anything. Marcel and I shared a cabin, but in sailing you're always being lumped in with people. Privacy isn't a priority.

Among those on board was Rachel Dunn, who had been sailing for a few years longer than me, and who became a lifelong friend. We also had Rupert Wynne – better known as 'Bear'; and Hollywood, a complete plonker who had earned his nickname by being so shallow and vain. By an amazing coincidence, an old schoolmate of Trevor's, called Martin Barnes, was also part of the crew.

We left in October, doing a nice easy sail to Puerto Banus in Spain. After a good night out, John told everybody to be back on board *Southern Star* by 10 a.m. For some reason, Hollywood nipped off again at the last moment without telling anybody. We were a couple of hours out, on our way to Gibraltar, when Martin piped up, 'Has anyone seen Hollywood?'

We searched the boat. We had his passport, his clothes and his wallet, but not the man. We debated carrying on without him but in the end turned around. Suddenly, a speedboat appeared in the distance. Hollywood had hitched a ride and was chasing us.

The weather turned nasty in Gibraltar and kept us there for ten days. It felt more like ten years. I hated the place. Other boats were also delayed and we spent most of the time drinking and partying. Rachel, Brownie, Martin and I chartered a light plane and flew to Morocco for a day. Brownie bought a parrot from a street trader and called him Rocky. He was to become our mascot on my first voyage across the Atlantic. He ate his way through the panelling on *Southern Star* and attacked anyone who wasn't Brownie.

The storms were coming in one after the other, without a break. Fed up with waiting, John decided to leave anyway. Under dark skies we passed the Rock and sailed into the strait. We put up a spinnaker – the first time I had ever seen one up close. Instantly I was terrified by its power and by how fast we accelerated.

'Do you want to helm?' John asked, handing me the wheel.

'Are you sure?'

'That's how you're going to learn.'

My knuckles turned white as I gripped the leather on the stainless steel wheel. I had my legs braced apart as if frightened the yacht might take off without me. John stood there for hours, teaching me to helm. I can still remember the lessons because he made everything seem so simple.

'All you have to do is follow the wind,' he said, describing how to sail with the spinnaker.

'But the wind is behind us.'

'Yes. And all you're trying to do is keep the spinnaker full of air. That's why you're following the wind. Feel it over your shoulder. Don't turn your head. Watch the sails.'

He taught me how to judge the curl of the edges of the spinnaker and to look at the telltales – the small ribbons that fly off the back of the sails. Whenever I looked down at the compass and the course, he'd say, 'Get your head up, Tracy. Look at the sails. What are they telling you? You can't just steer a course and forget about the wind.'

This was the first time somebody had tried to teach me how to sail. On charters I wasn't allowed anywhere near the bridge. Suddenly, I discovered how being at the helm made me part of everything around us. Instead of just sitting on a moving object, I was a functional component just like the wind, or the waves, or the sails. *Southern Star* was 90 feet long, yet so receptive. A subtle movement of the wheel would alter its course and speed. I could feel this is my hands and feet; in the breeze on my cheeks and the curve of the sails. I had become part of an amazing interaction between the sea, the wind and a vessel fashioned by human hands. It was a huge learning curve. Apart from being terrified half the time, I was also badly seasick. Thankfully, *Southern Star* was a metal boat and the decks could be easily washed off.

By the time we reached Tenerife, I was getting used to the large swells. After a few days' break and the inevitable partying with other crews, we set off for Antigua. I couldn't believe what was happening to me. For the first time in my life I felt part of a team. I wasn't a lowly stewardess on the outside looking in. I had a watch.

Nobody on board could really understand my enthusiasm and it made them laugh. People usually hate going on watch – particularly when it means getting out of a nice warm bunk – but I didn't care. To me this was new and exciting.

The man in the cricket jumper was naked and sprinting across the outfield. He had somehow put his legs through the sleeves and pulled the jumper up so that his wedding tackle could be seen through the V-neck.

'You see that guy?' said Julian Gildersleeve.

'The streaker?'

'Yeah. That's who I was telling you about. You should ask him for a job.'

I looked at the unclothed figure of Paul Van Beek, hurtling across the lawn of the Inn at English Harbour, Antigua.

'I think I'll wait until he gets changed,' I told Julian.

I had been in Antigua for less than 24 hours, having arrived on the last day of Agents' Week – one of the biggest events of the year – in November of 1982. This is when all the charter agents turn up to see what boats and crews are on offer for the season. They then head home and begin taking bookings.

Southern Star wasn't going to be chartering in Antigua, which is why John had been in no hurry to get there. He was heading up to St Thomas after dropping me off.

We had sailed into English Harbour in the afternoon, with Nelson's Dockyard dominating one side and Shirley Heights the other. I fell in love with Antigua even before we'd lowered the sails and anchored.

Customs came out and John took responsibility for me because you couldn't bring somebody into the country unless they had either a work permit or a flight off the island. I had neither. John said I was sailing on to St Thomas with *Southern Star*. Hopefully, this lie would hold up until I found a job and another skipper sponsored me for a work permit. I rarely had more than a few hundred dollars to my name – only what I could earn doing day work. Most of this went on living expenses and having a good time.

I spent my first night in Antigua watching a revue called *Fincham's Follies*. Traditionally, the yachties put on a show for the agents on the last night of Agents' week. The impresario, Tony Fincham, had been a leading light in Antigua since he sailed there on his yacht *Freedom* many years earlier.

The revue was held at Antigua Sails, a sail loft run by another colourful character, Reena, a South African. I laughed from beginning to end. Among those on stage that night were Filthy Phil Barrett, Patrick Banfield and Peter Mullins. They were to become lifelong friends, along with many others I watched doing ridiculous things.

Antigua was still relatively undeveloped in those days. There were no sealed roads, just dirt tracks that were graded once a year after the rains. Chickens ran through the streets and stray dogs slept in the shade of trees. The wonderful smell of fried chicken and frangipani filled the warm air.

Nelson's Dockyard had once been the base for the British Navy in the great age of sail, when a young Horatio Nelson headed the squadron of the Leeward Islands. The fort and dockyard were gradually abandoned in the nineteenth century and fell into disrepair. It lay in ruins for decades until the Nicholson family started a restoration project. Like so many other expats living in Antigua, they had sailed there many years earlier and never left. The Antiguan government had taken over the restoration when it recognised the tourism potential of the only Georgian dockyard in the world.

My first priority was to find a job. Each Sunday during the season the boat bums and yachties hold a social cricket match on the beautiful big lawn belonging to the Inn at English Harbour. Of course, this is an excuse to get rolling drunk and forget most of the finer points of the game, including how to walk and talk.

While watching this high farce, I met Julian Gildersleeve, the skipper of *White Quailo*. Julian told me that another skipper had lost his stewardess the previous day when she fell off the back of a speedboat and sliced up her leg on the propeller. As he spoke, I watched Paul Van Beek streaking across the pitch wearing only his cricket jumper. He and his girlfriend Jo Jo Tobitt were English and had been in the charter business for years. Paul – better known as 'Pig' – was the skipper of *Sealestial*, an Ocean 70 and a proper luxury charter yacht.

I went to see Jo Jo the next day, but came away thinking I'd failed the interview. She didn't seem to like me at all. Later that afternoon, I got word that she was looking for me. The job was mine.

As *Southern Star* sailed away the next day, I loaded my gear on to *Sealestial* and started work with a new crew. Jo Jo proved to be a true free spirit, with boundless energy and the soul of a poet. I could barely keep up with her as she organised parties and food for cricket matches. She and Pig made a great team, although both had fiery temperaments. His exploits both on and off the water were the stuff of legends and he was regarded as an outstanding seaman. The fourth member of the crew was the deckhand Paul, a young Englishman and the calming influence on board.

Being a stewardess on a sailing boat was a lot different from the same job on a motor boat. With only four crew members, everyone had to pitch in, which meant I cleaned, cooked, sailed, scrubbed, shopped and did transfers.

As in Greece, we normally did short hops between bays and islands. Very few people who chartered the boat wanted to go sailing properly. They were more interested in sunbathing and seeing the islands. During the season we went as far north as the US Virgin Islands and to St Lucia, Dominique, St Thomas and Bermuda. Arriving in Grenada in November, we discovered that US combat troops had just invaded the island.

Grenada's self-proclaimed leader, Maurice Bishop, had been murdered in a coup attempt, prompting America to step in. There were warships in the bay and soldiers everywhere. Some of the buildings along the shore had been bombed and burnt.

Our passengers were *Sealestial*'s owner, Papos, and his girlfriend Judy who lived in New York.

'It didn't look like this last time I was here,' said Pig, as an American Navy launch came out to meet us. We tied up alongside the one dock that hadn't been destroyed. In the distance, Government House was still a smouldering heap. Elsewhere, however, things seemed remarkably normal. The shops were open and a bustling market sold fresh vegetables and fruit.

The Americans were in control of customs and immigration and we had to report to the military control post with our passports. Having settled the formalities, we stocked up the boat and then found a local dance in a warehouse. Reggae music blared out and the bottles of Carib beer were icy cold. As I sat talking to Pig a vision of manliness walked up in a uniform, complete with combat rifle. I thought I had died and gone to heaven.

'Could I ask your permission to dance with your daughter?' he drawled in a southern accent. Pig immediately hated him.

'She does what she wants to do. She's nothing to do with me,' said Pig.

The GI was about six feet four, and with his close-cropped hair and smoky blue eyes was the most gorgeous man I had ever seen in my life. He gave Pig his gun to hold. He obviously didn't know Pig at all – he's the last person in the world you'd hand a gun to.

We danced, or more correctly, I stood on his feet while he danced. He had to hold me up otherwise we couldn't have a conversation. Brad Croslin was everything I had ever imagined a GI to be and he literally swept me off my feet.

The warehouse slowly emptied and reluctantly Pig gave Brad his gun back. Brad took me back to the boat in his jeep. I smuggled him on board and squeezed him down through the front hatch. My quarters seemed even smaller with someone his size.

I smuggled him off again five hours later feeling very pleased with myself. I could have lost my job if the owner had caught me.

Brad and I arranged to meet the next day but he didn't show up.

I had the name of his barracks – a commandeered hotel – and took a taxi to the front gate.

'I want to speak to Brad Croslin,' I said to the MP who wore a white hat and gloves. He disappeared for a few minutes, leaving me standing behind the cyclone fence.

'I'm afraid Private Croslin isn't available to see anybody for the next few days.'

'Why not?'

'He's in the stockade.'

'Pardon?'

'Solitary confinement.'

'What did he do?'

The soldier grinned and gave me a wink. 'He went AWOL last night.'

It turned out that Brad's jeep had been stripped of everything, including the tyres. He had to walk back to his barracks and then do some serious explaining.

Just my luck. I was only in Grenada for two days and my new boyfriend spent the entire time locked in a military jail. I managed to see him once before we sailed – a quick goodbye through the cyclone fence.

'I'm sorry about all this,' I said.

He grinned. 'Don't worry. It was worth it.'

We exchanged details and began writing to each other. I've still got his dog tags and a label from his uniform that I sewed on to one of my T-shirts. Brad was perhaps the first real gentleman that I ever went out with. He wrote me beautiful letters full of wonderful descriptions and insights. After Antigua he took me camping in the Blue Ridge Mountains in Virginia and we shared a sleeping bag under the stars. He told me that he had my picture up in his locker at Fort Bragg.

As always, I fell madly in love and began racing the relationship to a conclusion. It's as though I've got the life expectancy of a butterfly and have to do everything in the shortest time. Brad and I managed to see each other twice over the next twelve months. But long distances aren't good for relationships. I became distracted and the gap between letters grew. We lost touch. I tried to find him again a few years later but the US Army isn't very forthcoming about giving out details on its personnel. Shame.

Sailing had started to dominate my life like nothing before it. I felt as though I was learning something new every day. So much of sailing is about balance and counterbalance. The wind is trying to push the boat over, while the weight of the keel is keeping it upright. As the boat heels over, it wants to turn into the wind. By steering away from the wind, you harness the energy to create forward momentum.

Race Week, the highlight of the yachting calendar, came at the end of the charter season in April. Yachts and crews from across the Caribbean and America turned up for the regatta. I volunteered to work on the committee desk with Klaire McNeil, a good friend. Together we learned how racing yachts are rated and handicapped.

Although a few people take it very seriously, Race Week is primarily a time for parties and farewells, with some sailing in between. On the final evening, a prize-giving was held on the lawns of Admiral's Inn, the old gunpowder magazine at Nelson's Dockyard. The next morning I woke up and everyone had disappeared. It was as though I'd fallen asleep for weeks, not hours. The charter boats had sailed for Florida or the Mediterranean. Most of the crews had hitched a lift, or flown out. Anyone who hadn't found a ride could be stuck in Antigua until the next season.

Pig and Jo Jo were leaving *Sealestial*. They had a house in Oxford, England, and spent part of the off-season there, seeing friends and family. Meanwhile, Paul and I had agreed to sail *Sealestial* to Fort Lauderdale for the owner. I hadn't decided what to do after that. For the first time in my life I had a few thousand dollars in my pocket. Doing back-to-back charters meant I had little time to spend it.

After a month in Florida, I drove north, along the east coast, with my new Kiwi boyfriend Gino. We stopped at loads of places before finishing up at Newport, Rhode Island. I met up with Julian

Gildersleeve again who was looking for crew to take *White Quailo* across the Atlantic to the Med. It meant flying back down to Antigua to help get the yacht ready.

I liked the idea for a lot of reasons. One of them was that Gino was back in Antigua for the off-season. We could spend more time together. This great idea lasted until I arrived and discovered he was two-timing me. When will I ever learn?

English Harbour became a completely different place in the off-season. Suddenly, I began meeting people like Jol and Judy who only came out during the summer when the tourists and yachties had left town.

After working on the boat for six weeks, Julian gave the go-ahead to leave. We sailed from Antigua in June 1984, looking for the trade winds to take us across the Atlantic.

Two days out, he said to me, 'Can you navigate?'

'No.'

'What are you going to do if I fall over the side, then?'

Pray? I didn't have a clue.

'Right then, it's time to learn.'

Navigating had always seemed like black magic to me. It didn't help that mathematics was my weakest subject at school. I'm dyslexic with numbers and learning to navigate is all about latitudes, longitudes, angles and degrees. I had to work really hard. Nowadays, with satellites and global positioning systems, finding your location in the middle of a vast ocean is as easy as pushing a button. Julian, however, wanted me to learn the traditional methods, which meant using a sextant, cosines and logarithms. Get one number wrong and basically it puts you somewhere else on the planet. Finding out where you went wrong is the difficult part because it means working your way back through the numbers, checking each of them.

It still amazes me how you can spend weeks sailing across a seemingly featureless expanse of water, without signposts or markers, and then suddenly emerge slap-bang into the middle of the harbour you were heading for. One degree out and you'd have missed it by sixty miles.

Navigation proved to be a fascinating subject. I loved the feel of the sextant – one of those solid, beautiful objects that is wonderful to hold because it is so functional. Everything about it is exquisitely designed. So simple, yet so practical.

Julian taught me how it worked in practice before telling me the theory. He showed me how to bring the sun down on to the horizon, using the mirrors and then measure the angle at precisely the right time.

It is the sun's angle to the Earth's surface at a particular GMT that helps plot location. Normally, you take a sight and then two more readings a couple of minutes apart. The noon sight gives you a cross-reference point. Then the horrible mathematics start and you go to the tables.

Apart from the sextant, the most important piece of equipment is an accurate watch. Much later I had the privilege of being able to hold John Harrison's first marine chronometer. He was the humble clockmaker who in the mid-1700s solved one of the great mysteries of maritime history – how to plot longitude.

Like most great discoveries, the answer was blindingly simple. He designed an accurate clock that could be carried on a ship and set to the time at Greenwich, England, which also marked the prime meridian – 0° longitude. By reading the clock at noon local time it is possible to work out a time difference. The Earth revolves 360° every 24 hours (or 15° per hour), so the time difference, multiplied by fifteen, will give the ship's longitude.

At first this seemed like gobbledegook to me. Then Julian showed me how it worked in practice. The blinkers fell off and I wasn't frightened of the numbers any more.

I learned more about sailing in those few weeks than some yachtsmen pick up in a lifetime on the water. On deck, steering beneath the stars, I plotted our course across 3,800 miles to Portugal and then to Majorca.

EIGHT

Two minutes before the gun my heart began to pound. Shouting filled the air and white sails blocked out the horizon. I glanced nervously about. Seasoned sailors leapt over the yacht as nimbly as mountain goats.

I couldn't believe the jostling. We had 60-foot yachts closing in so tightly that surely there had to be a collision. With a minute to go, we skirted the starting line, ready to turn and surge across. I didn't understand the tactics of forcing rivals across the line early and making them go back around the buoys. The ratchet winches rattled and skippers yelled commands.

Some yachts were dead in the water, spilling all the air from their sails. Others were shadowing the line to get a running start. A jet black yacht carved across our bow, so close I could have reached across and grabbed the side rails. Julian yelled a mock complaint. The other skipper grinned.

The gun sounded. We swung 60° and surged across the line. Sails billowed as we caught clean air. Behind us, the black yacht had misjudged its run. We had stolen its wind at the gun and left it floundering.

This was my first experience of yacht racing and I couldn't believe how excited I felt. I didn't really see myself as a competitive person when it came to sailing, but now I wanted to win so badly. I thought the buzz would diminish after the start, when the field had spread out and I couldn't tell who was winning or losing. But the sense of urgency didn't go away. It seemed to rub off from those around me. Our crew was so competitive it wouldn't have mattered if we were sailing a bathtub.

White Quailo had arrived in Sardinia to compete in the Swan Regatta. Swan is one of the most popular styles of yacht in the world because it can cruise as well as race. The owners have formed their own clubs and hold their own regattas. In our case, *White Quailo*'s owner Annie, a wealthy Australian divorcee, was determined to enjoy life and add some silverware to the mantelpiece. She had flown to Europe for the regatta and crewed the boat with a bunch of reprobates who also happened to be brilliant offshore racers.

Apart from Julian, we had Kym 'Shag' Morton, a Tasmanian, and his best mate Butcher, who arrived at the boat each morning and puked up because he was so hungover. Then he'd put on a magnificent display of seamanship, before getting drunk again that night.

We were all living in the crew house and racing during the day. Annie and her boyfriend Rocky, who owned another Swan 46, made sure we had every creature comfort.

Most of the other boats had cruising crews, whereas we had pure racers and blow-ins like me. Simon Le Bon, the lead singer of Duran Duran, was racing on *Yellow Drama*. On shore we'd all meet up at bars and restaurants, discussing the day's events and the races ahead. The courses changed each day and the last event was a longer race from Sardinia to the South of France.

Shag took perverse pleasure in stationing me on the grinder – the two-handed winch used to tighten the sheet lines and trim the sails quickly after changing course. I don't think he trusted me with anything else. Normally hulking strong people do the grinding but Shag put me on one side and Butcher on the other.

'Call that grinding? My grandmother grinds faster than that,' he shouted, as I pumped the handles. I had to remember to duck as the boom swung across during the gybes. I got caught so many times it's a wonder I have any brain cells left.

When I finally remembered to duck, I smashed the grinding handle into my mouth, knocking a tooth clean out. Blood poured down the front of my T-shirt.

'Oh, my God! Oh, my God!'

Judy took me down below. Shag followed a minute later. 'What's wrong with her?'

'She's knocked a tooth out.'

'Oh, I thought she'd damaged something important – like her hands.'

Annie flew me home to the UK and paid for a dentist to have a crown put in place. Then she flew me out to St Tropez where I met up with *White Quailo*. It had raced from Sardinia without me, which guaranteed that we won our class in the race.

The celebrations were surprisingly muted. It was almost as though it had been expected. We cleaned the boat, washed down the sails, repaired broken gear and packed everything away.

Julian decided it was time I learned how to take an engine out of a boat. 'I'm too busy to help you,' he said as he disappeared.

I spent the next three days up to my neck in grease in the bilges. At one point, I went to borrow some tools from *Matoaka*, a classic wooden ketch moored nearby. This is where I found Julian, with a beer in his hand, drinking with the skipper Steve Carson.

'I hope you've learned an important lesson about working by yourself,' said Julian, handing me a beer and grinning. I didn't know whether to drink it, or pour it over his head.

At some point during the regatta, I had made a decision. I wanted to keep racing. I couldn't imagine going back to charters. Other people's pleasure is hardly a reason for living, whereas racing seemed more than enough.

Up until then, sailing had been a way of life, not a career. I had never regarded myself as having any ambition. I didn't see a ladder stretched out in front of me that I had to climb. As long as nobody asked me to do too much cooking or cleaning, I could get by. Now I felt differently. I had become a thinking person and the need to win became overwhelming.

Offshore yacht racing is very much like polo. Very wealthy owners, who might not necessarily be particularly good sailors, surround themselves with the best crews and buy the best boats in the hope of winning trophies. There is no prize money involved – purely prestige.

Somehow, I had to get on these champion boats. It was easier said than done. If it hadn't been for Julian I'd never have sailed in the Swan Regatta. This was my Catch-22. To get experience I needed to race, but unless I had experience nobody would take me on.

It wasn't an issue of gender, as far as I knew. Only later did I discover that very few women sail on the ocean thoroughbreds. These are big boys' toys.

White Quailo was staying in the Mediterranean so I caught a ride back to the Caribbean on *Matoaka*. We had a great crossing with some wonderful sailing.

Meanwhile, Julian flew back to Antigua and when I arrived he let me stay with him on his boat, *Sunbeam*. Before long, I had a job cooking on a charter boat called *Marivent* where I spent the season.

Mum and Trevor came out for a holiday. Since finishing school Trevor had been dabbling in motor racing and showing a lot of promise. I took him on as a steward on *Marivent* and bullied him into shape. By the end of the trip he knew precisely how to set a table and serve from the left. Eventually, some of the passengers began sympathising with him and took to requesting paper plates so he wouldn't break them when he washed up.

Mum still regarded me as a tearaway, but she could see that I'd calmed down a lot. Sailing had been good for me. I seemed to be sticking to one thing whereas before I'd bounced between places and jobs, without any sense of direction. Being on the boat gave us both a chance to talk and it was like renewing a friendship. Neither of us mentioned my teenage years. These were best forgotten, or left for another time when the years had softened the edges. Instead, I wanted her to see my world and be reassured that I was finally happy.

While visiting Julian one day between charters, I began looking through his small library of books above the chart table. I pulled down a copy of *Cape Horn to Port* by Erroll Bruce and began leafing through the pages. It was the official account of the 1977 Whitbread Round the World Race. Here was an event to capture the imagination – an epic journey of 27,000 miles through the most dangerous oceans in the world.

Suddenly, I saw Julian's photograph. He'd been aboard *Heath's Condor*, a maxi, which had been in the thick of the action. On the second leg from Cape Town to Auckland, gale force winds pushed *Heath's Condor* to a point where the speedometer went off the scale. It covered 267 miles in a single day.

A crewman, Bill Abram had been flung over the side, without a safety harness, when a deflated spinnaker on the deck suddenly filled. He managed to catch a life-ring and then disappear into the swells as the rest of the crew tried to turn the yacht around.

The sails were dropped and the engine started, but the propeller malfunctioned. The sails had to be raised again. By then, the crew had lost sight of Abram. Suddenly, somebody noticed a flock of albatrosses circling the water. They were like rescue aircraft marking his position.

Stories like this fired my imagination. When Julian returned to the boat, I bombarded him with questions. What was it like? Did you get scared? How did you cope?

He described an amazing adventure, full of camaraderie and good times. 'Most of us were racing cruising boats back then. Nowadays it's getting more professional,' he said.

Over the following days, I read *Cape Horn to Port* and pestered him with more questions. I was fascinated by his stories of races won, disasters, near misses and the freezing cold. No other event put so many competitors at such risk for so long and so far from help. Could I do something like that? Did I have what it takes?

Very few women had ever competed in the Whitbread. The general consensus seemed to be that women had no desire to be that wet, cold and miserable. Either that or they simply didn't have the sailing experience or the strength to take a man's place on a crew. Yet it seemed to me that if I wanted to race yachts, why not aim for the Everest of the sport? If I wasn't willing to strive for the top, why bother climbing at all?

A few weeks later a striking yacht arrived at Falmouth in Antigua. The big old maxi looked virtually unsinkable. *Great Britain II* (*GBII*) had sailed in the previous two Whitbread contests. More importantly, it was about to go round again. *GBII* couldn't hope to compete with the newer, sleeker maxis so it was making up the numbers of cruising-boat entries.

That night I went to see the skipper, Bob Salmon.

'What does one have to do to get on board your boat for the Whitbread?' I asked.

'It's a charter boat this time,' he said. 'I'm only taking paying crew.'

To raise the necessary funds Bob had decided to offer hobby sailors and wealthy businessmen the chance of the ultimate adventure holiday. They could pay for their spot on board.

Professional sailors don't pay to go on boats. I'd never be able to live it down. Bob could sense my disappointment. He offered a compromise. 'I'm looking for two people with sailing experience. There won't be any wages – just free places on board. I've filled one place. Are you interested in the other?'

'Definitely.'

'Well, how about coming on board as cook?' he said. 'Who knows, I might even be able to pay you a bit.'

We discussed the details and Bob shook my hand. I agreed to meet up with the rest of the crew at Cowes Week in Britain in the summer of 1984. That would give us three months to get the boat ready for the race.

In the meantime, as the season ended in Antigua, I sailed with *Matoaka* up to Newport, Rhode Island, stopping in Bermuda on the way. I spent a month in Newport, doing the odd day job for my new boyfriend Scotty, the skipper of *Jubilation*, a 50-foot racing yacht. The crew house was very New England, with white picket fences and wooden shutters on the windows. I spent most of my time in the cellar doing the crew's washing, as well as the cooking and shopping.

Newport is regarded as one of the world's great sailing cities. For 126 years it was home to the America's Cup — the longest unbroken winning streak in sporting history — until those uncouth Australians came and spirited the cup away in 1983. The New York Yacht Club across the bay was still in mourning. It had been so confident of never losing the cup it had bolted the trophy down.

Newport reeks of money, but hasn't been over-commercialised. Americans aren't totally devoid of style. Amazing mansions overlook the Atlantic, built by famous families like the Astors and Vanderbilts.

I was only beginning to realise how class-bound the sailing world could be. In the grand scheme of things I was still a peasant. Of an evening at the Wharf Delhi I'd sit at tables with people who chatted unassumingly about boats they had sailed and races they had won. I saw pretty quickly I should keep my mouth shut. They told stories of America's Cup campaigns and legendary acts of seamanship. The names they mentioned were part of sailing history.

Could I really hope to be part of this world? Did I want to be? They didn't seem overly friendly.

A few hours after I'd gone to bed, I had a phone call from Whitey, the skipper of a boat called *Excalibur*. 'Are you up for a two-day charter?'

'No,' I said honestly, feeling hungover.

'Come on, say yes.'

'When?'

'Now.'

'Whitey. Let me sleep.'

'It's a really important charter. I could really do with some help. There's no cooking involved. They're bringing all their own food. It is just looking after the guests. We'll be over at Martha's Vineyard. It's lovely.'

A long pause followed as he waited for the information to sink in.

'OK then.'

'I need you down here now. We have to get the boat ready.'

I fumbled through my kit and pulled out my cleanest T-shirt and a smart pair of blue shorts. Splashing water on my face, I brushed my hair back into a ponytail. The sun had just come back as I walked along the harbour foreshore. The first thing the light touched were the tips of the masts that formed a leafless silver forest on the water.

Excalibur was a beautiful 50-footer with a gleaming blue hull, wooden decks and a nicely varnished interior. Definitely among the elite cruising boats, it normally wouldn't leave the dock for less than $5,000 a day.

Whitey poked his head up from the sail locker. 'Morning, sunshine. You look like shit.'

'Thanks to you.'

'You should blame the brewery.'

He tossed me a chamois and I began wiping dew from the decks so that it wouldn't stain the varnish. Whitey emerged with a cup of coffee.

'Once we clean up we have to pick up the food from Goat Island.' He motioned across the harbour.

'Who's catering?'

'One of the big hotels.'

'So who is the charter for?'

Whitey shrugged. 'I still don't know. We won't know till we get there.'

I frowned. 'That's odd.'

'It's all very hush–hush.'

We started speculating on who it might be. Teddy Kennedy perhaps, or maybe Jackie O.

An hour later we motored across to Goat Island and went stern to at a pier opposite the Hilton Hotel. A catering van pulled up and kitchen staff carried wicker picnic hampers down the dock. As the food kept coming, I wondered how many people we were supposed to feed.

I stowed the baskets in the galley and then joined Whitey on deck as we set sail for Martha's Vineyard about fifty miles to the east. It was a nice leisurely trip and I managed to catch an hour's sleep before we reached Edgartown, the major town on the island.

As we arrived, the coastguard directed us to moor at the very end of the jetty, on the T-junction. There were two large coastguard boats tied up on either side of us. It felt as though we had been quarantined, or put under arrest.

A tall, square-jawed CIA type, in a dark suit, took us through the timetable for the following day.

'The guests will be arriving at nine o'clock. You will leave immediately. Coastguard vessels will escort you the entire time. You must keep radio frequencies open at all times . . .'

At no stage did he mention specific names. Whitey and I saw the bulge below his left armpit and thought it best not to ask.

That evening as we went out for dinner, two armed guards were stationed on the dock, keeping watch on *Excalibur*.

'Who *are* we picking up?'

'Maybe it's the President,' joked Whitey. 'I didn't think Ron and Nancy sailed.'

The mystery had become so intriguing that it reached the giggling stage as we came up with suggestions that ranged from Lord Lucan to Colonel Gaddafi.

Waking early, I wiped the dew from the decks and made sure everything was stowed away. Our guests were running late and arrived at ten o'clock. By then the coastguard vessels had left the dock and were waiting a little way offshore. A helicopter hovered overhead.

Four men in dark suits started walking down the dock. Behind them I could see a party of people. Craning my neck, I tried to make out who it was, but caught only fleeting glimpses.

Suddenly Whitey whispered, 'It's King Hussein of Jordan and Queen Noor.'

I looked past the Jordanian bodyguards and suddenly recognised the royal couple. She looked stunning in light coloured slacks and a jacket on top of a blue and cream striped T-shirt; all beautifully tailored.

King Hussein wore a collared, short-sleeve shirt, sailing slacks and deck shoes. The first thing that struck me about him was this smile from heaven. It lit up everyone near him and even the sternest of bodyguards couldn't help but smile back at him.

Whitey made the introductions and the King and Queen shook my hand. I wasn't sure if I should curtsy.

The other member of their party was Crown Prince Hassan, the King's brother. He wore a captain's hat, but I don't think he had done much sailing. As soon as they stepped on board, the security men declared, 'Right, cast off.' They kept their backs to us, scanning the shore, as we pulled away.

The King and Queen sat in the cockpit.

Whitey said, 'I've been told that we have to get you back to Goat Island by six o'clock. It's just a day sail, is that OK?'

'Yes, of course,' said the King.

'And would you like to sail or motor?'

'Definitely sail.'

'Fine.'

The sails went up. What a beautiful day. We had a perfect breeze and warm sunshine. Queen Noor explained that their eldest son had just graduated from university in Boston. They had a day to spare after the ceremony and had decided to go sailing.

The helicopter disappeared after a while but the coastguard continued shadowing *Excalibur*. The King's brother smiled and laughed the whole day and was absolutely delightful. He spent much of his time at the wheel, with Whitey giving him advice. I think he fancied himself as a sailor. Meanwhile, the King and Queen went up forward and sat talking. I wondered how often they got to spend time alone together. It was lovely to see.

At lunchtime they chose to have a light snack on deck. I unpacked the mountain of food and made up a few plates of bread, salad and meats. We could have fed an army.

Afterwards, I repacked the hampers and began washing plates in the galley. King Hussein materialised beside me with a tea-towel in his hand.

'You don't have to do that,' I said, quite surprised.

'No, it's fine. It gives me something to do. I haven't done anything all day.'

'That's the idea.'

'I know. But I like to be busy.'

He dried a serving dish and set it on the table. I wondered how often he had dried dishes in his life.

'So tell me, Tracy, is this your normal job?'

'Well, I'm just working on this boat for a couple of days. I'm in Newport at the moment working on different boats.'

'So you move from boat to boat?'

'Yes. Some of it's cruising and I try to do a bit of racing.'

'It sounds like an interesting way of life. How long have you been doing it?'

'Since I was eighteen. I'm twenty-two.'

'Where is your family?'

'My father is dead, but Mum is still alive. She's in England with my younger brother.'

'Do you ever get the chance to go home?'

'Occasionally. Hopefully, I'll get home before I start the Whit-bread Race.'

'Oh, what's that?'

'I've managed to get myself a place on a boat doing a round the world race. They say it's the toughest race in the world. I've never done any long distance offshore racing. It's really exciting.'

'Isn't it dangerous?'

'A little.'

The King kept up a constant stream of questions as he dried the dishes. In particular he wanted to know about the Whitbread. What sort of boats competed? How long were the various legs? What communications did they use?

We must have chatted for over an hour as we sailed towards Goat Island and Newport. That wonderful smile never left his face and he made me feel like the most interesting person in the world. Nobody had ever made such a strong impression on me.

'I'm fascinated by this race,' he said. 'Will you keep in touch with me, Tracy, and tell me how it goes?'

His request seemed very genuine. 'Yes, of course,' I replied, unsure of what else to say.

The tea-towel now hung casually over his shoulder. 'I'll tell you what,' he said. 'When I get back to Jordan I will call your mother and tell her that I've seen you and that you're OK.'

'You don't have to do that.'

'I know, but I want to. It must be very expensive to call.'

'I write her lots of letters.'

'Yes, but I'd like a call.'

I found an old envelope in a drawer and scrawled down Mum's name and the telephone number. The King then gave me his card. 'This is the address of the palace,' he said, 'and also my direct line. If you ever need anything, please call me. And write to me. I want to know about this Whitbread race.'

Excalibur arrived at Goat Island later than expected. It was just on dusk and the sunset painted Newport in a golden glow. The security guards were flapping on the dock about the delay. Suddenly, the Royal couple had gone – as quickly as they arrived. It was as though they had never been there.

'Wow, what a great day,' said Whitey.

'What nice people,' I echoed.

Two months later, in July 1985, I managed to hitch a ride across the Atlantic on *Jubilation*. I had to be back in Britain for Cowes

Week to meet up with *GBII* and start preparations for the Whitbread.

It was my fourth Atlantic crossing and by far the hardest. We took a northern route, stopping in Newfoundland on the way. With only summer clothes and no foul-weather gear, I was totally unprepared for the bitter cold. I scrounged and begged gear off people. The fog barely lifted the entire trip. *Jubilation* was set up for day racing rather than long-distance offshore sailing. The makeshift bunks and galley were miserable and bare. I hated the trip and was pleased to arrive in Lymington on the south coast of England.

I went out with the crew for a final crew meal and phoned Mum from a pub on the waterfront.

'You won't believe what's happened,' she said excitedly. 'I had a phone call from someone who claimed to be King Hussein of Jordan. I felt like saying, "Yeah, and I'm the Queen of Sheba".'

'You didn't say that!'

'No, of course not. I'm learning to expect the unexpected.' Mum raved about how nice the King had been. He told her how much he'd enjoyed the day charter.

'He's phoned four times since then.'

'Why?'

'He wants you to call him. He's in London.'

I scrabbled for more change in my pocket and dialled the direct line. I was put through to King Hussein.

'Tracy, it's good to hear from you. How was your Atlantic crossing? You must come up and see me. Do you have any time? Come up to London.'

'Well, I think so . . . when?'

'Tomorrow. Come and have dinner. We'll talk about the Whitbread.'

The race fascinated him and I almost felt that, in different circumstances, he would have loved to take part.

I packed my few possessions and took a train home to Reading. Mum and Peter had finally split up and she had left Wales, happy never to see it again. Things had apparently got so bad that Trevor,

Gregor and Uncle Arthur had taken matters into their own hands. They hired a removal van, drove to Wales, loaded all of Mum's things into it and brought her back to Reading.

There was no money left by then, but she managed to get a council flat in Purley. She seemed happier than I could remember for years and Peter's name was never mentioned. But each time I saw her, I felt a twinge of sadness. Although still a strikingly beautiful woman, her multiple sclerosis was slowly but surely becoming more evident. It showed in little ways, that only those close to her could see. The loss of balance and the slight slurring of her words; the awkwardness of movement and pauses in mid-sentence.

Yet she continued to fight these symptoms with everything she had. To me she personified the 'mind over matter' theory of medicine. She would not go quietly. She would fight onwards, as if each day had to be won anew.

My relationship with Mum had been tempestuous for most of my adolescence. We are very similar in so many ways: both strong willed, independent and single-minded. That's half the problem. Mum has described her relationship with her mother as being very similar. Across three generations of my family, mothers and daughters have fought each other and loved each other with equal amounts of passion and energy. In a way I feel as though I have been given the combined strength of all these amazing women.

It was nice to be home again. Mum's new flat was spotlessly clean and there were plants and flowers hanging from the window boxes. We chatted about family and friends – the marriages, births, christenings, birthdays and holidays. Although sailing had given my life some semblance of stability, I'm sure Mum would have preferred me to settle down, or live closer. She didn't say anything. As long as I was happy, she had no complaints.

Now I had a dinner engagement with a king and absolutely nothing to wear. All I owned were T-shirts, sarongs and shorts. These are great for bumming around the islands, but hardly fit for royalty. The best I could do was a pair of green and white striped trousers, with a rusted stud clasp, and a vaguely presentable T-shirt. I wore my cleanest pair of deck shoes.

Despite spending long periods away from home, I had always kept a car. This is a very loose description of my old Vauxhall Viva; rust bucket might be more apt, or car wreck. A mottled green colour, it had two red doors, neither of which opened. Instead, I had to hook my fingers over the glass in the driver's side window and force it down. Then I wriggled through the gap.

I drove into London and turned into Kensington Palace Gardens. There were two policemen at a sentry gate at the entrance to the exclusive street. They eyed me suspiciously as I pulled up.

'Does King Hussein live up here?'

'On the left,' one replied, staring at my car.

In the rear mirror I could see them watching me as I drove away. I parked outside a beautiful house with a Jordanian guard in full military uniform standing outside. Then I crawled out the car window as he watched with a bemused look on his face.

'Is King Hussein there, please?'

Amazingly, he didn't bat an eyelid.

'Do you have an appointment?'

'He invited me for dinner. I'm just back in the country. I've been sailing.'

I have no idea why I was telling him my life story. Nerves, I guess. He spoke into the intercom and then invited me inside the gate.

'What about my car? Can I leave it there?'

'I'll keep a close eye on it,' he said. I caught a hint of a grin.

A butler met me at the door. I wish I could remember his name because he had been with the King for years and was absolutely charming. The marble reception hall led off to a series of function rooms on the ground floor. King Hussein had a private apartment that took up one of the upper floors.

As I went up in the lift I had a sudden attack of nerves. What does this guy want with me? I asked myself. He's a king. I'm a boat bum.

I felt guilty about it afterwards for he was such a perfect gentleman. Later, I discovered that a lot of people in Britain and abroad had had similar experiences with King Hussein. He seemed to collect people that he found interesting and stay in touch with them. As a ham radio operator he scanned the airwaves befriending schoolboys, scientists and anybody he felt could teach him something about life.

We spent the evening talking about the Whitbread. In particular, he was interested in the communications side and satellite navigation. As an experienced pilot, he knew how to navigate in the air and wanted to learn about the differences. I didn't have a lot of self-esteem and was still unsure about tackling the Whitbread, but he made me believe in myself. He thought my plans were amazing and that made me feel special.

'I'm really sorry, but can I use your phone?' I asked.

'Is there something wrong?'

'No. It's just that it's Mum's birthday today.'

'Yes, of course. You should have said something earlier. You must let me talk to her again.'

From that evening onwards, King Hussein never forgot Mum's birthday. He sent her flowers every year along with a card.

As the evening ended and I crawled through the window of my Vauxhall Viva, I knew that I had made a friend for life. He would follow my career and watch over me like a proud father. Everybody needs a mentor. Perhaps I had found mine.

NINE

A month before the start of the Whitbread, the yachts and crews gathered at Gosport, Portsmouth, on the south coast. The voyage from Plymouth was the first time our crew had sailed together – not the ideal preparation.

GBII had been renamed *Norsk Data* after our new sponsors, a Norwegian computer company. The previous four weeks had been a real eye-opener. I was beginning to realise that I'd signed on to a project with no money. Everything had been done on a shoestring budget, which meant patching gear.

As the paying punters began to arrive, my anxiety grew. I was used to being the least experienced person on board a boat. Here I was the most experienced, along with Karl Gillette, the other 'free fare' member of the crew and Bob, the skipper. We had three people who knew what they were doing and twelve others who were winging it with little or no knowledge. Weekend sailing hardly equips you for sailing around the world.

I had also discovered that I knew lots of people who were on the various boats. Skip Novak was skippering *Drum*, Simon Le Bon's boat, with a crew of gun sailors and rogues including 'Filthy' Phil Barrett, whom I'd started going out with.

Atlantic Privateer had guys like Shag, Paul Standbridge, Arthur

Radford, Hagar the Horrible and Eric Soper. They were true pirates of the yachting world, with enormous experience and talent.

I spent most of my spare time with the boys from *Drum* and *Privateer*. Each time I drove back to Plymouth and my motley bunch, I felt depressed. We were very much the poor cousins compared to the big money teams. To make matters worse, our paying passengers were rather snobby towards Karl and me – as if we were hired help and somehow beneath them. Maybe we were, but it was an odd attitude to take when their lives were going to be in our hands once the serious sailing began.

I stocked up the boat. Freeze-dried food was still in its infancy and beyond our financial reach. Instead, our provisions came in cans and boxes, adding enormous weight to the yacht. The first leg was to Cape Town in South Africa. I had to feed fifteen people, three meals a day for six weeks.

As I battled with my budget, I couldn't help sneaking glances at the sleek maxis around us, with all the crews in uniform. I kept telling myself that if I could get through this race, it might give me enough experience to get on to a better boat next time. Saying that, there were only about five women in the entire fleet of 250 sailors.

In the final few weeks there were loads of parties – half of them hosted by the boys from *Drum* and *Privateer*. At one point we had so many people dancing on the first floor of *Drum*'s crew house that the beams sank four inches into the walls.

Simon had an enormously high profile and the media flocked to report his every move. Ironically, sailors who race are called 'rock stars' and here was a real rock star among them. They deserved to celebrate. A month earlier *Drum* had lost its keel and turned over in the Fastnet race off the coast of Cornwall. Simon and three others were trapped in the hull. The Royal Navy had rescued the crew and towed the boat ashore.

Surely they couldn't be ready in time for the Whitbread. The 77-foot sloop was pulled out of the water, put into a shed and worked on for 24 hours a day. They put on a new keel, mast and sails. A lot of that was down to Simon. He comes across as being a really laid-back guy, but is incredibly motivated. He also inspired tremendous loyalty in his crew, who were desperate to do the race.

On a grey foggy day, 28 September 1985, thousands of spectator boats dotted the Solent. *Drum* and *Privateer* were there in all their finery. By comparison *Norsk Data* looked like a clunking dinosaur. It wouldn't have mattered if we were ready to race – the Corinthian spirit can go too far and can be downright dangerous.

Bands were playing on the docks and people lined every vantage point. Thousands of flags fluttered and last farewells echoed across the water.

'What am I doing? I must be crazy,' I whispered.

Trevor, Mum and the entire Edwards clan of aunts, uncles and cousins had come to see me off. Thankfully, Mum had no real idea of the dangers I faced. I think she imagined the Whitbread to be much the same as any other sailing, except longer.

There were so few women in the fleet that I was a novelty. Most of us were cooks, which meant answering questions from journalists about how we were going to keep 'our men' fed and watered on the voyage. I sounded like the little woman baking below decks while the serious business went on above me.

The fog lifted slightly as we sailed down the Solent. We passed the striking cliffs of the Needles and the red and white striped lighthouse that looked like a stick of Blackpool Rock.

The first hour was like a sailing lesson for most of the crew. Karl and I shared a few looks and raised eybrows. It was too late to pull out now. The next stop was Cape Town. We would just have to knuckle down and get on with it. Ahead of us, the rest of the fleet raced away.

My favourite moment of all was when the last spectator boat turned for home and left. *Norsk Data* was alone. I felt as though we were sailing through a gateway that opened up into the oceans of the world. There was nowhere that we couldn't go.

At that moment I experienced a strange sensation – a fleeting feeling of panic that I'd never see England again. And a strange sense of missing people I'd only just said goodbye to.

It's bad luck to talk about getting home and even worse luck to talk about not getting home. Best say nothing at all. And you never stand and watch the land disappear. Turn your back on it quickly and look forward.

I had never had these feelings when I'd sailed to America or the Caribbean. The difference this time was that I was sailing around the world. When you journey towards some distant point, there is a beginning, middle and end to the voyage. But when you circumnavigate the globe there is almost no middle or end. Instead, you have a constant forward motion, rather than a conclusion. The end means getting back to where you started.

All of these thoughts occurred to me as the land disappeared and the breeze picked up. Karl's voice broke into my musing.

'There's someone chasing us.'

I looked up. A speedboat raced over the swells. As it came closer, I recognised the man near the stern. He was standing up waving something in his hand.

It was my dentist. Nothing surprises me any more. 'Catch!' he shouted, tossing a small package on board. I opened it to discover a cap that he'd made yet again for my missing tooth.

'Get it put in in Cape Town!' he yelled, as the boat turned for home.

The first leg to Cape Town stretched out before us. I had never sailed such a distance and the whole concept of having all those miles ahead felt amazing.

The next few weeks proved to be a mixture of the sublime and the ridiculous. I loved the sailing, but hated the politics and back-biting. Many of the paying clients seemed to think they were on a holiday cruise. They were far too relaxed about watches and would turn up late, or not at all. I'm not blaming them − they didn't know any better. Things should have been explained more clearly to them.

As expected, *Norsk Data* was soon well back in the fleet. I followed the real race from radio updates. Twice a day at the 'chat show' all the yachts would call each other, giving positions and information. This was also a vital safety channel.

A large low pressure system was sliding across the South Atlantic towards South Africa. We were too far north for it to bother us, but the leading yachts were directly in its path.

There is something quite beautiful about the swirling satellite images of a deep low pressure system. To most people it will always remain just a picture, but to an offshore sailor it starts to tell a story. It is the same with the isobars on an atmospheric pressure chart.

Nine miles above the approaching storm a river of air was accelerating through the troposphere. Called the jet stream, this belt of strong westerly winds is the dividing line between the warm, tropical air masses of the central latitudes and the cold, polar air masses. It is also the engine that drives our weather. When the core of the jet stream is centred over a low pressure area, it draws air up and away from the surface, causing the low beneath to deepen and intensify. Because nature deplores a vacuum, cold polar air rushes towards the depression from the south, while warm tropical air is drawn from the north. As these air masses flow into the centre, they are deflected by the rotation of the Earth and begin to spin.

On 22 October the leading five yachts were hit by the storm. They were forced to beat through headwinds, taking a fearsome pounding. *Atlantic Privateer* took the biggest hit and lost its mast. They were given permission to motor straight into shore, where they managed to get hold of sewage pipes and tried to build an ingenious makeshift mast. They motored back to where they lost the rig and set off again. Unfortunately, the new mast couldn't stand the strain and came down. *Privateer* was forced to motor into Cape Town, wrecking any chance she had of winning overall. I felt desperately sorry for the crew.

Drum also narrowly avoided disaster. When Simon and the boys reached Cape Town they discovered the hull had started to delaminate. This meant that the outer skin of the carbon-composite hull had started to peel off, allowing water to enter the honeycomb-like interior. It weakened the structure of the boat and made it heavier. In addition to this, *Drum* almost lost the keel again.

By the time I glimpsed Table Mountain with its white linen covering of cloud tinged pink by the sunrise I couldn't get off *Norsk Data* fast enough. The daily fights and lack of teamwork had worn me down. Here was a real lesson on what not to do. You don't throw a group of people together and simply expect them to sail a boat from A to B. We had no leadership and no understanding of how a team works. There had been no planning and precious little preparation. I was as much to blame as anyone else – I gave up on the project before we reached Cape Town.

Karl and I both decided that we wanted to get off *Norsk Data*. At the same time, both of us wanted to finish the Whitbread. This meant finding a place on another boat. With 250 crew there was always a chance that someone would be injured, or personalities would clash. Unfortunately, being a woman, my only hope was to get on a boat as a cook.

We had a month to find a place before the race re-started. I began praying for one of the cooks to leave, or get run over by a bus, anything . . . Then I heard that Jim, the cook on *Privateer*, had suffered a stroke. I felt so guilty.

I was due to cut the crew's hair that day, which meant that Shag, the skipper, was a captive audience. It also put a pair of scissors in my hand – an important psychological tool.

'I heard about poor Jim,' I said. 'That's terrible luck. I guess you're looking for another cook.'

'Don't even think about it,' Shag said. 'Not in a million years.'

'You don't know what I'm going to ask you.'

'Yes I do. You want to be our cook.'

'Yes, but . . .'

'Listen, Tracy, if we were going to take a girl, it would be you. I have no doubts that you can do it. But this is a male crew. We cannot have a girl on the boat.'

'Why not?'

'Because we can't. It creates problems . . . tensions. It's an all-male crew. You understand.'

I pestered him for the next three days. I wrote up menus for the next leg and did a budget. I offered to cook meals in the crew house. Time was getting on. They had to make a decision soon.

'We're not taking a cook,' said Shag. 'We'll all take it in turns.'

'That won't work. It's a recipe for disaster. You know that.'

'Tracy, I'm not taking a woman on board.'

I sensed him starting to weaken. Was that a tiny chink in his armour?

Then I did a really bad thing. I went to see Padda Kutell, the wealthy South African owner of *Atlantic Privateer*, who had a magnificent house just outside of Cape Town. Over tea on the terrace, I started bending his ear. 'Look, you need me on the boat. I'm the only available cook. Shag says he doesn't want a girl on the boat, but let's face it, it's your boat. I know everyone. I can sail. I can mix with the boys.'

Padda had a twinkle in his eye. My enthusiasm appealed to him. 'Look, if you can get Shag to agree, I have absolutely no problem with it at all.'

So I went back to Shag. 'Padda's told me that I can be on the boat.'

Shag raised his eyebrows. 'He said that?'

'Yep! He knows you need a cook. I'm available. No problem.'

Shag discovered the truth just before we sailed but by then it was too late. I'd worn down his resolve. There was also a bit of, 'OK, you want to do it; you want to find out what it's like. Fine. These guys are going to annihilate you. You're going to hate it. It's going to put you off sailing for life.'

I didn't appreciate Shag's reasons for not wanting a woman on the boat. I understand them now. I wouldn't allow a man on an all-female yacht. It is so invasive. Guys have a great time being guys together. They don't want some bloody woman cramping their style.

That's what Shag tried to tell me, but I thought he was being a pig.

'You're going to cry,' he said. 'You'll be miserable, you'll hate it. By the time we get to New Zealand, you'll want to get off this boat so fast that we won't see you for dust.'

'Right,' I said accepting the challenge.

'Right,' he echoed.

The stage was set.

Poor Karl, on the other hand, hadn't been able to find another ride. I was amazed when he went back to *Norsk Data*. He obviously had more stamina than I did. I admired him for that.

On 4 December the race began again. With ten minutes to go until the gun, I asked myself the same question: What have I done? I looked around the boat and thought: How well do I know these guys? Maybe Shag is right.

Most of the previous week I'd spent getting the boat stocked and organising menus. I spent very little time with the rest of the crew and didn't know how they'd receive me. Perhaps I'd be an embarrassment. Maybe they'd worry about having to tone things down.

All of these thoughts were making me feel sick as we prepared to cross the line. Suddenly a message came over the radio and a coastguard boat came speeding towards the fleet. I had an awful sinking feeling this would have something to do with me.

'Do you have a Tracy Edwards on board?' they announced over a loud-hailer.

'Yes,' they groaned.

'She's left her passport behind.'

I could hear the guys muttering to each other. 'Bloody typical!' 'This is just the start!'

Off we went and I tried to keep a low profile for the first few days. They say that the way to a man's heart is through his stomach. That's how I intended to win them over – with my cooking.

Because freeze-dried food was still rather experimental and hard to find, I regarded myself as being so clever for having found a supply from a camping store. I bought boxes and boxes of the stuff.

'What's this?' asked Shag, staring at the bright orange porridge on his plate.

'Chicken and noodles,' I said.

'It doesn't taste like chicken and noodles.'

'It tastes like crap,' said Marco.

The next night I served up mince and peas. It tasted exactly the same as the chicken and noodles, except it was a dull orange.

Within two days the crew was ready to mutiny and throw me overboard. I deserved it. We were sailing the longest, toughest leg of the race through appalling weather. The guys were cold, wet and hungry. One of the few pleasures they could look forward to was a hot nutritious meal and I served them crap.

My only saving grace was that I bought loads of biltong – strips of meat dried and cured in the sun – which they loved. I also stocked up on Tabasco sauce, which was good for hiding the taste of the freeze-dried food.

Shag had been right about many things. I found it difficult to become part of the crew. Nobody was keen to have me on deck and I had to sneak up there when I could.

The Southern Ocean was terrifying. We surfed at incredible speeds in 60-knot gales. This was full-on ocean racing in the middle of the most frightening stretch of water on earth. We had a skipper who knew no fear; who would push the boat to the very limit because he knew no other way.

I saw my first iceberg and I couldn't believe how beautiful and menacing it looked. As we sailed quite close to it, I could see an extraordinary number of colours in the white walls. I could hear the ice groan and creak as the waves smashed against it.

The sailing was exhilarating, terrifying, miserable and magnificent. I lived a whole lifetime in that six weeks. All the maxis were so close that we had to keep pushing. At one point Shag stood on deck and declared that we were going to keep the spinnaker up for as long as possible. 'If there's too much wind to take it down, I'll shoot it with a flare gun.' I tried to pretend I hadn't heard that.

This was real racing. These guys were deadly serious. I began to realise how my presence might inhibit them. In heavy weather I was a liability. If I went on deck to help, somebody always kept an eye on me. This put undue pressure on the crew, which they didn't need.

Even when the guys realised I could look after myself their natural protective instincts were to treat me differently. During a fierce storm, the cry went up for all hands on deck. I had crawled into my sleeping bag a few hours earlier, sick and exhausted. I dragged on my wet weather gear and scrambled through the hatch. As my head emerged, Paul put his hand firmly on top of it and pushed me down. The hatch slammed shut. I hammered on the inside, screaming at them, 'Let me out! Let me help!'

Later, when the danger had passed, Paul came below.

'What did you want?' he asked.

I lost the plot. 'I'm one of this crew, for God's sake. There was a call for all hands. I wanted to help.'

He looked surprised. 'Tracy, I was thinking of you. I didn't want you to get hurt.'

This was the attitude I had to overcome. Yet I have nothing but admiration for these men. They were so focused and single-minded. It was bizarre to watch this. I had seen them on land as a bunch of party animals that never trained and drank like fish. Now I saw another side to them – the slick professionalism and amazing courage. Here was a great team with a great leader. I had never come close to being a part of something like this before.

As we neared New Zealand, two maxis had broken clear, *Atlantic Privateer* and *NZI Enterprise*. Rounding the North Cape we were neck and neck. After 7,000 miles of racing it came down to a duel – a sprint along the New Zealand coast to Auckland.

Pete Montgomery, a radio commentator who watched the final stages, coined the phrase, 'the gladiators of ocean racing'. All day we shadowed each other in a tacking duel. Neither boat could open a gap of more than a few hundred metres.

By late afternoon we neared the Hen and Chicken Islands.

Should we go inside or outside? We came across a boatload of fishermen with cans of lager in one hand and rods in the other.

'Which way is the best way to pass this island?' shouted Shag.

'Down the inside.'

NZI, who should have had the local knowledge, chose the outside. For the first time we pulled ahead by half a mile.

We came into Auckland Harbour still in front. In the darkness it was impossible to know by how far. A spectator boat put a spotlight on the spinnaker of *NZI* behind us. They were getting closer. Where was the finish line?

Suddenly, the gun went. What a feeling! Thousands of people were cheering on the docks. We had won by seven minutes – the narrowest winning margin in the history of the Whitbread. It was the greatest moment of my life.

There were tears in the eyes of some of the guys. They weren't so rough and tough after all. *NZI* ghosted alongside us, as we came into the mooring. They, too, were standing along the guard-rail, some of them in tears.

'We had to win one leg,' shouted Shag, sympathetically.

'Yeah, but did it have to be this one?' came the reply.

Later, we learned that 25,000 people had packed the harbour to watch the final stages of the race. There had been a nine-mile traffic jam into Auckland. I also discovered that I was the first female competitor in the history of the Whitbread to finish first in a leg.

That night we partied and I didn't feel like an outsider any more. The guys accepted me – if not for my sailing ability then for the good luck I'd brought them. Sailors are a superstitious breed. I'd gone from public enemy number one to younger sister in the time it took for the gun to sound.

'Just put some decent food on the boat,' said Shag, as he wrapped me in a bear hug.

Janni swung out across the water in a huge arc, lifting his legs at the last moment, letting his back touch the surface before surging into the air again. He was suspended from the mast, taking a wild ride for the cameras.

On deck, Simon Le Bon had the helm. With his sun-bleached hair and deep tan he looked every inch the pop star. Three models in bikinis were cavorting behind him. One of them was a teenage Rachel Hunter, with freckles sprinkled on her nose and a girl-next-door face. She was already famous in New Zealand for advertising flavoured milk. The scene looked like something out of a pop video. *Drum* carved through the water, with its spinnaker flying. The Bay of Islands appeared majestically out of the morning mist. There wasn't a cloud in the sky.

It had nothing to do with music. An Italian clothing company had hired *Drum* for a TV commercial. They took the boat up to the Bay of Islands and put these gorgeous models on board. None of the boys were complaining.

Unfortunately, some of the press made a big thing out of the day. Simon had started dating Yasmin, who was portrayed as the beautiful woman he'd left behind while he gallivanted about the south seas with local beauties. I was amazed at how well Simon put up with being followed around by photographers and reporters.

Mum and Trevor came up to the Bay of Islands to watch the filming. They had flown out from England to see me during the stopover. I managed to get Mum an apartment in the same complex as the *Drum* crew. Simon and the boys loved having her around and she mothered them constantly.

It was so good for her. The divorce from Peter had dented her confidence – or perhaps it was the years of bickering. Now I could see the old spark in her. I liked her coming to see my world and to meet my friends. Not only that, she liked them. Like a child, I was still trying to impress her. Now she was seeing a side of me she hadn't seen at close quarters before. Particularly the wild, partying side. She had to stop herself admonishing me for the hi-jinks and alcohol abuse. I wish she could have seen me sailing. Then she'd have seen the side of me that was professional and passionate about winning.

After six weeks in Auckland we set off again. The next leg proved to be a disaster. We made the wrong decisions and fell behind quite badly. We went to 61° south, so deep into the Southern Ocean that we risked hitting icebergs and growlers (floating ice).

The rest of the maxis went north and had better weather conditions. *Privateer* spent days beating into fierce headwinds towards Cape Horn. The conditions were horrendous and I thought I was going to die. I'd be cooking and puking up into the sink at the same time.

The guys were more sympathetic now, but I had to keep working. They'd become like my big brothers – seventeen of them – and I was their little sister.

'Basic' Bill and I had a bet on who could last the longest without washing. The leg was likely to be five or six weeks long. 'Basic' was an American and a legend in his own lunchtime. He earned his nickname for being the basest individual that anyone had ever met. He always went further than anybody else did when it came to being disgusting or over the top.

All of the guys had become more relaxed about having me around. Strangely, if any of them had a problem, they wouldn't talk to each other, but instead came to me. We had a doctor on the boat but nobody ever consulted him.

'Tracy, can you have a look at something for me, please,' asked Hagar, appearing embarrassed. I looked at him nervously and nodded.

Ian had a mass of red hair and a bushy red beard. He looked like a Viking – hence the nickname 'Hagar the Horrible'.

He motioned me to follow him. In a quiet corner, where all the sails were piled up on the windward side, he started taking his trousers down.

'Hagar, I'm not sure . . .'

'Just have a look.'

He bent over and showed me a large hairy arse. 'What do you think that is?' he asked.

'What exactly?'

'That lump.'

Steeling myself, I looked closer. Sure enough he had a large lump on his left cheek.

'Why don't you go and see the doctor?' I suggested.

'Are you kidding? It'd be around the boat in three seconds. You're the only person I trust.'

'OK.'

'What do you think I should do about it?'

It was obviously a growth. I suggested that he should tie cotton around it. That's what they do with lambs to get rid of their testicles. 'Then it might drop off.'

Hagar thought this sounded a reasonable idea. Cotton didn't seem to work, so we settled on an elastic band.

The story did get round the boat, but Hagar didn't blame me. I think he began telling people. Eventually, the entire crew was waiting in anticipation for the 'dingleberry', as it had been christened, to fall off. The jokes went on and on, until Hagar finally began threatening that when it fell off he'd put it in someone's food. It was about the size of a conker and had started to look like a testicle.

One afternoon, Hagar took me aside and handed me a lump of tissue paper.

'What's this?'

'Shhhhh. It's the dingleberry.'

'What am I supposed to do with it?' I whispered.

'Put it in Basic's dinner.'

Gingerly I took the dingleberry, but I wasn't about to let anybody eat it. I couldn't do that to Basic – not least because it might have killed him. Instead, I got some resin, moulded it into shape and put an elastic band around the top.

That night, as Basic tucked into his spaghetti and meatballs he came across the fake dingleberry. Without blinking, he popped it into his mouth and munched away. This was a man's joke, played on a man in front of other men. He couldn't back down. To this day, he still believes he ate the real dingleberry.

After weeks of appalling weather, we finally reached Cape Horn. Ironically, the skies were blue and the sun shone. The huge cliffs of the Cape reared out of the Ocean and looked as impressive as I had always imagined them to be. It felt eerie sailing past this landmark that was a tombstone to so many sailors. Their graves were beneath the boat as we cut through the grey water.

The mood on board was strangely sombre. Basic managed to bring everything down to his level though, with the suggestion that he sleep with the cook to celebrate. Luckily I knew him well enough not to punch his lights out.

This was my coming of age as a sailor. Cape Horn is the most legendary of sailing landmarks. To this day I wear a silver ring in my left ear – just as the old salts did – to remind me of that moment.

Having taken different lines across the Southern Ocean, the fleet bunched up again as we sailed up the east coast of South America. *Privateer* went too close to the Falklands and we joked about seeing the whites of the sheep's eyes. *UBS Switzerland* took the best line, along with *Drum*.

We finished nine hours behind *UBS* and twenty minutes behind Simon and the boys. *Drum* deserved a good result after all its problems on the first leg.

After the highs of Auckland, I experienced the lows. Nobody felt like partying, but we did anyway. The last thing I remember as I slowly disappeared beneath a table was a bet with Henry that I could drink him under it. When I woke up the next morning, the guys had carried me back to the boat and tied me in my bunk just in case I sleepwalked.

I also lost my bet with Basic. After forty days without washing, I had a shower in Uruguay. Basic, true to his reputation, went another two days on land reeking so badly it made my eyes water.

During the voyage the guys had discovered that in Cape Town I had started going out with Patrick Banfield on *Drum*. This is the sort of information I tried to keep very quiet. In Uruguay they presented me with a T-shirt which on the front said, 'Property of

Atlantic Privateer'. On the back it said, 'One crate of beer'. I happily wore the T-shirt with no idea of its significance. A few days later, I realised that the crew had put a price on my head – one crate of beer.

Our stay in Uruguay was enormous fun. Various members of the crew spent time in prison but once they sobered up they were back on deck. Padda threatened to sack everyone at various intervals but never did.

Gregor and Trevor came out for a few weeks. Trevor had become even more of a hero in my life. I had the fire and passion, while he was thoughtful, logical and unselfish. While I'd been gallivanting around the world, he'd been looking after Mum, living in a one-bedroom flat in Purley. I was so proud of introducing him as my brother. He got on with everyone and was never fazed by any situation.

As we left on the final leg, Simon asked Trevor if he could stay with Yasmin for a few days until her flight left for London. As we left the dock on *Privateer* I have a lasting memory of Trevor and Yasmin standing side by side, waving us off. All the guys on board were muttering, 'The lucky, lucky bastard.' Trevor has never forgiven me for not taking a photo.

We sailed for home. Light winds delayed everyone through the Doldrums – an area of complete calm or very mild winds. These are created by the slackening of trade winds that fail to reach the Equator and rise upwards, channelling air vertically instead of across the water. We all tried to find the right course in the fickle conditions. *UBS* got it right again, going a long way east towards the coast of Africa. They finished two full days ahead of the fleet.

This was a good leg for me as the guys finally let me steer, even though I could hardly see over the wheel. By then we were well behind.

The sight of Portsmouth Harbour filled me with mixed emotions. A great adventure was ending and I had no idea what I was going to do next. I couldn't go back to doing charters. The Whitbread had spoiled me. I would never be happy pottering around the Caribbean or the Med.

Sitting in the cockpit next to Paul, I glanced out at the approaching strip of green and asked: 'Do you think an all-female crew could do the Whitbread?'

'Don't be silly.'

'Wasn't there someone who tried?' I'd read a story in a yachting magazine about an American yachtswoman, Miranda Delmar-Morgan, who attempted an all-female challenge.

'Yes. She didn't get on to the water,' said Paul.

I kept pestering him to give me reasons why women couldn't do the race. Finally he said, 'Look, Tracy, do you really want to do it? Is that why you keep asking me all these questions?'

'I don't know. I don't know if I could sail with a bunch of women. It's just . . .' I didn't finish the sentence.

The crowds had gone by the time we reached Gosport. It was half-past ten at night and they had shut the bar at the marina. Good old England! Welcome back. Elsewhere in the world, they had kept the bars and restaurants open all night, knowing the Whitbread fleet was coming in. At Gosport everything shut down on time.

The next morning I wandered down to the dock and found it deserted. The crews and skippers had gone. They had flights or trains to catch and other places to be. There was no farewell party, or final fling; no gala dinner where we could swap phone numbers and promises to stay in touch. I took the train home, feeling very sad. What else in my life could ever touch this?

TEN

OR those next few weeks I wandered about Mum's flat in Purley and visited friends. Close as I felt to my family, none of them could really understand my sense of loss. I had no idea what I was going to do next. The only certainty in my mind was that I wanted to race around the world again.

It was four years until the next Whitbread. Next time, I didn't want to spend the race below decks, slaving over gas burners. I wanted to sail and to have my own watch. Again, I knew that I'd face the problem of being a woman in a sport dominated by men. Why weren't more girls interested? Surely there were enough women sailors to see more in contention.

The germ of an idea had formed in my head. It kept nagging away at me. Could an all-female crew compete in the next Whitbread? Could it be a team just like the crew on *Privateer*?

I went to see Admiral Charles Williams, chairman of the Whitbread Race Committee.

'What would you say if I told you that I wanted to enter an all-female crew?'

'I'd advise you to go away and have a long think.'

'But there are no rules against it?'

'No.'

'Well, I'm thinking of launching a project.'

He smiled wryly, but not in a patronising way. 'I can see you're very determined, Tracy. Go and talk to other people who've put Whitbread projects together. Listen to what they say.'

I did as he said. First I told Patrick about my idea. He and I were still seeing each other and I knew he'd be brutally honest if necessary. Patrick is the Biggles of English sailing. He would have made a very pukka naval officer, which is why people often tease him, even though they love him dearly.

I pitched my idea in a very negative way, expecting him to tell me I was crazy. Instead, he defended the plan.

'Why not have a go?' he said.

'Because I wouldn't know where to start.'

'You've done the race before. You have the contacts. You know what it takes.'

'I'm twenty-three years old. Who'll listen to me? Who'll give me the money?'

'You're not the sort of girl who dies wondering, Tracy. There's only one way to find out.'

Next I sounded out some of the guys from *Privateer*. We met up at a pub, the Olde Ship, in Bursledon. If anyone laughs at me, that will be it, I told myself.

'Listen guys, what would you say if I said I was going to put an all-female crew together to do the next Whitbread?'

In the silence that followed they looked at each other. Finally, Hagar announced: 'Well, if any woman is going to do it, I figure it will be you.' Others echoed his thoughts. None of them realised how much the project hinged on their reactions.

I told Mum as we sat at the kitchen table of her flat, drinking mugs of tea. She had never been fearful of me sailing because she knew so little about the risks involved.

'I have four years to the next race,' I said. 'I want to raise money and build a new yacht. Then I'll pull together a crew and we'll train for a year beforehand.'

Mum said nothing at first. She stared into her teacup as if the answer lay inside. 'You've never stuck at anything, Tracy, what makes you think you can stick at this for four years?'

I didn't have an answer. Perhaps she was right.

Just as these doubts threatened to overwhelm me, Mum added, 'You have amazing willpower, Tracy. If you can harness that resolve and see it through, you'll do a fantastic job.'

I had a lot of thinking to do. Even if I could stick with it, what chance did a twenty-three-year-old boat bum and cook have of convincing anyone that she could do this?

I didn't have the profile of Harold Cudmore, Lawrie Smith or Robin Knox-Johnston. Nor did I have the experience. That's why I didn't even contemplate being skipper of the challenge. I pictured myself as part of the crew, or perhaps the navigator.

During the Whitbread, I had written letters to King Hussein from each of the stopovers and occasionally called him. He enjoyed following my progress and told me that I should come and see him as soon as I returned.

Meeting again at his house in Kensington, we had a long discussion about my new plans.

'You have to do it,' he said. 'It is a fantastic idea.'

'But I'm not sure I can pull it off.'

'Of course you can, but you must be skipper.'

'I've never done it before.'

'We all have to start somewhere. You've done this race. You're going to raise the money and build this boat. Nobody is better qualified than you are. This is your project. You must be skipper.'

The most frightening aspect was the money. Even my rough figures, scribbled while sitting at the kitchen table, added up to £1.8 million. Half of that was to design and build a new yacht. This was pie-in-the-sky stuff to me. I'd never had more than a few thousand dollars.

A week later I sat on a dock in Hamble with a boat builder, Syd James, discussing the cost of building. Syd introduced me to a friend of his, Howard Gibbons, who sat and listened to me talking.

From the dock we moved to the Ship and Syd bought the first round of drinks.

Howard had a big bushy moustache and a strong, handsome face. He'd been losing his hair for years, despite being in his early thirties. He barely said a word, apart from prompting me with more and more questions. He could see my passion and became caught up with the details. Howard had once been a sports journalist working on a south coast paper. Then a friend asked if he fancied delivering a yacht to the Caribbean. That was it for Howard. He sent a postcard to the newspaper, quitting his job.

Since then he'd been drifting. Like me, he'd been looking for something to fire his imagination. Syd told him about my plans for the Whitbread and the sheer audacity and novelty of the project appealed to Howard.

'You need someone to do the PR and help you raise the money,' he said.

'Yes.'

'I can do that.'

I didn't have to ask him why. I could see it in his eyes. Howard was as captivated by the idea as I was. He shuffled his other work to give himself one day a week on the project.

I had been living out of a duffel bag for nearly six years, rarely owning more than a few T-shirts, a sarong and a pair of jeans. Now I had to find a base and settle down. I chose Hamble-le-Rice and considered renting a house. Then Mum sprang a surprise. My father had set up a trust fund for Trevor and me when we were very young. That money was now available.

In August 1986 I moved into a modern, four-bedroom house in Hamble Manor Court. Apart from the bricks and mortar, I had nothing except a kettle, a TV and a wastepaper bin.

On the first day Howard arrived with a typewriter and desk. He didn't have a chair so we turned the bin upside down for him to sit on. We started from there – typing letters to suppliers and making lists of companies to approach for sponsorship.

I still wasn't absolutely sure if I wanted to do this. Did I have it in me? At the first sign of trouble would I pack up my things and run away to sea?

Howard had a gift for persuasion and a bulging book of contacts. He always knew a man, who knew a man who knew the answer. It's strange because I don't normally trust people like that. They make me feel as though they're telling me one thing and thinking another. With Howard it was different. I liked him immediately. He never doubted the project could succeed and he never lost faith in me. I was diving into deep water, swimming against the current, but he was the rock I could cling to whenever I grew tired or despondent.

On my first day at the house I had an impromptu house-warming. Howard had brought a bottle of wine, but I didn't have a corkscrew so I went next door to borrow one.

My neighbour turned out to be tall, slender and dashingly good looking. I held up the bottle of wine. 'Hello, I'm Tracy, I'm you're new neighbour. Have you got a corkscrew?'

His name was Simon Lawrence, a property developer whose company had built many of the houses in Hamble Manor Court.

'It's just a little housewarming,' I said. 'You're welcome to come over.'

'Great.'

'Ah, you had better bring a wine glass . . . and a chair.'

Simon laughed and followed me back. There was a great deal of ribbing from the others. 'Typical Tracy. She goes to get a cork-screw and comes back with a man.'

Simon got used to me borrowing things. We became good friends and he eventually lent me my first £2,000 to start the project. It meant that we could buy a chair for the office and start sending out letters.

In September, I flew to Australia. Patrick had invited me to Fremantle to watch the trials for the America's Cup. He and Paul Standbridge were sailing on *White Crusader*, the English entrant being skippered by Harold Cudmore.

It felt almost like a stopover for the Whitbread because I knew so many of the guys competing for the various countries. There were other legendary names involved too, like Denis Connor and Lawrie Smith.

Seeing the teams operate at close quarters gave me a chance to learn how the various projects were put together. The America's Cup was like a Formula One event. By comparison, the Whitbread was more of a long-distance rally. The depth of planning and preparation was staggering. Apart from having two boats and all the spares, there was a huge support team working on shore. After months of training and tinkering with the boat, the actual races took a matter of hours.

I found the hierarchy interesting. Someone like Harold Cud-more was far more than just the skipper. He was the figurehead, around whom the money had been raised from sponsors. This gave him obligations far beyond simply sailing. There were media and corporate commitments; race functions, team meetings and con-tracts to be signed.

All of this should have frightened me away. Instead, I returned from Australia even more determined. I still wasn't sure about being skipper, but that decision could wait. Now I had to put together a budget and begin raising money.

Patrick had offered to design the boat. Initially, we talked about a state-of-the-art maxi, to compete for overall line honours. Then I wondered if an all-female crew could handle a yacht of this size and keep up with the men. Perhaps we should walk before we ran.

Howard had put a basic structure together and a list of priorities. The first was to come up with a name for the project. Then we had to get a boat. Finding a crew was another issue again. Were there enough women sailors in the world who could do the race? Would any of them want to?

I'd hoped that Patrick might become the project manager, but he was too tied up with the America's Cup. Howard took on more responsibility and slipped into the role almost by default. Publicity wouldn't be a problem, he said. The novelty of an all-female crew would generate headlines. We decided to make the first official announcement at the Southampton International Boat Show early in September. There had to be no suggestion of being 'possible' Whitbread contenders. From the very beginning we had to act and talk as though we were a racing certainty.

Howard had a friend who owned a restaurant opposite the boat show venue. He agreed to let us use it for our press conference and we printed up media packs for journalists. For want of a better name, we had settled on the ponderous 'First All Female Whitbread Challenge'.

Dozens of reporters turned up at the restaurant. There were TV lights in my eyes and radio microphones cluttering the table in front of me. I sat alongside Howard feeling incredibly nervous.

When my turn came to speak, I managed to stumble through the details of the project. I had a lot to learn about presentation. Few of the journalists were impressed. The articles that followed were more tongue-in-cheek than anything else. Ian Wooldridge of the *Daily Mail* wrote the only positive piece suggesting that we could actually do it.

Howard set about writing a sponsorship proposal and researched a list of likely companies and their addresses. Meanwhile, I began gathering details and advice. The end result was a massive document that could have been the doorstop at St Paul's Cathedral. It contained everything we knew about the race – the route, budget, training, preparation, publicity . . . you name it. Unfortunately, it contained so much information that the message became lost in the details. A lot of company bosses simply ignored it.

The rejection letters were normally polite, which is more than I can say for some of the meetings. At one appointment, I was ushered in to see the managing director of a large manufacturing company. Usually, we didn't get past junior management level.

A middle-aged 'suit' with thick glasses leaned across the boardroom table and said: 'I don't want to be rude, Miss Edwards, but the thought of twelve of my wife sailing around the world is so horrifying, that I simply can't contemplate it.'

Howard had to grab hold of the back of my jacket to stop me launching myself at the man's throat.

I had dozens of meetings like this and couldn't always hide my anger at the arrogance and negativity. 'You have to stop attacking everyone,' Howard used to say. 'Everyone is entitled to an opinion. The reason that we're doing this is to change their minds. If they won't listen, then move on.'

I knew he was right, yet I still struggled to hold my tongue. Some of these men were blatantly sexist and had to struggle to deal with a woman. Right from the beginning I had decided that an all-female crew couldn't simply be male clones. We had to be seen for what we were – a bunch of nice girls who were going to sail around the world.

There were times when I started to doubt whether this philosophy would work. Nobody wanted to be associated with a project where 'nice girls' might make headlines for all the wrong reasons. Time and again I heard the same thing: 'What if someone dies? It's hardly good publicity.' Unfortunately, I had no way of proving that this wouldn't happen. We were breaking new ground.

Finding the money was never going to be easy, but I hadn't realised the depth of opposition that I'd face. We were generating loads of positive stories, but no promises of sponsorship. Meanwhile, hundreds of CVs were flooding into the office from around the world.

Yet for all of this momentum, I couldn't overcome the attitude that women were incapable of doing the Whitbread. Strangely, this wasn't coming from professional yachtsmen. Most of them were extremely supportive. There were one or two exceptions, however. One in particular – a very famous skipper from across the pond – told me quite brutally what he thought of my plan.

I was standing outside the beer tents during Cowes Week, when he strode off the dock. We were introduced. 'This is Tracy Edwards. She's skippering the first all-female crew in the next Whitbread.'

The yachting legend didn't bother to look at me for more than a moment. 'What are you trying to prove?' he said. 'You're going to kill everyone on board. Don't be so selfish.' Then he spun on his heel and walked away.

I was gobsmacked. Maybe he was right. What on earth *was* I doing taking a bunch of women sailing around the world?

Each time I grew disheartened, Howard managed to set things right again. Somehow, almost by accident, I had managed to surround myself with people who shared my dream. They all had different skills and were looking for something in their lives. I had no money to pay them. We relied on friends of friends to grant us favours, or lend us a few hundred pounds at a time.

One night, a group of us sat around drinking wine after dinner. 'What are we going to call this project?' I asked. 'We need something that grabs people.'

Howard added: 'And it has to be something that won't put off sponsors who want to replace the name.'

We were getting drunker and drunker. Neil Cheston, who'd been the sail-trimmer on *Drum*, started thinking out loud. 'What about Maiden, Great Britain? It's also a play on words – Made in Great Britain.'

Jaws collectively dropped. It was brilliant! Inspired. Neil looked quite sheepish. Where had that come from?

The project now had a name. A friend of Howard's, Keith Webb, designed a striking logo showing a mermaid on a boat above the words MAIDEN GREAT BRITAIN.

We set up a company of the same name to put the project on a corporate footing. Until then, the money we'd received had a whiff of charity about it, rather than proper corporate funding.

The shore team also began expanding. Fiona Edgecombe and Sarah-Jane Ingram joined the project. Howard called them 'the mad blondes' – not without reason. Both were beautiful, energetic and very talented. Fi set about learning how to run a limited company, while Sarah-Jane (SJ) became Howard's strong right hand. They both worked harder than I had any right to ask and the four of us, including Howard, became inseparable.

A strange thing happened as the project came together. I discovered that I had a skill for organisation and managing people. Even the most basic and boring facts and tasks interested me.

Suddenly, it wasn't just the sailing that I craved. It was the idea of putting together something that was bigger than one individual and getting it absolutely right.

Early in 1987 our prayers seemed to be answered. A financial services company promised to put up £250,000 to get the project started. Plans were made for a big announcement at the Earls Court Show in London. At the same time we planned to reveal that Tony Castro, a brilliant yacht designer from Hamble, would design a boat for Maiden's challenge.

This was the breakthrough we needed. Once people saw how much publicity we could generate, companies would be falling over each other to sponsor us.

On the eve of the boat show, the contracts were still unsigned. The company, however, expected us to go ahead and announce the sponsorship. Then I realised that we'd been duped. There was never any intention of giving us the money. The company wanted massive free publicity at absolutely no cost.

At the press conference I stood on a chair and bitterly announced that our 'sponsor' had stitched us up. It was a naïve and angry outburst. Afterwards, Charles Williams, chairman of the Whitbread Race Committee, took me to one side and offered some advice. 'Unless you learn to deal with your disappointment, Tracy, you'll never do this.'

I had tumbled down to Earth and the bump was painful. Welcome to the real world, Tracy – big business doesn't play fair. Charles and Howard tried to help me. They taught me how to deal with aggressive questioning and sexist comments. No matter how patronised or humiliated I felt, I had to smile and find a way to convince people that I was right.

It didn't help that the press stories had dried up. We couldn't offer reporters any new angles. We had no boat, or any money to build one. The yachting press began circling – waiting to write our obituary.

The old Tracy Edwards would have given up about now. Instead, for the first time in my life, I discovered that being bloody-minded is just as important as motivation and ambition. Little spurts had surfaced in the past in the schoolgirl who kept one step ahead of the bullies. Now it was on a different scale. I became more focused than ever before. The project was no longer just about racing. It was about finishing something that I had started – an entirely new concept for me.

People were joining our team all the time, often working for no money and sleeping on my floor. They were boat bums and crew hopefuls, who volunteered to lick envelopes and make phone calls. I felt humbled each time I looked around me. At the same time it gave me incredible self-belief and confidence.

Similarly, yachtsmen like Peter Blake and Robin Knox-Johnston – heroes of mine – were supporting me. When asked about Maiden in interviews, they said things like, 'Of course they can do it.' These were legendary sailors whom I barely knew yet they believed in me. I had to succeed otherwise I'd be letting them down. It was the same with King Hussein. I didn't want to disappoint him. A burden of expectation had been building up around me and instead of scaring me it made me more determined. I had never taken pride in anything like this before. In truth, I'd let a lot of people down. Not this time. I *had* to succeed.

In February 1987 the organisers of the Whitbread arranged a lunch for Prince Andrew and the Duchess of York. The Prince had agreed to present the prizes at the end of the next race.

Peter Blake and I were invited to the lunch and I sat next to the Duchess. She took a real interest in Maiden and kept asking me questions. It gave me an idea. During a quiet moment, I spoke to her equerry. 'We don't actually have the boat yet, but do you think the Duchess would agree to launch it?'

'Why don't you ask her?'

I did just that. As the lunch ended, she turned to say goodbye. 'I hope you don't think I'm being presumptuous,' I said, 'but I would really like you to launch our boat when she's ready.'

'I thought you'd never ask,' she said, flashing her trademark smile.

* * *

The generosity of some people amazed me. Henry Strezelecki was a Polish immigrant after the war, and through sheer hard work he had become a successful self-made businessman. He owned Henri Lloyd, a company making foul weather gear and offered us part of their stand at the Southampton Boat Show.

Another friend printed a load of boxer shorts with the Maiden GB logo. Someone else did balloons and badges. A travel agent gave us a holiday in Greece that we could raffle. And a local pub arranged a big night for the prize draw.

Naïvely, I began thinking we might even raise the money like this. Yet in reality we needed hundreds of thousands of pounds, rather than the odd one or two.

Each time the project had any publicity another spate of applications arrived for crew places. Fiona sifted through them and arranged interviews for those who appeared to have enough experience.

I knew from the outset that we were going to lack experience. Perhaps the only women in the world who were well practised in long-distance offshore racing were the French, and there is no way most of them would sail under someone like me. Instead, I would have to pick an amateur crew and we'd learn to sail the boat together. Simply being the first all-female crew to compete in the Whitbread wasn't enough. That idea had been quickly left behind. There was no point in being that wet, cold and miserable unless we wanted to win.

I needed girls who were determined and had the right person-alities. I'd been on a boat where people didn't get on and that was awful. We'd never win like that. We had to be the ultimate team – individuals capable of thinking for themselves, as well as being team players when it mattered. The other major necessity was a bloody good sense of humour.

By now I had gathered the nucleus of a crew around me. This was important because it showed journalists and would-be sponsors that it wasn't just me behind this. We were a team.

My next-door neighbour Simon Lawrence watched all this from

a safe distance. He wasn't a sailor and knew little about yachts. I liked that. At times I needed to talk to somebody normal about something other than the project.

I used to fall in love at the drop of a hat. This time I tumbled for Simon. You should never try to rationalise love, but with Simon I sensed a calmness and stability – traits that were lacking in my life. I lived within a storm and he was like a safe harbour. This time I consciously tried to slow the relationship down. Normally when I fall in love, the passion is almost scorching. Trouble is, once that passion begins to burn out then it's all downhill. This time I fell in love with someone who was a friend first.

Simon was so different from other men I'd dated. He wasn't a sailor, for a start. He was also a gentleman, which was a definite step in the right direction. He was a few years younger than I was, but it didn't seem to matter. We enjoyed each other's company immensely. Although Simon looked as though butter wouldn't melt in his mouth he could be really wicked. We laughed a lot together and respected our differences.

Mum liked Simon but thought he wouldn't be strong enough for me. He was just too nice. She knew me well enough to know that I tended to dominate people if they let me. I tried hard not to do that with Simon. I didn't want to lose him.

He gave me a Rottweiler puppy and I named him Punch. Soon a sign appeared on the office door saying, NEVER MIND THE DOG, BEWARE OF THE OWNER.

Through 1987 the project limped onwards, with growing debts. Any thoughts of building a boat had to be shelved. We no longer had the time. When the bank refused to lend us any more money, I borrowed money against the house.

None of us were being paid, except some of the crew. God knows what Howard was living on. Meanwhile, we kept working through a list of companies, asking for sponsorship. Each reply was the same.

Mum, who had moved from Purley to a house in Hamble, proved to be a wonderful sounding board and support. Whenever I was under pressure, I could talk to her about everyday things. She had the uncanny knack of sending me quotes or passages – many from the Bible – which proved to be amazingly apt. Just when a sponsorship deal collapsed, I'd open a letter and find a scrap of paper that said: 'When one door closes, a window opens somewhere.'

How did she know?

Mum fed me when I had no money and kept me abreast of the family's news when I didn't have time to call or turn up for get-togethers. Although she never complained, her MS must have been a terrible burden.

There are some forty types of multiple sclerosis and some attack the body quicker than others. Mum's led to a very slow, progressive destruction of the body. She came out of each small relapse a little bit worse than before. It might be a small change like pins and needles in her fingers or a twitch in her neck. Later she lost her balance more often, which was particularly distressing for a former dancer.

Daily she was the most stubborn, bloody-minded woman I had ever met. Much of her strength came from her faith. Religion had never been preached across our dinner table, or forced down my throat. For years after I left home I forgot about it completely. Then slowly, I began thinking about it again while I worked on Maiden. I don't know what changed in me. Perhaps I saw what it did for Mum. After all the dreadful things that had happened to her, if she could still believe in God then so could I.

When I first went travelling to Greece Mum gave me a book written by Reverend Norman Vincent Peale. It was called *The Power of Positive Thinking* and, typically, Mum had marked certain pages and underlined sections. During the Maiden campaign, she gave me the follow-up, *The Power of Positive Living*. Obviously she recognised when I needed a bit of help. This book has been everywhere with me since then – on all my trips around the world.

I still pick it up occasionally, whenever I'm unsure of what to do, or need encouragement. Some passages I can recite by heart:

> *Do not passively accept unsatisfactory circumstances, but form a picture in your mind of circumstances as they should be. Hold that picture. Develop it firmly in all details. Believe in it. Pray about it. Work about it. And you can actualise it according to that mental image emphasised in your positive thinking.*

That's what I do. When I want to achieve something I picture every aspect of it. Like *Maiden* crossing the starting line and the finishing line, in first place of course.

More than 350 British companies had turned us down. Meanwhile, the bank was taking my house piece by piece. For weeks I'd been going to dinner at people's houses because I couldn't afford food. Simon had been making me eat: he had seen there was nothing in the cupboards.

At times I had no dog food for Punch and had to scrabble for small change to buy a can. One night I gave him the only thing I had in the cupboard – baked beans. This ranks among my worst ideas ever. Punch became so windy he was almost rocket propelled.

Another fond memory of poverty was listening to Fi trying to explain to the VAT man why dog food should be VAT reclaimable. She spent half an hour skilfully arguing her case, but he wasn't convinced.

At the Earls Court Boat Show in early 1988, I finally dared talk to Howard about shutting the operation down.

'When do we call it quits?' I asked him. 'When do we decide that we're bashing our heads against a brick wall?'

Unlike in the past, Howard struggled to find a silver lining to the dark clouds. 'I can't see the wood for the trees any more,' he admitted. 'I believe 100 per cent that we can do the race and win. But I cannot see how to raise the money.'

'So what should we do?'

'We can't give up.'

'And we can't go on like this. Maybe we should scale things down for while.'

As much as the decision hurt, Howard agreed.

Early the next morning I gathered the girls together. Apart from Fiona and SJ, the nucleus of the crew and shore team was Marie-Claude Kieffer, Jenny Pocock, Nancy Hill and Dee Ingles.

I looked at them, remembering what they had all given up for me. Instead of feeling downhearted, I suddenly felt my strength returning.

'This is only a setback. It's not the end,' I said. 'I can't pay you any more. I have no choice but to let you go. As soon as we find a major sponsor, we'll get back together again.'

The girls understood. Some of them even offered to stay on, working unpaid.

'We will find a way to do this,' I said, believing it totally. 'We just need a little more time.'

I woke up at two o'clock one morning and phoned Howard.

'We have to buy a boat.'

'Do you know what time it is?'

'Yes. I'm sorry. But we have to buy a boat.'

'OK, I'll dash out and buy one tomorrow.'

'I'm being serious.'

'It's two in the morning.'

'I'm going to mortgage the house to buy the boat.'

He thought I'd gone completely mad.

'People are never, ever going to believe us unless they see that we have a boat,' I explained. 'Drawings and designs are beautiful but they're not real. They need to see something physical. We need a boat.'

I talked to Robbie Cook, a friend who had been helping out occasionally on the project. He began searching the world for suitable boats. Very sensibly I decided to ignore the top-of-the-range maxis, which were far more difficult to sail and fearfully expensive. Instead, we'd look for a smaller boat and compete in a different class.

The cynics in the yachting press reacted with typical scepticism. Andrew Preece wrote in *Yacht and Yachting* magazine: 'Edwards tells us she's now buying a boat instead of designing and building one for the Whitbread. No doubt she'll be parking it on her front lawn . . . We'll believe it when we see it.'

Robbie looked at several former Whitbread boats before tracking down a yacht called *Prestige* in Cape Town. The 58-foot sloop had raced in the 1981–82 race as *Disque D'or III*.

Having remortgaged my house, I flew to Cape Town a week later. The taxi took me to the commercial docks and I wandered through warehouses criss-crossed by trolley tracks and dotted with containers. Huge ships and tankers dwarfed the docks and cranes swung overhead. Surely this can't be the place, I thought.

Black workers in blue overalls scurried to and fro. Their shoes were too big for them and flopped along the dock like loose sandals. I stopped one of the workmen, who crouched to reach eye level with me. I showed him the piece of paper and he thrust out his arm towards a dilapidated warehouse. I continued walking, weaving between pontoons and docks. A sheen of oil stained the water, forming rainbow colours in the patches of sunlight.

Suddenly, on the outside dock, amid the huge ships, I spied a pint-sized yacht that would have been white if not for the dust and grime that covered its decks. It had been there so long that weeds had started growing on the hull.

'What a crime,' I whispered, saddened by the total neglect. There was no excuse for it.

The boat had been virtually abandoned, or written off as obsolete. Gingerly I stepped on board, half expecting to put my foot straight through the deck, but she was solid enough and just the right size.

Don't ask me why, but I fell in love with her. Perhaps I could visualise what she could become, or maybe I had an affinity with a

craft that, like me, had done one Whitbread and deserved the
chance to do another.

Being an aluminium boat, *Prestige* had enormous potential. She
could be opened up and welded shut again, allowing us to chop
and change the interiors and deck layout. A carbon boat can't be
altered in the same way.

I had a survey done and began negotiating a price. The
yacht's previous sponsor, Prestige Kitchens, wanted £150,000.
Howard told me to offer £100,000 and we finally agreed on
£115,000.

While in South Africa I managed to see some of the guys from
Atlantic Privateer. They couldn't believe that I was actually following through with my idea and buying a boat.

'My God, you really were bitten by the race, weren't you?'
joked Hagar.

'I guess so. Are you still sure I can actually do it?'

'Sure, why not? You've been there before.'

The yacht was in no condition to be sailed to Britain so I found a
shipping company in Cape Town and managed to beat them down
on the price by using my usual tactics of grovelling and begging.

They agreed to carry the yacht on top of some containers they
were shipping. It only cost me a couple of thousand quid. I flew
home to await the arrival.

There is no greater sailing truism than that a boat is the
equivalent of pouring money down a drain. Yet I knew that if
I was going to make the project happen, I needed a symbol as proof
that we were serious. Now I had one.

I arrived home and told everyone that I had bought a great boat.
I left out the details about the neglect and damage.

On the day the container ship arrived in Southhampton we all
went down to the dock to watch the yacht being offloaded. By
then the nucleus of our team was back together – all except for
Fiona, who had taken a good job offer. I didn't blame her, although
I missed her company and her amazing drinking stamina.

I couldn't see the yacht at first. It was nestled amid the containers on deck. Then a crane lifted and swung the hull clear. It still had weed hanging off the sides, which had dried and become crusted and grey.

'Isn't she lovely?' I kept saying.

There was silence around me.

'Oh, my God, it's our boat. Isn't it great?' I danced about.

The silence grew deeper.

Nestled in a sling, the yacht was lowered towards the water. As its deck came into view, I saw that it was covered in a fine red dust which must have blown from the Sahara as the freighter sailed up the coast of West Africa. Those around me grew even more subdued. What on earth had I bought?

The hull settled in the water and I clambered on board, trying to be upbeat. Some of the others were waiting to make sure it didn't immediately sink.

Neil Cheston had agreed to help us motor around to Moody's boatyard in Hamble. 'At least the engine works,' I heard somebody mutter, as it spluttered into life. We headed down Southampton Water and up into the Hamble River. Most of us sat on deck, sweeping away the dust. The mast lay alongside us, protruding from either end.

Jo Gooding, our cook, had gone below to check out the interior.

'Ah, Tracy, should the floorboards be floating?'

'What?'

'Is that meant to happen?'

I scrambled down below. We were sinking. Neil hooked up the bilge pump on to the engine because the generator didn't work. We kept pumping for the rest of the voyage and went straight to the boatyard.

Pam Hale, part of our shore crew and one of the most colourful characters in yachting, had dressed in a French maid's outfit, with high-heel shoes and fishnet stockings. She carried a tray with a bottle of champagne and a stack of plastic cups.

Looking very blonde and busty, she sauntered through Moody's boatyard, collecting whistles from the workmen. It is still one of the stranger sights that I've seen in yachting.

Before we could celebrate we had to quickly lift the hull out of the water before it sank. After lifting her up, the crane took her into a horrible corner of the yard – away from all the nice boats, just in case she 'infected' them. We shored her up with wooden beams, before opening the champagne and drinking a toast.

ELEVEN

MAIDEN didn't look particularly fair, or fetching. The yard blasted off the weed and paint with high-pressure hoses and sanders. Afterwards I gave the girls sledge-hammers and told them to remove the interior. Pretty much everything had to go, including the galley sink. Only the engine could be re-used.

My poor bank manager, bless him, let me mortgage the boat to pay for the refit. He was a very nervous man – quite rightly so.

We did all the work ourselves, getting advice from boat builders and electricians. Tony Castro helped design the exterior and interior. On deck we added new winches and halyards, as well as two grinders to help raise the sails at speed. Below was completely rewired and given a brand new set of electronic equipment.

Friends, family and yachties all volunteered to help. Bit by bit we pieced Maiden together, working weekends and evenings. The girls had taken over Fernyside Cottage in Hamble as our crew house. It was known locally as the Pink House – an appropriate colour.

As Nancy scraped away at the inside of the hull she came across some old carpet. As she pulled at it further she realised, to her horror, that it was covering the chocks on which *Maiden* now rested. The hole went right through the hull.

At another time she was pulling out a headboard in the galley when a shower of dead cockroaches fell on her head.

The guys in the yard were brilliant, showing us how to use the welder and other tools. It helped being a pretty all-female crew, but we were never too proud to ask for advice.

The interiors were built in my garage and then moved to the yard. We put insulation foam on the hull to stop condensation, having first laid conduits for the wiring and the plumbing.

Jo, our cook, decided how she wanted the galley and I designed the nav station. We all had just enough experience on boats to know what we needed. At the same time, we didn't have rigid or preconceived ideas. Being young and energetic, we turned our lack of experience into an advantage because we discovered new ways of doing things. We all had a vision of how the boat would look when it was finished. Not only did we want to repair it – we had to make it faster and stronger.

I was learning all the time about leadership. One important discovery was that the more people are made to feel part of what's happening, the more they *own* the project. This might seem like common sense, but it had a profound effect.

Even when they moved us out of the grotty corner of the yard, *Maiden* still looked a mess. It wasn't until we painted her in the Maiden GB colours – red, white and blue – that I finally knew that I had a boat. On her unveiling for the media, we strung a huge banner along the hull, saying, THIS SPACE FOR SALE.

We moved her from the boatyard to Port Hamble marina, knowing that we had a year to train and prepare for the Whitbread – if we could find the money. The project team had picked up a few minor sponsors – a container company and electronics firm – but we still needed about £800,000. Nearly half of this was to pay off our bank overdraft.

In Hamble the townsfolk had adopted the project and we had a great deal of support. All except for the yacht club, which refused to let the girls become even temporary members. The idea of an all-female crew was obviously a threat to the traditionalists. There were also the occasional snide comments in the pubs, when drunken louts and know-alls would shout, 'Watch out, here come the tarts from *Maiden*. Going to sail around the world are we, loves?'

One night I picked up the phone and heard a man's voice say: 'You're a disgrace to women. You should be chained up at home, you stupid bitch.'

I was horrified. I'd always imagined that I'd laugh if I ever had an abusive call or pervert on the line. Instead, I felt violated. It was as though someone had come into my home and spat on me. No, worse than that: because I couldn't see his face, I could never be sure if this man was somebody I passed every day in Hamble. How would I know him?

The calls began coming at odd hours, day and night. Somebody poured oil and petrol on the lawn in front of the house, killing the grass.

Simon said I should move in with him. 'I don't want you in the house by yourself.'

I laughed. 'I'm never in the house alone. It's a hotel.'

Things soon escalated. At three o'clock in the morning the police arrived. I came downstairs in a T-shirt.

'We're arresting you on suspicion of dangerous driving and leaving the scene of an accident,' the officer said.

'Excuse me?'

'Your truck has been involved in an accident.'

'But my truck is parked outside.'

'No it isn't.'

Someone had stolen my truck and crashed it into a brick wall. I don't know if it was a joy-rider or someone targeting me, because stupidly I had left the keys in the ignition.

The police took me to the station and insisted I take a blood test. What were they going to charge me with? Being drunk in charge of a bed!

'That's ridiculous. I wasn't driving the truck. I've been at home all night.'

We argued the point until I convinced them that I had nothing to do with the accident. This should have been the end of the incident. Instead it finished up – more than two years later – on the front page of the *Sun*:

COPS DRAGGED ME NUDE FROM BED, SAYS YACHT GIRL.

The story went on to claim that I'd been arrested for suspected drink driving after apparently going out on a 'wild binge'. It wasn't until the end of the article that the year was mentioned, or the fact that no charges were laid.

Although I'm not the sort to scare easily, now I began to worry. What if someone tried to damage the boat? I felt a lot more relaxed after we hired a security firm to watch *Maiden*. I also asked Trevor to come and stay with me for a few weeks.

He was making an impact as a promising racing driver, competing in Formula Vauxhall. The Jim Edwards School of Racing had chosen him as the young driver they wanted to sponsor for a year. Trevor raced in *Maiden*'s colours, with the mermaid logo.

In August Simon moved in with me. Apart from being in love with me, he had endless patience. Who else could have put up with my late nights and spur-of-the-moment decisions?

Being an old boat, *Maiden* couldn't be 'launched', she had to be 'christened'. Howard contacted Buckingham Palace to remind them that the Duchess of York had promised to perform the task. The response arrived by return. The Duchess was heavily pregnant and couldn't possibly co-operate.

Howard and I wrote an impassioned plea. I felt like suggesting a joint christening – we could do *Maiden* and the new baby as a job lot. Fergie sent a charming letter back, saying that she had no intention of disappointing us. She'd be there on 20 September.

We still hadn't found a major sponsor who could rename the boat. Negotiations were under way with Digital Equipment, the world's second largest computer company, which had offered

£500,000 from the British division and recommended the US parent company put in £300,000. I contemplated how quickly we could change the name from *Maiden* to *Digital Dancer*.

With seven days until the christening, no contracts had been signed and our overdraft stood at £350,000. The bank was getting very nervous. We risked losing the yacht and all my assets.

In desperation, I phoned King Hussein and explained the situation. I had never asked him for help, despite his offers.

'Is there any way a company in Jordan would be interested in sponsoring us? It need only be enough to clear the overdraft, or pay for a winter racing programme.'

'Leave it with me,' he said.

Two days before the christening I had a phone call from Ali Ghandour, chairman of Royal Jordanian Airlines and a close personal friend of King Hussein. Although he made no clear commitment, he arranged a meeting to discuss sponsorship.

Only hours earlier, Howard had gone to the bank, hoping to extend the overdraft for a little longer.

'You must be very relieved that this money has come through,' said the manager.

'Pardon?' replied Howard.

'You must feel so justified.'

'Yes,' said Howard, thinking quickly. 'Absolutely. And, how much money *did* come through?'

'Three hundred and fifty thousand pounds.'

King Hussein had cleared the overdraft.

'You must come to Jordan to see me,' the King told me. 'You will like Ali Ghandour. He's a good man.'

On 20 September, at the Royal Yacht Squadron in Southampton, the Duchess of York sprayed a bottle of champagne across the foredeck of *Maiden*, declaring that she didn't normally like wasting good bubbly. It was her first official engagement since the birth of Princess Beatrice.

The dock was packed with TV cameras and photographers. Most of them had come to see how much weight the Duchess had lost since the birth. I didn't mind. We made headlines in every national newspaper.

Yet the day's most important event went entirely unnoticed. We had found ourselves a sponsor.

Two weeks later I flew to Jordan with Howard and Keith Webb, the designer of the *Maiden* logo. Royal Jordanian Airlines put us up in a hotel in the centre of Amman, the capital.

The following day we had a meeting with Ali Ghandour, a delightful man, and other senior executives from the airline. There seemed to be a real symmetry between RJA and Maiden GB. A lot of people had laughed when King Hussein had floated the idea of a national airline for Jordan. It seemed pretentious for such a small and not particularly wealthy Arab country.

The King was passionate about flying and started the company with a single aeroplane. He called it Alia Airlines after his second wife and great love who had died in a helicopter crash. Through a great deal of determination and persistence the airline grew and became Royal Jordanian.

Over a series of meetings we hammered out the details of the sponsorship. RJA would put up an initial £100,000 to fund a winter race programme. This was enough to fit *Maiden* out with new sails and gear, but not enough for naming rights. The *Maiden* name was to remain, but we would incorporate the airline's striking livery – grey, red and gold.

King Hussein also gave us permission to use his personal mark, a crown, on the new logo which Keith was to design for the project.

Howard and I stayed in Amman for an extra few days, hoping to see the King. One morning, as we both lay by the pool, I was summoned to the phone by hotel staff. It was the King's butler, whom I'd met several times in England.

'A car is being sent for you. You are to come to the palace.'

There was no mention of Howard, so I went on my own. A black limousine with tinted windows swept me through the bustling streets to the gates of an airbase. All of King Hussein's palaces were within military bases, no doubt for security reasons.

'Is Howard not with you?' the King said, beaming his famous smile. He wore an open-neck shirt and trousers.

I apologised. 'I didn't know if he was invited.'

'Of course. I want to meet Howard. I'll send someone to fetch him.'

Later Howard told me the story of how he was lying on a sun-lounger when a shadow fell across him. A man in sunglasses and a dark suit said: 'Get dressed. The King wants to see you.' He wasn't the sort of messenger you keep waiting.

The King served morning tea and then asked: 'Have you seen much of Amman?'

We shook our heads. 'We haven't really had the chance.'

'But you must. Come. I'll show you.'

We drove to the centre of the airbase and the King strode into a hangar. He began pulling on a pair of flying overalls. I looked at Howard and shrugged. Two co-pilots fell into step on either side of the King and we marched towards a large military helicopter. 'Hop aboard,' said Hussein, as he adjusted his helmet microphone.

Strapped in our seats, I watched the King run through the pre-flight check list and then give a thumbs-up to his co-pilots. The rotor blades roared above us and we lifted off. Within minutes we were sweeping over the city.

The King kept up a running commentary as he flew, pointing out landmarks and historical sites. We could talk to him through headphones and mikes.

We flew out across the desert above bedouin camps and over the wind-carved valleys of Wadi Rum.

'You see that mountain,' said the King. 'That is where Moses pointed out the Promised Land to the Palestinians after they fled from Egypt.'

Minutes later we hovered above the Dead Sea – the lowest point on Earth. 'This is the only time I ever want to see you below sea level, Tracy.'

After nearly two hours in the air, we landed in the grounds of a large modern hospital in Amman. 'My mother is ill,' explained the King. 'I promised to visit her. I'll see you before you go.'

He waved and crouched low as he ran through the downdraught from the rotors. Seconds later, we took off again and the pilots delivered us back to the airbase where a limousine waited. As we slid inside, the driver announced, 'I shall pick you up tomorrow morning at ten o'clock.'

'I beg your pardon?'

'A helicopter will be waiting at ten. I shall pick you up at 9.30.'

'Where are we going?'

'To the King's palace in Aqaba. You shall visit Petra on the way.'

'Right. OK.' I wasn't about to argue. Instead, I postponed our flights.

Two Royal Jordanian Airforce pilots flew us to Petra the next morning. Neither of them had ever visited 'the rose red city, half as old as time', so we convinced them to come along with us.

We hired horses – which made Howard decidedly nervous – and rode into the ancient city through a crack in the cliff-face. The crevasse wound for half a mile through sheer rock walls, just wide enough for us to ride in single file.

In 8,000 years the ancient city of Petra had never been conquered by force because of these natural defences. The Romans had tried and so had Alexander the Great.

The crevasse opened suddenly and the Treasury towered above us carved out of the solid rock. I felt like a Lilliputian who had just discovered Gulliver. The sheer size and scale of the buildings was breathtaking.

The rose granite shimmered in the sun and the cliffs around us muffled the sound of the horses' hooves. The silence was deafening. I sat and stared in wonder, completely gobsmacked.

Suddenly, my own achievements were put into perspective. These people had carved a civilisation out of stone, harvesting water from natural springs and building sophisticated aqueducts through the mountains. If they could do this, then surely I could skipper an all-female crew around the world.

We had lunch at a hotel before flying on to Aqaba. Again the palace was at the centre of a military base. It bordered the no man's land between Jordan and Israel. High fences stretched into the distance, with watchtowers and machine-gun posts. Egypt and Saudi Arabia lay across the waters of the Red Sea.

We were the only people staying at the palace and the staff put Howard and me into a double chalet. They were mortified when we explained that we weren't 'a couple'.

When I glanced at the visitors' book, I recognised the name of the last guest to stay. Sean Connery had been filming *Indiana Jones and the Last Crusade* here.

'Nobody is going to believe us when we get home,' said Howard.

'I'll believe you,' I said. 'Days don't come much better than this.'

The crew had been assembled in ones and twos since the project began. All of them were at least competent sailors, but they also had to have specialist skills such as engineering, sail-making or rigging.

Jo Gooding, our cook, was an old friend from school. Sally Creaser had come from Scotland for her interview and I liked her immediately. She was physically and mentally strong, with a wicked sense of humour. Nancy Hill lived locally and sort of drifted into the project. Dawn Reilly had great references and flew over from America for a week's trial. Mandi Swan, a sailmaker, had sent a letter from New Zealand.

I needed a strong deck 'manager' and chose Marie-Claude Kieffer, a brilliant French yachtswoman. She brought with her Michèle Paret, a top helmswoman, and Jeni Mundy, an electronics specialist.

The rest of the twelve – average age, 25 – was made up of Mikaela 'Miki' Von Koskull (helm), Tanja Visser (foredeck), Angela Farrell (sail trimmer) and Claire Russell our doctor, whom we taught to sail. Eight countries were represented in the crew, including Scotland, Wales and England.

After a lot of soul-searching, I'd decided to skipper *Maiden* as well as navigate. Normally, the tasks are separate because they're so demanding. Navigators tend to get blamed for bad weather and poor results, whereas skippers can stand back, avoid the flak and then claim all the glory if the yacht does well.

I loved navigating and very few women had my experience. One drawback of doing both jobs was spending long hours below deck studying the daily charts and weather faxes. I didn't want to lose touch with events on deck.

Almost from the start, I clashed with Marie-Claude. She was fiery and opinionated, but I could handle that. Others on the project, many of whom had volunteered their services free of charge, were less able to cope.

I told myself that all of these things wouldn't matter, once we were on the water. The team would pull together and sailing would surmount politics.

With our immediate funding secured and a new set of sails on board, we began training in earnest. *Maiden* showed that she was competitive, but she was still too heavy. Other boats in the race were made of carbon and were going to be quicker in light airs.

Although we had a good rating, in terms of handicap, our chances of being first over the line in our class were still regarded as being very slim.

I didn't believe the physical difference between men and women would become an issue. This might have been the case in close-quarters racing when tacking duels require enormous strength on the winches. Long-distance sailing is different. The result hinges more on tactics, courage and the ability of each helmsman to get every ounce of speed from the boat.

Our first big test would be the Route of Discovery Race from Cadiz, near Gibraltar, to Santo Domingo in the Dominican Republic. Most of the Whitbread fleet was taking part and this was our chance to prove ourselves.

My nerves were on edge for a week leading up to the race. I had stomach pains and a neck so stiff I had to wear a surgical collar. My doctor told me that if I kept going at the same pace I'd miss the Whitbread.

'I personally will put you in hospital for six months,' he warned.

Of course, I took no notice of him. The project still hung in the balance. A good result in the Route of Discovery might get us the rest of the money. A failure could consign us to history.

On a bright, sunny day, hundreds of supporters came to wave us off from the Royal Southern Yacht Club in Hamble. I took the wheel as *Maiden* sailed down the river. We did a couple of spinnaker runs on the Solent – showing off our new colours – and then set sail for Spain.

This is what we should have been doing all along, I told myself. Not sending out proposals or talking to press. We should have been sailing.

Maiden felt wonderful beneath my feet as she surged towards Cadiz. The sound of laughter filled the air. The dark days disappeared behind us with every mile and so did our financial worries. I felt as though I'd never been away.

Maiden had been turned into virtually a new boat during the refit. Watertight bulkheads designed to protect the yacht if we hit a whale or floating debris took up the first dozen feet of the bow. The next compartments were for storing sheets and other gear. The engine had been boxed to create a workbench where Dawn could repair equipment. Opposite, lay the day fuel tanks. These were vital to power the water-maker, navigation instruments and radios.

There were twelve bunks, in decks of three, with just enough stowage space for each of the girls to have a Ziploc bag of personal belongings. We rigged up a pulley system to keep the bunks level when the yacht was heeled over.

The sails took up the central area, along with a sewing machine to repair any damage. Next came the food storage lockers and galley. We had to sit on the floor to eat.

Opposite the galley, the nav station was the nerve centre of the boat. It had a computer, two satellite navigation systems, a weather fax, emergency beacons and the radios, both short and long range.

Near the aft hatch we had stowage for tools, wet weather gear, safety harnesses, flares and more sails. On the starboard side was the yacht's sole washbasin and head (toilet).

Most of the crew positions had been settled, but a few of the girls were still on trial. In stiff winds, we crossed the starting line on 4 December, heading for the Canaries.

Five days later, as we rounded the first mark in the bay off Las Palmas, our weather fax stopped working. We had no way of finding the best winds, or storm fronts. I had to make a decision. Did I simply follow the fleet, or should we strike out on our own, following the legendary trade winds that blow across the Atlantic?

Marie-Claude wanted to go north – the shorter route because of the curvature of the Earth. I chose to go south because I knew from experience where the trade winds would be. I didn't fancy trying to find the breeze without a weather fax. Nor did I see the point of following the maxis. Within a few days their extra speed would put them too far ahead for their weather forecasts to do us any good.

For two days I regretted my decision. We wallowed in the Atlantic swell, almost alone except for *With Integrity*, a Whitbread cruising entry which had followed us south. After a good start we had quickly dropped back from fifth to thirteenth in a twenty-boat field. I prayed to the Gods of the Wind.

I was aiming for 20°N, 20°W, hoping to find the trade winds. They arrived in a rush, filling the sails and my lungs to bursting. We had 25 knots of gorgeous nor' easterly, pushing us along at a steady 11 knots.

To the north, storms and severe headwinds hit the rest of the fleet. Gear began failing and tempers began to fray. One or two tried to come south, but by then it was too late. *Maiden* crept back into the race and into the lead.

As we crossed the finish line in Santo Domingo, I looked across to see one of the maxis tied up at the dock. A part of me felt sad, but I knew we could never compete with these giants. The male crew had lined up along the dock. They were shouting to us, 'You're first! You're first!'

Then I looked around and realised that we had finished second overall and first on handicap. We had beaten all the other Whitbread yachts, including Pierre Fehlmann, the winner of the 1985–86 Whitbread Race.

Later, at a reception in the Spanish Embassy, all the girls dressed up in striking black and white dresses. What a cool entrance! The male crews gave us an ovation. We not only looked good, we had proved a point. We weren't simply in the Whitbread to make up the numbers.

Yet despite having achieved the best result by a British yacht in a trans-ocean race for years, we still couldn't get sponsorship from a British company. We went back to over 300 companies that we had tried already. The answer remained no.

With eight months to go until the Whitbread, we still couldn't guarantee that we'd be there. Hauling *Maiden* from the water again, we began the crucial last refit, unsure of how we'd pay for it.

Our overdraft had blown out to £100,000. Howard and I were liable for it. We went back to Ali Ghandour at Royal Jordanian Airlines. I felt embarrassed telling him that no British company would invest in *Maiden Great Britain*.

'We're going to be a big story,' I told him. 'People are going to sit up and take notice.'

We showed him a video of *Maiden* in action, and photographs of the Duchess of York on board. After three hours hammering out the details, we emerged with another £450,000 – enough to get us halfway through the Whitbread. At least I knew that we'd make the start.

In August, a month before the race began, Simon took me on a holiday to a beautiful hotel overlooking Loch Lomond in Scotland. It was very romantic, with huge log fires and long bracing walks through the mountains.

After dinner one night, we sat by the fire finishing a bottle of

wine. Simon began a ridiculous spiel that sounded like Hugh Grant
in *Four Weddings and a Funeral*.

'What I mean to say is . . . ah . . . if you're not doing anything
after the race . . . well . . . I don't know whether you want to do
this . . . I mean . . . so do you think that you and I might . . . you
know . . . get married.'

I was amazed that anybody would want to spend any more time
with me than they absolutely had to. To start with, I didn't have a
very good track record with men. I'd been through enough of
them.

At the grand old age of twenty-six, I suddenly thought, why do
all my relationships last two seconds? Am I going to finish up on my
own? Here was this lovely guy, who was handsome, gentle, stable
and a calming influence on my life. I'd be a fool not to marry him.

TWELVE

ROPES were gently lobbed into eager hands. I eased *Maiden* forwards, opening a gap of inches . . . and then feet . . . with the pontoon. This gap would grow to 6,281 miles before we set foot on land again.

All the show; the bold front that I put on for the rest of the world; the bravado that said, 'I can do this and nobody will stop me', suddenly evaporated. Maybe they were right, after all. Maybe I can't navigate well enough? What if I lose the race for us? What if we all die?

Yet I had no butterflies. Instead I felt remarkably calm. I glanced across at the pontoon. There were so many people crowded on to it, I thought it might sink. I saw Mum's face. She looked so small and so proud. Trevor stood alongside her. My aunts and uncles had come down from Reading, with my cousins.

We eased into the channel behind *Rothmans*, another of the British entries. It was being skippered by Lawrie Smith and reportedly had a budget of £6 million. There were twenty-three yachts taking part in the Whitbread – the biggest entry in the race's history.

I'd been up since six in the morning. Simon made me coffee, while I had a bath and finished packing. He'd been really upset the night before. He didn't want me to leave.

'We're getting married in August,' I laughed. 'We'll have our whole lives together.'

He wouldn't tell me what was worrying him. His long silences could be unnerving. I knew that he didn't understand this passion of mine. Why did I want to be wet, cold and miserable thousands of miles from home? Why risk my life? To Simon, offshore racing was the equivalent of digging a hole at the bottom of the garden and shovelling money into it.

We drove to Southampton and I walked down to the quay. I stood watching the Whitbread boats. What a magnificent sight! They looked like racehorses straining in their halters.

Howard arrived and we hugged each other. No words were necessary. It had taken us four years of blood, sweat and tears. Who'd have thought?

An all-woman crew had never done the Whitbread. Now we were the first. Just a fortnight earlier, I had made the difficult decision to ask Marie-Claude, our most experienced crew member, to leave. Cutting her loose had nothing to do with her seamanship. It came down to a power struggle that had been brewing ever since the Route of Discovery Race when we argued over tactics. There had seemed to be two skippers operating on *Maiden*, which confused the crew and tested their loyalty unnecessarily.

For a long time I was reluctant to do anything about the situation. Finally, I had no choice. I told her my decision and called the rest of the crew together. There was silence. Marie-Claude had introduced Michèle and Jeni to the project. I was afraid they might leave.

Ultimately, they stayed, but I felt as though I was now on trial. They were watching me and I had to prove that I could take them round the world.

The Solent was covered in a patchwork of sails and a thousand spectator boats. How do I negotiate my way through this? A Royal Navy frigate, HMS *Ambuscade*, had anchored at the starting line. On board were the Duke and Duchess of York. I could just make out the royal party, surrounded by dignitaries and flanked by naval officers.

The radio buzzed and crackled. Fergie called to wish us good luck. 'How are my girls?' she asked. 'Nervous, I expect. I want you to go and win. I'm relying on you.'

'We'll do our best,' I said. We gave her three cheers from the deck as we passed close by the frigate.

Prince Andrew fired the cannon at 12.15p.m. I misjudged the start badly, because of worries about the spectator boats. We were last across the line – hardly an auspicious beginning. It should have been a magic moment, but instead I cursed myself.

We trailed after the maxis down the Solent. Michèle took the wheel and I went below. Finally I cried. I sat just inside the hatch, with my shoulders shaking and tears trickling down my cheeks. I thought of Dad. I wished he could have seen this.

We ploughed through the chop of spectator boats, acknowledging the cheers and blasts from air horns. Suddenly, I couldn't remember how impossible this was supposed to be.

A few days earlier, a journalist had asked me, 'What is it about you? Why are you sitting here on this boat, when so many people much more qualified than you and much more able to do this race are not here? What have you got?'

I pondered this for a while and said, 'I have faith.'

I could see this wasn't the answer she hoped for. She wanted me to give her some formula, or recipe for success. I didn't have one.

Mum always used to tell me to try my absolute best at things and give it 100 per cent. 'If it doesn't happen, it wasn't meant to,' she said, 'but if you haven't given your absolute best you'll never know.'

I remembered this. How awful it must be to never know.

Mum and Trevor were following on a motor launch that also carried most of our shore crew. As we headed past the Needles and out of the Solent, the boat blew its horn and turned. Mum waved, sad but happy. All at once we were alone.

The first leg was 6,821 miles, across the Equator and the South

Atlantic to Punta del Este in Uruguay. Throughout the first day it rankled that I'd misjudged the start so badly. This had played into the hands of our critics.

The *Daily Express* wrote, the following morning:

> *Hardly rated to be in with even a prayer, despite trial success, the all girl crew in the round the world yacht race were given a stirring and 'Britain expects' style send off by the Duchess of York on the weekend . . .*
>
> *As most of the fleet disappeared over the horizon, Maiden was left trailing well behind.*

Almost without noticing, we let our rivals slip away. In less than 24 hours, *Rucanor* and *L'Esprit* were thirty miles ahead of us. The big maxis powered away, in a race among themselves to be first to Uruguay.

I couldn't figure out why we had done so badly. Some of the girls weren't racing the boat enough. It was difficult to stay focused on such a long race, but unless we pushed hard we risked being left behind. None of the other crews were holding back.

We were caught in a large high pressure system that slowed the fleet. *Maiden* preferred heavier airs and we constantly experimented with different sail combinations.

Twice each day, morning and evening, we had a 'chat show' when the fleet swapped news and positions. I posted the plots for the girls. Hopefully, it would spur them on.

By pushing harder we managed to stop the rot, but closed the gap only slightly. Three days into the race, on my birthday, the wind strengthened and we were finally sailing.

I'd just finished dinner – freeze-dried curry and rice – when we broached spectacularly in a sudden gust. In seconds we had 30 knots of wind and too much sail aloft. I scrambled on deck. We were surfing down swells at 14 knots, with the boat shaking and vibrating. A mountain of spray exploded over the cockpit. Foam and water swept over the decks, trying to rip us off.

'Clip on,' I screamed, wanting everyone in a safety harness. The noise of the sea and wind tried to drown me out.

We put a reef in the main and I turned on the radar. There were three ships nearby, but we had no hope of seeing them in the waves.

Tanja had to go out along the boom to put a reef line through. I'd never seen her scared of anything until now.

She clung to the mainsail as she edged along the boom with the reef line tied to her waist. It took a long time as *Maiden* bucked in the seething water. Every few minutes Tanja was swamped by tons of water and had to gasp for breath. Numbed by the cold, her fingers struggled to put the line through the sail. It seemed an eternity before she crawled back to the mast. She came down smiling – more in relief than triumph.

Even with just the main we were doing 11–12 knots and being laid right over. We put in a second reef just before the wind hit 35 knots. Then we hoisted the 2.2 chicken chute – so called because it's very small and bulletproof. The boat goes slower but is more controlled.

The seas grew worse, putting enormous pressure on the rig. I decided to take the spinnaker down and got everyone on deck. Tanja stayed at the wheel. Michèle shouted instructions. The sock was dragged down to snuff the billowing spinnaker.

Suddenly, the sheet shackle broke and the spinnaker went everywhere. Three of the girls were trying to drag it in and stay on their feet. All wore safety harnesses. The deck lights were swallowed by the darkness and I could barely see a thing.

It took five minutes to drag the spinnaker below. It had torn in two places. My heart was still pounding as I swung through the hatch. I'd missed the evening chat show. My birthday cake, with candles, sat untouched on the stove.

Even with more wind, *Maiden* struggled to make an impression. I wasn't making the right decisions quickly enough. I should have gone further east towards the French coast.

Each morning I wrote down the positions of the fleet. *Steinlager II* was way out in front, but we were holding our own as we passed Madeira on 9 September. My decisions had finally started proving right. We swept past *Creightons Naturally* and closed to within five miles of *L'Esprit*.

The weather was scorching.

On 10 September I wrote in my diary:

Just after sunset the wind dropped to nothing and we glided silently, slowly forwards, with Clannad playing, surrounded by an angry blue and black sky filled with clouds and the moon's silver rays sprinkling over us. How do you explain this feeling to anyone? It is here and now and even after being here I won't remember it exactly as it is. How do you capture it? It is one of the moments that everyone in the world deserves at least once. And I have had so many! I must be the luckiest person in the entire world. What did I ever do to deserve this wonderful, wonderful feeling?

We took six days to crawl through the Doldrums at 100 miles a day. At one point, I sat stark naked and sweaty in the nav station, chatting to Admiral Charles Williams at the Southampton Boat Show. If only he'd known.

There was laughter from the deck. The girls had started talking about men. We were only two weeks out of port and they were already missing sex. I wondered what the guys would have said if they'd heard us talking about them?

It was too hot to sleep, or to eat or to move. I felt as though I was being cooked alive in the nav station. During the day, the deck heated up until it was impossible to walk or stand upon it in bare feet. The girls on watch took turns to hide under a small bit of shade from the main.

We ate our meals on deck – desperate for a cool breeze – and I often slept lying on the sails. The maxis were a thousand miles ahead and racing towards Punta del Este.

My moods were up and down, with each new report of our

position. Twice we closed to within five miles of *Rucanor*, but then suddenly slipped behind again. I read the riot act to the girls about sunbathing on deck, smoking on the grinders and making too many hot drinks.

Match racing is easier because you see your opponents. In our case, they were somewhere over the horizon. We had to race them in our minds and stay focused.

The girls were blossoming as people and sailors. There were no rivalries. The only competition was at the helm between the watch captains Dawn and Michèle and that made the boat go faster.

On 19 September we passed the halfway mark. Two days later Howard radioed to say that we'd overtaken *Rucanor*. There were cheers on deck. The celebrations were short-lived. We suffered a horrid few days, beating into squalls. There were leaks in the port compass housing and the winch seals. My charts were sodden and so were the electronics.

The girls were wet and exhausted. At least they were learning how to keep their clothes dry – an important lesson for the Southern Ocean.

For two days we stayed ahead of *Rucanor* and for another four days we kept within sight. Now the girls knew we were racing. Every mile came at a cost. At one point, we faced eating nothing but crackers and chocolate for a fortnight, when salt contaminated the water tanks. Without fresh water, we couldn't reconstitute the freeze-dried food.

While trying to fix the water-maker and pump out the bilge we hit a squall of 36 knots in thirty seconds. The boat heeled on its side, the mast almost touching the water.

I scrambled on deck wearing only a T-shirt. Sally battled with the wheel, while Michèle and Tanja tried to take the headsail down. The driving rain made it impossible to see or breathe. Where did the air and water begin? I mumbled the words of a psalm, as I let off the vang and main sheet.

That five minutes of madness almost cost us the mast, the race and our lives. Miraculously there was no major damage.

That evening, 24 September, we closed to within four miles of *Rucanor* but discovered that *L'Esprit* had overtaken us. It was the closest we were to get to either of them. Eleven days later we arrived in Punta del Este. We were third from last in the fleet, but third in our class.

This was no consolation. I felt as though I had let everyone down. My decisions had cost us dearly. I should have covered *Rucanor* when she gybed in the Doldrums. I should have fought harder at the start and headed east towards the French coast. All of these judgements were easy to make in hindsight.

Just finishing the leg was a first for an all-female crew, but that wasn't good enough for me. I wanted to win. A lot of this desire came from the calibre of people who had been drawn to the project. It seemed an insult to them if we simply aimed to get around.

Despite a warm welcome in Uruguay, I felt lonely. I missed Simon and the house and the dogs. We'd spoken a few times on the radio, but it's hard to say 'I love you' when half the Whitbread fleet are listening.

Simon didn't say much when we spoke. He let me do the talking. We'd sold my house in Hamble and bought a place together just down the road. Simon was renovating it while I was away. We'd purposely decided that he wouldn't come and see me at any of the stopovers. I needed to concentrate on the sailing and couldn't afford distractions. I also knew that he'd never understand the tremendous bond that had developed within the crew. Much as I loved him, he could never be part of that.

We had three weeks in Uruguay to recover and patch the boat. Most of the damage to *Maiden* had been minor wear-and-tear. Parts had to be replaced and others strengthened.

The Duchess of York continued to take a great interest in our endeavours. Her mother Susan Barrantes had a polo ranch just across the border in Argentina. Sarah was visiting her and issued a lunch invitation to the entire crew.

We had nothing posh to wear and eventually turned up in our trademark pink shorts and grey shirts.

As the minibus pulled up outside the polo club, I felt decidedly under-dressed. The gardeners looked smarter than we did.

Susan Barrantes was absolutely charming and put us all at ease. We sat at the main table as guests of honour. Waiters placed a small plate in between each place setting. Off to one side was an amazing buffet, with seafood, cold meats, salads, fruit, you name it. After five weeks of living on freeze-dried gunk, it was almost cruel to make us wait.

Sally looked at the plate and whispered, 'This isn't going to fill us up.'

'We can go back for seconds,' said Dawn.

'And thirds,' echoed Tanja.

We kept going back and forth to the buffet, filling up. This went on for ages until I finally noticed that everyone else in the room had stopped eating and was just looking at us.

Finally a waiter sidled up to me. 'Miss Edwards, I think maybe I should point out that this is only the first course. We're waiting for you to finish before we can move on.'

Oops!

We had a great day, watching the polo and being totally spoilt. The Duchess made a little speech, urging us to win the next leg. Easier said than done.

The Southern Ocean awaited – the last place on God's earth. Nothing interrupts the open water that circles the bottom of the world. With no continents to break upon, the swells go on for ever. The result is a vast desolate wilderness of screaming winds, giant waves and freezing empty cold.

This is where *Maiden* and her crew would fall apart, according to our critics.

Like hell!

THIRTEEN

THE sun emerged briefly on the edge of the horizon. For a moment I thought it might actually defeat the cold grey clouds. It was wishful thinking.

The living conditions were now unbelievably squalid. Sleeping bags were wet, foul weather gear had begun to leak and a week's supply of chocolate couldn't buy a dry pair of socks. Condensation on the inside of the hulls began leaking into every nook and cranny. I couldn't turn the pages of a book without tearing them.

Mum used to tell me, 'Take off your outdoor clothes when you come inside. Otherwise you won't feel the benefit when you put them on again.' Mums are always right (Mackenna, please take note). I was so tempted at times simply to crawl into my sleeping bag, leaving on my layers of thermals. Instead, I forced myself to take off every layer except one. That way I would feel the benefit when I got dressed and left the warmth of the bunk!

The other secret to staying warm is lots of thin layers. First I wore a pair of special socks that prevented my feet from perspiring. Then I had a pair of silk thermals that felt nice against the skin. This was followed by another pair of slightly thicker socks, a silk thermal top, a normal layer of thermal underwear, another pair of socks and a third set of thermals made of thin woollen material.

I then put on a pair of Gore-Tex booties with a rubber sole, which slipped into my proper boots. I had a turtle fur wrap that protected my neck and a woollen balaclava to cover my face. I had a foul weather jacket, hood and trousers.

Another ritual was to change my socks every three or four days because the inner layer had got damp. I would clean my feet with wet wipes and dump talcum power (the best thing ever invented) into every crevice. In the constant dampness it was important to keep your feet dry.

Miki had been wet, cold and miserable more times than most of the girls. Her back had also been giving her problems but she didn't complain. That amount of pain would have some people crawling around on their hands and knees, but not Miki. When the going gets toughest, she comes into her own.

Instead of being depressed and miserable, Miki had a childlike spirit and the ability to laugh at any situation. A lot of the younger girls didn't quite know how to take this and were never quite sure when Miki was being serious or not.

They'd be huddled in the galley, looking disconsolate and Miki would swing through the hatch and declare, 'Call this wet! What are you lot moaning about? In my day we used to break ice off the boom to put in our gin and tonic.'

The girls were catching every hour of sleep possible, trying to conserve energy and make the days go quicker. Dragged out of bunks to change the headsail, they arrived on deck hollow-eyed and grimacing, but never complaining.

It had been a fortnight since we left Punta del Esta in Uruguay. We still had 4,500 miles to sail before reaching Fremantle. Despite good boat speeds all day, *Rucanor* had narrowed our lead to less than sixty miles. Conditions seemed to be perfect for the Belgian boat. I found myself almost wishing for a hurricane. *Maiden* needed stronger winds to stay ahead.

We had installed southern hemisphere compasses in Punta Del Este but these seemed to be sticking and giving odd readings. This made it very difficult to steer a straight course and most of the time

These are my mother's
parents, George and Jean.

My parents' wedding, and yes, it did
tip down!

My parents met on the carting circuit, but unusually for the time, my
mother was the driver and father the mechanic.

I have to admit I was an incredibly cute baby. I don't know what happened after that!

Trevor and I in 1966 with Grandma Bint, or 'Mrs', as she was affectionately known by almost everyone.

My brother Trevor and me on holiday in Majorca, the year before Daddy died.

Some of my wonderful family; *left to right*: Uncle Arthur, Auntie Edna, Kerry, Mackenna, Kaia and Gregor.

1973, aged 11; Oh no, those legs!

This is Niki-Sue May and me at Arts Educational, 1974.

This picture is going to embarrass my cousin Gregor – it was our *Grease* phase. It didn't last long, thank goodness.

Suzy and I at Gowerton with some other friends, 1978.

My first boat, *Kovalam,* 1981 – so smart in white stewardess uniform. It didn't stay white for long.

The worst job on *Kovalam* was red leading, and I got it every time.

Some strange goings on in the Nav station on *Kovalam* with Jaynie, Mike and Robert.

Doug and I on *Kovalam* just before he sailed off into the sunset.

Majorca, 1982, looking for a boat to Antigua. I don't seem to be taking it as seriously as I might have done!

At the helm of *Southern Star* on the way to Antigua. My first Atlantic crossing.

I knew I was going to like Antigua as soon as I got there. This is the second night! Ruth, Wendy, Rachel (in fetching black wig), Bear (underneath there somewhere), and me with something weird on my head.

Jojo and Paul on *Sealestial*, Christmas 1982.

My adoptive Antigua parents, Jol and Judy, outside their book shop, Jim's Locker, in English Harbour.

The gorgeous Brad Croslin, during our camping trip in the Blue Ridge Mountains.

This was the *Atlantic Privateer* crew reunion during the 1989-90 Whitbread race. It was messy and involved hangovers.

Left to right: 'Filthy' Phil Barrett, Patrick Banfield, and Neil Cheston. *Drum* crew extraordinaire and all round good guys.

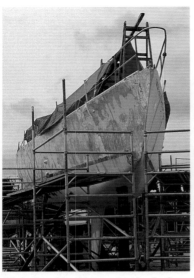

Unbelievable. This is *Maiden* before the refit.

The Duchess of York christening *Maiden*.

The unbeatable and fantastic *Maiden* crew.

Howard Gibbons and Pam Hale, *Maiden* shore crew and dear friends.

the girls steered by the electronic compass. This wasn't ideal because it didn't react as quickly as a floating compass.

Each time the wind strengthened it cleared the fog which rolled in again when the breeze dropped. Over the next 24 hours we managed to claw ten miles further ahead of *Rucanor*. The news lifted everybody's spirits and I heard Jeni and Dawn singing on deck.

I spent all day trying to plot the best course. That evening I called Simon. I hadn't spoken to him since the last night in Uruguay. It was so nice to hear his voice.

'I'm coming to Fremantle,' he said, excitedly.

'But I thought we said . . .'

'I know. But it's Christmas. I won't have seen you for three months. I'm only human.'

I laughed. 'You do realise that half the fleet are listening to us.'

'So what? I mean it.'

Simon talked about the new house, which sounded like a bomb site.

'Is it going to be ready when I get home?' I asked.

'I'll tell you in six months.'

When the call ended I could still hear his voice in my head. I missed him so much. At the same time, I was worried about how he'd cope with me. The race had become all-consuming.

The girls had bonded so closely as a team that anybody on the outside was going to find it very difficult to break down or reach through to us. I hoped Simon would understand this and wouldn't ask me to choose.

He had become my best friend – a fact that I was only just beginning to appreciate. But I couldn't shake the fear that he didn't really know me. No, that's not fair on Simon. It wasn't his fault. If anything, I had changed dramatically in the previous three months.

Discovering that I could skipper my own boat had a profound effect on me. I felt as though I'd been set loose, after having spent years in a cage. How could I give this up? There was so much I still had to do. I wanted to skipper a maxi in the Whitbread and ride a horse across the Andes and drive in the Paris to Dakar car rally. I could learn to fly a helicopter and write a book.

How could I do all these things? There wasn't time. In August I'd be married. I wished that somehow I could squeeze another ten years of experiences and adventures into the next nine months. Then perhaps I could happily settle down with Simon, without any 'what ifs' or 'if onlys'.

I had never been so happy at sea before. I felt totally and utterly free as if the last strings had gone. I know this sounds strange, considering I'd spent ten years living out of a knapsack and travelling the world.

I was so totally in love with my life, that I struggled to picture where Simon would fit into all this. Does that sound selfish? I told myself that the reason I felt so free was because of Simon. He was my anchor. I could go away sailing the world, safe in the knowledge that he was at home waiting for me.

I wrote these things in my diary as I huddled in the nav station, waiting for the next positional report. Jo had started dinner and steam billowed in the freezing air of the galley.

Having eaten like a horse, I wondered if I'd been getting fat under all the layers. It would be a novelty to see my body again.

The barometer had risen, along with the wind. Above me I could hear the ratchet sounds of the winches as the sheets were adjusted. Three dark shapes were hunched over and braced against the elements. The foul weather gear kept us relatively dry, although with so much water coming over the cockpit, it found ways of leaking through. These were the conditions in which *Maiden* excelled. They were frightening but fast. Come on, girls, we *can* do this. We *have* to stay ahead.

The slightest mistake would allow *Rucanor* to slip past us. I felt under enormous pressure, but I also felt more capable than I had on the first leg to Uruguay. The crew had helped. They had never questioned my judgement or decisions.

★   ★   ★

That night, 12 November, during the regular 'chat show' between boats, *Creightons Naturally* relayed the message that they had a problem. There were no details but the skipper John Chittenden asked me to call later.

Creightons didn't deserve any more bad luck. A day after leaving Uruguay it had been forced to turn back with a damaged mast. It had rejoined the race 1,000 miles behind *Maiden*, pushing hard to claw back the distance.

I radioed *Creightons* again, but missed the first part of the message. The second part sent a chill straight through me. 'A man fell overboard today. He was in the water for twenty-five minutes. He has been resuscitated but is suffering from hypothermia and possibly pneumonia.'

I changed frequencies to six megahertz to get clearer reception. Sounding upset, John Chittenden asked if Claire Russell, our medic, could stand by to give them advice on treatment.

Four people had now gone overboard on the leg, including Claire, who had been saved by her safety harness. Twenty-five minutes in these waters amounted to a virtual death sentence.

I stayed up with Claire for the 1 a.m. call from *Creightons*. The injured crewman wasn't named but his condition was stable. I sensed a degree of shock on board. What a nightmare it must have been – a crew-mate lost in the inky blackness, knowing that you have only minutes to find him.

Maiden was heading slightly north now – gently, gently – hoping to be on the right side of the next low. At last report *Rucanor* was ninety miles astern, with *L'Esprit* a further fifty miles back.

By morning there were icebergs on the horizon. At least they showed up by radar this time. Claire took over from me at 4 a.m. and stayed in constant touch with *Creightons*. I slept for nearly four hours – completely exhausted.

Mid-morning John Chittenden radioed that he had a message he wanted us to telex to race headquarters. Their radio wasn't working and wouldn't be powerful enough to make contact.

Claire took it down in longhand. Jo and Nancy were in the passageway listening.

> *At 03.32 on Sunday 12th November the yacht gybed heavily running before a westerly gale. The weather runner broke and the yacht gybed again breaking two of the grinder pedestals. The main was taken down and the lee runner was rapidly being set up when we were hit by large seas at 03.45.*
>
> *The yacht broached on the second sea and our poled out yankee was set aback breaking the spinnaker pole. Two men, Bart van den Dwey and Tony Phillips, were swept overboard. Both men were equipped with life jackets flares and personal EPIRBS [emergency position beacons]. Two life rings and a Dan Buoy were sent in after them.*
>
> *The headsails were dropped and the yacht motored back on a VHF/DF bearing. The first man was located with the aid of parachute flares at 04.15. Bart van den Dwey was successfully recovered and resuscitated.*
>
> *At 04.32 Tony was recovered and resuscitation begun and continued until 07.17 without success. Bart's life jacket was inflated when he was recovered. Tony Phillips' was not. We think Tony hit a stanchion as he went overboard, it is thought unlikely he was conscious once in the water.*
>
> *The two EPIRBS were recovered but the two life buoys were not. Two crew members went into the sea to assist with the recovery. Barry Mercer and Julian Morris went in three times. The sea temperature was 7°C and there were heavy seas running. Both actions were, in my mind, heroic, Julian's in particular. Twenty-four hours later, Bart is recovering well from hypothermia and shock.*
>
> *From John Chittenden, skipper.*
> *Ends.*

I gaped at Nancy and Jo in disbelief. Claire looked numb, but didn't let it show. As John finished, she said, 'I copy that loud and clear'.

For a long time nobody said a word. Then I started to shiver. I imagined the fear of those men as they tumbled into the darkness. What a terrible way to die – the panic, the struggle for life and the insidious, creeping cold.

The news of such a tragedy is bad enough when you are safe on land, but in the same ocean, barely 1,000 miles away, it hit me like a fist. I stared into the depths of the sea and no longer saw it as a friend, but a monster.

Andrew, the radio operator on *Creightons*, asked me to relay a question to the parents of Tony Phillips. What did they want to do with the body?

Really there was no choice – they would have to bury him at sea. Suddenly, I had visions of having to ask someone the same question about one of us. What are we doing here? I wondered, suddenly questioning the dangers. This was my dream. What right did I have to ask others to put their lives at risk?

Nothing could console those on board *Creightons*. I didn't have the words to ease their pain. I struggled to deal with my own. John had asked us not to tell the rest of the fleet what had happened until the parents of Tony and Bart had been informed.

I spent all day trying to get the telex through, via Cape Town or Portishead. At the same time, I couldn't get any weather maps through on the fax. The wind had continued to rise and it made for a wild old ride as we nudged into the raging fifties. The same gale that had hammered *Creightons* had now caught up with us.

Waves were breaking over the cockpit and the freezing spray felt like bullets against the skin. As each wave engulfed the bow, it rolled across the deck, smashing into the helm. The recess filled and formed a jacuzzi around the knees of the watch crew. Then it drained from holes at the stern.

Some of the waves were almost vertical and arrived with a sickening finality. The wind screamed as it parted through the wires, telling us that we had no right to be here.

The mood on board *Maiden* was the blackest it had ever been.

The laughter on deck had dried up. Instead, we seemed to contemplate our own mortality and say our prayers for Tony.

Periodically, the ghostly shapes of icebergs drifted out of the mist.

'It's like driving through a minefield with a blindfold on,' said Miki. Of all of the girls she seemed least affected by what had happened. Miki is a realist about sailing and the Southern Ocean.

'I can't understand why the ice is so far north,' I said. 'Not even the satellites are picking it up.'

Twelve hours later, I had a message from race headquarters. Tony's parents wanted him buried at sea. I relayed the message to *Creightons* where things sounded better.

Later that day, John Chittenden asked me to relay the message to the rest of the fleet about what had happened. I read his telex out loud during the chat show. The lump in my throat seemed to be choking me and I fought to stop my voice breaking.

The same response echoed down the airwaves – a shattered, 'Yes, copy' and then a quick sign off. Each operator wanted to grieve amongst crew-mates.

Exhausted I crawled into my sleeping bag. The compass continued to act up and as I slept *Maiden* sailed off course. By morning we were twenty miles further north than I intended. Adding to the problems, the sat nav also packed in. Now I had to pray my calculations had been right, and I had no way of checking them.

I felt like screaming in frustration. Surely *Rucanor* would have caught us overnight. All that hard work for nothing.

Jo looked at me through the gloom as she soaked some freeze-dried food in the galley. Our breath clouded in the air.

'I can't bloody believe this,' I muttered. 'The radar is rubbish, the compasses don't work, and I haven't had a position from the sat nav in 24 hours.'

'At least the weather fax is running again,' said Jo, trying to cheer me up.

'It would be, if we hadn't used so much fuel charging the batteries to stay on the radio to *Creightons*.'

I scraped my hands through my greasy, tangled hair and squeezed my eyes shut.

'You did the right thing,' she said.

'I know.'

It was so frustrating. If all our equipment had been working we'd have been a hundred miles further ahead. We'd have satellite positions instead of working on dead reckoning. As it was, I couldn't even use the sextant because the sun had become distant memory, locked behind a solid blanket of grey cloud.

Despite all of this, we were still ahead. How long could we hold on?

For the next ten days the sat nav refused our best efforts and our prayers. I woke through each night to check on it. We had a horrible wind angle that saw *Maiden* plunging into troughs with such force that my teeth rattled.

Suddenly, the breakers failed, cutting our electrical power. Everything went down at once and I woke Jeni Mundy, our electronics expert. We spent three hours going round in circles trying to figure it out.

My temper had started to fray. As the skipper, I wasn't allowed to let my feelings show. I had to put on a cheerful face and rally the troops. Right at that moment I wanted to be home curled up in front of the fire with Simon, watching *EastEnders*.

I had never been so highly strung on a boat before. I knew the girls were probably moaning about me. If things didn't improve they'd want another navigator. I felt like punching walls except my wrist already hurt too much. Sally had managed to slam it in a hatch earlier in the day.

On top of all this, Howard had radioed me with the latest news on our finances. Our money would run out in Fremantle. Without a further cash injection from Royal Jordanian Airlines or another sponsor our race would be over. If this was going to be the last hurrah, then we had to win.

Come on *Maiden*. Come on girls. Go! Go!

★   ★   ★

Four days later, on 18 November, *Rucanor* had closed the gap to only 23 miles. Fleetingly, the sat nav and compasses began working again before giving up the ghost. Becalmed for several hours, we took down the main and repaired broken battens.

I'd been awake for 19 hours straight, trying to decide whether to go north or south of the Kerguelen Islands. The course had become everything to me. I ate, slept and breathed it.

The race would now come down to tactics. If *Rucanor* went north of Kerguelen, should I do the same? Was it best to shadow our rival, or ignore her? The pressure had reached the point where I almost felt it would come as a relief if *Rucanor* did overtake us. At the same time, I refused to give up. I kept thinking of all those people who wrote us off. Then I pictured our supporters who had never stopped believing in us. Nobody expected us to be out in front like this. The Southern Ocean was supposed to break us. We *had* to win.

I stared at the charts until my neck stiffened and my eyes grew fuzzy. What a stupid place to put an island. If we gybed north-east, leaving Kerguelen on our starboard side, we would bypass the Kerguelen Plateau, a region notorious for rogue waves and pumped-up seas.

Any plateau in the Southern Ocean has to be approached cautiously because it can have the same effect as a sandbank close to shore. Huge swells sometimes break over these comparatively shallow areas, creating dangerous waves and confused seas. But to go north-east would add miles. We couldn't afford to let *Rucanor* overtake us. The psychological advantage would be lost.

A high pressure system had settled over us, taking its toll. As the air temperature rose, the birds returned.

On Tuesday, 21 November, under blue skies and cottonwool clouds, we surfed along at 16 knots. *Rucanor* and *L'Esprit* had taken more miles from us, but the distances were deceptive because of our different latitudes.

The barometer had started to fall as a new frontal system approached. The waves were 12 to 15 feet, coming from behind, with the boat surfing and slamming heavily.

On Thursday we passed 38 miles south of Kerguelen. The winds and seas were pummelling us, but at least daylight brought the comfort of seeing the wet fist before it landed. Jeni set a new record speed for *Maiden* – 17.1 knots. We were all too frightened to celebrate. The yacht shifted violently sideways as I pulled on my foul weather gear. I had to put both arms up to stop myself crashing head first into the bulkhead. I glanced at the navigation instruments. We had peak gusts of 42 knots and seas that had climbed all night.

It took me twenty minutes to get ready. My fingers were so cold that Velcro fasteners were annoying obstacles. I scrambled on deck to help change the headsail. The first wave that crashed over me was so cold it made my head hurt. I felt like screaming abuse at it, but saved my energy.

'This is more like mountain climbing than sailing,' shouted Jeni, as I slid next to her in the cockpit. I looked up quickly as a wave rose, crested and broke over the bow. Water rushed across the deck and tried to drag open the hatch covers.

The spinnaker tripped itself twice that day. Each time it came down from the top of the mast with the sides stretched to breaking point. What a great way to completely destroy it!

Then the reacher sail went up and we wiped out badly. *Maiden* was pushed right over on her side. Water poured through the cockpit, dragging people under and spitting them up again coughing and spluttering. Being below deck wasn't much better as girls were thrown from bunks, or catapulted into bulkheads. I finished up on my face in the galley, next to a bemused Jo.

The day continued, miserable, cold and very wet. Everybody seemed pretty pissed off, but philosophical. At least we were going fast and in the right direction.

I was on the crew's back the whole time – not letting them relax for a second on deck. We could win if we didn't let up. I didn't want any of them making the mistake of thinking: it's a big ocean out there, we can take our time.

Michèle eventually lost it and yelled at me, 'This is not a race around the buoys, Tracy!'

She was trying to tell me that we didn't need to change sails so quickly or trim them all the time. She was wrong. During the second leg on *Atlantic Privateer* we had beaten *NZI* by only seven minutes after 7,000 miles of sailing. Every second counted! I had to make the crew understand this.

At the next 'chat show' I waited anxiously for the positions. Hallelujah! We had rounded Kerguelen not just in front, but with a massive advantage. Although we still had 1,500 miles to go, I finally realised that we could win the leg.

For the next three nights I didn't sleep. I tossed and turned, wondering if we were holding the course and what the wind had done. On deck the girls did brilliantly. They, too, sensed that history was in the making. We just had to hold on.

With raw nerves and a dodgy stomach, I gritted my teeth at each 'chat show', waiting for the positions of *Rucanor* and *L'Esprit*, our closest rivals. I could feel them both willing us to make a mistake.

Four days later we had extended our lead even further, but conditions were miserable. We had 56 knots of wind. I left the spinnaker up as long as I dared. Hurtling down the waves at breakneck speeds, our hearts were in our mouths.

Wind channelled between the huge waves and lifted the white caps, atomising the foam into a fine spray. As the boat reached each new crest it lurched and then dropped into the hole. The swells seemed closer together and steeper than before.

In gusts of 65 knots we tried to take down the spinnaker. We needed the whole crew on deck. As the spinnaker pole came forward – the most dangerous part of the operation – Jeni hung out over the boiling water that was disappearing beneath the bow. She tripped the spinnaker and released it so that we could lower the halyard and pull the huge expanse of cloth in by the sheet.

As the spinnaker tripped, *Maiden* slid sideways. We broached suddenly, with the starboard side vanishing beneath foaming water. The combined force of water and wind kept pushing. The mast touched the waves. On the port side, the keel had lifted clear – eleven tons of lead, forced to the surface like a bobbing cork.

My mouth went dry. The watch crew reacted instantly. The mainsail was dumped and we grabbed the spinnaker to bring it in. We had to stop it filling and taking us over again.

Gravity took hold, forcing the keel under again. The mast lifted, pausing for a moment in mid-air as the sea spilled from the sail. Then it kept rising. Water had covered everything, leaving us soaked through and gasping for air. The spinnaker was shredded.

Down below, I sat wedged into a seat, writing my diary. 'I must remember not to do this again . . . Please, God, don't let me forget this hell . . . I can't blink without planning it first. Everything is such an effort it has to be thought out in advance: How will I do it? How long will it take? How wet am I going to get? How many people do I need?'

Even as I wrote the words, I could hear laughter from the cockpit. The human spirit is indomitable.

Maiden spent ten days with no satellite navigation, just working on dead reckoning. I cursed our luck, but it was nice to navigate the old-fashioned way – without pushing buttons. It made me think a bit more before deciding our course.

Those last few days were manic. Although I believed we could win, there was still a mental barrier to cross. Being out in front means you think differently. You don't take the same chances.

I wrote in my diary:

We are absolutely exhausted. I feel as if I have been walking on a cliff edge in a strong wind for weeks. My emotions are up and down – high as a kite one minute and the next suicidal. The girls are so tired they have to concentrate on not falling asleep on deck. We eat, sleep, work, eat, sleep and work.

As I write this, there are 700 miles left. I don't think we could hold on for much longer. Everyone has pushed to the limit and there is still not a whimper of complaint. These are eleven very special women.

We all feel twenty years older and look it. The trust we now share is immeasurable. You might know someone all your life and not trust them as much as we do each other.

I have seen the most extraordinary acts of selfless caring, heroism, courage, will power, kindness and achievement. If nothing else we have to win just to vindicate all that.

L'Esprit now has not let up for one minute; they wait for us to break the boat or just to break. I have been terrified, ecstatic, depressed, confident, unsure, brave and cowardly. I am ashamed I ever doubted we could do this. Proud of myself and, for once, not tearing myself apart or looking for faults.

I have finally found all the good bits I knew were there somewhere in me. I think the girls would say the same about themselves. Of them, I am so proud I could burst.

I hadn't slept in four days. I kept popping caffeine tablets. I trusted Dawn and Michèle implicitly, but I still couldn't let go. The last 24 hours were the worst. That's when I knew that we were going to do it.

We came up out of the Southern Ocean surprisingly quickly. One minute it was stark, cold and bleak, and the next we had blue sky and warm sunshine. It was as though we'd emerged from hell into the real world.

The Australian mainland appeared as a thin dark line against the horizon. We sailed up the coast towards Fremantle. Two helicopters came out and buzzed above us. Why were they making such a fuss?

We crossed the line at midday on 3 December 1989. The sun shone in a perfectly blue sky, almost making a mockery of what had gone before. Newspapers called it the longest, toughest leg in the history of the Whitbread. Seven people had gone overboard, including Claire. One had died.

We finished thirty hours ahead of *Rucanor* and took an overall lead of sixteen hours in our class. It was the best result by a British yacht in the Whitbread for twelve years.

As we crossed the line, horns and whistles sounded. Thousands

of people had left their homes and offices and now crowded the
dock. All I could think of, as we approached, was: Please don't
crash the boat into the dock, Tracy.

Admiral Williams waited on a pontoon beneath the crowd. TV
cameras and photographers surrounded him. I caught a glimpse of
Simon. I could only wave. The crew had lined up along *Maiden*'s
deck. Admiral Williams handed me the Beefeater trophy. I turned
to the girls and held it above my head. They went wild.

Afterwards, we took *Maiden* round to the marina. As we were
coming in I noticed a middle-aged couple standing on the dock.
He wore a grubby vest, stretched tight over his beer belly, and she
looked mousy and overworked.

'I see the Sheilas made it in one piece,' he cracked.

His wife whacked him in the stomach. 'They're first, you
arsehole.'

The maxis were lined up. The skippers and crews stood as one
and cheered. It was the high point of my life. These were my peers.
No matter what happened in the rest of the race – nobody could
take this win away from us.

FOURTEEN

Two glasses of champagne gave me a lovely buzz. That's what happens when you haven't had a drink in six weeks. I looked around for Simon and couldn't see him anywhere.

TV reporters and journalists were eager for quotes. We spent over an hour answering questions, before we could begin stowing the sails and collecting dirty laundry.

I was high as a kite. Complete strangers wanted my autograph, or to take my picture. Where was Simon? Then somebody told me that he'd stormed back to the hotel because I hadn't paid him enough attention.

'For God's sake, I've only just arrived.'

I felt angry and disappointed. I hadn't slept in four days and we had just triumphed in the longest, most difficult leg in Whitbread history. What did Simon expect? Much as I loved him, he had to understand that the race came first, at least for now.

I found him at the hotel. Instead of the big romantic reunion we hoped for, we finished up fighting. I was exhausted and he was jet-lagged: it was hardly ideal. Then I noticed that my shore bags were in the room. Simon had taken it upon himself to move my things out of the crew accommodation and into a hotel. I think he envisaged that we would spend the stopover together – away from the distractions of the race.

'What have you done?' I demanded.

'I thought you'd like to stay with me.'

'No.'

'But I've come all this way.'

'Yes. But I should be with my crew.'

'You've just spent four bloody months with them, Tracy.'

I don't blame Simon for not understanding. How could he possibly appreciate what we'd all been through? There were times in the Southern Ocean when we'd almost died. We had trusted each other with our lives and triumphed. That's why I wanted to be with my crew.

There is a very famous old saying, 'Ports rot ships and men.' Every skipper will tell you how true this is. That's why we dread stopovers. Crews become bored and disaffected when they spend too long on shore. Costs blow out and disagreements come to the surface. Already a lot of the boats had changed personnel because of these problems. I couldn't afford to let that happen to *Maiden*. For the male crews it was often easy to find a replacement for someone. I didn't have this luxury. I had to keep my team together.

Simon stayed in Fremantle for the next ten days. He grew tired of trailing around after me. I had sponsorship meetings and media commitments. Damaged gear had to be repaired and new compasses found for *Maiden*. I had to study weather charts and talk to meteorologists.

Before Simon went home we had a long heart-to-heart about our relationship. Although neither of us admitted as much, we both had concerns about the future. I'd always promised Simon that I wouldn't do another Whitbread after this one. Now he worried that I wouldn't keep my word.

For my part, I began to realise that perhaps he was right. Maybe this was an obsession. Did I really believe that I could settle down afterwards and become Mrs Simon Lawrence – housewife, mother and ex-yachtswoman?

The race had always come between us. It had existed in the background from the very first day we met. Now we had to hope that when it was all over, we still had a future together. I told myself that I was being melodramatic when I thought like this. At home, in familiar surroundings, it would all be OK again.

Maiden's victory had created an enormous stir in the UK. It had been inconceivable that we could win a leg of the Whitbread, but suddenly we were headline news in all the papers.

This created a degree of resentment in some of the other crews. The British entry *Rothmans* had a budget five times larger than ours, yet nobody was writing about them. *Maiden* had journalists queuing up for interviews and Howard had to work overtime to keep up with the demand.

Royal Jordanian Airlines hadn't intended to send anyone out to Australia, but suddenly senior executives were scrambling to get flights. Their investment was about to pay off big-time. The irony, of course, was that our sponsorship money had now run out. *Maiden* – the most talked-about yacht in the world – wouldn't be going anywhere without more funds. Not surprisingly, the Jordanians arrived with their chequebooks in hand, determined to keep us in the race.

This was a huge weight off my mind. For the first time in four years, I could go to sleep at night without worrying about how I could raise money. More importantly, I could now concentrate purely on sailing.

Fremantle turned on scorching temperatures for so early in the summer. We set about repairing *Maiden*, in particular the stress damage to the mast. Mandi spent a lot of time re-splicing worn rigging and sheets, while Nancy stripped all seventeen winches and cleaned them.

Already it was clear that we had the best shore crew in the race. This came down to the people and attention to detail. A container had been sent to each stopover with spares, sails and equipment. Simon Le Bon's brother Johnny was in charge of this. We had forty-seven sails for *Maiden* and chose twenty on each leg. We had to know in advance which sails we needed on the various legs. These would then be packed and sent in the container.

Our social director, Pam Hale, was a vital member of the shore crew. I used to joke that she was in charge of parties, but her role was far more important. She had to keep up morale and help SJ with logistics. A typical example of their attention to detail came when we arrived at the crew apartments in Fremantle. Our shore clothes had been unpacked and toiletries put in the bathrooms. There were even fresh flowers in the rooms.

Many of the other crews soon recognised our organisation and professionalism. They began asking favours of Howard, wanting gear sent in our container because they knew it would get there. We also had them coming to see how Mandi did things because she was such a good rigger.

As I sat on deck one morning, the very tall figure of Peter Blake strolled along the dock. He's one of those yachtsmen who inspires absolute awe in other sailors because of his achievements. In the race among the maxis, he had won both legs on *Steinlager II*.

'Well done. That was some great sailing,' he said.

I was gobsmacked. He spoke to me!

I felt the same way at the presentation night. *Maiden* won more prizes than any other boat in the fleet. We were first over the line in Division D and first on handicap. Dawn and Michèle both picked up awards for outstanding seamanship and I was voted the Communicator of the Leg for my radio work during the crisis on board *Creightons*. Claire also won a special award for helping save Bart's life.

We had won the respect of our peers and silenced most of our critics. At the same time I felt a little annoyed that we were being written up as being 'super' women.

'You're a special bunch of girls,' people would say.

'No we're not,' I answered. 'All women can do this if they have the training and the desire.'

Even the most strident of our critics had been forced to eat their words. Bob Fisher, the doyen of sailing journalists, wrote a charming apology in *Yacht and Yachting*:

> *OK, so I take it all back. I'll admit I was more than a touch cynical about the potential of the all girl crew on* Maiden, *particularly their ability to handle the Southern Ocean legs. I formed my opinion without finding out that the* Maiden *ladies were a terribly determined bunch. Now, eating everything I have said, I praise them unreservedly for their efforts.*
>
> *It is twelve years since any British boat won anything in the Whitbread. For* Maiden *to take out both the line honours and handicap first place for the second leg is a sterling effort which should make others who were even more cynical than myself sit up and take notice . . .*
>
> *When* Maiden *arrived at the reception dock in Fremantle, the twelve girls were on deck. They looked like an ordinary bunch of girls in pink shorts and Royal Jordanian T-shirts, but they were anything but ordinary . . . They proved beyond all doubt that they are quite an extraordinary group of women to whom I raise my glass.*

Unfortunately, not all of the yachting journalists were won over. Some had been so rude about us they found it difficult to climb down from such a great height. They still viewed *Maiden* as a novelty, which is why the next leg became so important.

The short sprint to Auckland of 3,000 miles would come down to tactics and match-racing, according to the experts. This would favour the male crews, with their greater experience and strength.

Our major rivals were smarting over having been beaten. One skipper had been overheard saying that our win had been a 'fluke'. This was laughable. We had beaten *Rucanor* by thirty hours. Even so, if we fared badly in the next leg, such ridiculous claims might gain acceptance.

On a stormy summer's day the fleet set off for Auckland. This time I nailed the gun. *Maiden* crossed the line squeezed between

Steinlager II and *Fisher and Paykel*. If I looked one way I saw Peter Blake and the other way Grant Dalton. What a moment! We led the Division D boats down the coast towards Cape Leeuwin.

The next morning at eight o'clock GMT, we rounded the Cape. I couldn't get a satellite navigation fix and our electronic compass was 10° out. I looked at the chart and realised there were two reefs nearby. We were too close to the mainland.

I changed course, heading south to find more wind and to cover *Rucanor* and *L'Esprit*.

On Monday morning, Jo and I were up early filling the Christmas stockings. The girls woke to find one on the end of each bunk. Our shore team had given us a calendar of naked men, which was quickly passed around to great amusement. We also opened a few bottles of champagne that Jo had slipped on board.

I spent hours on the radio to Portishead waiting to get calls through for the girls. Each of them had the chance to call home for Christmas.

For the next week we had a succession of cool fronts bursting across us from the west. The maxis ahead of us would radio back to get precise times on when the fronts passed us because we were experiencing weather that would hit them in a few hours. I did the same with the trailing yachts like *La Poste* – the smallest boat in the fleet.

The third leg was so short, I feared it might be hard to motivate the crew. Perhaps it would feel more like a delivery than a race. I was wrong. *Rucanor* and *L'Esprit* were so close that we couldn't let up. Less than thirty miles had separated us since Fremantle. These guys were serious about revenge.

On New Year's Day we passed halfway, making good speed, with Tasmania to port. Late in the morning we gybed. The spinnaker suddenly tripped, coming away from the pole. A fury of wet cloth billowed from the mast, straining to break free.

The cry went up for all hands on deck. I scrambled up to help, not really thinking. Grabbing hold of the spinnaker, I tried to hold it down. Suddenly, it filled. My feet left the deck. Sally snatched me

out of mid-air before I disappeared over the side. I had no harness
or life-jacket. I had broken every rule I had drummed into the girls
for weeks. I should have known better. We'd all seen what could
happen on the previous leg. An hour later I was still shaking when
Jo brought me a cup of tea.

'Did it flash before your eyes?' she asked, referring to my life.

'Twice,' I said. 'I'm only twenty-seven.'

With just the mainsail, Miki had *Maiden* flying at 19 knots. We
put the reacher up and Tanja pushed us over 20 knots. It's amazing
how differently we all perceived danger. We were all much more
confident. Once we would have taken the spinnaker down in 40
knots of wind. Now we waited until it hit 50.

Rucanor was thirty miles behind but *L'Esprit* only a mile away.
With a thousand miles to go, we were beating into dreadful wind
and waves. *Maiden* seemed to belly-flop into every trough, shaking
herself to pieces. It jarred every bone and set my teeth on edge.

Because of her flat bottom, *Maiden* often felt like a huge
surfboard with a mast. The downwind passages could be terrifying,
particularly with the spinnaker up. We were sliding left and right,
sailing on the very edge of control. People can't steer properly
when they're frightened. They tense up and turn away from the
wind.

At one point during the first leg, *Maiden* had been surfing down
swells and broaching severely in a storm. I suggested we take down
the spinnaker and pole out the blast reacher.

The girls had looked at me as though I was crazy.

'They do that on cruising boats,' said Michèle, screwing up her
nose.

She was right. It is an old cruising boat trick when the wind is
absolutely astern. The blast reacher is a small headsail, cut very high
up. It can be poled out on the opposite side to the main, creating a
goose-wing effect. This also produces much more stability and
stops the boat from broaching.

The girls were horrified at the thought. 'What if anyone sees us?
We'll be a laughing stock,' said Dawn.

'Listen. Don't preach to me about cruising and racing,' I told her. 'I've done the Whitbread before.'

Very sceptically they agreed. 'Just don't tell anyone we ever did this.'

The new configuration was a revelation to them. They loved it. It gave us speed as well as stability. *Maiden* was no longer broaching and the fear had gone out of steering.

Now on the third leg, in identical conditions, we came across *L'Esprit*. She had her spinnaker up and the crew was battling to stay in control. I suggested unleashing our new secret weapon – the poled-out blast reacher.

'What if they see us?' echoed Michèle, still feeling self-conscious.

'Oh, please!' I replied. 'This isn't a beauty contest.'

We poled out the blast reacher and the impact was immediate. We waltzed past *L'Esprit*, as though they were standing still. So much for tradition!

We kept sight of each other for the next few days as they tried everything to bridge the gap. One morning we sighted them closing fast. *L'Esprit* came out of the water trying to circle past us. She took the fastest line, and the better course. There was nothing I could do. We had 40 knots on the nose and she seemed to be handling it better than us.

As she passed us, she suddenly swung to starboard. Something had happened. The entire crew was on deck, dragging the main down. Later we discovered that the main halyard had gone.

By next morning we were seven miles ahead. The barometer had dropped and the seas flattened. We had 625 miles to go. Auckland couldn't come soon enough. The following day, 6 January, we spotted the coast. Now we had to hold on. At dawn, local time, we rounded Cape Reinga on the tip of the North Island, with 200 miles to go.

The entire crew was on deck, gazing in our wake, watching to see *L'Esprit* come round the corner of the cape. Anybody watching would have wondered if we were trying to sail backwards.

We timed the gap – half an hour.

'Here I go again,' I muttered. 'I've been here before.'

What followed was almost an action replay of the battle between *Atlantic Privateer* and *NZI* in the previous Whitbread. It had come down to a sprint along the east coast of New Zealand to the finish line.

L'Esprit was lighter and faster off the wind than *Maiden*. We needed stronger breezes, none of which had been forecast. We zigzagged our way down the coast, never more than a few miles apart. It played havoc with my nerves as we constantly searched for wind.

Mandi had been a dinghy sailor around the coast of Auckland. Our only hope of staying in front rested with her local knowledge. She took us quite close to shore, normally a gamble because the land can steal the breeze. At the same time the land creates breezes of its own as wind channels through the valleys. You just have to know where to find it. At times we sailed within a few hundred yards of shore. Without Mandi I would have been nervous. I could see waves crashing over rocks and submerged reefs.

Maiden found the favourable currents, while *L'Esprit* had no wind further out to sea. Slowly we began pulling ahead. As it grew dark, we lost sight of *L'Esprit* when they didn't turn on their navigation lights. This was obviously a ploy, but I didn't blame them. Unable to keep track of our rival, we had to stay focused and concentrate on our own work.

We arrived in Auckland Harbour at about one in the morning. Again Mandi knew all the little currents and the effect of the tides. There were so many lights on the water I couldn't find the two small green lights that marked the finish line. I kept running down to the nav station and checking the charts.

'Just keep on this course,' I told the girls.

The crew from *Fisher and Paykel* had chartered to come out and greet us. The guys were having a party and Bob Fisher was decidedly worse for wear. 'Yeah, girls, way to go!' he cried, clutching a bottle of wine. The rest of them burst into song, 'There she goes just a walking down the street . . .'

Then one of them shouted, 'You're going the wrong way. The finish line is over there.'

All the girls looked at me.

'No, I'm pretty sure we're right,' I said, suddenly having second thoughts.

I could see them thinking: the men must be right.

I kept reassuring them and at the same time thinking: please let me be right. Five minutes later we crossed the line. The guys hadn't been trying to send us in the wrong direction. They were simply wrong.

Our shore crew arrived in a launch to escort us back to the dock. As we entered Princes' Wharf, Sally commented on all the birds that were roosting on the wharf's main shed.

'They're not birds,' I said. 'It's people.'

A crowd of more than 14,000 had turned up to greet us. They clung to every vantage point and spilled on to the streets of the city. A local radio station had announced our imminent arrival and people had left their homes in the middle of the night to welcome us to Auckland. Mandi had tears in her eyes. What a way to come home!

Just under an hour later *L'Esprit* crossed the finish line. They were magnanimous in defeat, standing on deck and applauding as they returned to the dock.

Auckland stayed awake to party. Various pubs had adopted each of the boats and we stayed at the bar drinking until the sun came up.

I didn't think we could win the third leg. Now I started to dream of winning the entire race. We had extended our lead in Division D to almost eighteen hours. *Steinlager II*, which headed the maxis, had nowhere near this sort of lead.

Waiting for us at Auckland was a cable from King Hussein. He'd sent it on New Year's Eve.

To the Skipper and crew of Maiden,
   I have been following every moment of your epic voyage and am immensely proud that Royal Jordanian and through it the

*Hashemite Kingdom of Jordan is associated with this exceptional
endeavour and the making of history in the yachting world.*

Again congratulations for being the first in so many ways.
*Your courage and dedication is unsurpassed and your assistance to
other yachts in times of great distress is commendable. As we enter
the 1990s I send you all my warmest good wishes for a very
happy and successful year and look forward with great pleasure to
congratulating you all in person on your epic achievements.*
Wishing you continued success.

Hussein.

As I finished reading it, Howard gave me another piece of news.
British sailing journalists had just voted me the 'Yachtsman of the
Year'. It was the first time in its thirty-five-year history that a
woman had won the award.

The ceremony coincided with the stopover in New Zealand. A
live broadcast was organised, beaming pictures back to the London
International Boat Show. Peter Montgomery, a veteran New
Zealand broadcaster, stood on a stage by the dock, with *Maiden*
nearby. He began reading out the names of previous winners of the
award – people like Sir Francis Chichester, Edward Heath, Robin
Knox-Johnston, Chay Blyth and Harold Cudmore.

'You told me you weren't going to cry,' said Howard, handing
me his handkerchief.

'I know. I know. I can't help it.'

'Do you know something about this award?' he whispered.

'What's that?'

'It's the first time it's ever been won by a boat bum.'

FIFTEEN

THE race re-started on 4 February and *Maiden* fell behind almost from the gun. I made several tactical mistakes and we rounded the first mark last in our class. The next three days were frustrating as we languished in light winds.

I couldn't decide whether to dive south or go gradually. Instead I chose to stick with *L'Esprit*, even though she was slowly pulling away from us.

Despite our slow progress the mood on deck remained amazingly positive. We still had plenty of time to claw our way back before Uruguay.

Early on day three we had a message from Bruno Dubois. *Rucanor* had hit a whale during the night. The rudder had been damaged and they were taking in water. They were turning back to Wellington for repairs. I felt desperately sorry for them. It would cost them at least six days.

By not diving south as quickly as possible, I'd allowed *L'Esprit* to open a gap of more than fifty miles on us. At the same time, a high pressure system wouldn't let us go. Where was the wind?

Playing catch-up means taking risks. I chose to dive radically south. If it worked, I'd be a genius navigator. If it failed, we'd lose even more miles.

We reached 57°S – down among the icebergs. Our compasses were messing up again, giving readings that were 10° out. This made it almost impossible to set a course and confidently know we were following it.

That evening, during the 'chat show,' a front passed through. Suddenly we had 35 knots of wind from behind. Within minutes it had swung 100° and started going north. I raced on deck. The rain was being driven sideways and felt like icy needles against my cheeks.

The spinnaker was dragging us sideways. 'Get it down and gybe!' I cried.

As the girls tried to snuff it out, we crash-gybed. The boom swung savagely from port to starboard. Miki didn't duck quickly enough. It smashed into her head, sending her sprawling across the deck. We dragged her back into the cockpit.

'Miki! Miki!'

She was out cold. Claire scrambled out of her bunk.

'Is she going to be OK?'

The lump on her head was the size of a cricket ball and had already started turning blue.

We'd managed to get back on course and the watch crew began cleaning up the tangled knitting of halyards and sheets. Miki opened her eyes. She was groggy, but managed a smile. I sighed in relief.

Every decision I made seemed to be the wrong one. By 15 February we were caught too far south. *L'Esprit* was ten miles north and sixty in front, with loads of wind. We had nothing.

I felt as though I had let everyone down, especially the crew. None of them showed their disappointment. We suffered for the next three days in appalling conditions. It was bitterly cold on deck and at night we manned the radar, keeping watch for icebergs. The girls were soaked to the skin, their hands and feet numb from the cold.

On 18 February our fate was compounded by the loss of the generator. We had no heat to dry clothes and the bilges were swimming. I had to limit use of the radios and sat nav until we could fix the problem. Yet we needed the radar on at night to monitor icebergs.

During the morning, a huge wave came over the port quarter. Michèle was hurled against the wheel with such force that the wheel broke. I bent her backwards and she collapsed in a ball of pain, unable to move.

'How bad is it?' I asked Claire.

'I can't be sure. She may have bruised her spine, or worse.'

That night I navigated by torchlight, keeping watch over Michèle as she lay in her bunk. Meanwhile, Dawn and Jenni spent hours trying to get the engine and generator working. Angela and Nancy had to hand-pump the bilges. Water had been pouring through the mast screws, saturating the sails below. Our clothes and bedding were soaked. This is the real Southern Ocean – an icy hell.

'Remind me never to do this again,' I told Miki, who still nursed a sore head.

We were pounding through the waves, making it impossible to stand up, or do the most routine chore. I dressed while kneeling down, avoiding the floor and the wet bodies. It took me twenty minutes because my fingers were so cold. The air temperature, away from the wind, was 4°C.

I had to keep reminding the girls to eat properly and drink plenty of fluids. They were so exhausted it was easy to forget, or not to bother.

Dawn and Nancy bled the engine and managed to get it going. Now we could start recharging the batteries. Hopefully we'd have the radar by nightfall and I could make some radio calls. Several boats, including *L'Esprit*, had offered to turn back to help us if Michèle's injury proved to be serious.

For the moment, I'd told them we were OK. If the situation worsened there were good medical facilities in the Falklands, but that was more than a thousand miles ahead of us.

The wind kicked in during the afternoon and I almost saw the 'fasten seatbelt' sign come on. We put a reef in the main and flew the chicken chute. *Maiden* was like a kite trying to tear itself away from the string. It twisted and turned, sliding down waves that reached nearly halfway up the mast.

Dinner finished up over the galley floor when we broached. Seafood chowder and potatoes mingled with salt water and spilled coffee. Poor Jo was almost in tears. Every few minutes green water broke over the cockpit. We pounded into the troughs and accelerated out again.

Angela and Claire managed to cheer me up when they began talking about how strange it is that men would turn their boats around for us in the middle of the Southern Ocean when they'd never think of opening a door for us on shore. I had to laugh.

Through all this chaos and misery, we slipped further behind *L'Esprit*. I could have kicked myself. I had made almost exactly the same mistake that we'd made on *Privateer* four years earlier – gone too far south.

To compound matters, I discovered that the New Zealand weather charts we'd been using were wrong. All the boats that had relied on them were faring badly. Those that used satellite weather pictures were doing much better. I tried to get new charts from Buenos Aires.

On 23 February we began clawing miles back, although I feared we'd left it too late. The leading maxis *Steinlager II* and *Fisher and Paykel* had already rounded Cape Horn. We were still two days away.

Apart from being a personal milestone for the girls, rounding the Horn would create another piece of sailing history. An all-female crew had never done it before.

The big day dawned grey and cold. We had passed Diego Ramirez Island during the night. I could see it etched against the clouds by the rising sun. A Chilean Navy vessel made radio contact. It planned to rendezvous with us to take photographs of the historic event.

The girls were all on deck, rugged up against the cold. The mist slowly lifted and the mountainous cliffs to the north grew darker. Nobody spoke.

Here was the meeting point of two great oceans. It is also where two weather systems converge. That's what makes it so treacherous. We had survived the Southern Ocean and turned the corner.

Jo opened a bottle of champagne.

'A toast to King Neptune,' I declared.

'And to going north,' echoed Dawn.

Within a week we'd reach Punta del Este, Uruguay. Then I could drown my sorrows and put the disastrous fourth leg behind us.

I'd been doing a lot of thinking about Simon and the future. Was I really getting married in six months? I couldn't make up my mind how I felt. I wasn't the same person who had kissed Simon goodbye at Southampton. I still loved him, but would he love me?

Having the girls around was like living with eleven agony aunts. They tackled someone's love life each day – offering loads of free advice. Unfortunately, I finished up being more confused than before.

I'd spoken to Simon from Auckland. Our new house had been totally gutted and the builders had started on the interior walls. It's amazing how I could suddenly think of colour schemes and curtains while deep in the South Atlantic.

In the past eight days we had clawed back eighty miles on *L'Esprit*. Heading north along the coast of Argentina, we hoped to narrow the gap further.

The good intentions came to a shuddering halt on Tuesday, 27 February. Jeni scrambled on deck, crying, 'We're sinking! We're sinking!'

The boat was full of water. When *Maiden* heeled over it reached as high as the second tier of bunks. All hell broke loose. Dawn waded straight into the rising water, trying to figure out where it was coming from. She directed the others to look in particular places.

'It can't be the mast screws. We're taking in too much water.'

'What if we tacked?' I suggested.

'It depends where the leak is.'

The water level seemed to be rising by the minute. For the first time in my sailing career I contemplated losing a boat. The fact that I couldn't swim had always been a comfort. An old salt had once told me that most people drown because they strike out for shore and don't make it. If you can't swim, you cling to wreckage.

It was scant comfort to me now. I radioed the Race Committee in Punta del Este, putting them on alert. They contacted the British RAF base on the Falkland Islands and an RAF Hercules was scrambled. At the same time a Navy frigate was put on standby in case *Maiden* continued sinking.

The bilge pump had stopped working because the generator was full of salt water. We set up a human chain passing full buckets on deck and emptying them over the side. As fast as we bailed, the bilges seemed to fill. We had taken the headsail down and heaved to with three reefs in the main.

I could see my race ending. Surely we couldn't get out of this one.

'How's the engine coming?'

Dawn had been trying to get it started so we could stop bailing and start looking for the leak. In the meantime Michèle had the wheel and was having to tack to avoid various islands.

The Race Committee waited for more news. We began pulling the boards up from the cabin floor to check the bilges and bottom plates. Surely if we'd hit something during the night we'd have heard the bang.

Dawn estimated we had fifty gallons an hour coming in, but from where? Everything had been checked. There was no obvious place left. Surely we could see it.

I had to make a decision on whether to take the life-rafts from the lockers. It was the hardest call of my sailing career. Having the life-rafts ready could save us if we sank quickly. Yet the sight of them could have a disastrous effect on the crew's morale. I took the decision to wait.

With the engine working again and the pumps at full capacity, we averted the chance of sinking. We'd also noticed that the leak didn't seem as bad when *Maiden* was on a starboard tack.

'It has to be somewhere at deck level,' said Dawn, her hair plastered to her forehead. 'We've checked everywhere below the water level.'

'But why so much water?'

She shrugged.

After five hours we had pumped out the yacht and started sailing again. The source of the leak was still a mystery. All our hard-won miles of the previous days had been wiped out.

We limped towards Punta del Este and continued searching for the source of the leak. Suspicion eventually centred on the mast, where metal plates and screws were punched through the deck. Perhaps water had leaked through as waves came over the boat. We hadn't noticed the leak because crumpled sails were piled around the base of the mast.

I had my doubts. It didn't seem to explain the sheer volume of water. And why was it worse on a port tack?

We had other problems to contend with. After 23,000 miles the mast seemed to be shaking itself to pieces and the gooseneck fittings were looking suspect. What a bloody, bloody leg!

Five days later I wrote:

The last few days have been very strange. I feel almost a calm relief at not winning – no, that's not quite right. Not relief, just calmer than I thought I could be. I am not feeling aggressive or angry (very odd for me). I'm sleeping well, my dreams are peaceful, happy and comfortable and my stomach is fine (all equally unlikely).

I have sorted out my emotions, thoughts and fears. I've come to terms with them. I feel grown up – finally. Adult enough to face defeat fairly and squarely.

In a few days I will have to stand up and tell the world that I have messed it up. Yet I feel as strong now as when I told them how we won.

Early on 6 March, *Maiden* arrived in Punta del Este for the second time during the Whitbread. Strangely, a bigger crowd welcomed us than in October. Our glorious eighteen-hour lead lay in tatters. We were now seventeen hours behind *L'Esprit*.

In my heart I knew that our chances of winning Division D had evaporated. The North Atlantic lay ahead of us, including the Doldrums. *Maiden* had already shown that she didn't like light airs. Unless there was a freak weather pattern, or *L'Esprit* made a major tactical error, we wouldn't catch her.

The next leg was a short hop to Fort Lauderdale in Florida. It didn't feel like a proper leg. All of us wanted to be racing home. Now I wanted to get on with my life. I wanted to marry Simon and settle down. How else would I ever discover if this was my future?

A lot of the conversations on deck began to centre on what each of us would do after the race. *Maiden* had become like a home to us. We'd have to leave and go out into the big wide world again.

I felt incredibly close to the girls. Every crew in the race had changed personnel at some point, apart from *Steinlager II* and *Maiden*. Now, more than ever, I was convinced that this contributed to our success.

Perhaps in round-the-buoys racing you chop and change your crew to suit each race. But in the Whitbread you form a team, you bond, you work together and become strong. If someone has a problem, you deal with it. You don't just get rid of them.

On the light legs like this one, we could have taken two fewer crew members on *Maiden*. This would have saved weight and made the boat a fraction faster. I couldn't do it to the girls. We were a team. How could I suddenly tell two of them they were off the boat? I wanted to win, but there are things that are more important than crossing the finish line first. The spirit of *how* you compete is one of them.

The temperature had grown milder as we sailed north along the coast of Brazil, towards the Equator. The evenings were lovely and cool, with clear starry skies.

A mistake in the first hundred miles cost us dearly. After winning the start we edged too far from the coast, hoping to find more wind. As it turned out, we had the same wind as *L'Esprit* and *Rucanor*, but sailed a longer route.

The last leg had dented my confidence. I felt almost frightened of navigating. Instead of looking forward to each 'chat show', I felt nervous. If the news was bad my heart dropped into my stomach. I felt breathless and empty. If the news was good I bounced on deck, feeling elated and vindicated. What a way to live – always up or down. Now I knew why most boats had a skipper *and* a navigator. Perhaps single-handed sailing would suit me better. Then I wouldn't worry about letting other people down.

Halfway into the leg, I crawled out of my bunk to check our course. Tanja was steering 5° higher than I wanted. The instructions had been passed along like Chinese Whispers and been screwed up. We'd wasted eight hours. I sat in the nav station and burst into tears. It felt good. Maybe I should have done it earlier.

'If only the guys could see me now,' I muttered. 'They'd say, "I told you so. Women can't handle the Whitbread".'

I didn't care. I didn't want to be a man. Everybody should be able to cry sometimes. The lost miles, breakages and my own mistakes had compounded until I needed to let out my frustration. We should have won the previous leg when the conditions suited *Maiden*. On this leg we had an excuse.

A few days later I sat by the radio, listening to the charter boats chatting in the Caribbean. It made me feel homesick for the old days. As we sailed past Antigua my friends began calling. I chatted to Pig and Jo Jo, Julian Gildersleeve, Peter Mullins and Jol Byerly. They were like family to me. I wondered if they understood the part they played in getting me here.

I woke that night to a strange noise. The girls on deck were all imitating an ambulance: 'Neeee, nawww, neeee, naaaww . . .'

I went up to investigate. Dawn was using a galley spoon to flick flying fish from the deck into the water.

'What on earth are you doing?'

'We're the flying fish emergency unit,' she said earnestly.

I laughed till I cried.

If we couldn't win the leg into Florida, we decided to arrive in style. In preparation we spent a day washing our hair and getting ready. Then on the morning we pulled in to Fort Lauderdale, we all put on our swimsuits.

The British tabloids had been hoping for something like this since *Maiden* was first announced. Now they had their photo opportunity. A dozen tanned and very fit young women in white swimsuits sailed across the line.

On Pier Sixty Six the crowd roared in appreciation. Having shown them that we could win, now we proved we could lose graciously and with a sense of fun.

Florida in the springtime had its rewards. We stayed at the luxurious Embassy Suite, pampering ourselves and catching up on sleep. I didn't need to spend as much time studying charts and weather patterns. I knew the Atlantic. This was my back yard.

The phone rang in my hotel room. Jo and I were sharing a room.

'It's Buckingham Palace,' she whispered, holding one hand over the phone.

I thought it was a wind-up.

'No, it really is!' She nodded frantically.

I took the phone from her. She paced the room, unsure of what to do.

'This is the Honours Secretary at Buckingham Palace,' said a male voice with a very clipped private schoolboy accent. It didn't sound like Howard or Robbie Cook. Who else could it be?

'I've been instructed to inform you that the Queen has awarded you an MBE in her Birthday Honours List.'

'What for?' I asked.

'Well, ah . . . for services to sailing. You are Tracy Edwards, aren't you?'

'Yes.'

My God, this man is serious! He *is* from the palace.

'Before we can actually award the honour we have to check whether you are willing to accept it.'

'Oh, I see.' There was a pause. 'I guess that's OK.'

'Oh, good. Her Majesty will be pleased. Would you mind not telling anyone? This is very important. We like to announce all the honours at the same time.'

'Of course.'

'You'll be sent some further details. Good luck on the last leg of the race.'

'Thank you.'

My face had gone pale. Jo was dancing from foot to foot, eager to find out about the call.

'You've won an award,' she said, excitedly.

'Shhhhhh. You can't tell anyone.'

'But you won,' she said, her voice rising an octave.

'Yes.'

She let out a squeal. 'I won't tell anyone. I promise.'

I felt enormously proud. On top of everything else that had happened to me, this was almost too much. I had never imagined in my wildest dreams that the Queen would honour me. I had never aspired to it. Surely other people deserved it more. I felt like saying, 'I didn't ask for it. This is not why I did it.'

During those few weeks in Florida, I began to regret that we were heading home. In truth, I didn't want the race to end. 'If I could do this for ever, I would,' I told Howard as we sat on Pier Sixty One watching the last rays of light touch the tips of the masts.

'What about Simon?' he said. 'You told him that you'd never do another race.'

'I know.'

Howard could see that I was being torn between two loves that weren't compatible. To make matters worse, I'd heard that Nance Frank, a local yachtswoman, planned to race the first all-female *maxi* crew in the next Whitbread.

I reacted with a mixture of anger and incredulity. I didn't mind

that Nance had cashed in on *Maiden*'s arrival in Florida to further
her ambitions. What bothered me most was the possibility that all
our hard work to change the image of women's sailing could be
jeopardised. Nance had never sailed in the Whitbread. She had
never been through the Southern Ocean. It was an insult to think
that anyone could just walk into this race. That's how people get
hurt or die.

Maiden had shown that a strong, professional, well-funded all-
woman crew could compete with the men. I didn't want some
half-baked attempt to undermine this. We had all worked too hard.

'Can I ask you something, Howard?'

'Sure.'

'If – and it's a very big "if" – I decided to take part in the next
race, would you be my project manager?'

'I'd be honoured.'

Tears welled in my eyes.

'Why are you crying?'

'Because I don't deserve friends like you.'

The fleet left Fort Lauderdale on 5 May 1990 for one last hurrah.
We had nearly 4,000 miles to sail before the finish in Southampton.
If the leg had been longer, perhaps we might have been able to
catch *L'Esprit*. Enough people asked me the question. I kept telling
them that we'd try our best.

Already, I had begun thinking about the next Whitbread. This
time, if we had the money early enough we could build a new
boat. We could study the weather and the sails. We could spend
two years training the crew.

The wedding in August didn't even cross my mind. Instead, I
asked myself how long it would take me to find a sponsor. Surely
this time it would be easier. We could build on *Maiden*'s success.
Royal Jordanian Airlines was estimated to have received £26
million worth of publicity from *Maiden*. That's not bad for an
investment of £800,000.

I had to force myself to think about the present and the race to

Southampton. *Maiden* started brilliantly and was almost first over the line, with the maxis bearing down on us.

By the first mark *L'Esprit* had overtaken us and *Rucanor* and *Schlüssel* were just behind. It was so obvious that we were slower in light conditions. *Schlüssel* set off straight across the Atlantic on the shortest route. It was a huge gamble but they had nothing to lose.

I stayed close to *Rucanor* and *L'Esprit*. By next morning only a mile separated us. I had just woken and emerged on deck, when I noticed a giant water spout off to the starboard side.

'Isn't that amazing,' said Jeni. 'It's getting closer.'

'That's a tornado,' I said, gazing in awe. Then all hell broke loose.

'Drop the headsail! Drop the headsail!' I grabbed the leeward runner. Michèle, Jeni and Sally ran to the foredeck. I turned just in time to see *L'Esprit* and *Rucanor* rushing to pull down their headsails.

The tornado hit *Maiden* first. It picked us up like a child's toy. More than fourteen tons of aluminium and sail were spun round as though the keel were the bottom of a spinning top. We finished up facing in the opposite direction to where we started. The heavens opened.

In blinding rain we fought to get *Maiden* back on course. The deck was a mess of tangled sheets and lines. Initially, the damage appeared to be minor, but the stress on the rigging had been enormous.

Edging further north, we managed to take miles from *L'Esprit* and edge past her on 8 May. Our good tactics gave us the lead for two days. *L'Esprit* took it back again when I dithered over whether to carry on along the Great Circle Route (further north) or follow the Gulf Stream. This cost us six hours. By evening *L'Esprit* was twenty-one miles ahead of us.

Am I mad to want to do this race again? I asked myself. Forget about what I said in Florida, I'm going home to Simon. I'll be happy with my house and my dogs. I'll go to the pub and the supermarket and walk in the garden. I'll pick up milk from the doorstep every morning and read the paper while listening to Radio One.

The water spout had damaged *Maiden*'s mast. Twice we had to virtually stop to make repairs. At one point I was so tired I made a decision to gybe and went back to sleep. When I woke I couldn't remember saying anything. Luckily it had been the right choice. Perhaps I should do all my navigating when I'm half asleep.

Simon called. He seemed a bit nervous about the house.

'It isn't quite finished,' he said.

'What do you mean?'

'Well, it could be a bit chilly. It hasn't got any doors or windows.'

Apparently SJ had been round to see him. She took one look at the gaping holes in the walls and told him he was deluding himself if he thought I'd be moving in with him.

'Listen, Simon, Tracy has been wet, cold and miserable for nine months. I have a feeling she won't like this.'

Bless her. She was right. Simon had come up with a contingency plan. He'd rented a little house not far from where the crew would be staying.

The nights had turned bitterly cold on the water. It almost felt like the Southern Ocean again. The radar scanned for icebergs through the night and we kept the emergency channel open.

The air temperature fell to 1°C and the nav station felt like a walk-in freezer. Dawn spent an hour on deck without her gloves. Her hands were so badly frozen they had to be thawed in hot water. The fingers were painful and swollen.

'Any longer and you'd have lost some of them,' Claire scolded her.

At 6 p.m. on 13 May we spotted a handful of fishing boats ahead of us. They seemed to be circling in the same place. I radioed ahead, asking if they'd seen any icebergs. Word came back that they were searching for a lost crewman. He'd been missing four hours.

'Poor sods! They're looking for a body,' I said sadly. The water temperature was only 4°C. Nobody could have survived more than half an hour.

They asked us to steer clear, so we changed course. All the girls came on deck to keep lookout.

I estimated that we had ten days to go. I was wrong. A huge high pressure system turned the mid-Atlantic into a giant parking lot. The wind dropped to nothing and we couldn't make any sort of reasonable course.

Most of the fleet was caught in the same weather system. Each 'chat show' was like a meeting of manic-depressives. All of us wanted to get home, but the weather was holding us back. The maxis were shooting off east because they couldn't get north and I was shooting north because I couldn't get east. At least it wasn't so cold.

A week later, we were still nearly 800 miles from Southampton. If this kept up we'd run out of food. We pushed into awkward waves, tacking against terrible winds. *Schlüssel* had skipped away but we had *Rucanor* in our sights. By Friday the 25th we'd managed to get upwind of our rival but not without paying a heavy price in broken gear and sleepless nights.

Saturday began with Jo's bunk breaking, catapulting her across the boat. Thankfully, she wasn't injured. I woke to discover water pouring into the bilges again. It was the same leak that had threatened to sink *Maiden* off the Falklands. By now we'd narrowed it down to the cockpit drains, but we couldn't reach them because of the foam insulation.

Everything on the boat seemed to be breaking or packing it in. I had visions of this being like the Wacky Races where *Maiden* fell apart as we crossed the line.

The generator stopped working and one of the halyards broke. Dawn burnt her hand on the engine. We had an emergency call about a boat in distress off the Scillies. For a while I thought we were the closest boat but another yacht proved to be nearer.

On deck the girls had suddenly realised that we only had a few days left together. The music had been turned off and they started chattering like mad – as if to make up for lost time.

On the 27th, with 150 miles to go, we began racing *Rucanor* in a classic tacking duel towards Lizard Island off the Cornish coast. Bruno played all sorts of games trying to break free.

At one point he began radioing *Maiden* so that I'd go below deck to answer. Then he'd order his crew to tack while I was occupied. It didn't work. Each time we saw them coming and matched them turn for turn.

In the last 24 hours of a 33,000 mile race, we tacked 100 times. We beat *Rucanor* to Lizard Island and matched her all the way to the Solent. Bruno and I both hoped to catch the ingoing tide, but we were too early.

He made a miscalculation and ran aground on the Shingles Bank. Here was our chance. Back and forth we tacked across the Solent, fighting against a fierce tidal rip. *Rucanor* was at our mercy, but we couldn't sail against the outgoing tide.

By the time *Rucanor* re-floated off the bank, she was still ahead of *Maiden*. We followed her down the Solent, still trying to take her. In the distance the water seemed to turn white. Thousands of boats had come to greet us.

'Must be some sort of regatta,' said Jeni, shielding her eyes to the sun. 'Will you listen to that noise.'

Air horns and bells were ringing. Within minutes we were surrounded by an armada of power-boats, yachts and dinghies. People were cheering us and chanting, 'Maiden! Maiden! Maiden!'

'Let's give them a show,' I said, already choking up. We broke out the spinnaker for one last time. A huge roar went up. There were 600 boats escorting us as we crossed the line at 11 a.m. on Monday, 28 May.

A single cannon blast marked our arrival. The sound could be heard as far away as Hamble. Four years of struggle had ended in a deafening bang. I always thought I'd cheer and throw my arms into the air. I didn't. I felt nothing but pain. My throat ached and tears welled up in my eyes. Instead of joy I felt totally desolate; as if my life had stopped. Then as quickly as it came, the feeling passed.

Michèle summed it up best. As she steered *Maiden* towards the finish line, Jo had asked her for her thoughts. In her wonderful French accent, Michèle said, 'I am just thinking that we have only a few more minutes of this very lovely story. Just a few more minutes – I am so sad.' Overall in the Whitbread, *Maiden* had finished second in division D and third in the combined division C and D. Although I had desperately wanted to win, I didn't feel disappointed. We had exceeded the expectations of almost everybody and captured the public's imagination.

As we slowly motored up the Itchen and turned into Ocean Village Marina, 20,000 people lined the quayside. Again the chant went up, 'Maiden! Maiden! Maiden!' A band played the national anthem.

Tears poured down my cheeks. I had never been so proud or so happy. I wanted to take this day and put it in a little box. I wanted to wrap it up – the sounds, sights, smells and feelings – so that I could open it up whenever I felt down.

Maiden had come home.

SIXTEEN

T HE headlines the next day made me feel very humble. TEARS AS TRACY HOME IN TRIUMPH read one of them. HOME ARE THE HEROINES, declared another. The *Daily Telegraph* said simply, HOME AT LAST.

Ian Wooldridge from the *Daily Mail* asked me if I was the same person who had left Southampton nine months earlier. How could I be? Too much had happened. All of us were going to find it very difficult to settle down to anything like home or a normal life again.

Libby Purves wrote perhaps the most perceptive article in *The Times* two days before our return.

'If I were Tracy Edwards,' she mused, 'almost home from the sea. I would be looking forward to a hot bath and a good therapeutic weep of relief that I had got my eleven crewmates back safely and was no longer responsible for anyone else's life.

'I would also allow myself a brief ten minutes of private crowing at the thought of those 300 companies who refused to sponsor our boat because they reckoned we would drown . . .

'I would not be human if I did not feel female biology lying in ambush. I am pushing thirty. I might get married, I might have children within the next five or six years. Somebody is bound to tell me that childbirth will be the greatest adventure of my life and only then will I think back with irony to the Southern Ocean.'

As I stepped off *Maiden* I fell into Simon's arms, exhausted and happy. I didn't care about the cameras, or the crowds. I felt older than when I'd left. He seemed so young.

'Welcome home,' he whispered.

He'd bought me a present — a new car. 'I didn't want my wife driving around in an old banger.'

Although neither of us said anything, both of us were having private doubts about marriage. Maybe that's only natural. I thought we had a chance, as long as Simon could be patient. I'd changed a lot in my time away. It wasn't going to be easy to have a roll of wallpaper thrust into my hand and a wedding band slipped on my finger.

If our roles had been reversed this wouldn't have needed to be explained. Women have been waiting for men to come home from the sea for centuries.

What neither of us expected was the media frenzy. Everybody wanted a piece of my time — magazines, talk shows, newspapers, publishers, charities, schools and yacht clubs. While I'd been off sailing, people had turned me into a celebrity. I wasn't looking for fame. That's not why I did it.

After *Maiden* I always assumed that I'd slip into a normal life on land. Simon imagined the same thing. For three years he'd taken a back seat and supported my dream. Now we could get on with our lives. The headlines, however, must have given him an inkling that this wasn't to be.

When I finished the Whitbread on *Privateer*, I'd been shocked by how quickly everyone disappeared. I didn't want that to happen again. A few of the girls had talked about staying around Hamble, so I arranged to rent a crew house. That way, we could spend a few weeks together and slowly re-start our lives.

This was absolutely the best way to do things, but Simon didn't see it that way. He wanted me back. Instead, I spent my time at the crew house or in the office.

A great deal still had to be done. Despite the sponsorship, I had personal debts of more than £60,000. And much as it saddened me, the only way to repay this money was to sell *Maiden*. It would also give me enough to pay the girls a bonus.

Howard contacted a yacht broker in Holland. I didn't want to sail *Maiden* on her delivery run. I said my farewells on the day before she left. I stood on the dockside and gazed across the decks. I knew every seam and weld mark. She deserved a good home. No more pounding Southern Ocean swells. Maybe some gentle, inshore cruising on Bank Holiday weekends.

The media frenzy showed no sign of abating. At the crew house we used to laugh at all the publicity. Fancy being recognised in the street! I couldn't get round Tesco's without being stopped and congratulated or asked for an autograph. People said such nice things.

At the same time, I didn't feel entirely comfortable. If you're truly famous everyone recognises you, so you act in a certain way. I could never quite be sure if someone knew me or not. I found myself not making eye contact, just in case. I didn't mind being approached in the street, as long as people were polite and friendly. In Hamble, however, some people acted as though they owned me. I'd be in the pub, chatting quietly to a friend, when suddenly a stranger would stand in between us and begin talking. I couldn't believe the rudeness.

Although I had trouble picturing myself as a 'sporting personality', the label had been affixed. Jackie Stewart, the legendary Formula One driver, invited me to a charity weekend at Gleneagles in Scotland. This biennial event featured various handpicked teams of showbusiness stars and sporting personalities, as well as 'lords and ladies'.

Billy Connolly skippered my team, which included his wife Pamela Stephenson, actor Anthony Andrews, his wife Georgina, and the pop star Paul Young and his wife Stacey.

The weekend was a wonderful affair, although I spent the entire time expecting someone to tap me on the shoulder and tell me I didn't belong. 'Sorry, there's been a mistake. We've confused you with someone who's famous. We do apologise. A taxi is waiting.'

Having Billy around helped. At one point, during the clay pigeon shooting, a fragment came back and hit me on the forehead.

'Oh, my God, they're fighting back,' he cried, diving to the ground. 'We're under attack. Take cover!'

Later, on the 'rabbit run', a clay disc toppled over instead of rolling across the ground.

Billy declared, 'Look at that! I'm so bloody good it committed suicide.'

Any sort of formal invitation filled me with dread. The Duke of Edinburgh Awards held a gala dinner in Manchester that was billed as the 'Night of a Thousand Stars'. It featured a host of lords, ladies and high achievers.

This is just the sort of glittering affair that afflicts me with terminal clumsiness. I have nightmares about spilling my wine over someone really important.

The invitation hadn't mentioned 'and partner' so I assumed that I was expected to go on my own. Simon and I were due to be married in two weeks and I had barely spent any time with him. He joked about seeing more of me on TV than in the flesh.

I arrived in Manchester early in the evening and booked into my room at the hotel. As I crossed the foyer I could see waiters and organisers making final preparations for the night. Upstairs I had a long soak in the tub and pondered what to wear. This had worried me for days and ultimately I bought two evening dresses – one a little more formal than the other – just in case.

Men have it so easy wearing black tie. For women it's a minefield.

At 7.30 I made a decision and put on a mid-calf gown that I had bought from Harrods. After one last equipment check in front of the mirror, I caught the lift downstairs.

The doors slid open. I took one look at what other women were wearing and stood rooted to the spot. The doors closed and I went back up again. They were all in long evening gowns.

Having changed, I came back down again, this time wearing a black velvet top with sequins and embroidery (it had cost me a fortune at Harrods) and a very simple long, black pleated skirt.

I didn't know anyone in the room. They chatted in small groups and politely laughed when appropriate. A waiter offered me a glass of champagne. I clutched it gratefully and pretended to be waiting for someone. In reality, I wanted to run back up to my room and forget the whole thing. I felt like a complete lemon, or worse still an impostor.

Glancing nervously through the crowd, I recognised one or two faces. One of them was Mary Peters, the golden girl of British athletics in the seventies. She was standing and chatting with a group of people. Suddenly she glanced across at me. Then she marched towards me and said, 'Tracy Edwards, I think you are absolutely amazing. Are you not with anyone?'

'No.'

'Well, come and stand with us.' She put her arm around me and drew me into a circle of people. 'Look who I found,' she announced.

What a relief! What a wonderful woman. I chatted and began to relax. People joined our little group and others broke off. Eventually, I found myself talking to a middle-aged Canadian woman whose husband was one of the sponsors of the evening.

'And tell me again, my dear, what did you do? Why are you here?'

'I sailed around the world.'

'Oh, how nice. Was it a holiday?'

'No, it was in a race.'

'Really. How interesting for you.'

She looked at what I was wearing, with barely disguised distaste. Her dress, of course, was right over the top. Almost like an echo, she relayed my answers to her husband, standing next to her, who was clearly not interested. He kept looking over my shoulder trying to spot someone with a title, or perhaps a fresh glass of Moët.

Abruptly, she announced, 'I think we should go and look where we're sitting for dinner. Do you know where you're sitting, my dear?'

'Ah, no.'

'Come with us.'

We walked over to a large board, where the names of guests were listed alphabetically, along with a table number. I looked for my name and it wasn't there.

'What was your name again?' the woman asked.

'Tracy Edwards.'

'Oh, how funny, you don't appear to be on the list.' She loved it. I died inside. Please, ground, open up and swallow me now?

'I'm sorry, my dear, but I can't see your name,' she said, gloating.

My stomach began doing backflips. Clearly, I hadn't been invited. I wanted to crawl away and hide.

Dinner was announced and people slowly began filing into the dining room. I stood outside, knowing that I'd soon be alone. What should I do? Make a run for it. I'll sneak back up to my room.

Just as I was edging towards the door, a deep voice made me jump.

'Tracy Edwards, you don't know me, but I know a lot about you.' An amazingly handsome man, with a huge handlebar moustache, shook my hand.

Oh my God, he's going to chuck me out, I thought.

'My name is Lieutenant-Colonel Sean O'Dwyer. I'm Prince Edward's equerry.'

'Oh, right. How do you do?'

'I'm fine. You met Prince Edward in New Zealand, I believe.'

'Yes, that's right.' He had presented the awards for that leg. I kept glancing at the door, watching the last of the guests disappear into the dining room. Any minute now, he was going to discover that I hadn't been invited. I had to get out.

'I'm really sorry, but you'll have to excuse me, I have to . . .'

'Of course, but I hope you don't mind, we've seated you on the top table.'

'I beg your pardon?'

'We've seated you on the top table next to Prince Edward because he doesn't have a partner tonight and neither do you. So if that's acceptable . . .'

'Thank you, God,' I muttered, a little too loudly.

'I'm sorry?'

'Ignore me.'

He had a wonderful smile. 'I'm sorry, I should have found you earlier and told you. So if you don't mind just waiting behind, you'll walk in with others from the top table.'

It was one of those perfect moments in life. As Prince Edward entered, with me alongside, we had to walk straight past the Canadian woman and her husband. I paused just long enough to lean close and whisper in her ear. 'I found my table.'

Hundreds of letters were arriving each week at the office. Many were from schoolchildren, who wanted an autograph, or to ask a question. There were also dozens of requests for interviews, personal appearances and charity launches.

Clearly, I needed somebody to help organise my life. The job fell to Tricia McMahon, who ran a sponsorship and PR company. I'd met Tricia while I was still trying to raise money for *Maiden*. She had read an article and volunteered to help. Her husband was Paddy McMahon, the show-jumping star, who had been one of my childhood heroes.

Trish drew up a weekly diary for me and made the arrangements.

People kept asking me what I was going to do next. I didn't have an answer for them. The next Whitbread was four years away. Did I really want to go again? For the moment, I felt it was my duty to make the most of *Maiden*'s success. The support for us had been so spontaneous and overwhelming that I wanted to thank people personally. It meant criss-crossing the country, talking at schools, opening fêtes and launching campaigns for cleaner beaches and 'learn-to-swim'. Often my expenses were covered, but I wasn't aiming to make a profit. Tricia handled that side of things.

Despite all the travelling, I still managed to organise my wedding to within an inch of its life. It became my next 'project'. I wanted everything to be absolutely perfect. The full fairytale bit. More than 250 guests came from all over the world, including people I'd sailed with in Europe and the West Indies. We set up a huge marquee in the carpark of the Royal Southern Yacht Club in Southampton. They had given me honorary membership.

I organised everything – the flowers, food, drinks, place cards, invitations, music . . . making sure that it was the best day possible. I wore a cream dress and Uncle Arthur gave me away.

So much work went into the wedding, it developed a momentum of its own. I kept wondering if I was doing the right thing. Then I told myself that everybody got pre-wedding jitters.

On the night before the wedding, I barely slept. I wanted to give Simon a call and ask him if he was sure. Did he have doubts? 'Don't tell me what you think I want to hear. Tell me the truth.'

In the morning, Uncle Arthur came to the house. The horse-drawn carriage waited outside. Dressed and made up, I came down the stairs. I'd drunk half a bottle of vodka to give me courage.

'It's never too late to pull out,' said Arthur. How did he know about my second thoughts?

'Hmmph! What are you talking about?'

'It's better to pull out now rather than later.'

The carriage driver had opened the door. I had my dress bunched in my hands, ready to step up inside.

'I know what I'm doing,' I said, trying to sound confident.

With my butterflies swimming in vodka, I strode into the church in Hamble and married Simon. The reception and party were brilliant and the day truly memorable, even if the photographs make it look over the top.

There was no time for a honeymoon. We had one night in a hotel in the New Forest. The next day I was back at work, rushing down motorways and catching trains to various appointments.

Often I was doing three or four engagements a day, arriving home exhausted.

The house still hadn't been finished, but we were getting there slowly. At least I could see how it was *going* to look.

Each morning Simon headed off to work. I walked the dogs, answered mail and visited the office. Another batch of invitations awaited answers. I couldn't turn anybody down – no matter how small. A third class at a small country school would write, or a local branch of the Women's Institute, and each time I agreed.

Four days after marrying Simon on 4 September 1990, I embarked on a whirlwind round of book signings for *Maiden* up and down the country. Among the first was at St Katharine's Dock in London, where the publishers had arranged for *Maiden* to be the backdrop.

Tricia and I met up beforehand for coffee at the Belgravia Sheraton. She had arranged a car and driver to take us to the dock. We left at about 2.15 p.m., driving along the Embankment towards Tower Bridge. The traffic was surprisingly light and we had a quick run. As we came up to the bridge the car kept going instead of turning right. I didn't know London very well, but I knew the driver had taken a wrong turn.

'I'm sorry, but I think you've just missed our turn.'

'Oh, right, where are you going?'

'St Katharine's Dock.'

'OK, sorry about that.'

He took a few turns and we slowly found our way back to Tower Bridge. Just as we were about to cross the lights, he suddenly veered off again.

'I'm sorry, but you've made exactly the same mistake. We need to go to St Katharine's Dock.'

'I'm sorry, love. We're early.'

'So what? I don't mind. It's nice to be early. I could have another cup of coffee.'

'OK. Right you are.'

I began to feel nervous. The driver kept glancing at me in the rear mirror. Why wasn't Tricia kicking up a fuss? Normally, she'd be ripping his throat out.

'Relax, Tracy,' she said. 'We have loads of time.'

Something wasn't quite right about this scene. Then it dawned on me. We're being kidnapped! Tricia obviously didn't realise. I couldn't say anything because the driver kept watching me strangely in the rear mirror. Glancing sideways, I noticed the car door on Tricia's side wasn't locked. Right! I told myself. At the next set of traffic lights, I'll push her out and jump. We'll both make a run for it.

Then I told myself not to be silly. People don't get abducted in broad daylight in central London. The man was clearly a complete idiot. How did he get a licence? We neared the same roundabout at Tower Bridge.

'If you don't turn this time, pal, you're in big trouble,' I told him, with just enough menace to have him worried.

By the time we arrived at St Katharine's Dock I had steam coming out of my ears. Unknown to me, I was being filmed as I slammed the car door and stormed down the footpath towards the boat.

A photographer wanted to get a quick publicity shot of me standing at the helm. I threw my shoes on to the deck and clambered aboard. It was frightening how quickly I changed from a furious harridan into a beaming 'sporting personality'.

As he fired off a roll of film, the centre hatch behind me slowly opened and the girls began to emerge on deck. I turned and let out a squeal of delight. What were they doing here? The publishers must have arranged this.

I gave them all big hugs and kept asking questions.

'Tracy Edwards?'

I turned to see Michael Aspel clutching his red book.

'I think you know what this is,' he said.

'Oh, my God, I'm too young. I'm not ready for this.'

'Tracy Edwards. This is your life!'

My first reaction was blind panic. I hadn't lived my life yet.

There had to be some mistake. Then I thought, Oh, my God, who have they dredged up? What guests have they chosen?

From St Katharine's Dock I was taken to the studio where the girls had a jolly time in the hospitality suite while I was locked in a Portakabin in the carpark for two hours.

An assistant showed me the clothes that Simon had brought for me to wear on the biggest evening of my life. He'd chosen an outfit that I wouldn't be caught dead wearing – white tights, white shoes and a blue suit.

I was furious. I had to borrow a pair of tights from the make-up woman, along with her shoes, and the hairdresser lent me her jumper.

I hated not knowing what was going on. How could people I knew so well have lied to me? All my worst fears began to surface. Hang on a second. What if Mum organised this? Her perception of my life was totally different from what actually happened. This was going to be a disaster.

As the show opened, I felt acute embarrassment. The girls were gathered in the audience, along with all my aunts, uncles and cousins.

Michael Aspel started his introduction. 'Tracy Edwards, you were born at Battle Hospital in Reading on the 5th of September, 1962 . . .'

I kept racking my brain. Who had they found?

'Do you recognise this voice?' he asked.

The answer was no.

It was Phyllis Kedge, from the Phyllis Kedge School of Dancing, in Reading. I was surprised that she was still alive and wouldn't have recognised her.

Next came an old school friend Anita Jones, from Arts Educational. I hadn't seen her in nearly fifteen years. Mike Corns and Jaynie, from *Kovalam*, were the next guests to emerge.

Not everybody could be there. The Duchess of York sent a lovely letter which Michael Aspel read aloud. She reminded me of the polo club lunch in Uruguay and then said: 'Before you left I had a message for you, Tracy. Do you remember? I said, "Don't let me down, girls, you've got to win. My street cred is suffering." I'm proud to say that you didn't.'

Robin Knox-Johnston, the first man to sail single-handed non-stop around the world, sent a filmed message:

'Hello Tracy, I know I speak on behalf of the whole world of yachting when I congratulate you on your achievement. To be awarded the MBE and to be elected Yachtsman of the Year just goes to show how highly we rate you. Good luck and calm seas in all your future voyages . . .'

The final message came from King Hussein.

'It has been some years ago since Queen Noor and I first met you, Tracy. Many may have had doubts regarding your abilities to accomplish what you set out to accomplish, but I am not one of them. Your qualities of leadership and your vision are what make you so unique. Well done.'

It was an amazing night. I felt enormously proud and also humble that so many people I admired had said nice things about me. The general consensus seemed to be, 'We knew that you had it in you, Tracy.' I thought this extraordinary considering I didn't know it myself.

Each week seemed to bring a new award or honour. I was voted Sportswoman of the Year and Sports Personality of the Year. *Maiden* swept most of the major sailing prizes and various crew members won special honours.

In September, the Prime Minister invited me to one of her famous mix-and-match parties, of people in the news. Mrs Thatcher had always been a heroine of mine because of her strength and determination. Although I didn't agree with all her policies, I liked the fact that she stuck to her principles and said what she thought. The fact that I lived in a country where the two most powerful figures – the Head of State and Prime Minister – were both women seemed enormously relevant to everything we had done on *Maiden*. Perhaps that's why I'd been invited to Downing Street.

Simon and I arrived at the big black shiny door and were ushered into a reception room upstairs. Here, Mrs Thatcher greeted everyone before we moved to another room for drinks.

Ben Elton, Stephen Fry and Hugh Laurie were there. I also recognised Will Carling and Adrian Moorhouse.

I stood in line, waiting to meet the PM. What would she say to me? Simon stood next to me. Alongside him was the English soccer star Paul Gascoigne, better known as Gazza.

Mrs Thatcher moved along the line with her husband Denis. My moment finally arrived. She shook my hand. The assistant next to her, whispered, 'Tracy Edwards, round the world yachtswoman.'

'How lovely to meet you.'

In the same movement – before she'd finished her greeting – she had handed me on to Denis. I went to open my mouth to say something but it was too late.

I had never been so disappointed in my life. Denis was really sweet and charming, but it wasn't the same. Not surprisingly, Mrs Thatcher passed Simon along even more quickly, if that were possible. She had eyes only for Gazza and the next morning's front pages. He was the man of the moment and the perfect photo opportunity.

Later, I came to realise that Margaret Thatcher was not the great champion of women's rights that I had always imagined. She pulled the ladder up behind her as she climbed. And she found it much easier dealing with men than women.

During the drinks I had a laugh with Will Carling and Adrian Moorhouse. We decided that the three of us were the least famous people in the entire room. It was still so strange to be classed as a 'celebrity'. When would people wake up and realise I was just Tracy Edwards?

The MBE was officially announced in July, but my appointment at the palace wasn't until 31 October. Other sporting MBEs that year were the middle-distance runner Peter Elliott, hurdler Colin Jackson and champion jump jockey Peter Scudamore.

I could only take two people with me to Buckingham Palace. I invited Mum and Trevor. I explained this to Simon and I think he understood.

On the morning of the ceremony, we drove to the palace and lined up with other cars at the gates. Eventually, they opened and the police directed us to park in the central square.

'I can't believe this is happening,' I said, as I glanced up at the palace.

Mum seemed to be walking six inches off the ground. She had spent weeks deciding what to wear.

Immediately we were separated. Trevor and Mum were taken with other guests to the throne room. Meanwhile, I followed an equerry to the White Ballroom where the other recipients of honours had gathered. We were all very nervous. I tried to be cool and not stare at people. Instead I kept silently whispering my mantra: 'Please don't trip over. Please don't trip over.'

A senior member of the palace staff gave us a short explanation of what was going to happen.

'Please, try to remember this. If you have any questions ask me. I don't care how many times I tell you this, you have to get it right.'

Oh my God, we've got to think as well.

'We are going to walk outside of this room and queue in a long line in the order I am going to give you. When you come up to the throne room you will walk in through the door, you will take sixteen steps forward. Do not look for friends or family in the audience. You will then turn to your left. You will take ten steps forward. You will then bow or curtsy. You will then take four steps forward and receive your honour. You will then shake the Queen's hand. She may say a few words to you, or she may not. You should not speak to Her Majesty unless she speaks to you. You then take four steps backwards. You curtsy or bow again. Only then are you allowed to turn around. You will then turn right and walk out of the room.'

As he spoke, I thought, Oh my God, I can't remember the first thing he told me. It flew out of my head immediately. Did he say walk backwards? He must be mad! If I haven't tripped over before then, he's made it a certainty.

The equerry knew exactly what we were thinking. He ran through the protocol three or four times.

I queued behind a lighthouse keeper from Northumberland. I kept looking at the grey hairs on the back of his neck and reciting my mantra: Please, don't trip over. Please, don't trip over.

The actual ceremony passed in a flash. Without turning my head, I tried desperately to catch a glimpse of Mum and Trevor in the audience. There were too many people. I walked in, turned left and counted my paces forward. Then I curtsied.

An equerry stood beside Her Majesty. He whispered, 'Ma'am, Tracy Edwards.'

She had amazing eyes and a nice smile. Her countenance was strong.

'It must have been so frightening, sailing around the world in a small boat like that,' she said.

'Some bits are frightening. It's also a lot of fun. We did pretty well.'

'I think you did wonderfully well. Well done.'

I almost turned round straight away. I stopped myself and stepped backwards. Out and along through the corridor, I joined the others. There was an amazing buzz. Finally I looked down at my award. A card read: 'For services to British yachting.' I felt incredibly proud but also quite sad. I wished that Dad could have been there to see me.

A lot of people scoff at the idea of an honours system. I think they're wrong. All sorts of people were at the palace that day, from lollipop ladies to lighthouse keepers. They had each given something to their community and their country. How can you begrudge them a brief moment of glory?

Outside I met up with Mum and Trevor. Mum couldn't stop crying. We went and checked out the loos before we left. I had to do that.

Photographers and journalists milled in the courtyard, taking photographs of happy threesomes.

'How do you feel?'

'Wonderful . . . proud . . . excited . . .' What can you say?

Tricia had arranged for us to have lunch at the rooftop restaurant of the Hilton Hotel. Simon, Howard, SJ and Dee Ingles were waiting there.

'You can see right into the gardens of Buckingham Palace,' said Tricia. 'It's the next best thing to being there.'

SEVENTEEN

FOR months I had been criss-crossing the country fulfilling engagements The diary seemed to be permanently full.

'Milk it while it lasts,' Tricia would say, but I didn't see this as a business, or a career.

I still hadn't decided about doing another Whitbread campaign. Howard had been hanging on, waiting for my decision. Some of the girls were also pressing me to decide. If I didn't go ahead, Miki had said she might launch a project. I quite liked this idea. I could lend her my support but wouldn't have all the responsibility and pressure. It might also convince Simon that I wouldn't run away to sea again.

At times I had so many invitations, I had to disappoint people. I couldn't please everybody. Unfortunately, local newspapers, searching for headlines, chose to write stories about how I had 'abandoned schoolchildren' or 'disappointed pensioners'. Didn't they realise I couldn't be in three places at once?

'You're not ruthless enough,' Simon told me. 'Just tell them no, you can't make it. You have a life.'

That was part of the problem. I didn't have any other plans. I had no new project. The right manager would have sorted these things out, but Tricia was more interested in 'keeping the momentum going'.

The media had written such wonderful things about *Maiden* that I wasn't prepared for the negative stories. That's why I took them so personally. It took me a long while to understand how newspapers worked.

Over Christmas and New Year I decided not to do the next Whitbread. I simply didn't have the time and I wanted a break from sailing. Miki announced her bid for the race and I supported her totally. She was more than capable.

Unfortunately, the *Sunday Mirror* saw it differently. MUTINY AMONG THE MAIDENS declared the headline. The story claimed that Miki and the rest of the crew had fallen out with me and that's why I wasn't part of the new project. Nothing could have been further from the truth. It was only natural that the girls should branch out on their own but the journalist, who wasn't a sports writer, had made no attempt to find out the real story.

In hindsight, I should have demanded an apology and set the record straight. Instead, I thought it so laughable I did nothing. I should have known that the same media that had labelled us heroines could very easily tear us apart.

The crunch came on Monday, 4 February 1991. Howard called me in Cardiff where I was working that day. He sounded upset. 'Have you seen the papers?'

'No.'

'Pick up a copy of *Today*.'

'Why?'

'It's Nancy Hill. She's given them a story. I can't understand it.'

Nancy had been the sail trimmer on *Maiden* and a bridesmaid at my wedding. I bought a copy of the paper at the off-licence and walked outside. The centre page spread repeated the headline: MUTINY AMONG THE MAIDENS. Beneath it, in smaller type, a subheading read: 'Tracy watched radar below deck for 17 days as we risked our lives on £40 a week. Now we're cast adrift while she rakes in millions.'

My heart sank. Oh my God, poor Nancy. What have they done to you? The story claimed that I had discarded the girls once we

reached dry land. I had treated *Maiden* like a one-woman show, and
the rest of them as though they didn't exist. 'Somebody made a
fortune out of it all right but it certainly wasn't us,' said Nancy. 'I
didn't get a penny.'

I called her up immediately.

'Nancy, don't worry about it. We'll sort this out. I know it's the
journalist's fault. They can't get away with making up lies like this.'

She seemed anxious and quiet.

'Look, I can't talk now. I'll call you when I get home,' I said.

Later that day, I phoned her again. 'Right, let's both issue the
writ together. We'll sue the paper and demand an apology. We'll
get all the girls together. All they're trying to do is prove that girls
can't get on. We'll show them all over again.'

Nancy said very quietly, 'They taped it.'

'What?'

'My interview. I did say some of those things.'

I was stunned.

'You bloody idiot!'

I felt like crying. Why had she done it?

Nancy had agreed to the interview because she wanted to
publicise her attempt to sail single-handed to the Azores Islands
and back on her father's £40,000 yacht. The reporter had taken her
for a drink at the pub and had a tape recorder. Then he simply
wound her up. He told her that I was earning millions of pounds
from public appearances and book deals. I'd stolen all the glory and
become fabulously wealthy, at the expense of the others. Jealousy is
a dreadful thing.

The reality couldn't have been different. I had to sell *Maiden* to
pay off my debts. The proceeds were also used to give the girls a
bonus of £8,000 each, which I paid the tax on for them. During
the race we'd operated a 'crew pool' for any money earned from
articles or photographs. This had been divided equally among us.
Rather than resenting my profile, most of the girls considered
themselves lucky not to be the centre of attention. I would have
swapped places with them any time.

All of us had the opportunity to use *Maiden* as a springboard to bigger and better things. Miki was doing just that by launching a campaign for the next Whitbread.

None of these things was mentioned in the article. Rather than being a major leap forward for women's sailing, *Maiden* was portrayed as a bitchy catfight, riven with disagreements and jealousy. Everything we had worked for and stood for was labelled as a lie. Our triumph was tarnished. I couldn't let this happen.

I gave Nancy quite a few more chances to retract her statements. 'I don't want to sue you. I want to sue the newspaper,' I told her. 'Are you going to tell the truth?'

'They have the tape,' she said, miserably.

'Yes, Nancy but they're lies. You weren't paid £45 a week. What about the tax-free bonus? No other crew in the Whitbread got that sort of money. I haven't made a fortune out of *Maiden* – you know that. You're going to look very silly when the real story comes out.'

'They've threatened to sue me if I back down,' said Nancy.

She was caught in an impossible situation. Even so, I didn't have time to sympathise. I had to save the project.

I issued the writ against *Today*. There were countless inaccuracies and many points of libel in the story. Most of these were easy to prove with paperwork. The rest of the girls supported me totally, but I resisted getting them involved. I didn't want them to have to take sides against Nancy.

The newspaper's lawyers huffed and puffed and said they were going to defend the story, but as *Today*'s case began collapsing, the pressure on Nancy became intolerable. Her parents called me up and begged me to drop the libel action because Nancy would get hurt.

'She should have thought about that before,' I explained.

It hadn't been entirely Nancy's fault, but I couldn't forgive her. Unwittingly or otherwise, she had cheapened all our efforts. Why did I have to keep defending *Maiden*? In every interview people asked me about the so-called 'mutiny'. My denials became more strident. I felt exhausted and angry.

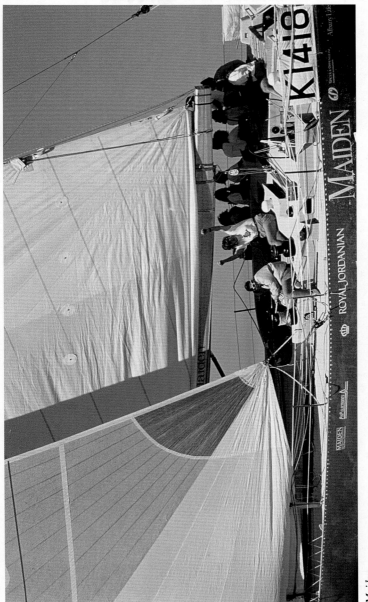

Maiden.

Arriving in Fort Lauderdale. Judging by the look on my face, I am not impressed with 4th place.

King Hussein sending me a wonderful message when I was on *This is Your Life*.

Happy to be home (or so we thought).
(© *Express Newspapers*)

The proudest moment of my life (before my daughter was born); with Trevor and my mother after receiving my MBE at Buckingham Palace in 1990. (*Evening Standard*)

Daily Express Sportswoman of the Year 1990. Gazza was Sportsman of the Year.
(© Express Newspapers)

The Duchess of York presenting me with the overall second prize for *Maiden*.
(© Express Newspapers)

This is me, Miki and Adrienne on watch during the Jules Verne in 1998, or as the girls would say, the 'Wrinklies Watch'.

Miki said it was going to snow, and so it did.

Breaking the Channel record in 1997 at an incredible 22.7 knot average speed.

March 1998, the tug tows us the final few miles to Chile, dismasted and exhausted.

Being a Rugby Union fanatic this was one of my greatest moments. It was also one of the best games ever, the 26/26 All Black/England draw. I couldn't talk for three days!

I am lucky enough to be involved with a few charities and NCH is one of my favourites. This is the fund-raising ball at Henley; *left to right*: Robert Powell, John Leslie, myself, John Thacker, Shirley Anne Field, Lucy Fleming, Simon Williams, Babs Powell and Christopher Cazenove. Babs Powell is, as I write this, racing around the world on a Challenge boat.

(Raymond Thatcher Maidenhead)

The ever-patient Gordon teaching me my new chosen sport, Clay Pigeon shooting.

Enjoying a joke with HRH Queen Elizabeth at the Scout's Association dinner. Her Majesty has a razor-sharp wit.

Mackenna's christening, July 2000, with her godparents; *left to right:* Suzy Mayhew, Fiona Brook, Mack and Tracy, Lord Moynihan, Mark Lucas.

Mackenna's first sail in Newport, Rhode Island. Mr Bill took us out on his boss's beautiful *Swan*. My dear friend Corrine is at the helm. I could be in trouble – Mack loved it!

Things with Simon weren't good. Although we'd moved into the new house, we rarely saw each other. I was travelling the country and he had properties to oversee. Even when we were together at the house, we trod on eggshells and avoided each other. Feeling the stress, I would snap at Simon for no reason, or slip into long silences. I felt lonely and confused. Poor Simon didn't know how to help. Everything he did annoyed me.

The libel case dragged on for months. My hopes of a quick apology evaporated. I had weekly meetings with lawyers, on top of my other commitments. I really needed a holiday but Tricia kept urging me to keep working.

From the beginning I'd tried to resist getting the girls involved in the libel action. I didn't want to drag them into a possible court case, but in the end it couldn't be avoided.

'We have to show the newspaper that it can't possibly win,' my solicitor told me. 'We have to put up a united front.'

The girls supported me completely and gave statements refuting the newspaper story and Nancy's comments. From that moment, however, I knew that our team had been irrevocably split. Everything I'd said about teamwork and our strong bonds of friendship now sounded hollow and hypocritical. The damage had been done.

On a personal level, I seemed to be constantly trying to patch up my life. All the girls had gone their separate ways and the *Maiden* project had been disbanded. I had to cope with things alone.

The speed of my elevation from boat bum to sporting celebrity created added pressures. I had been labelled public property and found myself pulled in different directions. Things were OK when the subject was sailing, but eventually the media began asking about my private life.

I had wanted *Maiden* to be the star, but journalists became more interested in my marriage. I felt like saying, 'No you're missing the point. That's not the issue.' It would have made no difference.

In August, Ross Benson, the diarist from the *Daily Express*, wrote a piece under the headline: ROUND THE WORLD TRACY OPTS FOR A SOLO BREAK.

One noble face absent from Cowes bustling marina has been that
of the diminutive round the world yachtswoman Tracy Edwards.
Instead of battling it out on the Solent during the world's most
prestigious yacht racing week, Tracy, 28, has surprisingly chosen
to go on holiday with friends 11 months after her marriage to
Simon Lawrence whom she has left behind.

A media storm broke. Within hours there were press photographers camped outside our front gate in Hamble. I couldn't move
without being followed and quizzed. Simon hadn't moved out of
the house, but he was spending most of his time away.

Periodically, a reporter came to the door. They were polite and
only doing their jobs, but I refused to talk. I didn't want to make a
statement. I didn't want to speak to anybody. The headlines talked
of 'a dream sunk by strain'. They weren't far from the truth.

For two days I crept out the back door, avoiding the cameras. I
kept the curtains closed so that nobody could peer inside. For the
first time in my life I had no more to give. I felt numb, absolutely
devoid of emotion and energy.

Jo Gooding came to see if I was OK. We sat at the kitchen table
and she tried to cheer me up.

'Are they still out there?' I asked.

She opened the curtains a chink.

'Why can't they just leave me alone? What business is it of theirs?'

'They're only interested because of what you've done,' Jo said.
'You act so persecuted all the time, but if you hadn't skippered
Maiden they wouldn't be camped outside.'

Jo was trying to make me feel better, but I totally misunderstood
her. Something snapped inside. I ripped the phone out of the wall
and threw it at her.

'Are you saying it's my fault?' I screamed. 'Are you saying I
deserve this?'

Poor Jo looked dumbstruck. I tore through the house, knocking
over furniture and tearing things apart. I screamed obscenities and
threw things across rooms. 'Why can't people leave me alone?'

Jo ran after me, trying to stop me hurting myself. I turned on her. 'LEAVE ME ALONE!' I screamed. 'GET OUT!'

I ran upstairs to my bedroom and locked the door. I curled up in a corner with my hands shielding my head. Rocking back and forth, I cried and cried.

Jo hammered on the door, pleading with me to let her in. I was talking incoherently and sobbing between words.

'Just go away,' I begged.

'No. Not until you let me in.'

She sat outside the door for what seemed like hours, listening to me crying and speaking softly.

'I can't deal with this any more,' I told her. 'I've tried to be strong. I've tried to keep going . . . can't show any weakness . . .' I dissolved into sobs.

'Right, I've had enough of this,' declared Jo. 'Open this door now or I'll break it down.'

She took me downstairs, poured me a very stiff drink and called Suzy Mayhew, our old schoolmate from Wales. I heard them talking.

'Can you come and get us? I'm bringing Tracy down to Wales. She can't stay here . . . Yeah, it's happened . . . I wondered how long she could keep going . . . She's collapsed.'

Jo started packing me a suitcase.

'I can't. I can't. I have all these talks. I'm committed. Tricia has booked . . .'

'Damn, Tricia. You need to rest.' Jo's anger startled me. 'You've done enough, Tracy. We tried to tell you to slow down, but you wouldn't listen. We've all seen this coming.'

Jo telephoned Tricia. 'Right, cancel everything in the diary for the next month. Tracy's taking a holiday.'

Tricia went berserk. I could hear her arguing down the phone. If it had been me, I'd have backed down, but Jo refused to buckle.

'She's doing nothing for a month. It's killing her.'

She hung up and turned to me.

Meanwhile, Suzy drove for three hours to Southampton. I sat at the kitchen table, feeling totally numb. For the first time in my life I was letting other people completely take control. I didn't know where I was going to go, or what I was going to do.

I had suffered a complete emotional meltdown. My unhappiness was like a real physical pain – a heartache that squeezed my chest until I could barely breathe.

Mild-mannered Jo had taken charge. She poured me another drink and called Mum. Then she managed to reach Simon and told him not to worry. I let her do everything. I didn't care any more.

Suzy arrived and parked out front. Inexplicably, the photographers had gone. It was almost as though they realised that I had surrendered and the chase wasn't fun now. Suzy and Jo led me to the car and put me in the back seat. I leaned my head against the window and closed my eyes.

I remember very little about the drive to Wales. The streetlights reflected on the glass for a few miles and then gave way to the darkness of the countryside. Everything rushed past me, while I sat frozen; my mind locked shut.

Suzy drove to her house in Upper Killay, Swansea. She had always given me somewhere to run away to. Even in those early days, when I argued with Peter, I'd escape to Suzy's house. It felt safe and warm. We sat and talked all night in the sitting room, drinking cups of tea and shedding more tears.

'Right, you'll stay down here for a while,' said Suzy. 'Relax. Chill out. Let everyone else do the worrying for a while.'

'But . . . but . . .'

'Just stop. Don't make excuses. Do as I say.'

Three days later I rented a house in Llangennith and moved in with my things. I called Simon and said that I'd be away for a while. We hadn't officially discussed the fact that our marriage was over, but we both knew it.

'What are you going to do?' he asked.

'I honestly don't know.'

EIGHTEEN

FOR the first time in my life I lived by myself. I'd always been terrified of being on my own, but now I really enjoyed it. I loved the solitude and sense of freedom. I loved being able to lie in bed with the Sunday papers without feeling guilty or having to share them. I could play classical music all day and watch black and white movies on Channel 4.

The house belonged to an old school friend of mine, Sally Price, and was nestled in a little lane that ran from the village to the beach. From the back I could look over the marshes and at the front there were open fields.

Sally's parents, David and Megan, lived next door and I'm sure they were under instructions to keep an eye on me.

After a while Suzy moved in with me. By then I felt like talking and having someone around. We spent many hours swapping memories of the past and mulling over the future.

Going back to Llangennith was like going home. I had never had bad memories of Wales, whereas Mum can't go near the place. I had blanked out all the bad bits. All I remembered were the good times with the likes of Suzy and Jo.

People were so wonderful to me. Even my former tormentors like Nicky Beynon and Sigmonde Wheeler became friends. We'd all grown up and grown old enough to recognise our mistakes. These were nice, simple, down-to-earth people, who didn't bat an eyelid when I turned up. They didn't ask me about *Maiden* or make cracks like, 'Did you leave your boat parked outside?'

I could walk into the King's Head at Llangennith and know every single person there. They ranged in age from Olga in her sixties to the kids of people I'd been to school with. Instead of talking about sailing or boats, I'd hear about how much someone's new tractor cost and what price lambs were fetching.

Paul and Anna, who owned the pub, were determined to make me feel at home. At one point Anna arranged spinning classes in the King's Head on Thursday nights and insisted that I go along. I enjoyed it immensely. These people had an amazing sense of family and of community. I belonged here. They didn't judge me or question my motives: they welcomed me as one of their own.

Up until then all that seemed to exist of me was a boat that had once sailed around the world and the negative publicity that overshadowed its success. I'd grown sick of talking about it. *Maiden* had consumed me. It was my every utterance and random thought. It had become my entire life.

This was my own fault. I had let it happen. I hadn't moved on. I gave the talks and the interviews. I kept the story alive. Although I didn't regret doing *Maiden*, I hated what it had done to me. It had twisted me up inside and made me feel persecuted and ripped to pieces. Never before had I felt sorry for myself.

Maiden had to be left to history. Now it was time to move on.

In Wales I spent my days horse riding and hanging out with Anna Stevens and her Shetland ponies. I took long walks along the beach up on to Rhossilli Down and went climbing to the top of Harding Down where Chris and I had once camped for the summer.

I spent the evening with Suzy, Jill Rees, Mary Nye, Gwenda, Anne Bevan and Jane Whitehead. There is a very strong matriarchal spirit in Llangennith that I'd never noticed before. These women enfolded me in their group and gave me the support I needed to start laughing again.

I still didn't know what to do with the rest of my life. I didn't want to go back to sailing. Maybe it might have been possible if I could have turned back the clock and recreated my life before *Maiden*. I knew that was impossible. Sailing for me would always be different now. It would forever be a competitive thing. It would be something that had to be done on a grand scale rather than boat bumming or day sailing. By the same token, I couldn't see a way forward. What else did I want to do?

I seemed to have stumbled upon this idea of ambition. Up until I began ocean racing there was never any issue of forwards or backwards in my life. I was simply out to have a good time. Now I'd become a thinking person, rather than someone who reacted. I had become a competitor and a team player. *Maiden* had been a battle for women, but I had never seen myself as a crusader of any sort. That took far too much energy. Up until that time I didn't have any strong feelings about equality or fairness. The anger came later when so many companies ignored us, or refused to give us an interview.

If I'd been happy beforehand, I could be happy again. Maybe it was time to walk away. Perhaps all my sailing life had been leading up to this. *Maiden* was the finale rather than the beginning. Now I could now go and do something else.

This didn't seem such a strange thought. Sailing had never been something I had aspired to do from childhood. In many ways I found the idea of starting afresh infinitely more exciting and thought-provoking than sticking around. I could draw a line in the sand and do something new.

If I didn't do this, then my biggest fear was that I'd finish up hating sailing. At that moment I was fed up with boats, and the people who sailed them.

All of this was a blur in my head. The internal dialogue kept bouncing back and forth. I didn't want to rush. I knew I had time. Tricia was pressurising me to go back to work, but I told her to back off.

In the meantime, my only official business was to keep in touch with my solicitors about the libel action.

Simon had been wonderful about the split. When I broke the news I told him, 'I'm leaving Hamble, I'm leaving sailing and I'm afraid you're part of what I'm leaving.'

'Does that mean you want a divorce?'

'I suppose.'

'I don't think I could have gone on for much longer,' he said, grinning.

It was one of those conversations where we laughed through the tears. Really sad, but a huge relief. Both of us had been waiting for someone to say something. We couldn't carry on in the same way.

'Did you always have doubts?' he asked, looking a little sad, but very strong.

'Yes. What about you?'

He nodded.

'Why didn't you say something?'

'Why didn't you?'

I shrugged. 'We should have talked more.'

'Silly buggers.'

It was such a lovely, open and honest talk that we seemed to turn full circle and become friends again. We decided how we'd split everything up and sell the house. Nobody argued or accused. I will always love Simon for that.

By then I'd made my decision not to go back. Tricia was told to cancel all future engagements. She tried to talk me into staying but I'd made up my mind. I'd done enough talking.

The summer of 1991 was when I dropped out of public life and disappeared. I broke with Tricia and I found a place to buy in Wales. At the same time, Mum moved from Hamble to Reading, breaking my last tie with the town.

I never went back. There was a brief flurry of articles about how I'd let people down. A few journalists managed to track me down to Llangennith but the village closed ranks and they never discovered my address. Eventually they stopped looking. I wasn't of interest any more.

The libel action against *Today* dragged on for almost a year before the newspaper settled. It conceded that the story was wrong on all counts – *Maiden* had been anything but a financial triumph and the girls had been well paid. The paper also admitted that I paid tribute to my crew at every opportunity in wages and bonuses. I had never tried to steal the glory, or accept sole credit for what we achieved.

Despite the printed apology and substantial amount of money given to two charities, I didn't feel victorious. Smears and lies can't be wiped out by a few paragraphs buried on page twelve. The wonderful spirit and teamwork that had typified *Maiden* had been tainted. Even worse, the girls had been forced into condemning one of their own.

I had one final lesson to learn about putting trust in people. I lent Tricia McMahon – my agent and friend – a large sum of money when she told me that she might lose her house in a dispute with an insurance company. To this day she has never attempted to repay it.

For the rest of the summer I immersed myself in Welsh village life, which was like a security blanket that kept me safe and warm. Among my new friends was Bev Pritchard who worked as a cook at the King's Head. She was a Welsh farmer's daughter, quite a bit younger than I was, but we shared a love of horses.

The King's Head had a women's darts team. I used to follow them around to their matches against rival pubs. Although I wasn't good enough to play, I enjoyed the laughter and celebrations afterwards. I wondered if I felt more at home in smoky Welsh pubs than I had ever done in Downing Street or dining with princes.

The other thing that struck me had to do with general happiness. I had gone off to see the world, while most of my friends had stayed in Wales. I used to regard them as stick-in-the-muds, who were wasting their lives. Now, surrounded by laughter, I found myself asking, 'Who is the happier?'

In the autumn I began looking for a house to buy. I wanted

somewhere with enough land for me to have horses. This had been a childhood dream of mine.

'Have you thought about College Mill?' said Angela Rees (Chris's mum). 'Gareth Watkins might want to sell.'

'I've never heard of College Mill.'

'Go back into the village, over the bridge and it's along on the right, through the gate.'

'What gate?'

I couldn't believe that I'd lived in Llangennith for so long and not noticed there was a house there. Bev had never heard of it either. She and I went exploring. We walked along the stream that led from the bridge and then hacked through bracken and brambles that tugged at our feet. Suddenly, a waterfall emerged from the undergrowth. It must have been thirty feet high, tumbling into the millpond. The sun filtered through the trees, creating beams and dappled shade. Dragonflies skidded nervously across the surface of the pond. It was like a fairyland from a Lewis Carroll story.

Hacking our way onwards, past the millpond, we emerged in the middle of a pigpen. I think pigs are really cute but they frighten the life out of me. Peter had once owned a wild boar called Honky who was the most terrifying animal in his menagerie.

Putrid mud sucked at our ankles as we backed out and walked around the side. We followed a crooked little path through a crooked little archway, to a crooked little gate. I didn't see the house until we were almost on top of it. Overgrown with brambles and bracken, it was falling down yet I had never seen anything so beautiful.

The original stone was still visible beneath layers of plaster and render. And from the front windows you could see the stream leading to the waterfall.

Bev spied the owner, Gareth Watkins. 'He's dressed,' she declared, sounding relieved. We'd been warned that Gareth liked to wander around naked.

Apart from being a naturist, he also experimented with being self-sufficient. At the back of the cottage he had built a medieval-style house with a barn underneath for the animals. He lived on top, with the animals underneath, using their body heat as a novel form of central heating.

We found Gareth feeding the chickens. He looked like an ageing hippie, with a weathered face and long hair pulled back into a ponytail. He had bright, smiling eyes and was so laid back as to be almost recumbent.

'I hope I'm not being rude, but I heard you were selling the house,' I said. 'I'd like to have first refusal.'

'We haven't quite decided,' said Gareth, sounding quite melancholy. 'Liz and I are splitting up. Depends on what she wants to do.'

Liz was his long-suffering wife. I think she finally got fed up with having chickens and pigs in the house.

'Here's my phone number,' I said, thrusting it into Gareth's hand. 'I'll give you a good price.'

As we walked out the front gate, I still couldn't believe this hidden treasure had been on my doorstep all this time. Nor did I think about how much work it would take to repair it. Here was a house straight out of my childhood. It reminded me of our house on the hill in Llanmadoc – the one Peter had never quite got round to renovating.

I bought College Mill in November 1991. As expected, it was falling down around my ears. Inside it was mouldy and ramshackle. The roof leaked and the only heating was a tiny wood-burning stove. The bathroom window was broken and wind and rain would whip through each time I took a shower. I loved it.

The house had some great stories. One night at the King's Head I got talking to Anna Stevens and we decided on a history project. She would research the pub, while I did College Mill. The search took us to the Bodleian Library in Oxford.

My mill dated back to 1165 and the reign of King Henry II. Much later, it had been owned by one of the Oxford colleges – hence the name. A tithe on the grinding of flour had apparently paid for the college to be built.

At the Bodleian I found a letter from the miller to the Dean of the College. He was complaining that the 'rude and lazy' villagers had failed to clean the millpond, which they were supposed to do by law once a year.

The mill ceased operating in the early 1900s and became a farmhouse. Some unusual people had lived there and at times, judging by the noises at night, I felt as though a few of them had never left.

Prior to Gareth, it had been owned by May and Rodney Williams, a local couple. When Rodney died, May had moved into the village because of her failing eyesight. She still owned most of the fields around the house. I went to see her to ask about buying some land.

She looked ancient, with snow-white hair, pebble glasses and a strong countenance. She had a wicked sense of humour and was quite batty. Although in her eighties, May kept a herd of cows, which she loved more than any creatures except perhaps her dogs. She gave me a glass of sherry – a ritual for visitors – and seemed quite pleased to learn that a woman had bought College Mill.

'I want to keep horses,' I told her when I asked about buying the land.

'Of course, dear,' she said, with a sparkle in her eye. 'As long as you make me a promise.'

'What's that?'

'You'll take me to the horse shows and auctions.'

How could I refuse?

I had always dreamed of having horses. Not just to ride, or to show, or to breed, but because I loved looking at them in the fields.

My equine love affair dated back to the coach house, when I used to imagine that we still had the stables downstairs instead of Dad's workshop. At thirteen I won a competition at the local gymkhana. The prize was £50 or a Welsh mountain pony. Peter was furious when I chose the pony. The little stallion was nothing but trouble. He was forever crawling under fences and sowing his wild oats.

The pony was already too small for me when I won him. I pressed Peter to let me have a proper horse. He eventually agreed – but only if I saved the money and properly fenced the fields. I worked for months and at last saved £65.

Peter took me to a horse auction – a horrible sale where most of the animals were bound for the knacker's yard. A few reasonable horses came in and out but none of them caught my eye. Towards the end of the sale, a bag of skin and bones was led into the ring. His long coat was matted with mud and filth. Ribs stuck out from his sides.

'That poor thing is dog food,' said Peter. Then his head spun as I started bidding against the meat man. 'I'll never understand women,' he muttered.

I bought the two-year-old gelding for £40.

'Why in God's name . . .' asked Peter.

'Because he has lovely eyes.'

I called him Sham and spent the next two years pumping food into him and getting the knots out of his coat. I rode him everywhere – playing Cowboys and Indians on the hill and having races without saddles and bridles.

Until Simon sold the house in Hamble, I didn't have the money to renovate College Mill. So I put buckets under the leaks, plastic over the windows and concentrated instead on the fields. Bev and I fixed the fences and bought my first horses – a stallion called 'The Yob' and a pretty mare called Daisy. Bev and her dad Leighton knew all about breeding and showing horses.

When I got sick of carrying buckets of water, I put water troughs in the fields with a system of pipes running through the hedges. I was out there every day, trudging through the frost and mud in my wellies. I became almost a strange reclusive figure in the village for a while. It's who I wanted to be. Most of the time I looked a complete mess, in mud-stained jeans, with tousled hair and chafed lips from the cold.

At no stage did I regret my decision to go back to Wales. Life on a farm is all about new beginnings. The first time I saw a foal being born, I started to cry. It was the most wonderful thing. It still amazes me, even though I've seen dozens born.

Most of my friends were married and having children. What they were doing seemed a lot more important than what I'd been doing. I felt as though I had moved out of a surreal, alternate universe, back into normality.

One morning during the winter I was feeding the horses when Daisy lashed out at me. She must have glimpsed me from the corner of her eye and thought I was one of the other mares coming to steal her food.

Both her rear feet hit me squarely in the small of my back. I flew ten feet through the air and came down face-first. The pain was indescribable. I lay there, grabbing handfuls of mud and grass, screaming silently. I wanted somebody to put a bullet in my head.

Luckily, Melanie Beynon was with me and she called an ambulance.

This is it, I told myself. I'm paralysed. I concentrated really hard and realised I could still feel my legs. Thank God!

The paramedics had to park on the road and trudge across a muddy field. They arrived to find a madwoman screaming at them not to move her. I didn't want gas or air, or drugs. I had to be awake. I was paranoid that they'd damage my spine if I lost consciousness.

They put a brace on my neck and casing on my back before strapping me to a stretcher. The whole village had heard the news by then. Bev came down from the King's Head and rode in the ambulance with me.

At the hospital they took X-rays and tried to clean me up. I had dried mud from one end to the other. Daisy had cracked two of my vertebrae and chipped my coccyx. The worst damage was to the muscles in my back, according to the doctors.

I spent the next six days flat on my back, floating in a chemical haze of painkillers. Even the drugs couldn't help me when I moved.

'I'd rather be dead than go to the toilet,' I told Suzy, when she came to visit. If I moved even a fraction of an inch, the pain went shooting through me like an electric current. Each time the doctors examined the X-rays they shook their heads in confusion and walked out. Oh great!

If I could lie in bed, I might as well be at home, I decided. First I had to prove to the staff that I could walk from one end of the ward to the other. With a Zimmer frame it took me thirty minutes.

At College Mill it took me an hour to get from the house to the mailbox and back again. This was using two walking-sticks and a geriatric shuffle. Bev, Jill and Suzy did my shopping for me and Bev fed the horses. Mary would come down with food she'd cooked, or take me to the pub.

The doctors had failed to realise that my hip had been dislocated. The truth didn't emerge until six months after the accident when I visited a chiropractor. By then the joints had calcified and I'd found a way of walking that compensated for the pain. When the hip was put back in place, I could walk normally again. Unfortunately, the delay guaranteed that I'd have back problems for the rest of my life.

By the following summer Simon had managed to sell the house in Hamble so I could start work on the cottage. Dick Barrow came with his digger and his workmen. First they cleared the undergrowth and tore down the old shacks and barns. Decades of junk had built up under the mud. We took a dozen skips of rubbish out of the place, along with the rusting shells of abandoned vehicles.

Trevor came down to stay and I put him to work. Inside the cottage, we ripped out pine cladding and the foam insulation behind it. The foam was networked with a thousand rat runs.

I had an architect draw up designs. He told me to take the banks of soil away from around the cottage because moisture had been pouring inside. We took the rendering from the walls. It was like opening a can of worms.

The roof had to be replaced, but once we took it off, the walls started to crumble. The roof had obviously been the only thing holding the place together. I had no choice but to demolish the cottage, numbering each stone. Then the builders put it back together again piece by piece like a three-dimensional jigsaw.

Not every discovery proved to be disastrous. Beneath the revolting brick hearth with a plastic beam we discovered a magnificent inglenook fireplace. And under the kitchen floor we found the old millstones.

It took more than a year to fix up the cottage. I also rebuilt the stables and barns, with the help of friends and acquaintances. I did a lot of the work myself because I had the time. I wasn't doing anything else except raising the horses.

During the haymaking season, all my friends would come and help, including some that had known me from sailing. Few of them knew what to make of the girl with grubby jeans, short hair and wellingtons. I looked more like a farmer than a skipper.

My new life was tremendously therapeutic and satisfying. But showing horses wasn't likely to make me any money. I had enough to last me a couple of years. Then I'd have to think about finding another source of income.

I had dropped out of public life so completely that people questioned where I had gone. Some assumed I was off sailing on distant oceans, or planning a long-term project.

My walls of privacy were thicker than the stone of the cottage and two years slipped by in the windswept beauty of Gower. I raised my horses and watched the seasons slip by. Perhaps things would have stayed that way, if I hadn't run short of money. At that time I had a call from Will Carling, the England rugby captain. I'd met Will at Downing Street a few years earlier and I'd also bumped into him later when I was giving a talk.

'How would you like to do some work for me?' he now asked.

'Doing what?'

'I've heard you talking. You're very good.'

Will had recently set up a company called Insights which was based on the premise that sports people have a lot to teach business people about teamwork, motivation and leadership skills.

I arranged to meet him in London, along with Jim Foley, who was running the company. 'You have to angle your talks a bit better,' Will explained. 'If you could draw out some of the things that you only hint at, we could really use you.'

By this he meant focusing on those areas of *Maiden* and the Whitbread which dealt with things like teamwork and leadership. How did I motivate the crew? What were the most difficult challenges? How did we overcome them by working together?

Already he had a strong list of speakers including Adrian Moorhouse, Gary Lineker and Mary Peters. I liked the fact that the talks were structured and more constructive. In the past, I'd tended to meander through stories, without any framework or particular message.

It was the summer of 1993. I was ready to go back into the big wide world again, albeit carefully. Softly, softly, this time, Tracy.

I began by doing two or three seminars a month. The money was so good I didn't need to do any more. The new talks had an added bonus. For the first time I had to consider why we'd been successful. What had made us a winning team? Why had I been a successful leader?

It wasn't a case of simply talking about *Maiden*. This was just the backdrop. Instead I spoke about interesting things that had happened in my sailing career that had taught me lessons.

The bitterness had gone. I no longer resented the questions, or regretted things that had happened. I began to realise that a handful of tiny incidents had coloured my view. Jo had been right. Each time I tended to over-react and feel persecuted.

Now I felt focused and calm. I could live happily in my Welsh bolt-hole, surrounded by old friends, and venture out every so often to give a talk. Even the miles of travelling didn't bother me. I now had a direction.

My favourite season on the Gower is winter. It is a wild, bleak and grey place with storms that come straight in from the Atlantic.

The wind whips the sea into a wild foaming monster that pounds the beach.

Standing on Rhossilli Down one afternoon, bent against the wind, I watched one of these storms. I looked towards the sea, with eyes squinted as though I could see a place a thousand miles away. The cold wrapped its fingers around my neck and sheets of spray slanted sideways, stinging my cheeks and eyelids.

Another year had slipped away. As much as I loved my life, I felt a strange longing. I still wasn't completely happy.

I remembered when Suzy's mother had read my tarot cards after *Maiden*. I was still a total sceptic, but the same thing happened as before – the last card she turned up was the picture of a man in ermine robes, standing on the parapet of a castle. He held a globe of the world in his hands, but looked past it towards his estates that stretched into the distance.

She had told me that no matter how much I achieved in my life, I'd never truly be happy. There would always be something more – something I couldn't get.

I'd once felt quite pleased to get such a card, but Suzy's mum had warned me to try to change it. Now I understood why. To be constantly searching for something more is a curse.

I watched the white water and foam spill over jagged rocks. Great white-tipped rollers arced upwards and smashed down, exploding into a fine mist that blurred the air. Once the sea has wormed its way into your heart and soul, there is no escape. You can pretend you don't care but it never leaves you alone. I found myself thinking about sailing again. I loved my farmhouse and my horses, but I needed something more.

I gave up trying to rationalise it. The best answer I could find was that I needed to be challenged. When my life becomes too comfortable I start to panic. I start looking for a new assignment and feel almost frightened of what might happen to me if I don't find one.

Now I began to wonder if I was ready to do another Whitbread round the world race. Perhaps I could get that first place instead of second. Or maybe I could skipper a maxi. We had come second on *Maiden*. I needed to come first.

I got back in touch with Howard, whom I'd missed a great deal. He was working with the British skipper Lawrie Smith on a current Whitbread project. The race was due to start in just a few months.

'I think I'm ready to come back,' I said.

'What do you want to do?'

'I don't know yet. I'm just sounding people out.'

A few weeks later I had a call from TVS, a regional television network that had planned a series of regular reports on the Whitbread. I was asked to be a guest commentator and I jumped at the opportunity. For one thing, I knew many of the people competing. It also gave me the chance to slip quietly back into the sailing scene.

Some of the reactions to my reappearance were amazing. People thought I must have dropped off the planet. 'One minute you were here and the next you were gone,' they said. 'We almost put out a missing persons report.'

Nobody could believe that I hadn't been sailing for nearly four years.

I enjoyed commentating on the race, although I found it strange being on the outside instead of competing. Being part of the media gave me a different perspective. I had never regarded journalists as 'the enemy', but when skippering *Maiden* I sometimes felt they didn't understand the pressures of such a punishing race. It is very easy to sit on the sidelines and be judgmental.

Now I was part of this same machine. I had to comment on the racing and various tactics adopted by the skippers. This meant making judgements and pointing out poor decisions. I tried hard to be as fair as possible, but TV producers see the world in black and white. Somebody has to be wrong and somebody right. There are no shades of grey.

'Sorry, life isn't like that,' I explained. 'Sailing isn't like that. A poor decision today could look like a stroke of genius in a week's time. This isn't like a soccer game. It lasts nine months.'

We filmed the programme at a different location each week. In between footage of the boats and commentary, I picked various topics to focus upon, like foul weather gear, food and safety. Surprisingly, I didn't feel any twinges of envy or desire to be wet, cold and miserable. This wasn't *my* race. Maybe next time I'd be out there.

I was beginning to see my time in Wales as a hiccup rather than a full stop. It was time to dust off my deck shoes. Howard, unfortunately, was committed to Lawrie Smith.

I called a couple of the girls to sound them out. Tanja was married with kids and Dawn was running her own America's Cup project. Others had serious boyfriends and promising careers.

I thought about single-handed sailing but gave that idea up quickly. I'd get too lonely. My only option was to put together a new crew.

The more I thought about it, the less convinced I was about doing another Whitbread. The politics and the stopovers were the main drawbacks. There were always people making rules and others trying to bend them. PR people battled with race people because their agendas were never the same. On the water it is just about sailing, but on the land there are all these other pressures.

Some of the legs of the Whitbread had grown ridiculously short because so many cities wanted to host the fleet. In the previous race the yachts had sprinted 350 miles – one day's sailing – between stopovers. It was hardly worth setting off.

Although the stopovers are great for the parties and making repairs, they are lousy for team building. The endless internal niggles that brew on a boat always come to a head on land. Partners and spouses arrive, pulling the crew in different directions. It's hard to keep focused.

The only way of bettering what *Maiden* had done was to win the whole Whitbread. This was certainly possible, but did I really want to deal with all the politics again? What were my other options? A different challenge. A new quest.

The real magic of the Whitbread for me had been the marathon six- and seven-week slogs. I wanted to spend more time at sea, not less. There had to be something out there like that.

In November 1994 Howard and I went to the Yachtsman of the Year awards at the Dorchester in London. Sir Robin Knox-Johnston and Sir Peter Blake shared the honour for their record-breaking non-stop circumnavigation of the world. I'd been so cut off from sailing in Wales, I hadn't even realised they'd made an attempt (two, in fact).

On a giant screen above the stage, images of the voyage were being shown. A giant catamaran, *Enza*, skipped across the water like a flat stone. It reached astonishing speeds, with water vibrating against the twin hulls and the wind generator propellers blurring until they became invisible.

Wow!

Peter Blake was interviewed. His eyes lit up as he talked about sailing the catamaran through the Southern Ocean. Despite all the dangers, it sounded like the most fun you could have with your clothes on.

I was sold. The challenge became clear. I wanted to break the world record with an all-female crew.

NINETEEN

S IR Robin Knox-Johnston was building a wall outside his cottage in Devon when I arrived. He seemed happy to have a distraction. With his bushy grey-flecked beard and curly hair he looked part man and part teddy bear.

'It's going to be dangerous,' he said, washing dirt from his calloused hands. 'It takes huge skill and concentration to sail a multihull in the Southern Ocean.'

'I want to break the record,' I said, boldly. I thought he'd tell me I was crazy, or to go back to Wales. Instead, he motioned me to follow him inside.

'You'll need the right boat. You should buy *Enza*. She'll need a refit.' He paused and glanced affectionately at a photograph of the big catamaran on the wall of his office. 'I don't know where you'll find the crew. Very few men have sailed a boat like that, let alone women.'

'We'll just have to learn.'

Sir Robin gave me a potted history of the Jules Verne Trophy. It had been created by a group of French sailors at a meeting in Paris in 1990. They issued a challenge to sail around the world non-stop in the fastest time possible. The French Ministry of Culture assumed patronage of the challenge and commissioned American sculptor Tom Shannon to make a trophy.

The first attempt at the record was almost a match-race between two huge catamarans, *Enza* and *Commodore Explorer*. They left in January 1993, racing across the Equator into the South Atlantic. Twenty-six days into the voyage, *Enza* hit a whale or floating debris and was forced to retire.

Peter and Robin were bitterly disappointed. They watched as Bruno Peyron, a Frenchman, took the Jules Verne Trophy. *Commodore Explorer* circled the world in 79 days, 6 hours, 15 minutes and 56 seconds.

Enza was shipped to New Zealand for modifications. Scoops were added to the sterns of both hulls, along with an impact skin beneath the waterline to protect against damage. In total, 12 feet were added to the 'big cat'.

A year later, on 16 January 1994, she set out again. This time her competition was a trimaran, *Lyonnaise Dumez des Eaux*, skippered by Olivier de Kersauson, another Frenchman. After a phenomenally quick start, Peter and Robin narrowly managed to hold their lead and *Enza* took the trophy in 74 days, 22 hours, 17 minutes and 22 seconds.

'It was 50 per cent fear and 50 per cent exhilaration,' said Robin, who likened the challenge to a Grand Prix that lasted for two and a half months.

Every element of the challenge excited me – the raw speed; the months at sea; the racing of the clock. Even so, a lot of the questions still had to be answered. Not least of them concerned money. For *Maiden* I had to raise £1.2 million. For the new challenge, I estimated, I would need £3.2 million.

Surely it wouldn't be as difficult this time. For one thing, I wouldn't have to face the same prejudices about women and sailing.

The entire project existed on a few pages of my notebook. First, I put together a list of companies to approach for sponsorship. In between feeding horses and repairing fences, I started making calls.

I was right about doors being open to me. I had no trouble arranging meetings. Unfortunately, I had no control over the

economic climate. The recession had started to bite and corpora-
tions were tightening belts. I sat in dozens of boardrooms and made
my pitch. Each time the answer was the same. Part of the problem
was getting people to visualise what they were investing in. The
idea of a yacht the size of a tennis court, with a ten-storey-high
mast was beyond their comprehension. No amount of line drawings or photographs could help me. Even more so than with
Maiden, I needed to show people a boat.

Early in November 1995 I called Nigel Irens, who had helped us
refit *Maiden*, on the off chance that he might know of something
for sale.

'*Enza* goes on the market tomorrow,' he said. 'Why don't you
give Ed Danby a call?'

Ed, a loud, flamboyant Kiwi, had crewed on *Enza* when she
broke the Jules Verne record in 1994. Later he skippered the big
catamaran, which was now based in San Diego, California. My
phone call caught Ed just as he was about to go sailing with a
potential buyer.

'How much is she?' I asked.

'£430,000.'

'Don't do anything until I talk to you.'

A week later I flew to San Diego. There were millions of dollars'
worth of yachts lined up at the marina, each a little bigger than the
next. I walked down the dock and marvelled at the clean lines and
polished decks.

The tide was half out, so that *Enza* lay beneath me. I gasped
out loud. Ed laughed. The catamaran was like nothing I'd ever
seen before. She seemed impossibly big with a carbon fibre
mast raked back at such an extraordinary angle that at first I
wondered how it could possibly stand up. The twin hulls were
like enormous missiles, joined by three cross-beams with green
netting strung in between. A central pod housed the nav
station.

None of the photographs or videos could do justice to the
catamaran. She was like a huge cat, coiled and ready to pounce.

Rather than mooring her to the dock, they had tied her down to stop her getting away.

As I gazed at *Enza* and walked her decks, I sensed that she was sizing me up as well. Probably thinking: God she looks a bit small to skipper me. I'll eat her for breakfast.

'So what do you think?' asked Ed.

I couldn't answer him. It was one of those very rare times in my life when I didn't know what to say.

Ed had gathered a crew together and arranged to go sailing. Once aboard, I watched in astonishment as he used the two little Yamaha engines, attached to the aft end of each hull, to delicately manoeuvre this monster away from the dock. Then we motored out of the inner harbour and I helped pull up the mainsail, which took six of us.

Then as Ed turned her away from the wind, he cut the engines and the headsail was unfurled. The next few moments will stay with me for ever. In 16 knots of breeze, we accelerated to 17 knots in a matter of seconds. I couldn't believe it! It takes a hell of a lot more breeze to get a monohull moving at that speed.

Enza glided over the water so effortlessly it felt like we were flying.

'Do you want to steer?' he asked.

I nodded like a schoolgirl.

Bracing myself, I gripped the wheel and was amazed at the ease of hydraulic steering and how responsive she was for a yacht that size. My monohull days were over.

It wasn't just the speed, although that was a part of it. On *Maiden* when we managed to do 17 knots it meant squeezing every knot out of her downwind or beating our brains out upwind with the boat heeled over on its side. It was a white-knuckle ride on the wheel with the crew looking at each other as if to say, 'My God, we're all going to die!'

Enza made 17 knots seem effortless. There was a magic, or indefinable something, about her that grabbed my heart and I felt the same excitement and exhilaration as I had ten years earlier when I first went sailing.

'There's no going back now,' Ed said, and he was right.

Two hours later, moored at the marina, he took me below decks. Up forward in both bows were the storage areas – great caverns into which food and spares are packed for long journeys. The port hull housed the galley – a rather grand description for little more than a two-burner stove and a sink – as well as the tiniest sleeping area for three people that I'd ever seen. The starboard hull contained three more bunks crammed into a tiny sleeping area. They could be hitched up and secured against the inside of the hull to create a few more precious feet. The head was so small I had difficulty imagining how a man could fit inside.

I was also surprised by how few sails *Enza* carried and their range. On *Maiden* we had taken twenty-six sails on each leg, changing them at each stopover depending on the weather conditions. *Enza* had only nine. Again this showed how efficiently she used the breeze.

The big catamaran had originally been built in 1983 for Canadair, a small aircraft manufacturer. Originally called *Tag*, it had been 80 feet long and rigged for single-handed sailing. The skipper Mike Birch hoped to break a lot of the single-handed speed records.

Apart from adding 12 feet to the twin hulls, Peter and Robin had also designed a central pod that acted as the nav station. It had two bunks for the skipper and navigator, as well as a chart table, generator controls and space for the array of comms and navigation equipment. The capsule had been nicknamed the 'God Pod' by the crew of *Enza*. This is because of the well-known yachting fact that God has an identity crisis – he thinks he is Peter Blake.

Where was I going to find £430,000?

Back in England, I mulled over the problem and began doing sums. Mum and Trevor acted as a sounding board.

'Please don't say you've mortgaged the farmhouse,' said Mum.

'I don't have a choice.'

She pressed her hands into her lap to keep them still. 'Exactly how dangerous is this voyage?'

'More difficult than *Maiden*,' I admitted, trying to be as non-committal as possible. 'If we have the right training we can do it.'

Mum sighed. 'Well, you've done it before. If you want it badly enough I know you'll do it again.'

Trevor thought I was completely mad, which is why he loved the idea so much. He'd just volunteered to drive aid trucks to Bosnia for a charity called the Serious Road Trip. Both of us would be risking our lives, although his was obviously the more worthy cause.

By mortgaging the farmhouse and borrowing from friends I raised more than half of the money, but I was still £186,000 short. The broker arranging the sale drew up a contract involving a series of payments. That would, hopefully, give me time to raise the rest.

Making the first payment of £44,000 was the worst moment. I knew that if I couldn't make the final instalment, I'd lose my house and my friends' money. It wasn't until a fortnight before the due date that I found the final amount. I read an article in *Country Life* about a prominent businessman and philanthropist who looked just mad enough to lend me the money.

I wrote to him explaining the project and he immediately posted a cheque for £5,000 for the yacht survey. Eventually, he couldn't stand me writing to him any more and phoned me unexpectedly one night in Wales.

'Is that Miss Edwards?' said a strange voice.

'Yes,' I said tentatively.

'You are the most annoying bloody woman I've ever come across.'

'I beg your pardon?'

'This is the poor sod you've been writing to for the past six months. How much more do you need?'

I blurted out, '£186,000.'

Right. Call my solicitor in the morning and get him to draw up a contract. I'm lending you the money. It's to remain strictly between us – no publicity – and I want it paid back in a year. OK?'

'Yes. Thank you. Thank you so much.' I started babbling and getting tearful. 'Can I ask you why?' I said.

'My solicitor tells me you can do this. He followed your voyage on *Maiden*.'

The call ended as abruptly as it started. I've never revealed my benefactor's name, but he's become a dear friend. I won't forget how he believed in me, despite never having met me.

At the end of March 1996, almost eighteen months after first contemplating the project and six months after deciding to buy *Enza*, I flew to San Diego and handed over the final cheque. I was now the excited owner of the biggest, fastest catamaran in the world.

Ed had agreed to be my project manager, responsible for the shore crew and the enormous logistical support we needed to reach the starting line. Hopefully, this would allow me to concentrate on pure sailing and finding the right crew. The initial challenge was to get *Enza* back to England. Because she didn't sail to windward, we couldn't take her through the Panama Canal – the quickest way home. Instead we decided to ship her as far as Florida and then sail her across the Atlantic.

This meant finding a container ship and the money to pay for it – a terrifying £80,000. I also had to find wages for Ed and arrange for him to move his wife and two young children to England. So many people were starting to rely upon me that I began to wonder. Had I gambled too much? Would I let them down?

My worst memories of *Maiden* and the mountain of debts came flooding back. I thrust them to the back of my mind and focused on the end goal. If I closed my eyes I could visualise us crossing the finishing line – the sea state, the colour of the sky, the helicopters buzzing overhead. I could picture it all.

While waiting for *Enza* to arrive in Florida, I flew back to England and continued the search for sponsorship. Four weeks later I returned to America to help sail her across the Atlantic. I needed the multihull experience. Jo Gooding left her job in Swansea to come with me and I also managed to recruit Angus Buchanan and Paul Standbridge, both of whom had sailed on *Enza* on separate record attempts. Ed met me at the airport at Fort Lauderdale.

'I've got some more bad news,' he said.

My heart sank.

'We had an electrical storm last night. Lightning struck the mast. The power surge has blown out all the navigational instruments.'

I relaxed. After the financial storm I'd weathered, a lightning bolt was a minor problem.

It took four days to get the big catamaran ready for an Atlantic crossing. I'd decided to rename her *Lady Endeavour* until a sponsor could be found. Early in the evening on 20 June, we untied the lines and motored out of Fort Lauderdale.

'Forget everything you know about sailing,' Ed told me, as we set the main. 'You have to start from scratch. Empty your mind and feel the boat.'

My heart beat a little faster with a mixture of fear and exhilaration. With my legs braced apart, I felt as though I should be strapped into a seat with a full harness, like in a racing car.

Digital numbers flashed up on the cockpit console – information about wind angles and speed. These had to be assessed in a split second, along with the waves in front and behind.

'Never stand in front of someone on the helm,' Ed said. 'They have to *feel* the wind on their face.'

I thought he was joking at first, but again he was right. Sailing the 'big cat' was entirely different from a monohull. I had a lot to learn.

For the first two days I was sick as a dog. It had been four years since I'd done any offshore sailing. We slipped easily into the watches. Jo and I had to get used to hauling sails around the netting and fell over loads of times. It was impossible to look cool on this boat because it moved so erratically.

We arrived at Falmouth harbour on the south-west coast of England, eleven days after leaving Florida. Our average speed on the crossing had been 15 knots, and that was without even trying.

Next morning, I drove up to Hamble to sort out accommodation. I managed to book everyone into a hotel for the first few nights and then found a flat to rent. I also rented a small office at

Hamble Point marina, where *Lady Endeavour* took up most of the outside dock. There was one desk, a chair, a phone, a fax and a word processor. We were ready for business.

Charlotte Buchanan, Angus's wife, had helped with the PR and marketing for *Enza*'s voyages. She now joined us to handle media and marketing. Sue Snow became the office secretary. We soon expanded into the next-door office and bought some second-hand desks and chairs.

By then I'd rented a house in Hamble for myself. The money situation hadn't improved but I took out a debenture against my company, Lady Endeavour Ltd, so I could borrow to keep things going.

Des Holmes, my bank manager at the Royal Bank of Scotland, was a pillar of strength. He and the bank worked hard to keep me solvent, as months went by without sponsorship. My only income was from the motivational talks I gave for Insight. Putting together a project of this scale meant I had to be a businesswoman, a PR expert, a management guru and a money-raising wizard. Unfortunately, I'm none of these things, but I did have the courage to ask people for help. Howard gave me a lot of advice, but he was still committed to another fund-raising campaign. I also called on other contacts from my *Maiden* days.

My first break came at a lunch for high-flyers in the City. I sat next to the managing director of Informix, an American computer software company. He expressed an interest in the project and we arranged a meeting at his offices.

Two weeks later I had a letter of intent from his marketing director. Although a contract hadn't been negotiated, I went ahead and borrowed enough money for the refit. I was about to learn another very big lesson about trusting people.

In the meantime, *Lady Endeavour* had her mast removed and early one morning a massive crane plucked her from the water. Without her rigging, she looked like a huge platform. We had a line tied to each corner, with someone hanging on each end. The catamaran weighed only nine tons and she swayed precariously.

After a lot of shouting and cursing, she finally settled on to the trolley cradles. It took another two hours and more cursing before we steered her to the entrance of the boat shed. By now a crowd had gathered to stare at this freakish craft.

My car was driven beneath her twin hulls and we tied the trolleys to the tow bar. *Lady Endeavour* was slowly pulled into place as the crowd of onlookers broke into applause. We all took a bow and retired to the pub for lunch.

The refit team comprised Brian Wallis, a laid-back Tasmanian and master mariner; Dave White, an expert Kiwi rigger; and Dog, an Australian accountant who wanted to be a sailor.

First they had to make sure that structurally *Lady Endeavour* could withstand the punishment of another circumnavigation. This meant stripping the paint off the hulls and checking every inch of the framework.

Each padeye, screw, shackle, block, winch, pump and piece of rigging had to be examined, improved or replaced. At the same time, the new deck fittings were set up in a more practical way, making the boat easier to sail.

New ropes and sheets were ordered and all the electronics in the nav station were replaced except for the radar and SSB radio which were the best available and virtually indestructible. We also changed the batteries, threw out the weather fax and installed laptops and a new satellite weather system.

With the help of Nigel Irens, who had originally designed the catamaran, we managed to remove two tons of weight and hopefully increase her speed. Her performance in light airs had not been good, according to Peter Blake, and could be improved. None of these changes made her any easier to live on – she was built for speed, not comfort.

After three months of work and £350,000, *Lady Endeavour* was ready to be relaunched and the mast put in place. Unfortunately, she wasn't going anywhere. I didn't have the money to pay the yard bill.

Inexplicably, our would-be sponsor, Informix, had gone

strangely quiet. Warning bells began to ring. I couldn't get hold of anybody at the company. Every telephone call and letter went unanswered. I cajoled, pleaded and threatened. *Lady Endeavour* was ready to launch, but without the promised money the project would collapse. Already I owed £900,000.

Finally, I gave the company until the close of business on 31 October to make the first payment. I sat in the office that day watching the clock tick past 5 p.m., waiting for the phone to ring. It didn't happen. Charlotte went over to the marina bar and bought two cases of beer. We drowned our sorrows and discussed our options.

We didn't have enough time to find a sponsor for an attempt on the Jules Verne in the coming January. To have come so far and achieved so much, it was heartbreaking to contemplate failure. I couldn't give up now. Defeat wasn't an option. I *had* to find the money.

With the help of Des Holmes and the bank, we worked out a strategy to keep the project ticking over. If I couldn't find sponsorship within three months, I'd lose my home, the boat and the life savings of many good friends. I felt sick.

I needed a slice of luck, or another mysterious benefactor. My 'angel' came in the rather strange guise of Andy Miller, a middle-aged businessman who ran a highly successful management consultancy company, Impact Plus.

Andy read an interview in the *Financial Times* and phoned the office in Hamble. I was understandably cautious of strangers bearing gifts, but I liked Andy's easy confidence and charm. He had a real enthusiasm for what I'd done with *Maiden*.

'I owe more than a million pounds,' I told him. 'I have two months to find the money, or I lose everything – even my friends.'

'We can't have that happen, can we?' He laughed. 'I can list ten companies who I think should sponsor you. Will you let me approach them?'

'What makes you think . . .?'

'This is a global event. You need a sponsor with global operations. Someone who can benefit from international exposure.'

A month later, Andy called again. 'I think I've found you a
sponsor. It's an international insurance company, Royal & Sun
Alliance. They've just merged and they want to advertise the fact
by sponsoring something global. They want to come and see you
before Christmas. Is that all right?'

I tried not to get too excited. I'd been here before. Yet somehow
I sensed that Andy had done it. My voice began to break. 'I will
never be able to thank you enough for this.'

'Yes you will,' said Andy. 'You can take me sailing.'

The following week I met Martin Booth the marketing manager
of Royal & SunAlliance (RSA) and Robin Courage from Atkinson
Courage, the PR company that would assess the sponsorship
proposal.

I watched closely as they first glimpsed the boat. They reacted
with a mixture of astonishment and awe. I'd started judging people
by their first response to the catamaran. If they didn't stare in
wonder and utter appropriate expletives, then I doubted if they had
a heart beating inside them.

Martin and Robin left Hamble loaded down with information.
They wanted to speak to people like Sir Peter Blake and Robin
Knox-Johnston. Did *they* think we were up to the challenge?

I had no money to buy Christmas presents that year. Nobody
minded, of course. The day was more than about giving gifts.

It was Aunt Edna's turn to host the family, which worked out
well because my house in Hamble was too small for all of us. As
usual Mum and I arrived early and made a nuisance of ourselves
while Edna fussed over a lunch that was like a work of art.
Meanwhile, Uncle Arthur cracked jokes and kept the drinks
topped up. Traditionally, after lunch we played a game of charades.

Sadly, there were two important people missing from the
celebrations. Trevor and our cousin Graeme were in Split waiting
for a shipment to arrive, which they would then drive to one of the

remote areas of Bosnia. It was dangerous work, but they managed to call from their base to wish us all a Merry Christmas.

Trevor was in great form, despite being in a place without electricity, food or alcohol. It sounded dismal but they laughed it off. I said a silent prayer for them.

On Boxing Day my cousin Gregor came to visit with his girlfriend Kerry and Kaia their little girl. Watching Kaia running about the house in a Christmas hat reminded me that there is more to life than racing around the world.

I even felt a pang of regret. I couldn't imagine myself having a child. A part of me wished that I could be like Gregor, Kerry and Kaia, who seemed so happy and secure with each other. If only I could be two different people. One of me could go sailing off around the world while the other stayed at home and raised a family.

I'm not saying it's right or wrong to go sailing in the Southern Ocean if you have young children. It's simply something that I couldn't imagine doing. It wouldn't be fair. What if something happened to me?

Back at work in the New Year, I began discussions with RSA at the company's head office in the City of London. The conference room was the size of my house.

Right from the outset, I knew we were starting negotiations from a less than favourable position. My solicitors at Denton Hall – Adrian Barr-Smith and Nick Fitzpatrick – nearly choked when I told them how much money I owed.

Secondly, we found a totally unexpected threat from a woman lawyer who worked in the PR field. She had approached me at about the same time as Andy Miller and asked for permission to look for sponsorship. The deal was fairly standard – she would get ten per cent of any money she found us. If someone else raised the money she would get nothing.

Without telling any of us, she had taken a job with Atkinson Courage, the PR company who would judge our bid for sponsorship. Despite the fact that Andy had arranged the introduction to RSA, she suddenly claimed that she deserved her finder's fee of ten per cent.

I couldn't believe it. Even before our negotiations started, I had a bizarre threat hanging over me of court action. And the woman trying to cash in was working for the company that had to judge our bid.

She knew how much we had put into this. She knew how hard we had worked and how much money I owed. Yet she was willing to jeopardise our big chance by making ridiculous claims. It was one of the worst examples of human behaviour that I had ever seen.

After several long meetings with RSA, I knew our fate would depend upon a boardroom vote on Friday 10 January. The lawyer had refused to concede, but had decided not to press her claim. In the meantime, I borrowed more money from the bank. In for a penny, in for a pound.

On the day of the board meeting, lone yachtsman Tony Bullimore was rescued from his upturned yacht *Exide Challenger* in the Southern Ocean. His keel had snapped in a savage storm during the Vendée Globe Single-Handed Race. Bullimore had sheltered for four days in a tiny air pocket beneath the hull. The pictures of his amazing rescue flashed around the world.

My heart sank.

'Oh, well, that's it,' I muttered. 'They won't give us the money now. They'll be thinking, What if someone dies on the voyage? What if they have to be rescued? The negative publicity would far outweigh the advantages.'

I sat in the office in Hamble waiting for the call. For most of the day there seemed to be a subdued hush over the marina. People who knew about the negotiations kept calling, hoping for news. Andy Miller phoned at least ten times, willing me to say yes.

'Sorry, Andy, still no word.'

We waited until six o'clock and then decided to leave. Clearly, the decision had been delayed. As I turned to leave, the telephone rang. A dozen people held their breath as I spoke to Martin. I must have been in shock because my face betrayed nothing. Slowly I put the phone down.

Charlotte could barely speak. Her voice squeaked, 'Well?'

I tossed my head back and screamed, 'WE GOT IT!'

The entire marina and half of Hamble must have heard the cheer. The office erupted in pandemonium. I laughed and cried at the same time – my favourite emotion.

Throughout 1996 the crew had been taking shape. Most of the girls had been recommended to me, or had heard about the project through word of mouth. I may not be the best sailor in the world but I have a knack for recognising others who are. This now served me well.

Maiden had been an exercise in making things up as we went along, but this time I chose my crew in a more structured way – picking the right people for the right job. I had also learned from experience that building a team is more important than hand-picking individuals.

Miki Von Koskull had sailed with me on *Maiden*. She's one of the most experienced yachtswomen on the planet, but took a lot of convincing to come with me now. 'I don't need to be wet, cold and miserable again,' she told me, being totally honest. That's the difference between Miki and me: she has a clear recollection of the horrible bits whereas I forget them and remember the good times.

Miki also had a chronic back problem, the legacy of a sport where you are constantly off balance and being jarred by the pitching of the boat.

I respected Miki's decision, but I really needed her experience, so I set about trying to wear down her resolve. Ultimately, I didn't convince her until I found my navigator. Adrienne Cahalan, an outspoken Australian, is arguably the finest female navigator in the world.

Miki was still wavering about coming with us, but finally told me, 'If you get Adrienne, I'll come.'

'You really feel that strongly about her?'

'I do.'

I faxed Adrienne in Sydney. She must have been standing by the machine because a minute later the fax came back. She had scrawled across the bottom, 'Yes, please'.

A taxi pulled up outside the crew house in Hamble a week later. Adrienne was sitting in the back. 'G'day, sorry it took me so long.'

What struck me first about her was her size. Apart from being tiny (half an inch taller than I am) she is so slight that I thought she might blow away in the first strong breeze. I couldn't have been more wrong.

Helena Darvelid had joined us soon after the delivery voyage from America. Friends had recommended her because of her experience on multihulls. She held the Round Britain and Ireland record and also the Round Isle of Wight record – both set on catamarans. Helena is every man's dream of what a Swedish girl looks like – blonde, blue-eyed and absolutely gorgeous. More importantly, she is also beautiful on the inside.

My other watch captain, Emma Westmacott, was probably the best all-round sailor on the boat. She came from a cruising background, just as I did, but it had left a chip on Emma's shoulder. Part of her wished that she'd risen through the ranks of yacht clubs and regatta racing – a more prestigious climb to the top. A legacy of this was that she constantly attempted to prove herself, when all of us knew she was a brilliant sailor.

'The young ones' – my collective term for Sam Davies, Emma Richards and Sharon Ferris – used to tire me out with their boundless energy and appalling taste in music. Emma was the baby at twenty-three, six months younger than Sam and eight months younger than Sharon.

Sam was the real party girl among them. Tall, slim, blonde and very pretty, she looked like a fashion model and would go out clubbing until the wee hours. Then she'd turn up for work the next morning still in her miniskirt and high heels.

Yet Sam was far more than just a pretty face. She had an

engineering degree from Cambridge University and had been sailing since the age of four. I gave Sam the role of 'rigger' – arguably the most highly regarded job on a yacht because of the danger associated with working 100 feet above the deck. It can be a terrifying place to be when the boat is powered up and the mast is moving in all directions. Just getting up there – strapped in a tiny harness – requires enormous skill, courage and strength.

Sharon Ferris had made her name as a dinghy sailor competing internationally and in the Olympics. Her name had been mentioned to me, but I didn't know how to get hold of her. Then totally by chance she phoned me in Hamble.

'You don't know me, I'm Sharon Ferris. I was just wondering if you have any crew places left?'

My first thought was, My God, what an appalling accent!

A few days later Sharon, our first New Zealander, swept into the office like a Force Seven gale – larger than life, breathlessly excited and very loud. She made a huge impact on all of us and when she left everything seemed so quiet. We needed size and strength on the boat – someone exactly like Sharon. In addition, she was an excellent sailmaker, who could make running repairs during the voyage.

Despite being the 'baby' of the crew Emma Richards had an impressive sailing record. She'd taken part in junior world championships at the age of twelve and later captained the Scottish Universities team. Initially, I thought she was too young, but Emma persevered. She turned up unannounced at the office – a pretty girl with a sprinkle of freckles on her nose – and tried hard to convince me, every day for a month.

'I'm so desperate to do this. I think I'd be really good . . . I'm hard working . . . I listen to people . . . I pick things up quickly . . . I . . . I . . .' She was blabbering and I could see her thinking to herself, please stop, I sound like a complete idiot. In truth, she sounded exactly like I had done fifteen years earlier.

Emma moved into the crew house the next day and proved to be a star. People could not help liking her; she just wormed her way

into your heart. The first thing I discovered about her was her
absolute honesty. She says what she means, and not many people
can get away with that.

I once began telling a story about *Maiden* and Emma announced,
'Oh, yes, I read about that at school. I must have been twelve.'

Thank you, Emma, I thought, feeling ancient.

I nicknamed her 'Oops' because she probably used that word
more than any other in the English language. Emma is accident-
prone. She doesn't cause major disasters, only small hiccups. If there
is a nail in the middle of a yard, Emma will step on it. She will drop
things, bump her head and lose saucepan lids overboard.

Within a month of starting, I began considering Emma as
possible crew, but I wanted to see her sail first. I pulled her aside:
'I'm putting you on a month's trial.'

Her eyes widened. She'd been convinced I was about to sack
her.

'Oh, my God! I won't let you down. I'll work really hard,' she
blabbered.

Emma was true to her word. She threw herself into everything,
never flagging. When I lost Claire Russell as my crew doctor,
Emma took on the role. She had a degree in sports medicine and
began working on the boat during the day and studying at night,
interrogating doctors about cold-water injuries, frostbite and hypothermia. She came back from the hospital with horrendous
stories of accidents and used to practise her sutures on a smelly
chunk of pig.

Despite all of her efforts, Emma's place still wasn't secure until Jo
Gooding pulled out of the challenge. Emma took over the role of
camerawoman for the documentary. Through sheer hard work,
enthusiasm and ability, she had made herself indispensable.

Hannah Harwood, Miranda Merron and the Frenchwoman,
Frédérique Brulé made up the rest of the eleven.

Hannah had been teaching sailing in Bahrain when I persuaded
her to join us. At first she wasn't sure about leaving her cushy life
and had to be convinced. She had represented Britain twice in the

Nations Cup and was the UK Women's Match Racing Champion in 1995.

Miranda looked like a hippie left over from Glastonbury but sounded like the product of a Swiss finishing school. She spoke six languages fluently and had captained the Cambridge University Ladies sailing team. I liked her the moment I met her, particularly her grace under pressure and sense of humour.

I put her in charge of safety on board and during training she began fining people 'drinks' if they failed to clip on their safety harness, or carry their emergency beacons. Of course, I became the worst offender. I was caught so many times running across the netting behind the outer beam that I should have just put money on the bar at the start of each week.

Frédérique – or 'Fred' as we called her – had more than 60,000 miles sailing behind her, including one transpacific and five transatlantic crossings. When she joined the team we launched a 'Teach Fred English' campaign. This was to make sure there was no confusion or misunderstanding when instructions were being given on deck. Her English improved enormously, although under pressure she still reverted to French.

By early May 1997, we were ready to relaunch the 'big cat' and announce to the world our bid for the Jules Verne Trophy. A huge marquee was erected in Ocean Village in Southampton, with seating for 300.

Standing on a podium, I looked at the sea of faces on the dockside. Most of them I knew. Apart from friends and family, there were so many others who had helped me along the way.

Sir Christopher Benson, the chairman of RSA, made a wonderful speech. As I responded, the girls filed out behind me and stood Navy-style on the middle beam of the boat. I introduced them one by one. At one point I looked straight at Mum. She looked so proud I thought she might burst. I struggled to hold back my tears.

Pete Goss, the single-handed sailor, raised a champagne bottle in one hand and a sword in the other. With a flourish, he sliced off the top and announced, 'I name this boat *Royal & SunAlliance*. May God protect her and all who sail in her.'

   Amen to that!

TWENTY

OUR challenge for the Jules Verne Trophy had been set for January 1998. We had eight months to get ready. The previous March, the Frenchman Olivier de Kersauson had set a new record of 71 days, 14 hours, 22 minutes and eight seconds. It had taken him four years and seven attempts to break the record. It had taken me that long to get the money, the boat and the crew for my first attempt.

The French have always had a love affair with multihulls, while most English sailors seem to regard them as alien craft or a weird experiment. People are always trying to reinvent things like the bicycle but it never really catches on.

In reality, a catamaran or trimaran uses the wind far more effectively than a traditional yacht. With a single hull, the wind tends to be pushing the boat over and spilling out of the sails. There are ten tons of lead in the keel keeping it upright but all this extra weight slows the boat down.

A monohull works on very basic principles of wind dynamics. If the wind comes from behind it fills the sails and obviously pushes the boat forward. When the wind is coming from the front (on the nose), or the side (on the beam) it pushes the boat over, which is called heeling. This makes the boat want to turn into the wind. By steering away from the wind, you harness this energy and create forward momentum.

These same principles apply to multihull but the wind has a different effect. A multihull moves forward so swiftly it 'creates its own breeze', which is called apparent wind.

The best way to explain it is to imagine that you're in a car. If you're stationary and put your head out the window, you'll feel the prevailing breeze. This is 'true wind'. But when you're driving along a road and put your head out a window, the wind you feel on your face is 'apparent wind'.

Now imagine the 'big cat' being propelled forwards by wind filling the sails. She is so light, stable and quick that she creates her own apparent wind. This comes forward as she goes faster, creating her own wind angle and wind speed. You may have a true wind speed (TWS) of 24 knots, coming from directly behind; you are moving at 10 knots so you have 14 knots of apparent wind. However, when the wind is on or forward of the beam, the apparent wind is more than your true wind. It is the apparent wind that drives the boat.

A catamaran with a 102-foot mast is like a big moving sail. The hulls are lifted higher in water by the air rushing between them. When this happens even less of the boat is touching the surface and it moves faster still. Add to this the effect of the apparent wind it generates and you have an explosive amount of power. In theory there is no limit to a catamaran's speed – the only thing slowing it down is the water.

The transatlantic speed record was our first challenge. Serge Madec held the record of 6 days, 13 hours and 3 minutes in the multihull *Jet Services*. Although I was determined to make a serious attempt, I also knew that we were still on a learning curve.

So far I had been relying a great deal on Ed and Brian Wallis because they knew so much about the catamaran. At the same time, I encouraged the girls to ask as many questions as possible. They were top-class sailors and soon began noting things they wanted to change. Ed, I felt, tried to stop this, although I didn't understand why. The phrase, 'We didn't do it like that on *Enza*' began to wear a bit thin.

A strange thing happens when you put a man on a boat with an all-female crew. No matter how confident and skilled the women are, they suddenly defer to the man. This showed whenever Ed sailed with us. He took control without even realising and pushed his opinions on others. Eventually, I recognised that until we got on the water alone we wouldn't discover things for ourselves. That's when the real learning would be done.

In late May we sailed to New York and began final preparations for the transatlantic record attempt. With everything in place, we had to wait two weeks for the right weather. Our meteorologist Bob Rice was trying to give us the best start possible. His job was to find us the best route through the approaching systems, by studying information from satellites, weather stations, buoys and balloons. Via e-mail, he relayed regular updates and advice from his head-quarters in Wolfeboro, New Hampshire.

Our window of opportunity finally arrived on Sunday, 22 June. Bob wanted us to cross the start line as soon as the sun came up and the thermals kicked in. I thought we'd need a crowbar to get Ed off the boat. I gave him a big hug and Helena threw the tug our towing line. For the first time in five years Ed watched his baby sail away without him on board. The lights of New York shimmered on the river as we glided along in the pre-dawn darkness.

We reached Ambrose Light at sunrise, when smog blurred the horizon in a hazy shade of pink. The moon disappeared and the breeze started to fill in. At 6.25 a.m., after a few practice runs to the start line, we finally wound up the catamaran and crossed the line doing 13 knots on course. The umbilical cord had finally been severed. We were on our own.

By 6.35 the next morning we had done 430 miles in the right direction – almost double *Maiden*'s best days' run. I was staggered at the speed and how the miles simply disappeared beneath the bows.

At the same time, we were getting used to life on board in the cramped conditions and freezing temperatures.

Shifting winds over the next few days meant a lot of sail changes. This took a huge amount of strength and energy, which made me aware of the importance of choosing the right sails. Sharon kept a log of all the changes, collecting numbers on the angle of sail and wind strength, so we could measure the effectiveness of each sail.

Reefing the mainsail was another problem because of the distance between the first and second reef. The catamaran had to be steered down (turned away from the wind) and six people were needed to pull the huge mainsail up the mast. If all went smoothly, it took twenty minutes to take a reef out and ten minutes to put one in. Ultimately, this might affect my judgement on when to reef.

By day three the temperature had fallen to below freezing as we crossed over the Grand Banks off Newfoundland. Icebergs had become a growing danger. As I plotted the ice reports on to our charts I found they were smack in the middle of our intended course. I started an iceberg watch on the radar as well as on deck, where we began using night vision glasses. Half an hour up forward was all anybody could manage because of the cold and the difficulty of hanging on with one hand and holding the glasses in the other. Any longer on deck and the mind began playing tricks and every white cap looked like an iceberg.

Despite the danger, we hurtled through the blackness at ridiculous speeds. My nerves were jangling as we raced over the entombed *Titanic*. Fog rolled in to make the night vision glasses next to useless.

As the navigator, I had to decide whether to take the more northern Great Circle Route, sailing fewer miles, or to sail east and avoid the threat of icebergs. I spent 24 hours agonising over the decision affecting our lives. Faster or safer? Faster or safer?

I chose to go east. No record is worth a life.

We had one more night in the iceberg zone, although the second field wasn't quite so terrifying. The hours of darkness seemed to drag on endlessly.

Having overcome one problem, another emerged. The high pressure system 200 miles ahead of us had a fifty-fifty chance of moving the wrong way and stopping us dead in our tracks. Bob Rice advised that if we put our foot down we might be able to punch through using the front we were riding. We spent all night smashing into nightmare seas with 40 knots of wind. It wasn't to be. By morning, the high had moved suddenly north and flattened across our path. The front stalled only twenty-five miles short of carrying us through the high pressure area. The wind died to 3 knots.

My disappointment was greater than my fear of icebergs had been. We had covered 1,516 miles in four days, well within the record, but now had a great barrier of calm conditions, preventing us from getting to the finish.

Two days later, with 900 miles to go, we abandoned the record attempt.

Despite the frustration and disappointment, we had learned a great deal about the boat. In particular, that she was worse than dreadful in light airs. A lot of weight had been trimmed during the refit but it clearly wasn't enough. We also needed better sails.

Back in Southampton, I spent a few weeks organising the changes and then flew to America to meet with Bob Rice. I wanted to learn about the weather patterns and discuss how we'd communicate during the circumnavigation.

Wolfeboro looked like the set for *Peyton Place* and every other New England village that I'd ever seen on TV. The wooden houses had shuttered windows, white picket fences and pick-up trucks in every driveway. The men wore jeans and logging shirts, while the women pushed prams down the main street and swapped sewing patterns outside the general store.

Bob Rice Weather Windows (BRWW) had rooms on the first floor of a low brick building in the middle of the shopping district. Caitlin Rice, Bob's rather eccentric but lovely wife sat at a desk at reception. A huge poster of *Enza* covered the wall behind her. Down the left side of the office were racks of telex machines, faxes and computer printers constantly spitting out paper. It felt like the middle of the weather universe. A mountain of specialised data was being analysed, ranging from sea temperature to wave heights, wind and currents. Added to this were eyewitness weather reports radioed to shore by thousands of ships at sea. These allowed meteorologists to immediately judge the accuracy of their forecasts.

Bob looked like Father Christmas with his snow-white hair and bushy beard. He barely moved his lips as he spoke and I had to lean close to catch each word. Rarely had I met anybody who had such a passion for his work. Bob could transform the most sterile black and white charts into seething masses of water vapour and pressure.

We spent hours discussing the likely conditions during the record attempt. I wanted to know what sort of winds we'd encounter and how far south would be safe.

In a smaller office, behind a screen, Bob introduced me to his two off-siders, George Donavon and Lee Bruce. George was older again and a self-confessed 'weather nerd'. I could just imagine him falling asleep at night reading the latest output from data buoys. Lee was cut from the same piece of cloth, with a similarly dry sense of humour.

These men were vital to our chances of success. They had to thread us through the high and low pressure systems, putting us in the right position to take advantage of the best winds.

Back in Hamble a problem was emerging. I should have had the courage to solve it sooner. Instead, I was to learn the hardest lesson of my life about leadership, self-belief and communication.

All but three of the crew came to me and poured out their worries and frustration about Ed. They complained that he treated them like idiots and didn't trust them on the boat. I knew exactly what they meant, but hadn't realised that they were also being affected. I assumed it was only I who copped Ed's criticism. I admire Ed enormously, but he is the only person I have ever met who can shred my confidence so completely that I question the very ground I walk on.

The problem went deep and I kicked myself for not seeing it sooner. Ed was a great project manager, but a lousy people manager. He was too dominating.

When I chose so many youngsters to crew *Royal & SunAlliance*, he had disagreed with me loudly and publicly. I wanted the youngsters because I knew they would enhance the team. A twenty-three-year-old dinghy sailor, without any ocean racing experience would look at the project with fresh eyes and an open mind. She would ask why things were done in certain ways and question standard practices. This is an asset, not a liability.

Ed couldn't see this. His stubbornness and inflexibility had already cost us dearly. Michèle Paret, who had been with me on *Maiden*, left the project because of a major personality clash with Ed. My failure to act earlier had cost me one of my best crew members.

The friction between Ed and me grew worse. We didn't seem to agree on anything. I defended him wholeheartedly to the rest of the crew and the crew to him but increasingly I felt more like a mediator than a skipper.

Slowly this began to wear me down. Maybe Ed was right. Perhaps I wasn't the right person for the job. For one thing, I'd failed to see that a wedge had been driven between the shore team and the sailing crew. I had been so immersed in the practical aspects of the project that I simply assumed the shore team would get on and do their jobs without input from me. Ed didn't think I had enough control. He claimed the crew was too young. At the same time, the shore team had started telling jokes about the crew and the skipper. One of them wrote limericks on her computer and showed them around the office.

Sadly, I had broken one of my cardinal rules about communication and sorting out problems as they develop. Instead of confronting the problem immediately, I backed off. Perhaps I was too tired. For three years I'd been riding an emotional roller coaster and teetering on the edge of bankruptcy. I should have taken a break after we found the sponsorship, and had a holiday. Instead, as had happened before in my life, I didn't listen to the advice of close friends who could see that I was working too hard.

In sporting parlance, I took my eyes off the ball and let the project disintegrate into bickering and disagreement. Isolated from the team and the shore crew, I felt completely on my own. More crucially, I had nothing left to give. The enjoyment and pleasure had gone

'I can't do this any more,' I told Ed in the office one morning. 'I don't have the strength. I'm going to bring someone else in as co-skipper. Once they're established, I'm going to leave the project.'

Ed said nothing to change my mind.

I can't described how utterly desolate I felt as I sat in the office that day. My dream lay in tatters. Ultimately, it hadn't been the debts or the long search for sponsorship that had crushed me. Nor was it that I couldn't find the crew, or wasn't a good enough sailor. I simply didn't have the support that I needed.

That afternoon Ed and Charlotte came to see me and didn't pull any punches. All the old gripes came to the surface. Instead of controlling the situation and defending my decisions, I just let them have their say. Anyone who knows me will find this hard to believe but I allowed myself to be crushed.

Later that evening, I sat on the sofa at home in Hamble, clutching my knees and rocking back and forth. I phoned Trevor and almost couldn't speak through the sobs. It was the second time in my life that I'd totally lost control.

'Sit tight. I'm on my way,' he said.

An hour later he arrived from Reading. I was still on the sofa, with a red puffy face and tears tumbling down my cheeks. I had no strength left. Even talking was an effort. I could still remember the last thing Ed had said to me as he shredded me verbally. 'I really will think something of you, Tracy, if you can bounce back from this.' I should have punched him.

Trevor put his arms around me. 'You can't let them do this.'

'No, I just want to give up.'

'You've worked too hard.'

'I don't care. I'll go away and take up crocheting or something.'

'Don't be stupid.'

I was inconsolable and Trevor stayed with me until I fell asleep. By morning, the sense of devastation had been joined by anger. I had admitted my fears and failings to my shore team and I felt that they had used that information against me. I had questioned my role. Maybe I wasn't tough enough on the girls. Maybe we weren't good enough. Deep down, however, I knew that this was as much about Ed's need for control as it was about my leadership style or me. Worse, I had let it happen.

Knowing the truth didn't help me overcome the problem; I didn't have the strength to fight another battle. Instead, I felt there was so much ill-feeling and distrust that it was best if I handed in my notice and let them all get on with it.

First I would talk to Royal & SunAlliance. I arranged to meet with Martin Booth the next day. Before leaving for London, I told Ed and Charlotte about the appointment. Suddenly, they seemed very supportive. I told them I would meet Miki Von Koskull and, depending on what Martin said, offer her the job of skipper.

When I arrived at Martin's office and told him that I was resigning from the project, he didn't seem surprised. 'I have lost the trust of those around me,' I said. 'I want to bring someone else in to skipper the boat. The project and the team are more important than one person.'

Martin said very little. Over dinner I discovered that he knew of my plans already. Ed had faxed him while I was on my way to London. He had written that they wanted me off the project because I was a lousy skipper.

My mouth dropped open and stayed there. If we hadn't been in a crowded restaurant I think my reaction would have been slightly more vocal. This was the ultimate betrayal.

'Close your mouth,' Martin advised sensibly.

I snapped it shut and sipped a glass of water. What had I done to warrant this?

Martin spoke very softly but with steel in his voice. 'You *are* the project, Tracy. It *is* you. You created it; you gave it life and you are the reason we are sponsoring it. Don't let us down and don't let your crew down. Stay.'

'My crew don't want me as skipper.'

'Who told you that rubbish?'

I didn't have to answer.

'Go back to Hamble,' said Martin. 'Ask your crew what they think. And while you're doing that just remember how hard you battled to get here.'

After the lunch I called Sir Robin Knox-Johnston, who has always been a hero of mine. He kindly agreed to stop off in Reading on his way home from London the next day. We met at the train station and went to the bar. I told him exactly what had happened and he listened in silence.

Finally, he looked at me and said, 'Tracy, you know in your heart what you have to do. Unfortunately, I don't think you're going to do it.'

'What's that?'

'You have to sack your shore team and choose a new one. You can't have disloyalty in a team.'

'But it's my fault that I let it get this far. It doesn't seem right . . .'

'We all make mistakes, Tracy. You will never be able to trust them again.'

I had a lot of thinking to do. Ed had just bought a new house and had a huge mortgage. What about his wife Ancki and the children? And how could I ignore the fact that he once lent me the entire proceeds from the sale of his house so I could pay the shipping costs for *Enza*?

I went back to Hamble and calmly replayed the events of the past year and, more importantly, the previous few weeks. I decided to give the shore team one more chance. From now on, I'd be more attentive. I'd involve them in crew meetings and keep them informed.

I called a meeting of the watch captains – Helena, Emma West-macott, Miki and navigator, Adrienne. As navigator, Adrienne

was also a senior member of the crew. We pulled chairs together
in the cluttered office, overlooking the marina. I asked Charlotte
to leave and when we were alone I took a deep breath and
started.

'I have something to tell you.' The general banter stopped
suddenly. They could recognise the tension in my voice. I looked
at their faces carefully. 'Each of you is here because you strengthen
this team. You are all skippers in your own right. You have all run
your own projects. This is a group with huge potential for conflict,
but each of you has special skills.'

I turned to Helena. 'Helena, you are the best multihull sailor we
have, with more multihull experience than the rest of us combined.
That's why we must listen to you when you tell us how things
should be done. Does everyone agree?'

Each of them nodded.

'Emma, you are probably the best all-round sailor we have on
the boat. You have learned more about the catamaran in a shorter
time than any one of us. Technically you are absolutely the best
person for the job. Does everyone agree?'

Again they nodded.

'Miki, you are definitely the best seaman. You have more ocean
miles, more sailing experience, more years on the water than any of
us. Your seamanship skills are huge and so is your knowledge of the
Southern Ocean. When you speak, we must listen. Is that agreed?'

'Yes.'

I turned to Adrienne. 'You are probably the best female
navigator in the world. I am going to listen to you. I am not
going to take it out of your hands. If you make a decision and you
want to stick by it, we follow you.'

Adrienne looked chuffed. 'Great, brilliant.'

I took a deep breath. 'For my part, I think I have more
experience than any of you in running this sort of project. I have
pulled together this team and I can keep it together. We all have
our strengths. We are not competing against each other; we are
working together to compete against people who think we *can't* do

this. I say we *can*. We can take ownership of this project back from where it has drifted. I can lead you.'

My eyes were blazing. I felt strong. 'There are some people who don't want me here. I've been very close to walking away. But I haven't worked this bloody hard to go quietly into the night. This is *my* project. I *am* the skipper. I only care about the opinions of one group of people and that is my crew. If you don't believe that I can do this; if you don't believe in me, then I don't want to be here. I'll go and do something else.'

Emma was the first to speak. 'You have to be the skipper, Tracy. You have to stay.'

Adrienne: 'I didn't come halfway around the world to lose my skipper.'

'The shore crew isn't sailing. We are,' said Miki.

I'd never seen Helena so angry. 'Don't listen to the bastards.'

When Ed, Charlotte and Sue returned, I announced the final make-up of the sailing crew. 'Miki, Helena and Emma are my watch captains. Adrienne is the navigator. And, of course, I am the skipper.' There was silence as we walked out. I didn't look at Ed's face. He didn't say a word.

Up until a few hours earlier, the project had seemed to be crumbling around me. Now I felt empowered. The team had given me my strength back and we shared an unforgettable sense of being unstoppable. Communication would be the key. I had let my crew down and it wasn't going to happen again. I had learned an expensive lesson about being a leader, one that I would never forget.

TWENTY-ONE

FOR six weeks we waited. The winter in England had been dominated by south-west gale force winds which made it impossible to leave. A multihull can't sail effectively into headwinds.

Three times during January we almost left Britain. Each time we were thwarted by pressure systems dipping too far south, or moving too fast or too slow.

Weather patterns change constantly and you can only predict five days ahead at the most. We were looking for a slingshot start – a weather system that would catapult the 'big cat' out of Britain as fast as possible. Unfortunately, the perfect system is unique.

Normally, the Azores high squats in the Atlantic and the low pressure systems slide along the Gulf Stream above it. We were looking for a low pressure system to be further south than normal and to park itself across central France, which rarely happens in midwinter. Air masses flooding into the depression would spiral anticlockwise and give us the start we needed.

That may sound simple and straightforward, but we might have waited ten years to get the perfect conditions. I didn't have the luxury of time. We had to reach the Southern Ocean during summer in that part of the world when the weather is kinder and the ice recedes. This meant leaving by the end of February at the very latest.

As the weeks ticked by there was a growing sense of unease and frustration. Our major sponsor, Royal & SunAlliance, had invested £3.2 million in the record attempt and, not surprisingly, senior executives were getting edgy. What if we didn't leave? Unthinkable!

Since Thursday, 29 January, I'd been watching the latest weather pattern develop in the Atlantic. On Friday, Bob Rice had dampened spirits by dismissing the situation.

I then spent all weekend pulling weather maps off the Internet and spreading them over the office floor at my house in Reading. I'd bought the house a few months earlier and moved in with Mum. Although she tried to remain independent, her MS had made living on her own out of the question.

At the crew house in Hamble, Adrienne also studied the weather maps. Throughout Saturday we watched and hoped. If a new high to the east of Ireland stayed north and didn't drop down, then a low would be forced south. If it didn't move too quickly, we might have a window.

The timing was also complicated by the fact that it could take us at least eighteen hours to reach the starting line at Ushant lighthouse on the north-west tip of France. If we waited too long to decide, the low might have moved and we'd be beating into headwinds.

On Saturday night I spoke to Ed. 'Bob isn't happy, but I think it looks promising. I'll try to let you know by lunchtime tomorrow.'

By midday Sunday, I still wasn't sure. The high pressure system was over the British Isles and the low centred just off the coast of Portugal. In theory this might give us at least two days of good wind and daily runs of around 360 to 400 miles.

What should I do? The wrong decision could see us 'parked' in the north Atlantic. The sponsors would panic and the press would write us off before we even reached the Equator. Then again, if we didn't go, there might not be another chance before the end of February. Was this the best compromise?

Bob Rice still said no. 'That low will come down so quickly, you'll be stuck with no wind after two days,' he warned.

I called him. 'Bob, we're not looking for a perfect forecast; that's unrealistic. We're looking for a good few days, that's all. This is just the start of the record. You can't tell what's going to happen down in the South Atlantic.'

I spent all of Sunday discussing the maps and synoptic reports with Adrienne. Every member of the crew was within two hours of the boat. By evening I still hadn't decided.

'This could be your last night at home – let's go for a drink,' said Trevor.

'Can we go and see *Titanic* instead?'

Trevor laughed. 'Typical.'

'It might not be showing when I get back,' I explained.

The sinking of the great liner had always fascinated me. I'd read dozens of eyewitness accounts and books, including all the conspiracy theories. We drove into Reading and I bought a jumbo-sized carton of buttered popcorn.

I had just settled into my seat when Bob Rice called on my cell phone. I dashed into the foyer.

'If you insist on going, it has to be in the next 24 hours,' he said.

'Agreed. I'll let you know when I've talked to Adrienne.'

I went back to my seat. The *Titanic* had left Southampton and was steaming across the North Atlantic, trying to break the record for the fastest crossing to New York. An iceberg loomed out of the darkness; engines were thrown into reverse; the ship swerved and my phone rang again.

Damn!

People muttered in the seats around me.

It was Adrienne. 'I think we should go.'

'I think you're right,' I echoed.

'Let's give ourselves eighteen hours to get to the starting line.'

'That should be plenty of time.'

Sneaking back to my seat, I struggled to concentrate on the rest of the film. Although relaxed and calm on the surface, underneath I was paddling like crazy. It's not often that you decide to sail around the world. The enormity of the decision horrified me.

The wheels were put in motion. Ed contacted the Speeds Sailing Record Council and began arranging helicopters for the media. I called the girls and told them to be ready in the morning.

At midnight, I crawled into bed and tried to sleep. My back felt terrible – it always happens when I get stressed. I woke at five with a dreadful suspicion that I'd done something drastic and irreversible. What was it?

Then I remembered – I'm going to sail around the world. I don't want to do this, I thought. I really don't. What the hell am I doing? I'm cornered. I can't get out.

The panic attack passed quickly, but the tightness remained in the pit of my stomach. Downstairs, I discovered Trevor sleeping on the dining-room floor. 'What are you doing?'

'The telephone extension wasn't working upstairs. I thought Bob Rice might call. I didn't want you to miss it.'

I gave him a hug.

We had a coffee and Trevor helped load my bags into the car. In darkness, I had to scrape ice off the windscreen and let the engine warm. Over the previous six weeks, I'd packed and said goodbye three times – would this be it?

Turning towards the house, I looked up at my nice cosy bedroom with all the bedclothes still crumpled and warm. Then I turned away from the comforts that I wouldn't see again for another two and a half months.

I drove along country back roads until I reached the M3 and then followed the motorway towards Southampton. The sky began to lighten as I passed Winchester. I love that time of the morning, before everything begins and there are no people about. Everything smells new and fresh. The day belongs to me rather than anybody else. It can be anything I want it to be.

At 8 a.m. I called the girls in the crew house. Miranda answered the phone sounding sleepy. She'd been awake for two hours, but didn't perform well of a morning.

'OK, load the sails; it's a definite maybe,' I told her.

'How definite a maybe?'

'It looks pretty definite.'

'So it's a definite definite maybe?'

This had become a running gag over the previous weeks as we waited for our window in the weather.

The office stepped up a gear. Press statements and bulletins were being prepared and there were dozens of requests for last-minute interviews.

My family arrived by mid-morning – the whole clan including uncles, aunts and cousins. Most of the girls had families saying goodbye and it was hard with so many journalists and photographers milling about.

As I stepped on to the dock, I gazed at the 'big cat'. No matter how many times I'd seen her, she always set my pulse racing. The sleek twin hulls looked like something that NASA might have developed and the mast was angled back like the top of an archer's bow.

I stepped on deck and swung down through the hatch into the God Pod. Adrienne was already at the chart table, checking the latest weather maps and beginning the navigator's log. I had to shuffle around her and crouch as I sat on my bunk.

'Welcome to the broom closet,' she said. Her bunk lay opposite mine, separated by a few feet.

'I hope you don't snore.'

'That's the least of your problems.'

For all its size on the outside, the *Royal & SunAlliance* had virtually no room below deck. The sleek design and aerodynamics had squeezed space to a minimum. To make matters worse, we had crammed the remainder full of technology, sails, food, water-makers, generators and spare parts. Everything had been given adequate space it seemed, except the crew.

The girls were itching to get on the water and leave. It seemed so long and drawn out – saying goodbye three or four times to the same people and then the awkward silences. All the press photographers wanted to get a picture of me kissing my mystery 'boyfriend'. We disappointed them by saying goodbye earlier.

I'd known Damian Foxall since he helped sail *Enza* across the Atlantic on the delivery run from Florida. We didn't start dating until much later, when the big catamaran was being refitted. Apart from being a brilliant single-handed sailor, Damian is Irish, with olive skin and penetrating blue eyes. It's an irresistible combination.

Some of the parents were fighting back tears. Many of them looked frightened for us. I can't imagine what must have been going through their minds as they watched their young daughters sail away. No matter how strongly they believed in us, I'm sure they were silently saying, Oh, my God, we should never have let them do this.

At 2 p.m. I ended the torment. 'OK, let's go!'

Ed started the tow boat, the lines were cast off and friends and relatives pushed *Royal & SunAlliance* away from the dock. I turned the wheel and the tow-line took the strain. The faces on the dock grew smaller and I could see people hurrying along the pontoon to the headland to catch a final glimpse of us as we disappeared round Calshot Spit into the Solent.

The tow boat took us halfway to the Needles and then let us go. With the mainsail up, we popped the big kite, a huge white spinnaker that seemed to be catching sunlight as well as breeze. It unfurled with a lovely crumpled 'snap' and Helena and Sharon worked the winches to take up the slack. Ropes were neatly coiled and stored, fittings gleamed and the first spray settled on my lips.

Three or four boats were still with us. Ed zipped past on a speedboat carrying photographers. 'You look great,' he shouted. My heart warmed to him.

Sam piped up, 'Right, who wants a cup of tea?'

I hadn't eaten all day – too nervous, I guess. At lunchtime, Sue Snow had done a run to the local deli and picked up about fifty delicious baguettes. She knew I liked chicken and avocado and ordered one especially for me. Even though she put it into my hand, I still hadn't managed to take a bite. Instead, I thought I'd bring it with me, but forgot in the commotion.

'Isn't that just the way,' I muttered. 'I'm going to spend the next two and a half months eating freeze-dried food and dreaming about that baguette.'

With more wind than we expected, we reached the starting line at Ushant ahead of schedule. Unfortunately, this meant we had to cool our heels until the race officials and media helicopters were in place. Having waited weeks, a couple more hours might not seem like much, but it annoyed the hell out of me. How long would our weather window stay open?

At 8.30 a.m. we all gathered on deck to talk through the start. Adrienne showed us the charts and synoptic reports.

'At the moment we have the wind from the south-east, but it should shift round behind us,' she said. 'If it doesn't, then we may have to gybe to get out past Ushant into the North Atlantic. That will lose us time. We want to start as close as possible to the island and be really flying when we cross the line.'

Adrienne looked to me for any final words. I knew there was little I could say that would make any difference now, but I wanted the girls to know how much I believed in them.

'I'm proud of the way you've worked and I want you to know that I have 100 per cent faith in each of you. The enemy is not here, amongst us – it's out there. We have to prove to millions of people who don't believe that we can do this that we can. If we work and stand together as a team we can do anything. If we don't stand together, we achieve nothing. You all know your jobs. You all deserve to be here. Let's go and do it.'

Ushant lighthouse looked like a barber's pole rising out of the sea mist. On the observation platform, Charles Bretan, of the Speeds Sailing Record Council, raised a compass. He closed one eye and peered across the marsh-green sea. Using marks on the dial he took a line of sight from Ushant to an unseen Lizard Island off the Cornish coast.

Below him, *Royal & SunAlliance* surged forwards. The twin hulls lifted. Twelve knots . . . 15 knots . . . 18 knots . . . still she accelerated. The winches cranked a notch tighter. Water vibrated against the hulls with a high-pitched hum.

'A lot of people are watching us,' I said, glancing at the media helicopters. 'If we do nothing else, let's get this one right.'

Charles Bretan glanced at his watch.

'*Royal & SunAlliance, Royal & SunAlliance* this is Ushant lighthouse. You crossed the starting line at 10.53 and three seconds on the 3rd of February 1998. Good luck and God speed.'

At that moment a clock was set running. It was to dominate my life like no other before it or since. Days were still 24 hours long, but they began and ended at 10.53. Time zones didn't matter, nor daylight or darkness: all that counted was how many miles were on the clock at 10.53 each day.

We had 71 days, 14 hours, 22 minutes and eight seconds to circumnavigate the world non-stop and match the record.

Each girl had taken her place in case we had to gybe to squeeze past Ushant into the North Atlantic. Emma W. had the wheel, Helena the main sheet, Miranda and Hannah were on the runners, Sharon patrolled the foredeck and Sam was stationed at the mast. Emma Richards scampered about the deck, filming for a live up-link.

I couldn't look at them without grinning.

More people had been to the moon than had attempted the record we sought. It had never been done by an all-female crew. The critics and the doubters said we weren't strong enough, or good enough sailors. They said that when it came to the crunch in the Southern Ocean – when the wind was screaming through the wires and we were surfing in mountainous seas – a woman would ease off, reef down and turn away from the wind.

Having listened to them for so long, I'd almost come to believe it. Maybe an all-female crew couldn't win the Jules Verne Trophy. We'd know in 71 days' time. Six hours after crossing the starting line on Tuesday morning, we were averaging 19 knots on a port gybe and eating up the miles across the Bay of Biscay. We had a good spinnaker run, although the seas were a little lumpy and awkward.

Adrienne briefed the crew on the latest weather fax. 'We're running away from this high,' she said, pointing to the chart. 'If it drops down to follow us we'll have to stay ahead of it. We're going to get a good first day's run, before we strike some light air. That's why we have to race our hearts out for 24 hours. Then we'll see what happens.'

As I looked at the map, I could hear an unseen clock ticking away.

TWENTY-TWO

'WHALE! Whale!'
I scrambled on deck. A pod of killer whales had dived about a hundred yards astern. I could see the patches of flat water, as if there was something below the surface.

'There!' shouted Helena.

A shiny black body broke the surface and curled upwards and then down again. Another appeared next to it and then a third and fourth. They blew almost together, sending fine spray 20 feet into the air.

Emma Richards dashed below to get the video camera. When she reappeared a minute later, the whales had dived again.

'What is it with me?' she says. 'It's like they know.'

Poor Emma. The same thing happened a day earlier with a school of dolphins. As soon as she went for the camera they disappeared. Yet if she didn't go, they'd surely hang around for ages, surfing the bow waves and performing.

'I'm banning that camera,' teased Helena.

I'd seen a lot of whales at sea and it never ceased to excite me. Maybe it's because there is normally so little to see in the middle of the ocean. It's one of the great beauties of sailing – being so isolated yet not alone.

One certainty of these sightings is that somebody on board will never quite catch the action – in our case Miranda. Every time she looked the spray had gone, along with the whale.

'There she blows!'

'Where?'

'There.'

'I can't see . . .'

Port side, port side. Nine o'clock.'

'Where? Where?'

'Oh, you've just missed it. Maybe it will come up again.'

Miranda thought we were playing games with her.

For the first time in my sailing life, I'd started a voyage without being seasick. For eighteen years I'd followed the advice of Mike Corns, my first skipper, who told me to eat, drink, puke and get on with it. I'm sad to say it hadn't made a blind bit of difference.

This time Emma Richards had suggested I use Stugeron. What a revelation! I felt like crying when I thought of all those horrendous days that I'd spent retching over the back beam. And then I'd hear myself telling journalists, 'Well it's just something I have to put up with because I love sailing.'

What a load of rubbish!

The smell of land had gone; wet earth and exhaust fumes had been replaced by salt air and sea spray that I could taste on my lips and feel drying on my skin. It was good to be back.

In the first 24 hours we covered 430 miles – the perfect start. Our gamble had paid off.

Yet already the high pressure system was catching us. 'We can't outrun it,' said Adrienne. 'When it lands on us, we're either going to park – which will be disastrous – or we'll manage to keep going. If we can limp along, we can hopefully get into the next weather system.'

Sure enough, by mid-afternoon on 5 February, the wind started to drop. At dinner it died even further and we shook out a second reef in the mainsail and put the big kite up again. The next couple of hours were glorious sailing as the waves flattened. Then the breeze fell to 10 knots and we decided to gybe away from the coast of Portugal.

All night we crawled through light variable winds. I lay in my bunk, watching the numbers on the console above the chart table. A mini–weather station, high up on the mast, constantly measured the wind speed and direction. Other instruments, on deck and below the surface, calculated air and water temperature, as well as boat speed. At the touch of a button, I knew how many miles we'd travelled in 24 hours and our global position to within a few feet.

The wind started filling in during the evening. At midnight, I crawled out of my bunk to do a watch for Sharon, who'd been up all day mending a torn spinnaker. I couldn't see the horizon or the waves. It was too dark. According to the instruments we were sailing at 23 knots, but I had no sense of speed. There were no reference points. It wasn't until we slowed down to 17 knots that I had the strangest sensation that we'd actually stopped moving.

Each time I came up into the wind, the cat accelerated until we had too much speed for the conditions. I had to decelerate by fractionally steering away from the wind. It felt as though we were zigzagging across the ocean.

'We might have a problem,' said Adrienne. 'A freighter has gone down, the *Mediterraneo del Defino*. There are containers adrift in front of us.'

'How close?'

'I'm getting positions from the Lisbon coastguard.'

Our radar could pick up a boat in front of us, but not containers or debris. If we hit something like that at speed, it would rip off an entire hull.

'There's no moon, we won't even see them.'

'Fingers crossed.'

As the sun rose on day six I didn't know whether to laugh or cry. For three days the weather had been grey and dismal with low visibility and awkward waves. Our nights had been spent avoiding areas of no wind or fierce squalls bringing wind from the wrong direction. And our days were gybing marathons as the wind swung back and forth.

I swear there was someone up there watching and playing games with us. We'd wait agonising minutes going in the wrong direction, wondering whether to gybe and hoping the wind would swing. When it didn't move, we got everyone on deck and into position. 'OK, let's do it.' Halfway through the gybe the wind would swing back.

'This is incredible.' I felt like screaming. 'I think we should bluff it.'

Sam looked at me uncertainly.

'Great idea,' said Helena.

I knew that I was being completely ridiculous but sometimes the wind pushes you to the limits of your sanity.

'What are we doing?' asked Miranda.

'We're going to pretend to gybe.'

'Excuse me.'

'We're going to pretend to gybe. We're going to set it all up and at the last minute not gybe.'

'Not gybe.'

'That's right.'

'Why?'

'Because we have to convince the wind that we *are* going to gybe.'

'That's the most stupid thing I've ever heard.'

'I know.'

Miranda shook her head and took up her position at the starboard traveller.

'Everyone ready?'

The 'ayes' came back.

'OK, let's gybe.'

Helena didn't steer down; Emma didn't wind in the mainsheet; one side of the boat didn't release and the other side didn't winch. It was the perfect 'non-gybe'.

I waited and watched the cockpit wind direction indicator. The seconds ticked by. Suddenly, the needle swung 20°. Helena steered closer towards the mark and the catamaran accelerated.

Cheers rang out.

Within fifteen minutes the wind had swung and started toying with us again. There was never any question about who had control.

Adrienne had been spending every waking moment studying the synoptic forecasts and maps. She even mumbled in her sleep about the weather. Success or failure would depend upon us putting ourselves in a position to take advantage of the best winds. If we got caught on the wrong side of a low it could virtually blow us backwards. Similarly, a high pressure system could park us up for days with no wind. The margin for error is surprisingly small. It can mean sailing in a corridor only a hundred miles wide to put ourselves in the right position for the next frontal system.

Bob Rice had been summoned to New Zealand for Sir Peter Blake's America's Cup campaign and left us in the capable hands of George Donavon and Lee Bruce. I found it quite surreal to imagine them sitting in their office in Wolfeboro, New Hampshire, surrounded by telex machines and maps, telling us what winds were coming and when they'd arrive. Often, I could look at the instruments above the chart table and say, 'Spot on, George,' or, 'Where's the southwester you promised, Lee?'

The perfect wind for us was about 25 to 30 knots, just behind the beam, although she could handle 40 knots further aft. And unless we could average a boat speed of 16 knots in the right direction we'd begin falling behind *Sport Elec*. Every mile counted and we had to sail with that sense of urgency. If someone on the helm underperformed by a single knot in the conditions, they had to be taken straight off the wheel. Apart from our own performance, Adrienne also monitored the progress of *Enza* and *Sport Elec*. She had the log books of both former record holders and knew exactly how many miles each of them had covered on any given day as well as the weather they faced, the equipment failures and crew injuries. At any moment I could pinpoint exactly how far *Sport Elec* was behind *Royal & SunAlliance* and how far *Enza* was ahead of us. They were like competitors in a phantom race. I would never be able to see them, but I knew they were out there — sometimes just beyond the horizon. I knew their skippers and the way they sailed. I knew what sails they had aloft and how fast they were travelling.

It wasn't just a race against the clock. We were sailing against ghost ships that had crossed these same waters in the past, sharing the same dream.

We started day six with *Sport Elec* 125 miles ahead of us. George and Lee wanted us further west, which meant sailing extra miles. They argued it would put us in a better position to cross the Equator and move quickly through the Doldrums.

The weather had grown warmer. T-shirts and shorts came out during the day. I felt revoltingly white and like an English tourist in the tropics. Ugh!

Below decks had become unbearable. Cooking in the galley meant swaying in a sauna the size of a cupboard, handling saucepans of steaming food for eleven people. Two small fans did nothing to stir the air; cotton singlets were soon plastered to skin and perspiration dripped from strands of hair.

I spent most of the night on deck, trying to escape the heat. Under a full moon the sea had gone silver. Phosphorus in the water created twin tails of soft green light that streaked out behind the hulls. It has something to do with the plankton or amoebas in the water that retain light from the moon and stars.

I love being on the deck at night. The isolation is complete. There are no lights in the distance or silhouettes against the sky. The horizons disappear in the darkness and the surroundings shrink to encompass a world that stretches barely a few feet in any direction. This is what I had dreamed about when I stood on Rhossilli Down, bent against the wind and watching the storm — to be out here again, mixing it up against the elements that could bring serenity one night and mayhem the next. Now I couldn't quite believe that I had finally made it.

A spark of silver flashed past my nose and slammed into the cockpit.

'Flying fish!' yelled Sharon.

Four or five of them smacked into the hull kamikaze-style. We scrambled to pick them up and toss them back. Sharon almost copped one between the eyes and whined, 'We need bloody crash helmets.'

I scooped one up from between my boots and tossed it over my shoulder. The fish were about six inches long, shaped like silver torpedoes, except for their amazing wings. They could glide as far as 200 yards and reach 30 feet in the air. Normally they manage to miss boats but our twin hulls probably confused them. I could imagine them thinking, Ha, I missed that sucker, just before they went splat into the other hull.

When the bombardment finished, I slipped into the God Pod to get a few hours' sleep.

The next bang shook me awake just before dawn.

Miki shouted from the cockpit. 'We've hit something.'

The words flipped a switch in my mind: suddenly I was awake.

'How bad is it?'

'The steering doesn't feel right.'

She hammered on the deck three times. 'All hands!'

I pulled on foul weather gear and boots, emerging from the hatch to see Hannah and Sam checking the hulls with torches.

'Feel this.'

I took hold of the wheel.

'What do you think it is?'

'Maybe something wrapped around a centreboard.'

'Or the rudders.'

Emma W. and Miranda were shining powerful torches into the water, trying to pick up any signs of damage or debris wrapped around the centreboards. The catamaran was still doing 16 knots.

Hannah checked the starboard rudder first and then looked across to the port hull.

'There's something wrapped around the rudder. It looks like a shark.'

I could see the dark grey shape bent almost double around the rudder. Its mouth gaped open and the torch picked out the whiteness of its teeth. Blood streamed out of its jaws. It must have been eight feet long.

'Miki, take us down,' I said.

She steered off the wind but we were still doing 10 knots.

Emma R. retrieved the boat hook from the forward hold. She gave it to Hannah, who tried to force the shark off the rudder. The pressure of the water and forward momentum of the catamaran made it difficult.

'Is it still alive?' asked Emma, sounding concerned.

'I bloody hope not,' said Hannah, frustrated. 'I can't move the thing,' she said. 'I'm worried about damaging the rudder.'

'Miki, are you dead down?' I asked.

'This is it. I can't go any further.'

'OK, pull the spinnaker down.'

We slowed to 5 knots.

Hannah tried again. The shark dropped off and floated to the surface, clearly dead.

'Oh, the poor thing,' said Sam, echoing Emma's concern.

Hannah snapped, 'Poor thing! What about my bloody boat?'

'It must have been old or sick,' I said, trying to make the youngsters feel better.

'Seems a bit silly to be sleeping on the surface like that,' said Sam.

'He probably thought that the chances of being hit by a 92-foot catamaran doing 16 knots were fairly slim,' said Adrienne.

'OK, sail back up.'

'What about checking for damage?' asked Hannah.

'We'll wait until the wind drops off. I don't want to lose any more time.'

*   *   *

Another scorcher awaited us. The nav station was so hot that I found it hard to breathe. When I tried to sleep, I had rivers of sweat running down my sides on to the sleeping bag.

In these warmer conditions, it wasn't just the big weather systems that affected us. Local weather such as squalls and rain showers could appear out of nowhere and create havoc in a few minutes. We could see them coming on radar and plot their direction and speed, but it didn't mean we could avoid them. The same wind driving them also drove us.

Adrienne and I watched a bright green blob on the radar screen. I went on deck to warn the watch. Helena had seen it coming. She had her foot braced against the winch and held the main sheet in her hands.

I looked over her shoulder and saw an intimidating black mass rolling across the water towards us. There is no way of knowing how much wind there is in a squall. Some of them look frightening, but then puff and fizzle out. Others can look innocent and then turn 20 knots of breeze into 40 knots within seconds, giving you no time to reef or take precautions.

We waited and watched it approaching. This one was bringing rain that looked like a huge curtain suspended from the black clouds above. Helena – as watch captain – took the wheel.

'How solid does it look on radar?' she asked.

'Pretty solid,' I said. 'Do you want to reef?'

'Not unless you want to. It's all guesswork.'

'I feel the need for speed.'

The sky above us went dark and for a few seconds it seemed as though the squall would be all sound and no fury. Suddenly, the wind kicked in, jumping from 16 knots to 24 knots and then 30. It changed direction radically and without warning. It punched us in the nose and then swung on to the beam – the most dangerous point of sail, because the catamaran is broadside to the wind.

Helena reacted instantly, as did Sam on the main sheet. The cat swung away, accelerating in gusts of wind that continued to swing through 180° and whip up spray. Then just as suddenly as it arrived, the squall passed over us and we emerged into brilliant sunshine. The wind fell to a steady 14 knots.

During the early hours the wind picked up and sent us skimming across the water as if running away from the sunrise. At 10.53 Adrienne did the calculations. We had done 241 miles in the day and picked up fifty miles on *Sport Elec*.

I felt elated. This was almost like a match race – one on one. I hadn't expected the excitement to be so constant. Somehow I imagined that the ticking clock would take away some of the thrill of racing but it wasn't like that at all. The countdown of miles sailed each day was a race in itself.

We were less than a hundred miles from the Equator and, officially at least, entering the Doldrums.

Adrienne tried to explain this to the girls that morning, showing them the charts and rattling off meteorological terms. 'These winds pick up large amounts of moisture as they pass through the Inter-tropical Convergence Zone and rise to form thunder clouds, or cumulus. When these reach the required altitude in the tropo-sphere, the colder air condenses the water vapour and the moisture begins falling . . .'

Hannah interrupted drily. 'That'll be rain then.'

The rest of us burst out laughing and Adrienne shook her head. 'Yes, that *would* be rain.'

True to form, Hannah had cut through the waffle and got straight to the point.

Throughout Friday the 13th of February Helena walked on egg-shells. Sailors are a superstitious bunch but I'd never known anybody who took it as seriously as Helena. She knew every old wives' tale and maritime curse, along with the associated piece of bad luck.

This had caused problems during the lead-up to the challenge. Royal & SunAlliance had arranged uniforms for the crew – shorts,

T-shirts, spray-jackets and fleeces in the company's corporate colours of green, blue and yellow.

Trying to kit out an all-female crew is an absolute nightmare because of the different shapes and sizes.

On the day the gear arrived, it was like Christmas morning in the office. People began ripping open plastic wrapping and saying things like, 'Oh, these are nice . . .'

'I like the socks . . .'

'Fleecy lining . . .'

Amidst them all, Helena pulled a pair of shorts from her box and exclaimed, '*Oh my God, they are green!*'

Everyone looked up.

'Yes,' I said, looking at the shorts.

'*Green!*' Helena dangled them from her thumb and forefinger, at arm's length.

'The colours of the boat are green, yellow and blue,' I reminded her.

'But they're green.'

'Yes.'

'We can't wear green.'

'What do you mean we can't wear green? Half the bloody boat is painted green.'

'Yah, that's not good, but I have let it go. But we can't wear *green*.'

'Why not?'

'Because it is bad luck.'

'What?'

'Yes, it's really bad luck. Green is a bad colour for boats.'

I thought she was joking. 'Oh, yeah, right.'

'No, I can't wear them.'

Strangely enough, I did actually remember this superstition. 'Hold on, Helena, it's bad luck to have women on boats. I think we're stuffed.'

'No, I can't wear this.'

'You have to wear them, there is no argument.'

'I can't.' She wouldn't even put them on to check the size.

Everyone else tried to convince her. Helena wouldn't budge. I left it for two weeks, hoping she might change her mind. Finally I had to say to her, 'Helena, you have a choice. I don't want to lose you, but either you wear the shorts or you can't come with us. It's as simple as that.'

She shrugged. 'OK, but I pretend they're blue. Aren't they lovely blue shorts?'

'Lovely.'

Six of the crew had never sailed across the Equator – Sam, Helena, Sharon, Miranda, Hannah and Emma Richards. All of them were dreading the prospect except for Helena. She actually looked forward to this rite of passage. Seafaring legends were important to her, as they are to most of the Nordic races because they have such a great maritime tradition.

On the night beforehand, Emma W., Adrienne and I spent two hours getting ready for the Equator Crossing Ceremony. This is one of the great seafaring traditions. First-timers are expected to ask permission of King Neptune, who normally demands a sacrifice.

Secretly, we made crowns from printer paper decorated with stars and jewels. The boat hook was transformed into a trident, with three pencils duck-taped to form the prongs.

For the previous week, Miki, Adrienne and I had secretly put all the leftovers from the galley in a yellow Tupperware box and sealed it up. The mixture contained chicken noodle stew – repulsive before it goes off – macaroni cheese, blackcurrant crumble (which gave it the colour), sweet and sour chicken, and egg custard. With temperatures of well over 100°F down below, the scraps had fermented and turned into rancid goo. I gagged whenever I opened the box to put more in.

Adrienne and Miki woke me just before dawn. They were like excited schoolgirls giggling to each other and putting on their costumes.

'How many miles to go?'

'Five.'

Hannah was on watch. I sent her down to make tea while we made the final preparations. Fred, Miki and Emma W. had joined us. The wind had died to 9 knots and I turned on the autohelm.

At one mile to go we put the plan into action. Fred and Miki began banging pots and pans over the open hatches. Bleary-eyed the poor victims staggered on deck. All except Helena, who bounced out, bright and eager.

Sharon followed her. 'What the fu—' Then she realised. 'All right, let's get this bloody thing over with.'

We counted down the final mile. The cockpit instruments put us only yards from the Equator.

'We're still north,' said Adrienne. 'Four . . . three . . . two . . . one.'

YEEEY AHHH!'

With that I straightened my crown and banged the trident three times on deck.

'Hear ye! Hear ye! The court of King Neptune is now in session. Any person guilty of a crime must be punished before they can pass into the southern hemisphere. Will all defendants who haven't crossed the Equator step forward.'

They all shuffled nervously.

'OK, take your clothes off,' said Adrienne.

'All of them?'

'Down to bikinis.'

Emma W. called the first person forward. 'Hannah Harwood, you are charged with being moody and insufferable if your boyfriend fails to send you an e-mail message. How do you plead?'

'Not guilty,' she mumbled.

'What is your defence?'

Hannah opened her mouth to speak but Emma stopped her. 'Silence! You can't speak in your own defence. We have given you a defence counsel.' She pointed to Fred. Hannah's jaw dropped. 'Oh, no.'

Fred's command of English had never been her strong point. 'I

don't think she eez guilty because ah, because, ah, what is the word
. . . because she eez, ah, how you say . . .'

'Right, enough of that, she's guilty,' I said.

Fred shrugged to Hannah, 'Well, I try for you.'

Sam was next.

Emma began, 'Samantha Davies, you are charged with having
brought a Valentine's Day card on to the boat to open on 14
February. The card in question is now pinned above your bunk.
How do you plead?'

Sam looked at Fred and then at me. 'Guilty.'

The court cases proceeded until all six had been tried and
convicted. Adrienne emerged on deck with the Tupperware
box and a ladle.

'King Neptune decrees that you are each sentenced to a ladle
down the back, a ladle on the head and a handful in the face.'

Adrienne, the Lord High Executioner, took enormous pleasure
from her role – too much so. She took the lid from the box and
grinned sadistically. The smell could have knocked birds from the
sky.

Everyone started gagging except Helena, who still had a huge
grin on her face. She bounced forward. 'Me first! Me first!'

'OK then, you asked for it.' Adrienne took a ladle and deposited
it squarely on Helena's blonde head. Another was smeared enthusiastically down her front and the last squashed into her face. She
then took the camera from Emma R. so she could be gooed.

By now the others were trying to run. 'We should have tied
them to the netting,' muttered Adrienne and she meant it.

Afterwards, we doused them with buckets of water and I gave
them their certificates allowing them to pass into the southern
hemisphere. The boat and Adrienne had to be washed down as
well.

As if by magic, the breeze picked up as the ceremony ended. The
autohelm was turned off and we set a spinnaker with the full main,
giving us 12 knots in the right direction. Perfect.

Adrienne had gone below to do her calculations. She emerged a few minutes after 10.53. We had crossed the Equator in 10 days, 20 hours and 48 minutes. More importantly, we were 182 miles ahead of Olivier. We'd won the first stage of our phantom race by half a day.

The sun was relentless and I spent all day in a T-shirt and swimming costume. Adrienne kept beheading herself on the fan put on her bunk to cool the Satcom M. No matter how many times she did it, she never learned to duck and the mutterings became louder and louder.

During the lull, we decided to drop the mainsail and repair a broken batten car. At the same time, Hannah went over the side to repair the rudder damaged by our collision with the shark.

Ahead of us, a huge high pressure system sat in the South Atlantic, blocking our path. A dominant high normally existed in that area, but this one was a lot further west. In the southern hemisphere, highs swirl anticlockwise, which meant we couldn't go east of it without facing headwinds. We would have to go round the back end.

'At this rate we'll be in Rio for Carnivale,' said Adrienne wryly. A message from Lee suggested even bigger problems:

CURRENT HIGH MAY BE SPLITTING IN TWO. WILL MAKE FOR
TRICKY SAILING. DATA IMPLIES THAT WESTERN HALF IS MOVING
EAST, SO STILL MAY BE ABLE TO COME DOWN WEST SIDE. WILL BE
LOOKING HARD AT THIS TODAY AND SUNDAY.
  SUNSCREEN NEEDED NEXT COUPLE OF DAYS. FEW CLOUDS,
LIGHT WINDS. 5–15 KNOTS THRU 5°S. WIND DIRECTION EXPECTED
TO MOVE TO 120–135 (SE) OVER THE NEXT 48HRS (AVG 10KTS) . . .
  REGARDS,
  LEE

Our 'high' was developing a split personality. We could finish with two pressure systems moving slowly east together. That would be like a solid wall stretching across the Atlantic, blocking our path.

We spent all night bouncing in horrible seas. I couldn't sleep. I gave up and started reading Rowland Huntsfords biography of Sir Ernest Shackleton. We'd decided on two books each on the voyage.

Shackleton had always been a hero of mine. The polar explorer led two expeditions to Antarctica in the early 1990s, but failed in both attempts to reach the South Pole.

In many ways I think we're remarkably alike, although I possess far more of his faults than I do of his qualities. He was a less than perfect man and I am a very much less than perfect woman. He battled the whole way through his life between normality and the path that he had chosen. He backed himself into corners and knowingly created situations that he had to fight his way out of.

Similarly, he tended to be quite selfish. Shackleton would focus on one thing, often to the detriment of everything else in his life, including his family. For years his wife lived alone in Edinburgh while Shackleton raised funds in London and disappeared on expeditions that lasted for years at a time. He rarely visited her and she almost forgot what he looked like.

Many establishment figures didn't regard Shackleton as one of their own. The Royal Geographical Society looked upon the British explorer Robert Scott as their golden boy. Shackleton, an Irishman, was a bit of an embarrassment to them.

I used to feel a little like that. The sailing establishment had once regarded me as an interloper who didn't have the right pedigree. I didn't come up through the traditional route of yacht clubs and weekend regattas. I'd been a lowly stewardess on a charter boat.

As I read the biography, I came across a passage from a Robert Service poem:

The trails of the world be countless and most of the trails be tried
You tread the heels of the many till you come where the ways divide
And one lies safe in the sunlight and the other is dreary and wan
Yet you look aslant on the lone trail
Yet the lone trail lures you on.

This seemed to describe how I feel about my life in words that I could never conjure up myself but wish I had. Most of my life I have taken the hardest path and made things more difficult for myself. Whenever there is a bigger more difficult challenge, that is the one I choose rather than a goal that is more readily achievable. And each time in my life that I've achieved everything that most people would want to achieve, I smash the whole thing up and start again from scratch. I don't know why this is.

The massive high beneath us still hadn't split and the outlook remained awful. We were being forced to go further west to get around it, sailing hundreds of extra miles.

I scanned the horizon looking for trade wind clouds. 'Come on, come on,' I muttered. 'We need some speed.'

We were still just ahead of *Sport Elec*. I felt as though the race had started again from the Equator.

The sloppy seas and squalls added to my bruises. I fell sideways and hit my knee on Adrienne's bunk. Later, I pitched head-first into the chart table. In a monohull you can often anticipate the movement and brace yourself against something. But the catamaran seemed to skid from side to side, as well as up and down. It was like a nightmare fairground ride. Water cascaded over the boat as we bashed headlong into waves. Some exploded into fine spray that could be blinked away by the eyelids, but others ploughed over the cockpit, burying the watch crew.

Every wave starts as a tiny ripple on the surface. As the wind blows, it catches these ripples and makes them grow. Then it becomes a self-generating event. The higher the wave, the more wind it catches and the higher it grows.

But it doesn't rise exponentially. Waves formed by a 40-knot wind aren't twice as powerful as waves formed by a 20-knot wind: they're seventeen times more powerful. Even when the wind drops the waves continue to generate by falling into the trough that precedes them. Gravity keeps them moving until they strike a landmass.

Every wave, no matter how big or small, moves at a speed of 21 knots. The *Royal & SunAlliance* could sail faster than this in the right conditions. This created the problem of nose-diving – surfing down a wave and colliding with the one in front.

At other times, in a headwind for example, we were sailing slower than 21 knots. This meant rising over waves and dropping into troughs that seemed bottomless until the boat shuddered. Then we'd rise up over the next wave.

In the early hours of our sixteenth day at sea the catamaran began surfing down a wave that it couldn't get off. It accelerated to 21 knots and buried both bows into the wave ahead. Instantly, we came to a shuddering halt as if hitting a brick wall.

Miranda was coming out of the sleeping area, about to go up on watch. She was thrown the whole way forward through the starboard hull, crashing into a bulkhead and twisting her wrist. Hannah had been getting undressed to go to the toilet. She rocketed forwards and bent two fingers back as she tried to protect her head.

It had been the worst nose-dive so far. The strain on the rigging is enormous when a boat stops that suddenly. Thousands of pounds of pressure reverberate through the carbon fibre mast. Every bolt and stay is put to the test.

New maps overnight showed the high pressure system *had* finally split in two. One half was moving east while the other seemed to be stationary. It couldn't have been worse.

George tried to be optimistic. He even suggested a sacrifice to Neptune to nudge things in our favour. I messaged back that we didn't have any virgins on board.

Where are you, Olivier? I asked silently. Are you trapped by the wind?

I knew the answers. *Sport Elec* was further north and also further east. Olivier had taken the shortcut. We were going the long way round.

For two days we crashed into waves. It was too hot to sleep. I lay on the bench seat, feeling clammy and punch-drunk.

One morning I forgot to take my seasickness tablets. The office had scheduled an interview with a local newspaper in Portsmouth. I lay on my bunk and chatted over the Satcom to a young journalist.

'Where is your next stopover?' he asked.

'Pardon me?'

'Where is your next port of call?'

'Well, with any luck, Southampton.'

'Oh.'

'We *are* sailing non-stop around the world. That's the whole point.'

The boat was moving constantly and I felt the contents of my stomach start to shift. My breakfast wanted to be somewhere else.

'How is everyone coping?' asked the reporter.

'Actually, I'm not feeling too good at the moment. Pretty seasick.'

I could hear him scribbling furiously. There was a silence as he tried to think of something else to ask.

'Can we leave it there?' I said. 'I hope you have enough.'

I managed to put the phone back on the cradle before my stomach lurched. On my feet, I ran for the door. Bursting out of the hatch, I put both hands over my mouth. In the cockpit, Sam, Emma W. and Adrienne looked down in horror. I didn't reach the back beam. None of them escaped.

Sam went below and got my jacket. She held it over me as I heaved my heart out. I was dying. My nose ran and tears stained my cheeks. I retched on a dry stomach, crying through the pain. The others helped me sit down in the cockpit. My stomach muscles ached.

Seasickness is a terrible, terrible affliction. I once heard said of it, that 'at first you're afraid you're going to die, then you're afraid you're not going to die'. Never were truer words spoken.

After two hours of vomiting, Emma Richards began to worry. I was losing too much fluid. I sat in the cockpit trying to drink from a water bottle, but each time it came straight up again.

'You have to take a seasickness tablet,' Emma said.

As soon as I put it in my mouth I retched. I forced myself to swallow and took a gulp of water. It hit the bottom of my stomach and bounced out again.

'There is another way to take a seasickness tablet,' she suggested.

'I don't want to know.'

'If you can't get it down your throat, you stick it up your arse.'

'What a charming bedside manner you have, doctor.'

'Do you want me to do it?'

'I think I can manage.'

The suppository didn't seem to help. Emma sat next to me, massaging my back. My stomach cramped in spasms.

'I'm going to give you some really strong sleeping tablets. If you sleep it will stop you being sick.'

Somehow I managed to keep the tablets down. I dozed off. Every fifteen minutes Emma woke me and gave me a sip of water. Then she let me sleep again. I was so badly dehydrated that her only other option was an intravenous drip.

When I finally woke, Emma was still beside me.

'What are you thinking about?' she asked.

'I'm wondering who I can bribe to do my next cooking day.'

She laughed.

'Who did I vomit over?'

'Pretty much the entire watch.'

'Oh, no.'

'And also Miranda's T-shirt that was hanging over the back beam. She'll settle for a pack of cigarettes and an apology.' Emma smiled.

The boat ploughed into a wave and shuddered. Emma grabbed the base of the bunk to stop being thrown forward.

We had 24 knots of headwind and a swell of 20 feet. The peaks seemed higher than the troughs were deep. We needed the speed to drive through the waves, but too much would shake the boat to pieces.

The next 24 hours were a blur of sickness, headaches and lethargy. Everything became an effort – to get up and look at weather faxes, to go on deck, to vomit. Too many days like this and the brain gets fuzzy and the body starts twitching through lack of exercise. I kept thinking of Bill Murray in *Groundhog Day*.

The twin highs were still blocking our way south, but the eastern high had started to move. Adrienne and I talked about little else. If we dived down the middle we risked having no wind at all. The western high would then most likely move back on top of us, giving us more headwinds.

The other option was to go round the outside, if only both systems would move east.

Adrienne and I favoured diving down the centre. George responded bluntly:

IF YOU START GOING FARTHER EAST NOW, THAT WILL JUST PUT
YOU CLOSER TO THE CENTER OF THE HIGH TOWARDS THE END OF
THE WEEK. THIS INCREASES THE LIKELIHOOD OF VERY LIGHT
WINDS. YOU MUST WORK THE WESTERN END OF THE RIDGE, NOT
THE CENTER, TO AVOID COMING TO A COMPLETE STOP.

YOU CAN'T MAKE A ROPE LONGER BY CUTTING OFF ONE END
AND ATTACHING IT TO THE OTHER END . . . REMEMBER, ENZA AND
OLIVIER DE KERSAUSON WERE IN DIFFERENT WEATHER PATTERNS SO
YOU CAN'T COMPARE THEIR SITUATION TO YOURS.

BEST REGARDS, GEORGE

Adrienne sent a message straight back, trying to placate him. She explained that we just wanted to discuss the options.

George replied,

I'LL SEE IF I CAN SQUEEZE OUT A STRATEGY THAT WILL ALLOW
YOU TO TURN LEFT SOONER THAN THURS/FRI.

I DON'T KNOW IF ANYONE HAS EVER BEEN KILLED VIA EMAIL,
BUT IF I SUGGEST YOU TRACK ANY FURTHER WEST, I'M SURE
YOU'LL HAVE ME WASTED.

At least he still had a sense of humour.

*   *   *

After nineteen days we were still in touch with Olivier, although he had gone east big-time. The wind was still heading us – stopping us from chasing him. We had blue skies and squall clouds, but the temperature has dropped quite suddenly. Out of shorts and into thermals in one easy lesson.

Now on the outskirts of the high, Adrienne and I decided that if the wind filled in we'd try to cut the corner and move east. It was our only hope of keeping in touch with *Sport Elec*.

All afternoon and evening we wallowed. Becalmed. The quiet was almost claustrophobic. On deck, beneath millions of stars, I listened to the sounds of water lapping against the hulls. The only other sounds were the ripple of sails, a winch pulled on, or a sheet let off. Sharon and Fred, the helm and trimmer, whispered quietly to each other as they edged the boat forward an inch at a time. Amazingly, they were getting 2 knots of speed with only 3 knots of wind.

After the constant movement and noise, now we had silence. This is what it must have sounded like on the old square-riggers a century ago,

At 1.30 a.m. I went to bed, unable to stand it any more. I woke every couple of hours and glanced at the wind instruments. The boat speed had fallen to 1 knot.

Adrienne barely slept.

Her head rested on the chart table.

'What do George and Lee say?'

'Tough it out and wait for the wind to come to us. Lee can't see any evidence of this on his maps. He says it doesn't exist.' Adrienne smiled ruefully. 'I told him our barometer says differently.'

I stared at the instruments as if hypnotised. A breath of wind shifted round the compass, unable to decide on a bearing. The barometer had climbed to 1025. We had sailed directly into an enormous parking lot.

Aaaaaaaaarrrgh! Why were we being persecuted? What had we done to deserve so much bad luck? It had been one thing after the other. I took a deep breath. Calm down, Tracy, you're still only a day behind.

I dozed off again and the wind picked up as I slept. By 7 a.m. it was coming from the right direction – the north-west at 7 knots. At last! During the morning it picked up to 12 knots. Setting the big kite, we were off again.

Now we had to make up for lost time. Olivier had stretched his lead to more than 400 miles. I knew he was watching our progress from his base in Brest harbour in France.

He'd been quoted in a newspaper saying: 'I am confident that even if the girls have been quite good until now and using the best of really imperfect weather conditions, my opinion is that the trimaran is a better all-round boat than a catamaran.

'We will be faster in the Southern Ocean. We own all the ocean records between Good Hope and Cape Horn. I wish the best of luck to the girls but I don't see any reason why they will catch *Sport Elec*.'

I felt like sending him a message: 'Keep up the good work as my team motivator.'

TWENTY-THREE

TIME had stopped being a measure of when I woke or went to bed. The hands on my watch still turned but they had no significance. We had 24 hours to do a certain number of miles – from 10.53 until 10.53. Nothing else was important.

In ocean races like the Whitbread you are counting down the miles until the next stopover. It doesn't matter if it takes five weeks or six weeks, as long as you cross the line first. This challenge was different. Instead of counting the miles to go, we counted how far we'd done and how long it had taken. Nobody ever said, 'Oh, God, there are still 18,000 miles left.' And none of us had a need or desire to reach the finish. Instead we *needed* to do 450 miles that day.

Sailing had never been more fulfilling than this. The sense of immediacy was electrifying. I wanted to make the boat faster and the clock slower. I wanted to reach up, put my fingers between the hands and hold them still – just for a few hours. Then we could squeeze a few more miles into the day.

On a cold and misty morning, the sea had turned transparent emerald at the tips, capped with white. The desolate, grey rollers stretched from horizon to horizon. There is something indefinable about the South Atlantic, yet I'd know this place instantly. I love it more than anywhere on Earth.

Emma W. swung herself into the God Pod and looked around, making sure we were alone. 'Has Helena talked to you?'

'No.'

'I think her arms are bad again. She doesn't want to tell you.'

Helena had problems with tendonitis and her elbows were scarred from past surgery. Before we left England a specialist had told her that the problem was caused by a back complaint. She spent two months being strapped up and doing physiotherapy. We hoped the problem had been sorted, but the colder weather had obviously caused it to flare.

'She's down there now, trying to get dressed. She's crying, they're so painful.'

I pulled on my gear and clambered across the netting to the port hull. Helena sat on her bunk in tears, trying to put her arms into a jacket. She was clearly in agony.

'How are the arms?'

'Oh, they're fine.'

'No they're not. They're hurting.'

'Yes, a little, but it's OK.'

'You're not OK if you can't steer. You're a problem for all of us. How many painkillers are you taking?'

'I just take a couple when I go up on watch.'

'Why didn't you tell me?'

She shook her head.

'I've said it to everyone, if you want me to take a watch, you only have to ask. Do you want me to take this watch?'

She nodded and wiped her nose. 'Yes, maybe if you could do this one.'

'When does it hurt most? Is it when you're steering?'

'Yes, but the worst is getting up from my bunk; going from being warm and getting into damp clothes.'

'OK. I'm going to do the next few watches for you. Then we'll try to work out an alternative plan. I don't want you to hurt yourself.'

I was angry, not so much at Helena, but at Emma Richards. As the crew's medic, she should have informed me.

'How many painkillers is Helena taking?' I asked her.

Emma looked at me and wasn't sure how far to carry the secret.

'I know about it,' I said.

'She's taking the strongest thing I can give her. You're supposed to take one tablet every twelve hours.'

'How many is she taking?'

'Two a watch.'

'Oh, Jesus, why didn't you tell me?'

'She made me promise. I felt caught in the middle.'

'Don't ever do it again. She could suffer an adverse reaction.'

'I know. She can't keep taking so many.'

I steered for Helena that day and tried to come up with a solution. The cold and damp would only get worse, along with her pain. She was a watch captain – a vital cog in the machine. I couldn't afford to lose her.

Bangs and crashes woke me. The hulls ploughed into waves and then groaned as they lifted and cleared water off the decks. Miki yelled from the cockpit: 'I think we should take a reef!'

Crawling out of my sleeping bag, I began getting dressed. Adrienne did the same, pausing to glance at the wind readings. The gap between the first and second reefs on the mainsail was quite large.

Emerging on deck, I could feel the spray biting at my cheeks. Hannah, Sharon, Adrienne and Miranda were already in position and clipped on. I took over the main sheet and Adrienne controlled the traveller.

'OK, when you're ready, Miki.'

'We're going now,' she shouted and steered down, holding the catamaran off the wind. At the same moment, I released the main sheet and Adrienne dropped the traveller. The boom swung away from the wind and lifted higher. The mainsail now swung over the leeward side of the netting.

Sharon released the halyard and began lowering the sail. The slackening cloth smashed violently all over the place. The reefing lines that are used to pull the outside of the sail down and keep it secure were now loose and flapping wildly, whipping through the air at astonishing speeds. One line cracked like a cattle-whip an inch in front of my face — a terrifying sound.

The reefing lines went from a point on the boom up the outside edge of the sail, through a ring and then back to the boom. Some of them were 30 or 40 feet long and could so easily snake around a head, take out an eye, or get caught on the SSB antenna and break it. Miranda was at the mast trying to get them under control.

We lowered the sail by 30 feet. The reefed cloth folded into a rope cradle formed by the lazy jacks.

Sharon volunteered to go out along the boom to put a safety strop on the outside edge of the sail. This meant that if a reefing line broke, we wouldn't lose the main. She clipped on her safety harness and began crawling on her hands and knees along the boom. This was equivalent to clinging to a three-foot-wide ledge on a moving mountain while having buckets of freezing water hurled at her.

Every few feet she reached a lazy jack and had to unclip her safety harness then clip herself back on again at the other side. As the boat pitched and rolled, she clung tightly and waited for an easier moment.

The boom is 35 feet long, but must have seemed twice that length in the darkness. Only the deck lights illuminated Sharon's bright yellow jacket, as she neared the end of her crawl.

She attached the safety stop and began to turn. Suddenly, the boat came up into the wind a little and a wave punched it back. The boom moved violently and Sharon was flicked off the end like an unwanted insect on a picnic rug.

She flew through the air and over the back beam. Without a safety harness she would have disappeared completely and most likely have died without ever being found. Instead, in a split second, the harness pulled her tight and wrapped around her neck as she tumbled over the beam.

The safety line wrenched her back but left her hanging there, unable to breathe, with her legs flailing desperately for something solid.

Miranda, Adrienne and I dived across the beam and grabbed any part of her clothing we could.

'Lift her, lift her!' I screamed.

Sharon's face was a mask of pure panic. She couldn't speak – the safety line was slowly throttling her.

As we lifted, I slipped my fingers beneath the line and pulled it past her chin and nose. She gasped a breath and gripped our arms as Adrienne unclipped the harness and we dragged her up over the beam into the cockpit.

Sharon lay there sucking air into her lungs and clutching her badly bruised neck. 'I thought my throat had been cut,' she wheezed.

'That was a pretty good dive,' said Miki.

'I reckon she would have got more points if she'd completed the pike,' added Adrienne.

Sharon managed a pained smile. She waited in the nav station until Emma R. made sure there were no other injuries. Then she insisted on going back to her watch.

During the night we crossed the Greenwich Meridian. We had already decided to keep all clocks set to GMT, regardless of the local time. This made it easier to plan radio schedules and was less confusing for the crew changing watch.

The big cat powered eastwards, with 27 knots of wind from the north-west and a long, following sea. The swells were 10 to 15 feet.

My eyes were puffy and I could barely see straight. I'd been doing watches for Helena and not getting enough sleep because we had to be up at completely different times to each other. However, I had managed to come up with an idea that might solve the problem of Helena's elbows.

Emma R., who wasn't part of the watch system, could steer for her. It wasn't the perfect solution because it meant that Emma wouldn't be available to pick up the camera and film for the BBC documentary. She had, however, shown a lot of ability when the girls had let her steer.

Emma's face lit up when I told her the news.

'She'll be your arms,' I told Helena. 'You tell her what to do.'

That afternoon I sat watching the two of them steer together for the first time. What an amazing sight! Helena stood with her back to the bows, leaning against the God Pod, looking at Emma. She spoke very quietly, 'OK, so now you have a good feeling of boat. Don't look behind you. Feel the wind on your face. Ignore what's going on around you. Just feel the boat.

'Now there is a very big wave coming up on your left. You are not going to look at it because it is not important. But you have to make sure that when it comes under the boat you are going to feel us swing a little to the right . . .'

Within hours we could see the numbers. Adrienne looked at me. 'I can't believe the speeds she's doing. Where does she get this from?'

We had discovered an astonishing talent. Never before had I seen anyone with such natural talent. I could actually sit and watch her steer, it was such a joy.

This sort of ability cannot be taught. It is almost a sixth sense that allows someone to feel, see and sense precisely the best line to steer for maximum speed; to make those tiny adjustments that keep the wind in the sails at the right angle and power the boat forward, without tipping it over. It's like running along a clifftop and never once slowing down or pulling away because you're scared of heights or the wind.

Although I revelled in Emma's genius, deep down I felt a pang of sadness. I had sailed for half a lifetime, but I would never be as good as this girl.

★   ★   ★

Riding along the top of a low we edged southwards at 17 knots. The front had arrived and the wind had swung more to the west. Steering became a true test of skill as horrible cross-beam rollers crashed into the starboard side, pushing the boat off course.

The banging on the bottom of the God Pod was horrendous. Waves slammed into the fibreglass pod, rattling every bone in my body. I tried to sleep through them while Adrienne sat tapping something on the laptop. The biggest wave so far came up beneath us and exploded against the God Pod. I was up, out of my bunk and halfway through the hatchway before Adrienne could grab hold of me.

'You're in your thermals and you're going outside.'

I was standing in a pool of water half asleep. What am I doing?

'I thought we hit something.'

'No, no.'

'Are you sure?'

'It's OK.'

We then began checking for cracks, lifting mattresses and looking in corners. We joked about waking up one morning and finding that the God Pod had broken free and the boat had sailed away.

'We'll be bobbing up and down all by ourselves,' I said.

'Would that be classed as mutiny?'

'Only if they don't come back and get us.'

For the first time, I felt a pang of homesickness. I began to daydream about my house in Reading, walking through each room in my mind. My favourite is the lounge with its squishy sofas and the french windows leading out into the garden. My dogs, Arnie and Hannah are curled up on the floor. Upstairs, Trevor is sitting at his computer, with his chair tilted back and a cigarette burning in the ashtray. Claire, my PA, is in the office fielding calls. My cousin Greg is painting the dining room.

After three weeks at sea, I craved normality. I wanted to be able to make a cup of coffee without having to make another ten cups

and remember what everyone had in it. I wanted to be able to go to
the loo without putting on all my foul weather gear and clambering
across the nets in the freezing wind and spray. I wanted to be able to
step out of my bunk and not stand in a puddle of water. I wanted to
be able to pee into the funnel of my pee bottle without it running
down my leg. But most of all, I was sick of the constant movement
and noise. I wanted to scream, 'Stop! Let me off! Give me a few
minutes' peace.'

In my diary I wrote a list:

GOOD BITS
- *We still have pens and pencils in the nav station and I have*
  acquired a pencil.
- *No more washing for a month. Hoorah!*
- *The chute has been in the oggin (sea) twice and not broken!*
- *Emma Richards's steering.*
- *My feet don't smell yet.*
- *I managed to get out of my second day of cooking.*
- *We saw our first albatross.*

BAD BITS
- *The wind is always up the backside.*
- *The boat keeps breaking.*
- *The chicken and noodles are disgusting.*
- *Helena's arms are still bad.*
- *My feet will smell soon.*
- *I owe Sam two bottles of champagne for doing my cooking*
  day.
- *An albatross attacked us.*

Trevor had been e-mailing us weather maps and ice reports.
Unfortunately, his latest batch covered the northern hemisphere
instead of the southern hemisphere.

When I pointed this out to him, he replied:

Dear Tracy,

Talk about picky! Okay, so the charts I sent may not quite
have covered the relevant areas but personally I think far too much
is made, these days, of this North/South business. It was all
much easier in the old days when the world was still flat.
Anyway, to keep you happy I've now sent the other charts but I
don't expect any of this nit-picking in the future.

On Saturday, 28 February the air temperature had fallen to 3.5°C
and the wind chill factor sliced it even further. The nav station felt
like a freezer and each breath condensed and seemed to hang in the
air like a speech bubble.

Most of the girls had packed away their foul weather gear and
started wearing their survival suits. They looked like babies in
romper suits with harnesses over the top and their hat and mittens
tied on with string. Cute! Adrienne called them the Teletubbies.

We were doing almost identical mileage to *Sport Elec*, except one
day later.

I had to speak to the girls about helming, advising that the watch
captains were to take people off the wheel if they were steering
dangerously, or too slowly.

'No one's ego is more important than the team. We all have bad
days,' I said. 'When that happens we can start trying too hard and
staring at the numbers. By then, you've lost it. If that happens, you
must be big enough to say, "I can't do this, somebody else have a
go."

'It's the same if you're getting tired. We can't afford to make
mistakes. Our lives are at stake. Do you all understand?'

Everything about our lives had become more difficult. Every sail
change and gybe took longer. It took fifteen minutes to get dressed
and thirty minutes to go to the toilet. Staying dry had become the
centre of my existence and woe betide anybody who got me wet.
Each of us had a limited number of dry socks and each pair had a
value beyond money or bartered chocolate bars.

Everyone developed their own little rituals because the practicalities of everyday life had become so much harder. In the port hull the girls faced the problem of getting up in nice dry thermals and having to dress in the galley surrounded by dripping bodies. Similarly, as each girl finished her watch, she had to undress, hang up her gear and back into the sleeping area, taking her boots off last.

The logistics in the starboard hull were almost as crazy. You had to be half contortionist and half magician to get dressed while two dripping people waited to use the toilet.

At other times, as you crawled tentatively from your bunk, somebody would swing feet-first down the hatchway, bringing a surge of water with her. The howls of protest could be heard from the God Pod. People took it personally and I didn't blame them.

One of my little rituals was to put my boots on the floor beneath the chart table, so that when I got dressed in my sleeping bag, I could reach them easily. One morning, I looked down and the boots had been moved. I lost the plot.

'Who the hell moved my boots?' I screamed.

Sam jumped about two feet in the air. 'Well, I did, I thought they might get wet.'

'Never touch my boots.'

'Water was dripping into them.'

'Never, ever touch my boots.'

'OK, OK.' Poor Sam looked at me as though I'd finally flipped.

We had 20 knots of boat speed, heading south-east and waiting for the next front. Every so often a squall moved through. During the afternoon they intensified and we had lots of sail changes.

Emma Richards had been getting incredible speeds out of the boat.

'I want her on the helm 24 hours a day,' Adrienne said, only half joking.

'That's not really possible.'

'I don't care. Tie her to the wheel. Look at the numbers.'

At that moment I was more interested in the radar screen. It had picked up an approaching squall that looked solid and nasty. I went on deck to warn Helena and Emma. R. Helena had seen it coming. Emma looked nervous.

'It's OK, it's only a squall,' said Helena. 'It's going to be about 30 or 40 knots of wind.'

'I've never steered in 40 knots of wind.'

'Well you're about to learn.'

'I'm not ready.'

'Yes you are. The boat is completely set up for it. It's not going to be a problem. We've sailed through it before.'

Emma looked at me for reassurance. 'Do you want someone else on the wheel?'

'No.'

The blackness crept closer. Because the apparent and true winds were coming from different directions, it felt as though the squall was running us down like a predator. Nothing we could do would shake it off.

Suddenly, the wind picked up and the boat began acting differently. Then the gusts rocketed. The catamaran started to power up. The raw energy gave me butterflies inside. The vibration of the water against the hull sounded like an express train rattling over the rails. This started as a low-pitched hum and ended as a scream. It's a lower pitch than the wind screaming through the wire stays and cables. As one hull lifted from the waves, there was a momentary lull and then the sound began again.

At the same time, the catamaran was sliding from side to side. It didn't have a rhythm or cadence like the rocking of a train. Instead it was like standing on a flatbed truck being driven by a schizophrenic driver who keeps hitting the brake and the accelerator, and swinging the wheel violently.

Everything on the boat becomes difficult – standing, getting dressed, writing, reading and eating. I had to hold on with one hand and type with the other.

The faster we travelled, the worse it became. After a while I realised that unconsciously, I was always braced against the movement. To be so tense all the time is exhausting.

Emma tried hard not to watch the wind speed indicator, but couldn't help glancing at it.

'Thirty-two knots . . . 34 knots . . . 37 knots . . .' Her voice was getting higher and higher.

Helena said, 'Don't look at the wind speed. You steer the boat. I'll worry about the numbers.'

Emma's legs were braced apart and she gripped the wheel tightly, as if fearful that the boat would take off without her. Her eyes were the size of saucers and filled with a mixture of terror and excitement.

The wind was screaming past my ears and we were hooning down waves at 30 knots. Helena never took her eyes off Emma's face and kept talking to her calmly.

Emma was singing, 'My first 48-knot squall! My first 48-knot squall!'

For twenty-five minutes she mastered the wind and waves, refusing to be put off by the blinding sheets of rain or waves crashing through the netting. Emma's arms must have been aching but she didn't let it show.

The port gybe was taking us further south, against the advice of George and Lee, but we couldn't go anywhere else. The starboard gybe would mean heading almost directly north and losing some miles. We had to claw back distance in the Southern Ocean and get closer to *Sport Elec*. Then the race could begin again from Cape Horn on the tip of South America.

Passing 50°S we entered iceberg country. From now on we kept a watch. It had been warmer than normal in Antarctica during the summer, which meant the icebergs had tended to break up and growlers float north. Countering this was well nigh impossible, particularly at night. Sailing at our speed, there was almost no chance that we'd see floating ice until it ripped off a hull.

Olivier had encountered floating ice at 60°S in April during his record attempt. The size of the individual pieces was too small to show up on satellite imagery, which is primarily how the growler fields are detected.

I had no intention of going that far south, particularly in a multihull, but both *Enza* and *Sport Elec* had been forced into deep dives south because of wind angles. Sometimes it becomes un-avoidable.

On the first day of March, we passed the Crozet Islands. Olivier was now two days ahead, but I was confident of catching him. *Sport Elec* and *Enza* had both suffered bad luck in the second half of their races. Our bad luck had been at the beginning. If we could stay in touch until Cape Horn then the race would begin again.

The negative thoughts of the past few days had gone. We were still 4,500 miles from the halfway point. This race wasn't over.

Midway through the morning the wind swung completely and came forward, just aft of the beam. We took the spinnaker down and put two reefs in the main. The wind rose to 32 knots, with waves of 30 feet and higher crashing over the starboard aft quarter. The cat was being thrown about and surfing down the faces of waves at 28 knots. It was too rough for that sort of speed. Half a dozen times we buried both bows beneath the water.

I sat in my foul weather gear for most of the day, in case I was needed on deck. Every ten minutes or so a wave slammed into the floor of the God Pod. Adrienne and I spoke to each other through clenched teeth.

Lee, bless him, proved to be a master of understatement:

NOTICE FROM YOUR OBS THAT WINDS HAVE PICKED UP
SUBSTANTIALLY (41 KTS AT 1439 GMT). YOU ARE NOW IN THE
TIGHTENED GRADIENT ON THE BACK SIDE OF THE LOW. WIND
SPEEDS ARE EXPECTED TO PEAK SHORTLY, BUT I STILL THINK
YOU'LL HOLD IN THE MID TO HIGH 20'S AND OCCASIONALLY A
TAD HIGHER, FOR A WHILE, AS THEY GO MORE SOUTHERLY OVER
THE NEXT 36 HOURS.

As dusk fell we had 40 knots of wind and 40-foot seas coming from behind. I was about to put the storm jib up but instead settled for a third reef. Not a moment too soon. The wind rose to 45 knots.

I had never sailed a multihull in these conditions – none of us had. I didn't know what 'the cat' would do next. Sometimes we bashed into waves and other times we skidded precariously sideways down them. In theory we had to keep the boat upright and keep sailing, but a storm like this doesn't follow any rules. One mistake on the wheel, even the tiniest miscalculation, and the catamaran would be lost.

I finally undressed and went to bed at 8 p.m. I didn't sleep. Each time a wave punched into the God Pod, my eyes flew open and I feared the worst. It was a long night, miserable beyond belief.

By morning the barometer had fallen to 992, which put us quite near the centre of the low. The seas were 12 to 15 feet, coming from behind, with the boat surfing and slamming heavily. We had covered 420 miles in 24 hours – good mileage for the conditions.

Hannah spilled into the God Pod, wearing her survival suit and dripping water. I recognised her eyes when she pulled off her mask.

'I feel like I've come to a fancy dress party and everyone has come dressed as Darth Vader,' she said, managing to smile. I knew she was scared. I didn't blame her.

By mid-afternoon we had a true wind speed of 30–35 knots and an apparent wind speed of 27 knots. The air temperature had dropped to 3.2°C but the barometer had edged up to 1010. Surely the worst was nearly over.

At 5 p.m. the wind began to moderate, although the seas were still rough. We shook out three reefs and began to relax a little. It's amazing how gusts of 30 knots can suddenly seem like a light breeze.

I went across to get a few mugs of coffee and came back over the netting. As I handed them to Miki, I looked down at the God Pod roof. There were tiny hairline cracks starting to form in the laminate. The girls began checking for delamination elsewhere. There was evidence of paint being ripped off by the force of the water and waves.

On Wednesday morning we were just off the Kerguelen Plateau, still riding on the back of the low pressure giving us southerlies. The next land above us would be Australia. If we could average 450 miles a day, we were nineteen days from Cape Horn. That was optimistic, but the lows were banking up nicely behind us. Olivier's lead was down to 715 miles.

The barometer began gradually dropping through the day from 1015 to 994. 'Batten down the hatches, it's about to blow again,' I muttered. Lee and George had said nothing about this one.

At 4 a.m. all hands were summoned on deck to raise the storm jib. We had 40-foot waves coming from behind, putting the fear of God into the helm and the watch crew. Each time we reached the top of one, it felt like being on a rollercoaster as it crested a rise. That first glimpse into the abyss is heart-stopping. As I felt the 'big cat' surf down the face of the wave, I grabbed hold of something solid and waited for the bottom.

The pounding was too much for us. We changed course, turning away from the wind. Minutes later I heard a sound like a gunshot. The starboard runner block simply blew apart. It took a split second and a few inches of movement before a safety strop took the strain. A shock wave reverberated through the mast and I thought the rig was coming down. The pressure must have been enormous.

Helena cried out from the cockpit.

I rushed up on deck and Sam looked at me. 'What do we do?'

'Gybe and put the other runner on so we can repair this one. Or maybe we can repair it as it is. I don't want to gybe if we can help it.'

Hannah arrived on deck.

'Can we repair it without gybing?' I asked.

'Yeah, I think so.'

I glanced at the safety strop. Without it, we would have lost the mast.

Hannah and Helena rigged up an amazing system of pulleys and ropes to take the strain. They also invented a new system to replace the runner block. We didn't have a spare. They weren't supposed to break

Meanwhile, the wind had risen to 45 knots and was howling through the wires. I sat wedged into a seat, with one hand braced against the bulkhead, trying to type my diary with the other hand.

Five hours after losing the runner block, Adrienne sent a 'please explain' message to George and Lee. Why hadn't they seen the storm coming?

> *Our position is 49°29S and 84°30Ee. At 0400GMT we opted to turn hard left to nurse the boat. The wind has been over 40–45+ for several hours and the boat was pounding so badly, a lot of gear was beginning to break. The wind has still not eased and I guess it won't for another 6–8 hours. Baro is finally rising again 994 after bottoming out at 992 at 0400. Seas very rough, 5–6 metres.*
> *Regards,*
> *Adrienne.*

The French yachting journalist Christian Fevrier had recognised the problem. As the unofficial statistician for the Speeds Sailing Record Council, he'd been following our progress with great interest. A day earlier he sent us an e-mail warning that the low in front of us had stalled and we risked catching up with it. He predicted winds of 40 to 50 knots.

If he'd seen it, why hadn't George or Lee?

Unflappable as ever, Lee responded:

HOPE NO PERMANENT DAMAGE ONBOARD, EQUIPMENT OR CREW.
NO INDICATIONS ON OUR DATA OF 45 KNOT WINDS, SO SHOULD
BE TEMPORARY.

Trying to forecast the weather so deep in the Southern Ocean is not a straightforward exercise. There are few weather stations or data buoys in the region and no weather satellites orbit directly overhead. Instead, forecasters have to rely on images from the edges of two other satellite photographs joined together to form one picture.

They also rely on devices called 'scatterometers' that fire micro-wave beams from satellites on to the earth to measure wind speed and direction on the ocean surface. All of this information is programmed into global numerical models run on supercomputers. Ultimately, weather forecasts are based on these models rather than direct observations.

I had lost all track of the days. Was it Thursday or Friday? I just knew it was day thirty-two. How many miles had we done? How many were there to go? Did we have enough time?

We were down to 53°S on a starboard gybe. Despite the cold, it was a lovely day, with blue sky and weak sunshine. After how rough it had been, I looked at the sea and thought it was saying, 'I was just playing with you. That's what I *can* be like, but this is my good side.'

We had gone from too much wind to not enough. The 'big cat' was heading north-east at 15 knots – too slow and in the wrong direction.

Miki looked up at the strange cloud cover. 'Looks as though it might snow,' she said matter-of-factly.

I figured Miki, being Finnish, probably knew a lot about the subject, so I didn't disagree.

Within minutes magical snowflakes began falling – first just one or two, and then thick flurries that swirled in the air spilling from the sails. We all reverted to childhood, cavorting about the deck, scooping snow into snowballs and miniature snowmen.

The snow flurries cleared towards dusk. It's not often in the Southern Ocean that you get a chance to see a sunset. This one was magnificent. Clouds on the very edge of the horizon forced the colour to leak across the sky, spilling out like a tie-dyed sarong caught in the breeze.

But for all its beauty the day had been cruel. We paid the price in lost miles. The gap with Olivier had blown out to 1,078 miles – three days' sailing unless we could improve our average speed. The lead was not insurmountable. At one stage *Enza* had been five days in front of *Sport Elec* and Olivier had caught her on the run home. At this stage of the race *Sport Elec* had been 3° in latitude further north than we were, a distance of 180 miles. Due to the curvature of the Earth, this meant we were sailing the shorter route, but also taking a greater risk with icebergs and getting caught on the wrong side of a low pressure system.

The margin for error is only one or two degrees in latitude – a distance of between 60 and 120 miles. Too high and we missed the winds. Too low and they beat us to pieces. It was like trying to thread a needle that was constantly being moved by the jet stream and the rotation of the Earth.

On Sunday 8 March, the barometer dropped seven millibars in seven hours. It was a wild old ride. We had reefed the main three times and had 40 knots of pure venom, blowing us eastwards. As darkness fell the wind reached 45 knots and the seas were pounding. We were now more than 53°S, less than 1,000 miles from the Antarctic ice sheet and the air temperature was 1.7°C.

As the wind reached 48 knots, I wanted to scream in frustration. I was scared. We were too far south. Why hadn't we learned from last time? Instead of riding along the top of the low, it was going to pass directly over the top of us, like a steamroller.

I knew what had happened. When you're falling behind in a race, the temptation is to find lots of wind to catch up. Adrienne was pushing too hard, but it was my fault for letting her.

We were caught between the proverbial rock and a hard place. To follow our best course meant having the wind at a dangerous angle and the boat being pounded. So we ran away from the wind, heading north-east but trying not to lose too much ground. This kept the wind just aft of the beam.

The noise was horrendous. Nothing ever stopped. Wind screamed through the wires, the hulls vibrated, waves crashed over us, people ran across the deck, 'Bang! Bang! Bang!' Blocks and winches were turned on the sides of the God Pod and the sound was amplified as it came through the carbon; the weather fax creaked, the wind generators whirled and people shouted in the cockpit.

My senses had been overloaded for too long. Please make it stop. Just for a moment, I wanted to stand still in a quiet field and look up at the trees, hearing absolutely nothing.

A wave slammed into the bottom of the God Pod. On my feet again, I looked towards the cockpit and heard Miki's voice: 'It's OK, Tracy.'

The catamaran seemed to slide sideways down the next wave. The cockpit disappeared under a wave. The weight of green water pushed the boat on to a dangerous angle, with the wind on the beam. The starboard hull lifted and seemed to hang in mid-air. Is this it? Are we going over?

My mouth went dry. If the hull lifted too far, one rudder would be out of the water. Every boat has a degree of roll from which she can no longer recover. When 48 knots of wind strikes a catamaran fully on the beam, the centre of gravity alters suddenly. Instead of the wind driving the boat forward, it is pushing it over. Two forces are locked in battle. The push of the wind against the sails is directly opposed by the downward pull of gravity on one hull and the buoyancy of the other.

Being 42 feet wide, the catamaran could be assumed to have a reasonable degree of stability, but the mast and sails counteract this. Effectively, we were on a vessel that was ten storeys high because of the mast and only 92 feet long. The taller the ship, the easier it is to capsize.

When the starboard hull lifted, the girls on watch reacted instantly. With only one rudder in the water, there was little the helm could do to save us. The fate of the boat rested with Miranda and Hannah controlling the main sheet and headsail sheet. These were dumped simultaneously, setting the sails loose and spilling the wind.

Suddenly, the wind lost its grip. Was it too late? The starboard hull paused for a moment in mid-air, until gravity regained the ascendancy. Slowly, it settled again in the water.

I was angry and frightened. Angry because we shouldn't have put ourselves in this situation and frightened because I thought we were going to perish in a cold wilderness, 1,000 miles from land.

So this is what it's like to be truly terrified. I squeezed my eyes shut and snatched gulps of air. Surely something would break inside of me.

I glanced at Adrienne, trying to draw strength from her. She, too, was terrified. I looked at her harder and longer than I should have done, turning away quickly. We nose-dived and I was thrown against the bulkhead at the end of my bunk. The decks groaned as they fought to rise. Water cascaded over the cockpit.

All night we fought, taking the seas astern and the wind from over the right shoulder. I had never been so frightened for so long.

My muscles were so taut they began locking up. My heart pounded until my chest heaved. How long could adrenalin keep me going? When would my body begin shutting down?

I couldn't show weakness or fear. Others were looking to me for reassurance. I heard myself say things like, 'Oh, we went through much worse than this on *Maiden*. It's fine.'

I was lying.

The moments that I have been most scared in my life have all been yachting moments. I remembered *Maiden*, deep in the South Atlantic, when she sprang a leak and almost sank. And later, on the final leg, when a tornado picked up the 19-ton yacht and spun it around in a complete circle.

I was scared when these things happened. Perhaps, for a moment, I thought I might die. But nothing compared to the fear I felt now. I sat in the nav station, dripping wet and typing on the laptop with one hand as I bailed with the other. Each time the boat accelerated down a wave or began sliding, I had to grab hold of the bench and brace myself.

A small label on the top of the computer read: 'IMPORTANT NOTICE: For comfortable and safe use please read the comfort and safety guide.'

I didn't know whether to laugh or cry.

A cry came from above. 'We've lost the numbers.'

The figures on the cockpit console and in the nav station had suddenly frozen in place. High above us, a single gust of more than 55 knots had destroyed the wind instruments at the top of the mast. We had lost all the information vital to steer the boat.

'What do we do now?' cried Helena from the cockpit.

'The best you can,' said Adrienne, unable to hide the tension in her voice.

The race or the record didn't matter any more. We were fighting to survive.

Steering without instruments is like driving down a country lane on a pitch-black night, with no headlights or brakes. The next corner might be a hairpin bend. It doesn't matter because you can't slow down.

Adrienne stayed at the end of her bunk changing motherboards and re-booting programs. We had no way of knowing if the problem was electrical, or mechanical. It was a process of elimination.

The girls did a brilliant job steering in the hours before dawn. Thankfully, the wind began to drop and crank around to a better angle. We shook two reefs from the mainsail and breathed a collective sigh of relief.

Right through the day we tried to fix the problem – still believing that the fault rested in the nav station. Software manuals and instructions were spread out in the God Pod and Adrienne cursed and swore as she leaned over the end of her bunk.

Slowly it became clear that the real fault rested a hundred feet above the deck. The windex instruments on the mast would have to be replaced.

Although the wind had dropped, sheets of foaming water still surged through the netting and the waves were enormous. I couldn't risk sending anyone up the mast in these seas. At the same time, we couldn't afford to spend another night sailing without wind readings.

By mid-afternoon I made a decision to try the repairs. I assumed

Sam would go up the rig, although she was still quite weak from hunger. She delayed and it wasn't until darkness approached that she asked if someone else could go instead.

I couldn't blame Sam. I had never seen anybody go up a mast in these conditions. Emma W. or Hannah were the most logical replacements because of their rigging experience. I asked Emma because she was lighter and very strong for her size.

'There's no way I'm going up,' she said, shuddering at the thought.

'Then we'll steer through the night without them.'

'This is ridiculous,' Adrienne answered. 'I'll go up.'

'No you won't. You've never been up the mast.' She was also built like a matchstick and would have blown away.

'If anyone *has* to go up, then I will,' I said.

'You can't, you're the skipper.'

Sharon had to be physically restrained from having a go. She had no experience and was too heavy.

Finally I asked Emma again. 'There's no pressure. If you say no, that's fine by me.'

'OK, I'll give it a go,' she said, sounding quite positive.

Emma wore her survival suit, with the new windex instruments strapped across her back. She carried a torch and a bag of tools slung around her waist. We taped a VHF radio to her arm so she could hit the call button and talk to us.

Gathered in the cockpit, we discussed each person's role. Miki would steer because nobody could match her skill at keeping the boat pointed dead downwind. She had to stop us accidentally gybing or accelerating away. We had one reef in the main and no headsail.

'I want Fred, Sharon and Sam on the halyard to take her up. Helena, you're on the winch.

'I'll have the other radio,' I told Emma. 'I'm going to watch you going up. I'll have the torch on you the whole way. If you get into trouble or you want to come back down, you say. Don't be a hero. We'll give this one shot. If it doesn't work, you come back down.'

Miki had us dead down, but the catamaran still rode the swell, moving around like a bucking bronco. I lay on the God Pod roof, pointing the torch up the mast. Water crashed over me, running down the back of my neck. I looked up at the mast and thought to myself: There's no way she's gonna make it.

Although we were only 15 feet from each other, Miki had trouble hearing my running commentary, so Adrienne sat between us relaying messages.

Emma stood at the bottom of the mast and tied herself on. Someone checked the knot and Emma tilted her head and took one look at the challenge above. 'OK, let's go.'

The girls sat along the beam and began pulling the halyard. Helena took up the slack on the winch. She edged upwards a few inches at a time. Wiping salt water from my eyes, I tried to keep the torch directed as the mast swayed. I could pick out the yellow of Emma's suit.

The radio crackled near my right ear. 'I need to go a bit faster,' she said, breathing hard. 'I just want to get up there.' She was having real problems hanging on and it was wasting her energy.

'Faster, faster.'

Sharon and Fred picked up the pace. Meanwhile, Miki was struggling to keep the boat down. Every gust of wind from a slightly different direction made the catamaran want to accelerate and start sailing. Miki's job would have been difficult at the best of times, but without wind instruments or being able to see the water, it was damn near impossible. Somehow she managed it.

Emma had reached the first spreader and had to negotiate the wires. I could hear her getting agitated. 'I need to go faster. I need to go faster. But you have to slow down when I say slow down.'

I tried to be as calm as possible. 'That's OK, Emma, you just tell us what you want.'

The higher she climbed, the more violently the mast moved. Suddenly, I heard the most chilling and terrified scream of my life. Emma's voice was so high-pitched and frantic I couldn't hear the words. She was screaming – not into the radio – but into the wind.

A wave crashed over me. The torch swung. For a brief second I lost sight of Emma. My heart leapt. The light picked her up again and she was still on the mast. Thank God! Clearly, she had a problem, but I couldn't see what it was.

Miki heard the words first. From the cockpit, she could hear Emma screaming more clearly than I could from beneath the mast.

'Her safety harness has come undone.'

Unbelievable!

Emma had to balance herself on top of the first spreader and do herself up again. She wasn't wearing gloves because they restricted her movement, but it took only a few minutes on deck before exposed fingers were too painful to move. Her fingers were like useless lumps of wood as she tried to re-do the harness rope. Over and over she tried, obviously terrified. She couldn't do it. Unless she managed to reattach the harness then she'd be trapped a third of the way up the mast. Bracing herself against the mast, she tried again. I watched her swaying precariously in the narrow beam of light. Miranda sat next to me with spare batteries for the torch.

A shaky voice came over the radio. 'I've done it.'

'I'm bringing you down. This is bloody ridiculous.'

'No I think I can do it. I really think I can.'

'OK, we'll take you up to the second spreader, but if you have problems again I'm just going to bring you down.'

Emma rose again, reaching the second spreader 80 feet above the deck. I could hear her crying into the radio, sobbing in fear and pain. Her fingers were half frozen and her limbs ached.

'Emma, we are going to bring you down. Listen to me.'

'No, it's OK, it's OK.' Her teeth were chattering.

'It's too dangerous. Come down.'

'No. I can do it.'

Without her permission, I couldn't bring her down. Emma's foot might be in the wrong place and she'd be caught in the rigging. She might die up there before someone could reach her.

The sobbing continued. I had never seen Emma cry.

She negotiated the second spreader and then yelled, 'Stop, stop, stop!'

There was a long silence. The torch struggled to reach her. I could see her clinging to the mast, her cheek pressed hard against the carbon.

'Emma, listen to me. Come down.'

'No, no, I'm OK.'

The silence continued. I waited for her instructions.

'Something is wrong,' said Miranda. We could see Emma shouting. Her radio had failed. Miki heard the message. 'She can't do it. She wants to come down.'

'Fast or slow.'

'Slow. Bring her down slowly.'

Helena controlled the winch, edging her down. It seemed an eternity before her feet touched the deck. I had never been so relieved to get anyone down a mast. Emma dissolved into tears and I put my arms around her. Her whole body was shaking.

'It's OK, it's OK.'

After unhooking the harness, I sat her on the beam and Helena and I held her close. I felt awful.

'I'm so sorry. I'm so sorry,' she sobbed.

'What for?'

'I let everyone down.'

'No you didn't. That was one of the bravest things I have ever seen.'

Miki turned 'big cat' loose again and we set a course that seemed to be fractionally north of east, although without a compass we couldn't be sure. It was the middle of the night (local time) and the aurora australis (southern lights) were just visible through the clouds. I sent Emma off to bed and did her watch for her.

I doubt if anybody has ever sailed a multihull the size of *Royal & SunAlliance* without wind instruments, especially in the dark. We had no way of knowing the true or apparent wind speeds and angles. We couldn't even see the telltales.

Concentration had to be absolute. Nobody could talk to the person on the wheel as she sailed the equivalent of a tightrope – keeping the boat fast but upright. After twenty minutes on the helm, your neck muscles were locked tight and your fingers had to be pulled back to let go of the wheel.

My feet were freezing. We were now passing almost 1,000 miles beneath central Australia and 500 miles north of the Antarctic ice shelf.

Conditions were so miserable that for the first time since the voyage began I found myself looking forwards to a point in the future. All I could think about was Cape Horn. When that seemed too distant an ambition, I concentrated on the next hour of my life. Suddenly, an hour seemed unbearably long. Instead, I existed from minute to minute, wrapped in misery.

I tried to start a mental checklist of my body. How was it holding together? My feet were painful; my legs were bruised, my ribs hurt from the last nose-dive . . . it sounded like an accident report.

Miki had only two hours off before starting another watch. When she emerged on deck in her drysuit I felt a wave of relief. I had managed to get through another few hours. She put an arm around me and shouted into my ear above the wind.

'It's just like I remembered.'

I could only see her eyes and they were smiling.

I shouted back. 'And you wonder why I forget.'

The mental effort of just surviving was so exhausting that I had to consciously try to shut down my mind when I crawled into my damp sleeping bag. For those few hours, I had to stop thinking and trust the people around me to keep me safe.

TWENTY-FOUR

O N day thirty-five Olivier's lead had blown out to 1,070 miles. This didn't worry me because the French tri- maran was about to encounter ten slow days, during which time it had dived south into iceberg territory to avoid headwinds. If we could deliver our best over the next week, we could narrow the gap to 400 miles – a single day's sailing.

We began the new day hurtling almost directly east at 20 knots, with one reef in the main and the staysail. The barometer had risen to 993 and the air temperature was a remarkably mild 5°C.

During a lull in the morning Hannah managed to replace the windex on the mast. After nearly three days, we had our wind readings back.

Lee reported that a broad band of stronger wind was moving through. Hopefully it would hold for the next two days. By the weekend, we would probably have to dip a few degrees further south to hold the breeze for any longer.

Given the forecast, Adrienne mentioned the possibility of breaking the Australia to New Zealand speed sailing record held by Olivier. He set the record in 1994 with *Lyonnaise Dumez des Eaux*, as *Sport Elec* was then called. Adrienne was itching to have a go. As we crossed the longitude of the southernmost point of Tasmania, we asked the office to start polling us every hour.

I spent the day doing watches for the girls. My feet were freezing, as well as my hands. We were riding the top of the low towards New Zealand, having come up into the wind while it was weak, so that we could run away as it strengthened.

In two days we closed the gap to 875 miles.

Lee had been predicting strong winds by early Thursday morning (local time), possibly as high as 50 knots. They arrived as if by invitation. We had 46 knots from a good angle and moderate seas. Fasten your seatbelts.

My feet had been painful for two days. When I finally allowed Emma R. to look at them she discovered mauve and swollen areas – the telltale signs of frost-nip, a minor form of frostbite. The cold had numbed my feet so much that the blood vessels had constricted and stopped the flow of blood. When feet are permanently wrapped in layers of socks and crammed into boots, you often don't feel the cold until it is too late. From now on, I had to be more careful.

The banging had started again. Adrienne and I, who were sleeping in the central pod, were in danger of losing our fillings or having compacted spines.

At lunchtime a wave emerged that was bigger than the rest. The catamaran hung on the crest for a moment, like a bodysurfer trying to decide if this was the perfect wave. Dipping forward and accelerating down the face 'the cat' had gravity as well as the wind driving her forward. Miranda tried to steer off the wave, but we had too much momentum. Out of control, we overtook the wave and slammed into the one in front. Both bows disappeared beneath green water.

In a split second we went from 32 knots to nothing. It was like hitting a brick wall at 37 miles per hour. The shock on the mast and rigging was enormous as 3,000 square feet of sail area came to a shuddering halt.

I was sitting in the head and instantly asked myself: Am I going to get hurt? In the starboard hull, Hannah and Miranda had failed to put their feet into the small nets at the base of their bunks. They became missiles and shot feet first down the hull. They flew past me horizontally almost flapping their arms, before hitting the bulkhead.

In the nav station, Adrienne was plastered over the chart table and had the wind knocked out of her, while in the galley Sam ended up in the sink and Fred with her head in the food cupboard.

The watch crew was thrown forward into the overhang, finishing in a heap, with nobody on the wheel. They scrambled back, before the boat spun on to the wrong angle and went over.

The wave now caught up with us and began lifting the stern. The bows were still buried, trying to displace tons of water. It was a classic pitch-pole situation. Either the wave would roll under us and away, or it would stand the boat on its nose and tip us over.

Mercifully, the wave rolled under us. It would not take us today. In a week's time it would break over the shores of South America.

The barometer had been dropping steadily, down to a low 987. It was a bumpy old ride, but the catamaran was sailing fast, averaging 21 knots. As we neared the line for Stewart Island, the southernmost point of New Zealand, Adrienne was grinning from ear to ear. 'We're going to break Olivier's record,' she said.

Confirmation arrived the following morning. We had beaten the speed sailing record between Australia and New Zealand by 53 minutes and 36 seconds. We had also bettered *Sport Elec*'s performance between Leeuwin Cape in Western Australia and South West Cape on Stewart Island by one day, 8 hours and 11 minutes.

Three weeks earlier, Olivier had boasted that he 'owned all the ocean records between Good Hope and Cape Horn'. Not any more, he didn't.

Adrienne had started to look at the long-range forecasts.

'You know, we're going to do this,' she said. 'We're going to be in contention at Cape Horn.'

I had clung to this hope for three weeks, through all our bad luck. From Cape Horn it would become another race. Olivier, here we come!

The cracks had widened on the God Pod and the delamination had grown worse on the hulls. Each time we nose-dived, the stress on the rigging was enormous.

Emma R. and Sam scrambled across the netting from the galley. 'You won't believe how much the hull is flexing,' said Emma, looking wide-eyed rather than nervous. The sides of the hull were supposed to flex a little as the boat moved, but not as much as they described.

I went across to the galley and made a cup of coffee. Sitting on the bench, I rested my feet up against the inner wall. A wave hit and my knees suddenly buckled. The side of the boat had moved by a foot. I felt sick.

The girls started checking the stringers. These formed the skeleton or framework of the hulls over which the fibreglass skin had been placed. The stringers were eight feet apart. As I feared, one of them had cracked and I could actually move the fibreglass with my hands.

We fanned out, crawling into the lockers and compartments to check the structural integrity of the catamaran. There was another crack in a starboard stringer, although it wasn't as bad.

'Is there any way of stopping the hull flexing?' I asked Hannah.

'Not at sea. Glue would take too long to set. I can't think of anything else to use.'

More than 1,200 miles away, a low pressure system was sliding beneath Australia. George had mentioned it briefly on Thursday, but it seemed to be a long way south and we had plenty of time to see how it developed.

Overnight the depression began sucking in air and spinning more quickly. The isobars edged closer together as the pressure dropped even further.

The deeper the low, the faster the air is sucked inside. These create the wind.

The storm was still several days away, but it couldn't be ignored. Adrienne and I watched the low intensify through Friday.

George advised:

A LATITUDE OF 54°S IS OK FOR RIGHT NOW, BUT WOULD FEEL
BETTER IF YOU COULD NUDGE UP TO 52°S–53°S BY MONDAY
1200GMT. BETTER WINDS WILL BE UP THERE AND I'D LIKE TO
TAKE YOU AWAY FROM THE CLOSED LOW CENTRE THAT IS
FORECAST TO BE MOVING IN FROM THE WEST ALONG 56°S–57°S.

SINCE WIND WILL BECOME MORE NORTHERLY, SUGGEST YOU
NOT DELAY TOO LONG IN NUDGING NORTH, ALTHOUGH WIND
SPEED AND SEAS MAY MAKE THIS DIFFICULT.

The 'closed low centre', as George called it, was spinning north-
wards and would cross our course in two or possibly three days. It
showed up in the satellite pictures as a huge swirling mass of cloud,
like a spinning Catherine wheel. On the atmospheric pressure
chart, the isobars were jammed so closely together they formed a
thick black line and the cold front preceding the low was 900 miles
long and curved like the front edge of a dorsal fin.

Meteorologists sometimes call a system like this 'a bomb'. At the
centre, the atmospheric pressure is so low that it almost feels as
though your eardrums are being sucked out of your head. As air
rushes in to fill the void, the system begins spinning faster and faster.

George predicted we could stay ahead of the storm until
Monday if we maintained a boat speed of 20 knots. Even so,
he recommended that we edge north to 52°S while we could.
Unless we climbed we risked being caught only 120 miles north of
the low's centre and being sucked into it. That would mean winds
of between 60 and 70 knots – a terrifying prospect.

Throughout Friday we tried to edge north. Unfortunately, it
was a horrible angle to sail. The wind direction was nor' nor'
east and the waves were beating us to pieces. It was tempting to
steer lower, nudging a little south of east. Olivier was so close
and a 500-mile day was possible if we kept sailing towards the
mark.

After four hours of trying to edge north, we were still stuck at
54°S. The barometer was steady on 987 and we were hurtling
directly east. My nerves were jangling. Sometimes I imagined that I

was holding the boat together through sheer willpower. Speed sailing, I decided, wasn't good for my spine or my nerves.

Having passed Macquarie Island to port, we were ten days from Cape Horn. Once we turned the corner, everything would be OK, I told myself.

George sent an update on the approaching storm.

A BOAT SPEED OF 19–20 KNOTS SHOULD KEEP YOU AHEAD OF IT UNTIL MAYBE 1800 GMT ON MONDAY. CLOSED LOW CENTRE EXPECTED NEAR 53°S 173°W BY MIDDAY SUNDAY, THEN 58°S 160°W BY MIDDAY MONDAY, THEN 60°S 140°W BY MIDDAY TUESDAY.

CENTRAL PRESSURE COULD GET BELOW 960 MILLIBARS AT THE CENTRE. THIS COULD PRODUCE WINDS ABOVE 50 KNOTS.

THERE IS ENOUGH SLOP IN THE TIMING AND POSITION OF THIS SYSTEM THAT I WOULD REALLY LIKE TO SEE YOU MORE NORTH TO SET UP FOR THE FRONTAL PASSAGE AND PROVIDE BETTER CLEARANCE TO THE LOW CENTRE (I'M IN MY GRANDMOTHER MODE NOW). SHOULD BE AT LEAST 52°S–53°S BY MONDAY 0000GMT.

YOU WONT BE ABLE TO AVOID THE HIGH WINDS ENTIRELY (SHOULD PREPARE FOR AT LEAST SOME GUSTS TO 50 KNOTS OR SO), BUT YOU'LL BE IN BETTER POSITION TO HANDLE IT IF FARTHER NORTH.

Adrienne groaned in disgust. The low had shifted north by 4 degrees.

'Twelve hours ago it was forecast to arrive on Sunday night, or Monday, with the centre at 57°S. George thought we'd be OK if we nudged up to 52° or 53°S.'

'We're almost that now.'

'I know. But they're now predicting the low centre at 53°S. He wants us even further north.'

'How far?'

'As much as 250 miles.'

It could hardly have been worse. We risked losing all the time we had gained in the past week. 'How bad do George and Lee think this is going to get?'

Adrienne showed me the numbers. Any low with a centre of 960 millibars had to be treated with the utmost respect. We had just been through two horrendous days that had put severe stresses on the boat and crew. Equipment had broken and there were cracks developing in the laminates around the port winches in the cockpit and near the hull beam joints. We weren't in any condition to handle 70-knot winds.

Adrienne tapped the keyboard with a pencil. 'You realise that if we go north now, we could lose any chance of this record. We've worked so hard to get this close.'

'I know, but I'd rather not kill us. As long as we are still in touch at the Horn, we'll catch Olivier in the Atlantic.'

In the back of my mind, I had the same concerns as Adrienne. By deviating north we could put ourselves too far behind. Weather forecasts in the Southern Ocean aren't always reliable. Three weeks earlier we'd waited for a front that didn't materialise. What if that happened again?

Even so, I couldn't ignore the warnings. We had to edge north.

By 2100 on Friday, the wind had eased slightly, but we still had 20 knots of boat speed over grey swells that rolled lazily beneath us. The visibility was poor and my feet were bad, but the ride had become a little more comfortable.

We were managing a course of 10° above due east and Adrienne sent a message to George saying that we expected to be at 52°S – or further north if required – by Monday. 'We don't want to hang around near a system like that,' she wrote.

Seven hours later we crossed the International Date Line – the 180° parallel – and I felt as though we were really on our way home. Hurtling along at 22 knots, I began to think we might even outrun the low. According to the storm warnings, it was moving east at the same speed as we were.

The wind dropped during the night, but each passing squall fired us forwards like a slingshot.

It was miserable on deck. The spray came in stinging sheets and water leaked through torn or worn drysuits. Down below wasn't much better. Nobody had any dry clothes left and their boots were soaked. Enormous willpower was needed just to drag oneself out of bed into the cold.

Even so, the doubts of the previous weeks had been replaced by a sense of expectation. People dared to whisper about breaking the record. It was within our grasp.

At 10.53 on Saturday we entered our fortieth day of the race. The storm was 48 hours behind us. *Sport Elec* was 650 miles in front. We had sailed 2,612 miles in five days at an average of 435 miles a day.

Cape Horn was now a solid reference point between the two yachts. Olivier had dived south and was sailing the shorter route, but we had 25 knots of true wind, moderate seas and good boat speed.

The barometer had fallen slightly but then steadied on 988. It was the first distant touch of the low pressure system.

George wrote:

HAD HOPED YOU WOULD BE FARTHER NORTH AND THUS IN A BETTER POSITION TO DEAL WITH THE LOW. IT MAY BE TOO LATE TO DO ANYTHING ABOUT THAT, SINCE WINDS WILL BE SHIFTING MORE NORTHERLY, THUS NOT ALLOWING FOR A VERY GOOD WIND ANGLE TO ESCAPE NORTH.

KEY NOW WILL BE TO STAY AS FAR AHEAD OF THE TROUGHING AS POSSIBLE TO STOP IT OVER-RUNNING YOU. BEST TO USE FAVORED GYBE TO GET AS MUCH EASTING AS POSSIBLE. NUDGE NORTH IF YOU CAN. DEFINITELY DON'T GO ANY FURTHER SOUTH.

UNFORTUNATELY, BY MIDNIGHT ON MONDAY THE LOW CENTRE MAY BE NEAR $56°$S $165°$W, WHICH COULD BE WITHIN A FEW HUNDRED MILES OF YOU. YOU COULD GET SUCKED INTO IT IF THE WINDS GO EAST OF NORTH NEAR YOU.

I WOULD STILL LIKE YOU TO BE AROUND $51°$S–$52°$S BY THEN, BUT DON'T THINK YOU CAN MAKE IT.

He also warned that the front could overrun us much sooner if our boat speed dropped below 16 knots.

We had left it too late to get north gradually. Our only options were to run, or to take a dramatic left turn that could immediately cost us any chance of the record.

Adrienne replied:

> George,
>
> If you want us to take a dive North at any time we can just do a left-hander and it will take us a couple of hours to get at least to 52.5°. We are on a very fast course slightly north of east and we'll proceed as in your report.

The storm was moving east at 30 knots, while we were travelling at only 20. It couldn't be outrun. It was 600 miles high and 1,500 miles wide. There was no way to go around it. The isobars were so close on the map that they merged into one.

Adrienne and I spent three hours discussing tactics and doing the calculations. We were in a no-win situation. If we dived north, sailing miles out of our way, the penalty would put us too far behind Olivier to catch him. If we didn't dive north, we could be caught on the wrong side of the low and face headwinds that would also deny us the record.

'Either way we're going to get the crap kicked out of us,' said Adrienne.

'But it won't be so bad if we dive north. It might mean 10 knots' difference in the wind.'

'That's true,' said Adrienne, but I knew she wasn't happy with surrendering even a single mile. She wanted to batten down the hatches and ride out the storm. 'I think we should heave-to during the worst of it and take a risk that we won't get headwinds. No risk, no record.'

I looked at her and wondered how she could fit so much strength and aggression into such a tiny frame. Until then, I thought there was nobody on Earth who wanted this record more than I did. I was wrong.

'No risk, no record.'

A decision had been made. We continued trying to edge north, but would not yet contemplate a dramatic left turn.

By midnight on Saturday the barometer had fallen to 984 and the seas had started to build. We were careering eastwards at 20 to 30 knots, racing to stay ahead of a storm. The wind had swung to slightly west of north, trying to stop us from edging higher. Adrienne wrote in the log: 'This will be touch and go.'

The girls were nervous. Everybody knew this dark, destructive force was coming. It had been following us for four days, shifting its path every time we moved.

The catamaran had started surfing in the following sea. Each time we tried to nose a little north, the waves pounded the God Pod like wet fists and the hulls reared up and slammed down into the troughs.

'We want to come down. We want to come down!' screamed Miki, with water dripping from her face. 'We're going to break the bloody boat.'

Adrienne said, 'Fine, we come down now, we get the shit kicked out of us in two days' time. We have to get north.'

By 3 a.m. we had three reefs in the main and the storm jib. This was the least amount of sail we could have aloft without pulling everything down and going bare poles. The wind had risen to 50 knots, from an angle way forward of the beam. Each time the girls tried to come up and steer the agreed course, they risked flipping the catamaran.

Three hours later we had gone south, instead of north. Not by much, but it was enough. We still had three reefs in the main, but had managed to put the staysail back up when the wind dropped to 35–40 knots. The barometer had fallen to 981.

Despite our efforts, the horrible wind angle was forcing us to sail fractionally south of east, putting us closer to the path of the storm. Occasionally the catamaran hit speeds of 29 knots, but the average remained at only 20 knots – not enough to stay ahead.

Adrienne sent a message to Lee.

Our position: 53° 45S and 165° 02W Would appreciate your urgent advice. We are in a position where it is extremely difficult for us to get north. We tried to when George asked us, however, the boat pounds so badly in these seas when we leave anything forward of the beam.

We are trying to maintain a course of directly east but are edging further south. We are nearly back at 54°S. Is it possible for us to continue averaging 20 knots in that direction and hope the front/system moves NE and we remain ahead of it?

If so, are we likely to get headwinds at some stage because we were unable to keep north?

If we turn north now we will be able to average 12-knots but this will pound the boat. What are our options?

Regards,

Adrienne.

Lee responded within fifteen minutes. He reported that the centre of the low was still deepening – a frightening prospect. For six to twelve hours before and after the front moved through, we could expect huge seas and winds of up to 55 knots, occasionally gusting to 60 knots between 55°S and 60°S. These storm force winds could extend further north, Lee warned. The tracking of the low had been erratic and there was no way to accurately forecast its position.

He did, however, manage to put a positive spin on a bleak situation. Once the first front had moved through, the wind should swing and make it easier for us to edge north. Moreover, if we managed to ride out the storm at 53°S, it would put us in a good position for handling the westerlies arriving by Wednesday.

'Brilliant,' said Adrienne. 'If we survive getting the stuffing knocked out of us, we'll be in great shape.'

Another wave crashed into the God Pod. Emma W. shouted from the cockpit. With a staysail and three reefs, we were over-powered, slamming into waves at 28 knots and having to steer a course that took us further south. I scrambled out on deck and helped put up the storm jib.

The waves had risen to 35 feet. They ghosted out of the darkness, blacker than the sky, with only the foaming crest visible until the wave began lifting the stern. A ball of fear wedged itself in my throat and I couldn't swallow. How desperately things had changed. I pressed my hands to my ears, trying to block out the noise. I tried to tell myself: Be rational, Tracy. You've been through this before. Calm down. Slowly, I felt my breathing become steady again.

Silently, I began to recite Psalm 27 – my favourite.

> *The Lord is my light, and my salvation;*
> *Whom then shall I fear?*
> *The Lord is the strength of my life;*
> *Of whom then shall I be afraid?*

Mum had always said to me, 'There is no point in only praying when you want something, or need to get out of a sticky situation. Instead, you pray for the strength and courage to get through it.'

That's what I did now. I had to be strong for the crew and make the right decisions.

The wind had risen to 45 knots. With a storm jib and three reefs we couldn't outrun the low. I tried to put a brave face on our prospects. The girls were being philosophical and getting on with the job.

All night we pounded into head seas, driven by 48 knots of wind. I imagined waking with the mast lying in my bunk. Trying to sleep was near impossible. I was airborne half the time. Every muscle was knotted and tense. When I did manage to doze, I woke with my heart thumping. I glanced at the navigation instruments and then pulled my sleeping bag over my head.

For the past four weeks we'd been constantly juggling between speed and safety. Before leaving Southampton, a journalist had asked me how much I wanted the Jules Verne Trophy. How hard would I push?

I told her: 'No record is more important than the safety of this crew. I will not jeopardise lives for the sake of speed.' Yet I knew I would push harder and take more punishment than ever before to get the record. I wanted it *that* badly.

Now I began to regret the decision not to turn north and sacrifice the miles. Had I gambled too much?

Daylight leaked through the black sky, turning it a gun-barrel grey. The wind angle terrified me. It was right on the beam, forcing us to steer down. The seas were awkward but had fallen slightly. That wouldn't last long. The pre-frontal system had come through just before dawn. Already the wind screamed through the rigging.

As I scrambled across to the galley a wave exploded through the netting and lifted me off my feet. For a brief moment I was airborne. I came down on my hands and knees, gripping the nylon mesh for dear life. I stared through the netting at the black, foaming water that surged between the hulls.

Miki yelled from the cockpit, 'Are you OK?'

'Yeah. Just washing the sleep out of my eyes.'

I could hear her laughing.

We had narrowed Olivier's lead to just 500 miles. Meanwhile, the satellite pictures showed the low was tracking as predicted. The next front would move through in sixteen hours.

Late in the afternoon the wind finally began to swing aft and conditions became a little easier. At the same time it strengthened and the waves began to build.

In the God Pod we chatted about home, our friends and things we loved to do. We joked about how far we'd go to avoid another trip into the Southern Ocean. It was amazing how attractive marriage, children, pets and mothers' groups had suddenly become.

Helena announced, 'I'm going to buy myself a cat. That way I won't be able to leave it behind because there isn't anyone else to feed it.'

'That's a pretty lame excuse,' I told her.

Hannah declared that she didn't need an excuse – wild horses couldn't drag her back.

Sharon was going to stick to Olympic sailing. 'That way I can go to the pub afterwards and go back to a nice warm bed.'

'What about you, Tracy?' asked Sam.

'I'll get married again.'

They all whistled. 'Bloody hell, that is extreme,' said Sharon.

The high spirits and smiles were a brave attempt at hiding apprehension and exhaustion. Cape Horn couldn't come soon enough.

When I finally got to bed, I slid into my sleeping bag and suddenly realised that I was lying in a puddle. The jib sheet track, the rail on which the jib is sheeted on the deck of the God Pod, had started to lift away and water had leaked into my bunk. My spare thermals and sleeping bag were soaked.

I wrote in my diary:

*How can I describe how utterly, utterly miserable this is? I fear it
is impossible. We just exist now. The days blur into one. We get
up to do what we have to do and then go to bed. I eat if I can
be bothered and sleep if I can. Everything is a supreme effort.*

The latest synoptic report put the low 500 miles behind us at 159°W. It had started dropping quickly south-east, giving us a glimmer of hope that it might pass beneath us. That idea was snuffed out when the barometer began dropping during the long night. The second front was coming.

The catamaran shifted violently sideways as I pulled on my foul weather gear. I had to put both arms up to stop myself crashing head first into the comms station. I glanced at the navigation instruments. We had 40 knots of wind on the beam.

It took me twenty minutes to get ready. My fingers were so cold that I couldn't grip the Velcro fasteners. I scrambled on deck to help take a third reef. The first wave that crashed over me was as cold as ice.

'This is more like mountain climbing than sailing,' shouted Hannah, as I slid next to her in the cockpit.

Wind channelled between the waves and lifted them into caps, creating a fine spray that peppered our skin like bullets. As the boat reached each new crest it lurched and then dropped into the dark hole. The swells seemed closer together and steeper than yesterday. White foam streaked down the grey walls like water being forced across the windscreen of a fast-moving car.

I looked up quickly as a wave rose, crested and broke over the aft quarter. Water rushed across the deck and tried to drag open the hatch covers.

Miki steered down, I released the mainsheet, Adrienne let the traveller go and Sam was at the mast to let down the sail. We managed the reef in less than five minutes. I worried about Sam crawling along the boom, but she'd become very good at this mountaineering act.

Swinging back into the God Pod, I wanted to catch up on the weather report. I felt the catamaran beginning to surf down a wave, accelerating so quickly that the hulls began to vibrate.

Get off it, I thought, get off it. I put my hands on either side of the hatch and began to climb out. At that moment we caught up with the wave in front and buried the bows. I tried to hold on but couldn't. My fingers were ripped from the frame and I flew backwards along the length of the God Pod. I landed against the chart table with such force that it almost broke me in two.

Winded and in shock, I sat on the bench. I knew my back had been hurt, even without moving. When the pain arrived, it came in such a rush that it knocked the air out of me again. The muscles down the left side of my spine began to spasm. I thought my ribs had been cracked. I groaned and squeezed my eyes shut. Hot tears blurred my vision. It wasn't just the pain; I felt sorry for myself, childishly so. Home seemed a long way away.

Emma R. emerged through the hatch. Gently she lifted my layers of thermals and began poking and prodding.

'I don't think you've broken your ribs,' she said. 'You've done something to your back.'

Tell me something I don't know, I felt like saying. Every wave that smashed into the God Pod felt like a needle being jammed into my spine.

'I'm giving you some painkillers,' Emma said, 'but the best thing you can do is to lie down and keep still.'

'OK, but you tell the boat to stop moving.'

'I'm good, but not that good,' she said.

I lay in my bunk, battling fear as well as guilt. I wanted to be out there, putting on a brave face and telling the youngsters that I'd been through far worse, even if that meant lying to them.

The wind had risen past 50 knots. The decks were awash and there was so much water in the air that it seemed possible to drown six feet above the surface. Miki clung to the wheel as the water drained away.

Rogue waves are an unspoken fear. These can emerge from nowhere and be two or three times higher than anything before or after. They can rear up, split at the top and have water rolling down the front and back, breaking in two directions.

A wave like this can snap a yacht in half or send it flipping end over end. From a distance it can look like an iceberg or the foaming crest can be mistaken for a cloud. Nobody knows for sure what causes rogue waves. They are freak events that occur randomly and without warning. Some experts blame undersea earthquakes. Others say that two or three waves join together or overlay the swells of a storm that might have passed days earlier. Such phenomena are difficult to research because there are so few eyewitnesses left behind and often the waves destroy the data buoys designed to measure them.

I felt helpless. Visibility had fallen to a few hundred feet, making it difficult to spot the squalls. The radar picked up a solid green mass sweeping in from the north-west. Clutching the wheel, Miki had her legs braced far apart as the boat pitched and slammed.

When the squall hit, the wind speed counter instantly hit 60 knots. We had the main, three reefs and no headsail but were still doing 15 knots and surfing at 25. There couldn't be any less sail unless we pulled it all down.

I had never seen Miki scared until that moment. Twice I had sailed around the world with her. On *Maiden* we went through winds of 100 knots and 60-foot seas, but that was on a monohull. The 'big cat' wasn't built for this and we couldn't slow her down. She careered down waves totally out of control and nose-dived to a shuddering halt.

My feet hit the bulkhead and the pain shot through me. 'We can't go on like this,' I said, looking across at Adrienne. She was wedged against the chart table with her back to her bunk. 'We have to slow down.'

'What do you want to do?'

'We have two options. Either we throw out the drogue (a sea anchor) to slow us down, or we take down the mainsail and put the staysail up. This would hopefully give us enough speed to man-oeuvre.

Either course of action had disadvantages. The drogue might stop us hurtling down waves and nose-diving, but if it slowed us too much we'd lose steerage. Dropping the mainsail was even more drastic. We wouldn't be able to pull it up again until the wind dropped. That could cost us a lot of miles.

Miki wanted to take the main down. Helena thought we should keep it up to stay in control.

I dragged myself to the comms station and talked to Ed. He suggested we use the drogues and only pull down the mainsail as a last resort.

'You should be a lot further north.'

'I know. We've been trying to edge up there.'

'Screw the mileage – just turn north.'

Adrienne still thought we should ride it out. Miki shouted from the cockpit that she wouldn't steer unless we dropped the main.

I had to make a decision. All thoughts of breaking the record had gone. We were trying to survive.

'We're going north,' I said.

'What about the main?' asked Miki.

'We'll take it down if we get 60 knots again.'

We changed course to nor' nor'east. Our situation hadn't improved but I tried to reassure myself that at least we were heading for safety.

The waves were 50 feet high. Any one of them could have destroyed the catamaran if it struck at the wrong angle.

Taking another painkiller I crawled into my bunk, convinced that we were going to die. How would it happen? Would a hatch give way on the deck, flooding the forward compartments? Or would we nose-dive and go pitch-poling end over end?

Two days earlier, in a 48-knot squall, I had thought it impossible to be any more scared. I was wrong. They were idiot words, swept away by the wind. Now I knew the truth.

True terror is so mind-numbing that it ignores adrenalin and the instinct to survive. It is a heavy slowness that spreads through the body. My brain wanted to close down. Events passed in slow motion and I lost all sense of time. A listless apathy settled over me like a warm duvet and I just wanted to close my eyes and sleep.

There were worse places to die than out here. A lot of good sailors had perished in the Southern Ocean. At least everything would stop moving and the noise would cease.

Five hours after turning north we had reached 52° 50S. I couldn't see the sail combinations from my bunk, but I could still read the numbers on the navigation instruments. The wind had fluctuated between 40 and 60 knots. The temperature outside was just below freezing with the wind chill. A sudden shift in the boat sent pain flooding through my spine. Reality slapped me in the face and I tried to shrug off thoughts of desperation.

'What have we got up?' I asked.

Adrienne was clinging tightly to the chart table. 'The main, three reefs and no headsail.'

'How are the girls?'

'Pretty scared.'

'How are you?'

'Ditto.'

She had sent a message to Lee reporting our escape to the north.

The barometer is 995 and rising rapidly. Sky clearing. Seas rough to very rough. We had a tough time today with 60+ knots in squalls. Please tell us only good news.

An hour later, we passed into day forty-three of the challenge. Despite having the living daylights beaten out of us, we had managed 466 miles in 24 hours. Unfortunately, as I'd feared, the escape north was costing us dearly. The gap to *Sport Elec* had blown out to 660 miles.

Many of the girls looked shell-shocked. Some were so frightened of the storm they steered too high and lost us more miles. I couldn't blame them. The cracks had widened in the God Pod. Two inches of water sloshed across the floor.

My sleeping bag rested in a pool of water and condensation dripped from the God Pod ceiling a few inches above my head. I wore three layers of thermal underwear, all of them damp, and hadn't washed in four weeks. My hair was plastered to my head and the wet pillow.

An hour before dawn, Adrienne sent a message to Lee asking when he thought we could turn back to the east. The winds had eased, but periodic squalls still battered us.

'What sort of day is it?' I asked Adrienne, recognising the dawn from the diffused light in the God Pod.

'It's a beautiful Southern Ocean day.'

I knew what she meant. Even in the midst of a storm, this ocean had a raw untamed beauty.

We nose-dived again at lunchtime. Adrienne and Emma W. were trying to cook scrambled eggs in the galley. A pot exploded upwards covering them with boiling egg mix that stuck to their skin and the walls. Adrienne was lucky to be wearing her wet weather gear but still suffered burns to her face and lower arms. The same nose-dive sent Miki flying headlong down the port hull, injuring her leg.

I felt sorry for myself. At least the girls were up there on deck, fighting for survival. I was crippled and helpless.

Adrienne wrote the daily journal for me:

> *Everyone is very tired but keeping their chins up. Steering the boat is a handful but some really good drivers have emerged from these conditions.*
>
> *It's so close to the Horn and we are so near to the record everyone is hanging in there. It will be a great relief to round the old rock. Let's hope tomorrow is a little smoother day.*

TWENTY-FIVE

'TRACY, Tracy, wake up.'

'What?'

I opened my eyes and looked up into the smiling face of Helena. She held a bowl and a spoon. 'I've brought you some dinner, I didn't think you'd be able to make it to the galley.'

I hadn't eaten since the accident because the painkillers made me feel nauseous.

'Adrienne is doing the cooking. She's wearing her survival suit just in case the pasta decides to leap up and attack her.'

I wanted to laugh but knew it would hurt. Helena helped me sit up. I glanced at the numbers above the chart table. The wind was a steady 50 knots.

'The waves are getting better,' said Helena. 'Adrienne thinks we might be over the worst of it.'

I drifted off to sleep again. At some point Adrienne came back from the galley. She sat at the chart table and began calling up the latest satellite weather maps. Her face had taken on the green glow of the navigation instruments.

'I reckon we should be able to gybe back in another couple of hours,' she said, showing me the latest map.

'What speed are we doing?'

She glanced at the dials. 'We're keeping it down to 15 knots most of the time. Occasionally we're surfing at 27.'

There was a movement to the left and behind me. Miki appeared in her survival suit, looking like an astronaut. I could only see her eyes behind the mask, but they were clearly tired and fraught.

For the next few hours I drifted in and out of sleep, unable to move. Each time the boat smashed into a wave, the muscles down the left side of my spine contracted and I groaned.

Adrienne woke after two hours and checked the messages. I watched her silently and realised how much weight she'd lost. Just after noon GMT, Lee advised us that we could turn back on to our favoured gybe. We had to wait another two hours between squalls before we could change direction.

We had never gybed in 44 knots of wind. Everybody was needed on deck, except the cripple in her bunk.

'OK, let's do it,' said Miki.

As the boat shifted downwind, Helena winched in the main until the boom was directly over the cockpit. As one side of the boat released the sheets, the other side was winding them on. The main swung from starboard to port and the wind filled the sail. There was a tremendous sense of achievement amongst the crew. After being hammered for so long, we had proved our resilience. We were back in the race.

The ride felt a lot easier with the wind behind us. Occasionally, the 'big cat' would take off and surf, but it wasn't happening so often.

I drifted in and out of sleep, fuzzy with painkillers.

Is this what you wanted, Tracy? I asked myself silently. Is this what you expected? Did you underestimate the challenge?

I found the answers: No. We're still here, aren't we? We're in the race.

A lot of the newspapers and yachting correspondents who had written us off at the start, or hadn't bothered reporting our progress, had changed their minds over the previous few weeks. We were being taken seriously. Survive until the Horn and then we'll come storming home. That was the goal.

At some point, Miki and Emma W. came down to talk to Adrienne and ask about the forecast.

'Can we put some more sail up?' Emma asked.

Adrienne nodded. 'We've been frightened but let's not let that affect us.'

I worried about putting up too much sail too soon. We all had a strong desire to grab back the lost miles, but that shouldn't override other considerations. There was still a lot of breeze and the seas were very rough. 'I don't want you taking reefs out too early. Be sensible,' I said. The reefs had lessened the amount of sail we had aloft. I didn't want us rushing to put it back up again while the seas and winds were still too heavy.

Some time later I woke again to the sound of heavy boots clattering over the God Pod and winches that cranked and echoed through the fibreglass.

'What's happening?'

'We're shaking out another reef,' said Adrienne.

I looked at the numbers. The wind had settled a little, but the seas were still horrible. Everything is relative, of course. Having encountered 50-foot waves, anything less than 40 feet seemed positively benign.

The barometer had risen to 1005 and we were heading slightly east-sou'east at 20 knots. We hoped to gybe between 53°S and 54°S for the next few days, before diving south to round Cape Horn.

For the umpteenth time I wondered if we were pushing the boat too hard. How did I answer a question like that? This whole challenge had been about discovering our limits and pushing back the boundaries of fear. It had never been our intention to just get round the course – we set out to beat the record. To do that, meant racing on the edge. It also meant injuries to the crew and damage to the boat.

We were 725 miles behind *Sport Elec*. Adrienne still believed we could catch them by Cape Horn. I thought we could narrow the gap to a day's sailing.

Six hours before dawn, we were heading due east with a boat speed of 18 to 20 knots – very fast for the conditions. Sharon had the wheel and Miki gave her constant advice on how to steer through the waves.

Sensing that there was something behind her, Sharon glanced over her left shoulder. A rogue wave with a face that was almost vertical came out of the darkness. Later, Sharon said it reached more than halfway up the mast, which made it over 50 feet.

She had time to utter, 'What do I—?' before the wall of water lifted the catamaran like a child's bath toy and balanced her on the edge of the tub. The bows tipped forward and we dropped into the mine. Surfing at more than 30 knots, Sharon tried desperately to pull away but there was too much momentum. We hurtled into the trough and caught up with the wave in front. Both bows speared into water.

My feet struck the bulkhead at the end of my bunk. The stern lifted as the freak wave caught up with us. Within a split second, the catamaran was standing on its nose. I looked across at Adrienne, who had just crawled into her bunk. The look in her eyes said: We're going over.

Crouched at the end of my bunk, I could feel the 'big cat' sliding and trying desperately to come back. It didn't want to go over. Gravity fought against the pressure of water and wind.

My back didn't hurt. I was too terrified.

Sharon had been thrown against the wheel and then past it, landing in the well alongside Miki and Fred.

For those few seconds the clock stopped. How ironic! All through the voyage I had been trying to hold back time and finally it had happened.

Why now? I wanted to cry. We didn't deserve this fate. We had sailed too well to finish our race ignominiously upside down and fighting for our lives.

The 'big cat' fought hard to come back. Ironically, the same wave that almost pushed us over now rolled underneath and brought the bows back up. The hull settled in the trough and the wind filled the sails with a suddenness that put more strain on the rigging.

Ten or fifteen seconds passed, perhaps longer. I gingerly tried to crawl out of my bunk. Everything not tied down or lodged securely had become debris. Adrienne's and my foul weather gear sloshed in water on the God Pod floor, along with flares, the spare safety harnesses and a laptop. The chart table was strewn with nav books, charts, pencils and e-mails.

I surveyed the damage as Adrienne tried to clean up. Above us, we heard the creaking and groaning of carbon fibre grating against itself.

Miki appeared at the door. 'The rig's coming down. It's coming down now.' She sounded so calm and matter-of-fact.

My brain screamed a single word, over and over. *No, no, no, no, no, no . . .*

I looked at Adrienne. 'Oh, my God, the record.'

'Sod the record! We're 2,000 miles from anywhere.'

'Send a mayday,' I said, struggling to pull my foul weather gear over my head and shoulders. Miki had already gone back on deck.

My first priority was to send a distress signal and let somebody know our location in case we had to abandon ship. Adrienne hit a 'distress' key on the laptop, which sent an automatic message to the search and rescue services in Falmouth, England. The duty officer would see the signal flash on screen giving the boat's name and position.

Our computer program immediately gave us a list of options, such as sinking, disabled or man overboard. Adrienne ran through them quickly and typed: '*Royal & SunAlliance. 92-foot catamaran. Lost rig. Position 52° 44S and 129° 49W. Disabled. Will advise if need help. Please stand by.*'

Miki yelled from above. 'The boom is over the port hull, the girls won't be able to get out.'

I picked up the phone linking the hulls.

Emma W. answered. 'What was that?'

'The mast has come down. You won't be able to get out of the hatch. Don't panic. Don't bother to get dressed, just grab your clothes. We don't know if the hull has been damaged. We're going to move the mainsail. I want you to climb out and come to the God Pod. You can get dressed here.'

Miki banged three times to wake Miranda, Hannah and Emma R. in the starboard hull. They gathered in the cockpit, wide-eyed with fear and still fastening their drysuits.

I scrambled on deck wearing just my mid-layers. My back no longer hurt – pure adrenalin had neutralised the pain. I couldn't see a thing. The deck lights had come down with the mast. Miki shone a torch over the devastation. It revealed itself a small piece at a time.

The mast had crumpled rather than fallen over. Initially, it had broken near the top at the third spreader. Miki had seen it break again at the second spreader and then at the first before it crumpled over the port side.

As I surveyed the damage, I felt as though my insides were being cut open and torn out. A wave slammed into the starboard hull and exploded over the cockpit and netting. I blinked away salt water that might have been tears.

Sharon was distraught. 'We just came down the wave. I couldn't get off. I did everything I could to get off . . . we had nowhere to go . . .'

'It's OK, Sharon. It's not your fault.'

'. . . and then the mast just came down. I have never ever willed something to stay up there so much in my life. "No, no, don't fall down." It was falling. Then it broke again. "No, no, you don't want to do that." And then it broke at the base. Oh, my God.'

It wasn't Sharon's fault, or anyone else's. Ultimately, the responsibility rested with me.

'We have to get the girls out,' said Miki, struggling to be heard above the wind. The bottom section of the mast lay across the netting. The boom and mainsail covered the port hatch.

'Hannah, grab a hacksaw in case we have to cut anything away.'

Using torches they picked their way through the debris and began lifting the boom. I went back to join Adrienne, who had been sending messages to search and rescue centres in Chile, New Zealand and Australia. The reality of our plight was clear from the map. We were 2,500 miles from New Zealand, 2,300 miles from Chile and 1,200 miles from Antarctica. We couldn't have chosen a place any further from rescue if we'd tried.

Having been freed, Helena, Sam and Emma W. arrived in the God Pod still wearing their thermals. Helena hobbled on a badly bruised knee but it had probably saved her life. If she hadn't fallen in the nose-dive, she would have been coming out of the hatch as the rig came down. The boom would have landed on top of her.

Sam was like a rabbit caught in a spotlight. Emma looked at me and I realised that she'd been saying the same thing over and over again: 'Oh, God, the record, the record.'

She put her arms around me. 'We nearly did it, Tracy.'

I almost cracked. I could feel the tears welling in my eyes and a lump at the back of my throat. No, Tracy, hold it together. Don't lose it. I had to be cool-headed; totally unfazed.

The heavy seas were bashing the rigging against the port hull. It might already have been holed. The catamaran wasn't likely to sink unless the watertight compartments had been breached.

Miki controlled things on deck. I had complete faith in her. She had been dismasted twice before and each time the crew had managed to put up a jury rig and sail to safety. I could hear her shouting instructions from the cockpit. I helped Sam get dressed.

'Are they coming to get us?' she asked.

'Yes, if we need them.'

'Is it going to be OK?'

'Absolutely.'

I sent a single-line message to race headquarters in Hamble:

'*Charlotte, we have lost our rig. We are sorting it out at this stage. We are in distress. The position is 52° 44S and 129° 51W.*'

Adrienne maintained contact with maritime rescue centres in Australia, Chile and New Zealand. If we discovered a breach in the port hull, we'd need their help quickly. The same was true if we couldn't rig a makeshift sail.

Miki and Hannah swung into the nav station. Both were breathing hard and dripping wet. They braced themselves against the bulkheads near the hatchway as the boat pitched and rolled.

'The mast is broken in three places and hanging over the port hull,' said Miki. 'The upper two-thirds are in the water. The only thing holding the sections together are torn pieces of mainsail and reefing lines.'

Hannah continued: 'We have water coming into the starboard hull but it doesn't look like a breach. I think a chain plate has been ripped from the deck and water is coming through when waves come over the top.'

'How bad is it?'

'I've told Sharon to turn on the bilge pump,' said Miki.

'OK, I'll turn on the generator. Is there any sign of damage to the port hull?'

'We don't know yet. We'll have to wait until we cut the rig away.'

'Do it as quickly as you can. You've got to cut away the rigging hanging over the side.'

Hannah said anxiously, 'We must try to save as much as we can. We can use it to make a new mast.'

'Yes, but if it does look like endangering the boat, you have to let it go.'

Both nodded in agreement. I continued: 'We got ourselves into this situation and it's our responsibility to get ourselves out of it. At the moment we don't need saving, but that could change very quickly.' As if to prove my point, a wave slammed into the bottom of the God Pod and rattled my spine.

'Miki, you're in charge of what everyone does. Hannah, you're in charge of the logistics of getting rid of the mast. I want you to tell Miranda that it's her job to make sure everyone stays on the boat. They won't be able to clip on easily. She won't be able to shine a torch in their eyes. Tell her to do a roll call every few minutes.'

The entire crew gathered in the cockpit and I caught glimpses of their faces in the torchlight as Miki briefed them. I knew they were all frightened, yet there was a tremendous sense of determination and resolve.

Miki and Hannah began issuing instructions. Tools had to be found. There were hacksaws in each of the hulls and in the God Pod. Wire-cutters and more blades were kept in the forward lockers. Emma W. took a torch and began picking her way through the debris.

Miranda kept watch as the darkness closed behind Emma and all that was visible was the bouncing circle of light in her hand.

'I want some of you to put on life-jackets rather than safety harnesses,' said Miki. 'I don't want you clipping on in case you're attached to something that's going over the side. Miranda, you'll stay in the cockpit and do the roll calls.'

I could hear their boots on the God Pod roof as they began cutting away the rigging. There are hundreds of yards of wire, ropes, reefing lines and torn cloth – all tangled together and wrapped around the broken mast. It looked as though a massive spider had wrapped its spindly legs around the hulls and tried to wrap us in its web.

Although the catamaran pitched and rolled, the broken mast seemed to act as a sea anchor, holding us solid in the water. Even without a sail we *were* doing 2 knots – what an unbelievable boat, she just wouldn't give up!

Waves crashed over the starboard hull and exploded up through the netting with even more force than before. Instead of coming from forward to back, as they did when we were moving, the waves erupted straight up, lifting girls clear off the netting.

The next four hours passed in a blur of hacksaws and wire-cutters. Miki and Hannah tried to bring in the second section of mast lying nearest the port hull but it broke and had to be cut away. The girls worked without a break.

At one stage, I came on deck to find Emma R. using a hacksaw blade with her bare hands because she couldn't find the handle.

As the first tinges of grey light emerged on the eastern horizon, the full scale of the devastation emerged. My heart felt ready to break. Debris littered the decks and netting. Padeyes and chain plates had been ripped out, stanchions had caved in, cracks had opened, ropes and torn sail dragged in the water. A thoroughbred racing catamaran had become little more than a floating platform.

I came on deck as the last of the rig was cut away. Miki sawed through the carbon fibre on the middle section of the mast. The girls all stood and watched in silence as she cut through the final half-inch. As it separated, the rig and mainsail slid over the side and disappeared. I felt as though I had watched the body of a friend being buried at sea.

We had managed to save 21 feet of mast. It now lay across the netting alongside the boom. I still didn't know if we could put it back up, or if it would disintegrate under the weight of a makeshift sail.

Hannah leaned over the port hull, examining it for damage. It appeared to be intact, although some of the padeyes had ripped out of the deck, creating small holes.

It was now fully light. The girls had been working solidly for six hours.

'Right, everybody in the God Pod,' I said.

People sat where they could find space and a few had to stay outside and huddle near the hatch. Sam had gone to make tea for everybody. Emma R. asked, 'Do you think we can break into the Sunday cake?'

'Emma, this is probably just the occasion to break into the Sunday cake.'

'Brilliant.'

She dashed across to the galley and returned with the fruit cake and a knife. As she cut slices and handed them out, I struggled to get my head around the bizarre sight of eleven women having a tea party in the middle of the Southern Ocean on a crippled yacht.

I looked at the faces around me. Miranda and Sharon were wide-eyed, as if almost in shock. Miki looked exhausted, but tried to make light of it. Sam had grown very quiet, which worried me a little. Little Emma looked to be almost in denial, the way she bounced and laughed, handing out pieces of cake. It was as if she'd said, 'I can't deal with this, so I'll pretend it hasn't happened.'

Hannah seemed angry and aggressive. I think she was pissed off at having endured weeks of misery only to discover that we weren't going to get all the way around.

Adrienne had been quite boisterous and upbeat. Although I didn't realise it at the time, I think she concentrated on me during those first few hours because she was so worried about me.

'Right, let's get down to business,' I said. 'I'm putting Hannah in charge of putting the mast back up. I'm not asking you if it can be done, Hannah, because it *has* to be done. I don't care what it looks like, as long as it works.

'Miki, I want you to help Hannah and give everybody their tasks. Sharon, you'll have to sew us some new sails. Adrienne will keep the emergency services updated and I'll stay in touch with the office and do any other comms.'

One of the reasons I had chosen Hannah for the voyage was her ability as a 'boat bodger'. Now she had her ultimate challenge – she had to make us a new mast.

For the next five hours the girls worked tirelessly. Hannah cut wooden spars from spare timber in the cockpit. These fitted inside the hollow top of the mast, bracing the outer edges apart so it wouldn't collapse. Four support cables were attached which we hoped would hold the mast in place once we pulled it upright.

There were two blocks at the front and one at the back, with a halyard going up and down.

The most difficult task lay ahead: how to lift the truncated mast into place.

Eleven hours after the disaster, we were ready to try. Miki and Hannah had rigged up a pulley system to hoist it upright. There were two lines leading through blocks back to the cockpit winches and to lines that were to be pulled by hand. Another line ran forward through a block and then came back to one of the winches.

With everyone in position, Hannah gave the orders:

'Sam, wind on a bit more . . . Not too quickly, Sharon . . . Steady . . . steady . . . keep it coming . . .'

The catamaran bucked and rocked in the swell, making the job more difficult. As the mast edged upwards, Hannah tried to make sure it was straight.

'OK, set it down.' Four people gripped the base of the mast and made small adjustments as it slid home. As the lines were cleated off, nobody felt like cheering. We didn't have the energy.

Sharon had prepared the storm jib as our first sail. With only 21 feet of mast, we would have to raise it sideways, with the corner that was normally sheeted in becoming the top. Clipping it to the halyard, it took her less than two seconds to hoist it aloft. Hannah sheeted it off and it bulged with the breeze. Ropes tightened on the winches and the new support lines creaked.

We were off again, with Miki at the wheel.

Adrienne asked the search and rescue services to stand down. We would give them positional reports every six hours. Meanwhile, I sent a message to Charlotte:

We are doing nine knots towards Chile. We will just head in the general direction of the coast at 50°S until we have some information on where to go.

It is really difficult trying not to show how much my heart is breaking at the moment and to keep people's spirits up at the same time. Adrienne is being great and mopping up the tears so we don't drown.

Lots of love and thoughts, Tracy.

Nobody underestimated the danger we still faced. We were deep into the Southern Ocean on a crippled yacht, directly in the path of two more fronts. George and Lee wanted us to get further north because the lows would catch and pass us quickly. The next would arrive within 48 hours, bringing forecast winds of up to 45 knots. I knew the jury rig wouldn't stand up to a severe storm.

Helena and Hannah began preparing the boat for the rougher weather, checking the drogues, tweaking the jury rig and filling any holes on deck with epoxy. Sharon and Fred worked for hours in the dungeon to turn the staysail into a main.

In London, a media release was drafted to break the news. As I read the statement, I seemed almost detached. So much had happened in the previous eighteen hours that I hadn't thought about the ramifications of failure. Here it was, set out for me; summed up in a few paragraphs:

Royal & SunAlliance, *the 92 ft catamaran skippered by Tracy Edwards with an all-female crew of ten, has been forced to abandon its attempt on the Round the World non-stop record for the Trophée Jules Verne.*

In pitch darkness at 0850 GMT this morning, on her forty-third day at sea having covered approximately 15,200 miles since setting off from Ushant, north west France on 3rd February, disaster struck Royal & SunAlliance. *In 40-foot seas and winds gusting from 30 to 50 knots, a huge wave came up behind them, lifting the stern and burying both bows in the wave ahead bringing the boat to a shuddering halt. About five minutes later, creaking could be heard from the top of the mast and the whole thing just crumpled over the port side and broke up as it hit the hull.*

The all-female crew, who are safe and well, are getting to grips with the new challenge of making the boat sailable and heading for land, some 2,000 miles away in South America. There is no possibility of pursuing the record.

At the time of the disaster, the boat had covered about 350 miles in the last twenty-four hours, and had averaged 435 miles a day over the last nine days in the relentless pursuit of the record of 71 days 14 hours, 22 minutes and 8 seconds set last year by Frenchman Olivier de Kersauson.

Speaking from the boat, Tracy Edwards said: 'We are

*disappointed beyond belief as we were so close to getting to Cape
Horn in such good time against the record. Words cannot describe
how we feel at the moment although the girls are once again
pulling on their reserves of strength to get through this.'*

These words didn't even come close to conveying how I really felt.
I was devastated. That night I cried silently, overcome by a sense of
having sacrificed four years of my life for nothing. I woke after six
hours, hollow-eyed and echoing inside. I didn't want to speak to
anyone or hear words of comfort.

It was as though someone had died and nobody knew what to
say. All of the girls were grieving; unable to talk about how they felt
because the shared sadness would have been overwhelming. I was
grateful for the fact that nobody mentioned what happened, but I
knew I couldn't hide for ever. Eventually, I would have to put on
my bravest face and confront reality.

At first light, Emma R. began filming some reaction scenes for
the BBC documentary. I didn't know if there'd still be one.

'I really can't believe this has happened,' I said. 'It wasn't meant
to. We have all been to the finish so many times in our minds. We
were so frigging close. We were going to be a day behind Olivier at
Cape Horn and we were going to burn him off on the way home.
We were going to do it. I just can't believe it.'

Next she interviewed Adrienne who, true to form, said: 'We
could have dithered around and made it, coming in behind Olivier
but ahead of where people expected. Instead, we took it as a serious
record attempt and sailed the boat like it should be sailed. We were
up to it, but the rig wasn't.'

I woke in the milky grey light of the God Pod. Adrienne's bunk
was empty. A sound of hammering puzzled me and then I felt my
chest. I took a deep breath and tried to slow my heart.

Had it all been a dream?

One glance at the blank navigation screens removed any doubt.
That's it for me, I thought. I'm never setting foot on a boat

again. I don't want to break records. I don't want to go sailing. I want to curl up in bed and never show my face again. From now on if I need a challenge I'll take up crocheting.

I had been wrong to do this. I had set myself too big a task; bitten off more than I could chew. And all those doubters would now be crowing, 'I told you so.'

They were right. I was wrong.

Tilting my head I saw Sam's legs at the wheel and could hear Sharon whispering. I wanted to hear her voice boom, but she had lost her Kiwi bluster and brightness. I wanted to hear Sam laugh and Helena tell a rude joke in her matter-of-fact accent. I wanted to hear Fred mix up her English words and Emma say, 'Oops' when she spilt something in the galley.

Most of all, I wanted to turn back the clock and start again. Not just 24 hours – I couldn't have stopped that mast coming down – but four years. I wanted to recreate that moment when the idea of winning the Jules Verne trophy first came to me. Then I would bury it so deeply that it never occurred to me again.

The shock hadn't dissipated. It had settled on the boat like a suffocating fog. The 2,000 miles to Chile stretched in front of us like a prison sentence. We were in the middle of nowhere on a floating platform with a 21-foot pole sticking up from the middle. Our once beautiful sails were cut up and hanging limply from the top.

There was not a breath of wind yet still the 'big cat' clawed her way eastwards at 5 knots. She had brought us through the most dangerous ocean in the world, battling conditions known only to a few sailors. Only when the sea picked her up and dashed her down did she finally surrender.

I had changed the watch system because we didn't need three girls on deck any more. From now on we'd sail in pairs, working three hours on and nine hours off. This gave everybody a chance to recuperate.

Adrienne and I barely slept during those few days because important decisions still had to be made. The girls seemed to hide away, cocooned in their sleeping bags. Nobody wanted to talk.

By Friday they began to spend less time sleeping. They emerged on deck or gathered in the God Pod to read their mail. Nobody discussed the race or the record. Occasionally, I felt an arm around my shoulders. 'Are you OK?'

'Yeah. Fine.'

As the girls started taking over, Adrienne and I retreated and slept.

I thought back to 1990 when *Maiden* sailed into Southampton at the end of the Whitbread. An armada of yachts, power boats and dinghies came out to meet us for the final three miles. I had never been so proud or so moved.

From feeling on top of the world I now scrabbled on the floor on my hands and knees. One minute I was right up there, a success story, the next minute I was nothing. The disappointment was almost suffocating. I had failed. I had let my family, friends and supporters down.

That night as I collected the e-mails, I found a message from Ed. He had sent me another poem by one of my favourite writers, Robert Service. It was a lovely gesture and very moving. Maybe Ed had more feminine qualities than I had first suspected.

The Quitter

When you're lost in the Wild, and you're scared as a child,
*   And Death looks you bang in the eye,*
And you're sore as a boil, it's according to Hoyle
*   To cock your revolver and . . . die.*
But the Code of a Man says: 'Fight all you can,'
*   And self-dissolution is barred.*
In hunger and woe, oh, it's easy to blow . . .
*   It's the hell-served-for-breakfast that's hard.*

'You're sick of the game!' Well, now that's a shame.
*   You're young and you're brave and you're bright.*
'You've had a raw deal!' I know — but don't squeal,
*   Buck up, do your damnedest, and fight.*

It's the plugging away that will win you the day,
  So don't be a piker, old pard!
Just draw on your grit; it's so easy to quit.
  It's the keeping-your-chin-up that's hard.

It's easy to cry that you're beaten — and die;
  It's easy to crawfish and crawl;
But to fight and to fight when hope's out of sight —
  Why that's the best game of them all!
And though you come out of each gruelling bout.
  All broken and beaten and scarred,
Just have one more try — it's dead easy to die,
  It's the keeping-on-living that's hard.

—*Robert Service*

When I phoned Trevor I could barely speak. Up until then I'd been holding things together. My voice started to break. Trevor sensed this and tried to do everything he could to make me feel better.

'I can't tell you how proud we all are of you. You were so close to doing it. You shouldn't see it as a failure.'

He was saying all the right things, the bastard. How typical! It made things even worse.

The office had been researching safe harbours in Chile that we might be able to reach and had come up with five possibilities — Valparaiso, Valdivia, Puerto Montt, Punta Arenas and Ushuaia (in Argentina). The final choice would depend upon how far north we could sail before running out of wind.

Unashamed looting and anarchy had broken out in the galley. I caught Emma R. and Sam raiding the food boxes for week seven and onwards. Emma and Sam seemed to have bounced back quickest. That's an advantage of being young and not being burdened by too many expectations or past disappointments.

Sharon was still unusually quiet and withdrawn. Despite our assurances, she still partly blamed herself for what had happened.

Helena had lost her bounce, but not her smile. Fred had inter-
nalised her feelings — a legacy perhaps of being a single-handed
sailor. Miranda seemed as laid-back and relaxed as ever. Miki gave
everybody a lesson on how to be the ultimate professional, even
with a broken heart.

I worried most for Emma W. Her single-mindedness and focus
on the end goal was so extraordinary that the possibility of failure
would never have entered her mind.

When I first collected the e-mails there were eighty-three
messages for us. By the following day there were hundreds, even
though our address was only known by family and friends. Tens of
thousands of messages poured into the office in Hamble — telephone calls, faxes, letters and postcards from around the world. I
had no idea how many people had been following our fortunes.

I began printing some of them out and putting them on the
noticeboard in the cockpit so all the girls could read them. Soon we
ran out of printer ribbons and I had to write them out by hand,
which took hours each day.

I found it awful reading the messages and headlines because
somehow it made the accident seem more indisputable. Nobody
could ignore the fact that the mast had fallen down, but once the
outside world found out, it seemed even more real than before.

Many of the messages were from well-known sailors like Sir
Peter Blake and Grant Dalton, as well as sailmakers, yacht clubs and
marinas. But the vast majority were from ordinary people who had
very little experience of ocean yachting.

Pete Goss wrote: 'We are thinking of you all and share your
disappointment at the dismasting. It could not have been any more
unjust, particularly as you had managed to overcome all the
frustration that had been laid within your path and had without
doubt the record in your hands . . . I hope you're all planning
another crack at the record. If anyone can do it, it is you lot.'

Christian Fevrier wrote a magazine article about the dismasting
with genuine sadness. 'Like most of you, I suppose, I was a bit
incredulous about their challenge. Day after day I was obliged to

change my mind. Their achievement, even though not successful, will stay in the ocean marathon story of one of the greatest sailing challenges of the past years.'

One of the messages that arrived in the office was in French. Translated, it read:

> *The courage, determination and seamanship that you and your team has shown during this Jules Verne Trophy attempt does not deserve this horrible dismasting. We share your sadness. You have just completed a magnificent journey around the bottom of the world. Courage, respect and friendship, from Olivier de Kersauson and Yves Pouillaude [his navigator].*

Despite all the kind words and messages of good will, I fought to keep my head above water. Everything had gone in an instant – my future, all my plans. I'd been tempting fate to plan for the future – I know that now. I was going to break the record and then move smoothly on to the next project. I wanted to put together an all-female entry for 'The Race' – a non-stop circumnavigation of the world involving the biggest, fastest multihulls ever built to celebrate the Millennium.

God knows what I'd do now.

I had never felt so helpless or vulnerable in my life. Failure had put me in a position of weakness and undermined all of my past successes. For the first time in my life I had failed to achieve something that I regarded as important.

That's it! That's me done! No more ocean racing. It won't happen again.

Yet even as I said these things to myself, I couldn't block out the fact that we were so bloody close. So, so close.

I kept asking myself questions. What could we have done differently? How much would it cost to refit the catamaran? Would it be better to build a new boat?

I lay in my bunk that night thinking of Ernest Shackleton's first expedition to reach the South Pole. Shackleton's triumph was in the fact that he didn't push on the final ninety-seven miles when his party came so close to reaching its goal. The honour of being the first man to reach the South Pole was within his grasp but he turned back because he valued the lives of his men more highly than personal glory.

They would have died for him – he was that sort of leader – but Shackleton had the courage to say, 'No, we are turning back so that we will live to come and do this again with everything we have learned.'

Before Shackleton could organise another expedition, the South Pole was reached by Norwegian explorer Roald Amundsen. Five weeks later, a British expedition led by Robert Falcon Scott also made it, but Scott's entire party died on the return journey.

Shackleton did go back. In the summer of 1914, he set off aboard the *Endurance* with the goal of crossing the Antarctic overland. More than a year later, and still half a continent away from his intended base, the *Endurance* was trapped in ice and eventually crushed. For five months Shackleton and his crew survived on drifting ice floes in one of the most savage regions of the world before they finally reached a small island off the Antarctic Penin-sula. Shackleton left most of his crew there and sailed almost 800 miles in one of the ship's lifeboats to South Georgia to alert rescuers. Every member of the twenty-eight-man expedition survived.

Everything about Shackleton's life seemed to be an attempt to learn from his mistakes. He was never too proud to admit that he was fallible and he regarded failure as simply another lesson learned. I once dared to believe that I had some things in common with this great man – even if they were only his faults. I had done him a great disservice. He wouldn't have crawled away with his tail between his legs. Nor would he have felt so sorry for himself or worried about what other people thought of his failure.

I knew what he would have done. I rolled over in my bunk and looked across at Adrienne, who was still diligently writing the ship's log.

'You know that we have to do this again?' I said.

'Yes, I know.'

'Bummer, isn't it?'

'Yeah.'

For the first time in four days I laughed. It didn't come a moment too soon. The mourning would go on, but at least I was starting to deal with the situation and refocus.

Dozens of questions began filling my head. Where can I find the money again? What will it cost? Who could I get to design a new boat? When can it be ready?

The words 'next time' now crept into the answers. 'Next time we'll do more light-weather testing on the sails. Next time we'll take stronger runner blocks and more spares.'

I couldn't walk away from this. I had never given up on anything in my life. If I did it this time then nothing would be the same – the farmhouse in Wales, my horses, my dogs, my life . . .

This wasn't the end of the challenge – it was only halfway. Olivier had made seven attempts before he took and captured the Jules Verne Trophy. Peter Blake had taken two attempts. Nobody had ever succeeded on their first attempt.

None of these thoughts gave me any comfort. When I looked at the mountain of work that lay ahead, I asked myself: Can I really go through it all again? God Almighty, why couldn't we have done it the first time?

I heard shouting and laughter from on deck. Hannah had put a sign outside the God Pod saying, 'Normality will be resumed as soon as we know what normal is.'

The human spirit is amazing. My crew was amazing.

The decision had been made to head for Puerto Montt. It would take another ten days to reach the Chilean coast as we continued crawling eastwards. Each hour blurred into the next. Time no longer had any meaning.

Charlotte called and announced excitedly, 'The RAF is coming to find you on Friday.'

'What do you mean they're coming to "find" us? We're not lost.'

'They're in Chile for an air show. A newspaper has arranged with them to fly out and see you. They want to publish a picture in the paper on Sunday of the jury rig and all of you waving from the deck.'

I didn't like the sound of this. To begin with, how was it being portrayed? We had fought bloody hard to get ourselves out of trouble and I didn't want a photo opportunity to be misconstrued as a rescue attempt. We didn't need rescuing.

'Oh, no it's nothing like that. The RAF is calling it a training exercise.'

I still wasn't convinced.

'Do you want them to bring you anything?' asked Charlotte.

'We don't *need* anything.'

'I know. But they can drop you off some goodies like magazines and newspapers, just to brighten up your days.'

I thought she was joking and told her we were running low on beer and crisps.

Four days later, we woke to a wet, misty and grey Friday. The RAF Nimrod radioed when it was still 500 miles away. The weather didn't look promising for a drop. The extremely low cloud and mist had cut visibility to only half a mile. The sea state was two metres, with the wind dying off in a pre-frontal lull. The Nimrod would have to drop below 300 feet to get beneath the cloud.

Emma W. and Sam had made a banner that read, 'Thanks RAF' and tied it to the forward netting. We had also spent the previous few days discussing how we could pick up the containers. I gave us less than 50 per cent chance of pulling it off, particularly when I saw the swell. If the catamaran lifted on a wave at the last moment, the canisters would simply slide by us. There could be no turning back to get them.

'Hannah this is your operation. How do you want to do it?'

'OK, we've already established the size and weight of the

canisters. They're bright orange cylinders, with no handles and weigh 200 lb. each.'

'No handles?' said Sharon. 'That's a bit stupid.'

'It's because of how they're launched,' I explained. 'They're being shot out of the torpedo tubes so they can't have anything on them that could snag.'

Hannah continued: 'We have to get them the first time. Even when we drop the sails we'll be doing three or four knots.'

I turned to Emma R. 'The RAF wanted feedback on these containers and how we pick them up. They've never filmed a drop in a real-life survival situation with a container coming out of the plane and landing in the water. They want us to film it – that's part of the deal.'

Hannah explained the plan. The Nimrod would drop the cylinders 300 yards ahead of us and we would aim to sail directly over them. We would keep the sails up as long as possible to give us steerage and drop them at the last moment, while we were still moving forward.

'Hopefully, if we gauge the wind and drift correctly, we'll ease directly over the top of them,' said Hannah.

'That's going to be really difficult,' said Miki.

'That's why they're going to drop a smoke flare which will give us the wind direction and drift. We'll try to steer the boat over it.'

Hannah had rigged up a huge net along the back of the boat hanging from the aft netting. It had a pulley system that would scoop up the cylinders when they floated between the hulls.

Soon everyone had been given her task. Hannah would control the net, Helena had the wheel, Miki would let down the main, while Sharon and Fred dropped the headsail. Sam and Emma W. stayed on the aft netting to grab the canisters and I was to run back and work the winches with the pulley attached, to help lift them. Emma R. and Miranda would help with the winches in between filming and taking pictures.

Adrienne stayed on the VHF trying to remember her radio

protocol. The RAF insisted on calling us Romeo Sierra Alpha (RSA), sounding very matter-of-fact and businesslike.

When still half an hour away, the pilot announced, 'Romeo Sierra Alpha, this is RAF Nimrod, we have you on radar.'

Every so often Ed came on the radio, sounding like a little kid on the adventure of a lifetime. I could imagine his face lit up in awe. Later he announced, 'That was the best day of my entire life' and then wisely added the proviso, 'apart from when we had the children of course.'

The Nimrod had to refuel in mid-air to reach us and a very excited Ed gave us a running commentary on the operation. We were all nervous, none more so than Emma R., who felt as though the success of the entire mission depended upon her being able to capture the drop on film. I tried not to remind her.

Already I had decided that the training must have been for us rather than the RAF. They had the easy job. We had to pull two heavy cylinders with no handles and nice smooth surfaces on to a catamaran doing 4 knots, with no sails or engines in a three-metre swell.

With ten minutes to go, we all took our places. At 16.40 silence descended on the boat as we waited for Adrienne to update us.

'Three minutes away.'

'Which direction? Which direction?' asked Emma.

Adrienne indicated the starboard side of the mast.

With thirty seconds to go, the pilot began a countdown. We had the VHF switched up on deck and listened in total silence. With fifteen seconds to go, I thought they must have been looking at something else on radar. Why couldn't we hear them?

'Ten . . . nine . . . eight . . .'

Shouldn't we be able to see them?

Suddenly, I heard a low hum that I could feel deep in my stomach. The Nimrod appeared from behind our staysail and out of the mist 150 feet above the water. They were so close I thought they were going to take the rest of the mast.

All of us screamed. The shock was amazing and the emotion

indescribable. I will remember it all my life. This huge monster roared past us looking beautiful, just beautiful.

'Romeo Sierra Alpha, Romeo Sierra Alpha, we have visual contact with you. You're looking good.'

Then Ed came on to the radio even more excited than we were. 'Oh, my God, I can't believe it, we came out of the clouds and you were just there. So close. Amazing. Just amazing.'

The Nimrod circled several times, measuring the wind angle and direction. We were relaying details about the sea state, in between waving and cheering. The first smoke flare arced from the underbelly of the jet and splashed into the sea 300 yards in front and slightly downwind of us.

Helena steered us towards it and we managed to have it drift perfectly between the twin hulls. The Nimrod came from behind and flew directly over us, very low. I could see the flashes of cameras in the windows. The first canister plunged into the water from 150 feet and almost disintegrated on impact. The top came off and it filled with water. I leapt all over the mainsail, pulling it down, as Miki called from the bow, directing Helena.

'OK, OK, you're fine. Come down a bit. Come down a bit.'

Everything went smoothly, with the canister floated between the hulls, until the last moment, when it looked as though it would slide between the port hull and Hannah's net. Emma W. and Sam lay on their stomachs, reached down and grabbed it. Others hung on to their legs and then hauled the sodden canister aboard.

Adrienne told the flight crew to drop the next canister a little further upwind. Even so, it almost got away from us, escaping the safety between the hulls and bobbing down the starboard side of the boat. We were 10 feet away, with Hannah trying to reach it with the boat hook. Suddenly, Sharon launched herself off the boat. I looked up to see her feet leaving the deck and grabbed hold of her trousers at the last instant. It was the only thing that stopped her disappearing over the side. Hannah managed to get a boat hook on to the cylinder and we pulled it aboard.

Complete success.

The Nimrod dipped its wings as a final farewell, and the captain, Wing Commander Sid Brown, came on the radio. 'This is RAF Nimrod departing for Santiago, I hope you have a good and uneventful journey back to Chile.'

'Nimrod this is *Royal & SunAlliance*, thank you very very much from all of us down here and if any of you are still there when we get in, then maybe we'll have a couple of beers together.'

'I'd be delighted to have a couple of beers with you.'

Inside the canisters we found 72 cans of beer and a huge bag of crisps. Charlotte had taken me literally. There were also magazines, newspapers, press cuttings, a game of Trivial Pursuit and a Lonely Planet *Guide to Chile*.

It had been so long since we had touched alcohol that none of us could manage even a whole can of beer. Cheap dates, or what?

By Monday, 30 March we were less than 450 miles from the Chilean coast. A tugboat, the *Rum Allipen*, had spent two days steaming towards us, having left Puerto Montt on Friday. It was due to rendezvous with us at first light on Tuesday morning.

After fifty-five days without seeing another face, or even a sight of land, it would be strange not to be on our own any more. It was going to be a shame. Even though we hadn't broken the record and we'd been stuck on a slow boat going home, I had to admit to having enjoyed the peace of the past few days.

At the same time I was looking forward to seeing some familiar faces waiting for us in Chile. Martin Booth, the marketing manager of Royal & SunAlliance, had flown across, along with Robin Courage, Charlotte and Ed.

The tow could not have come at a better time. The wind had been dying all night and coming aft. We were making less than 4 knots.

In the stillness before dawn, Adrienne talked to the tugboat on the SSB and VHF radios. As the sun began rising, Miranda spotted our tug silhouetted against the distant glow. It was still a small dot on the horizon. With perfect timing, the wind died to the faintest breeze as the tug neared. We ghosted along, feeling the warmth of each other's company and reflecting upon what lay ahead for each of us.

Adrienne would go back to her job in Australia – trying to persuade her bosses not to sack her when she wanted to do the Jules Verne again.

Emma Richards and Sam were talking about sailing two-handed and trying out for the British Olympic team. Sharon had encouraged them. She planned to go back on the dinghy sailing circuit to prepare for Sydney 2000.

Hannah had vowed never to set foot on another ocean racing yacht as long as she lived. She would go back to Bahrain and teach dinghy sailing in the nice warm waters of the Gulf.

Emma W. talked about going to the Caribbean with her boyfriend and then emigrating to Australia. Fred had decided to do the Figaro single-handed circuit and would have no trouble getting sponsorship after her exposure in France.

Miranda would return to Italy and her boyfriend Max. She'd go back on the J24 sailing circuit and slip so easily into the lifestyle that none of the locals would believe she wasn't raised on pasta and Chianti.

Helena had talked to me about helping set up the next project and Miki was going to take a long, long holiday somewhere warm, where she could forget about being wet, cold and miserable. She might even spend the rest of her life deciding what to do next.

As the tug came nearer, I had an awful feeling of impending reality. This was it! Much as I wanted to get back, another part of me wanted to stay out here for ever. I wanted to tell the tug: Go back. We're OK. We want to stay here a little longer. I don't want to get to land. I want to stay with these people who are now such close friends. At home we'll all go our separate ways and I may not see them for months or years. If I go back now, I'll have to answer questions. It's going to be the end of a dream. I don't want to wake up.

The large orange tug arrived alongside us and I saw the grizzled unshaven faces of the Chilean crew. They gawped in amazement.

They had absolutely no idea of what they were coming out to tow and the 92-foot catamaran looked more like an oil rig than a yacht. Even more astounding was the sight of eleven women standing on the deck.

'They're not doing anything. They're just standing there gawping,' said Helena, as the tug circled us slowly.

'They're frightened of us,' said Miki.

'They either think we're from Mars, or all their Christmases have come at once,' I suggested.

The men pulled out cameras and began taking pictures. Nobody at home was going to believe them unless they had proof. Eventually, they got the tow-rope ready and threw us a line. Hannah hitched it on and Adrienne signalled by radio that we were all set.

The rope pulled taut and the catamaran eased off. The 'big cat' was so fast and smooth through the water that she kept overtaking the tow-line and surfing up behind the tug. I put someone on the wheel to make sure that we didn't collide.

The tug steamed towards Darwin Channel at a top speed of 10 knots. The captain explained to Adrienne that there was some nasty weather coming. None of the crew had been this far out and all of them were nervous. They wanted to get us into the fjords as quickly as possible.

By late afternoon the following day we entered the first of the fjords. The mountains rose dramatically on either side of us and we navigated the narrow channels between them. I sat on the boom watching the stunning scenery and smelling damp earth for the first time in nearly eight weeks. Penguins swam alongside us, riding the bow waves.

The channel opened quite suddenly into a huge bay with glaciers sweeping down to the shore. The water was mirror-calm and reflected the scenery in perfect detail.

The tugboat captain pulled into a bay just short of Puerto Montt and we spent the evening there. I had a long chat with the girls about the plans for the morning. Charlotte and Ed would bring out fresh clothes for us. The TV crews and reporters would be kept away until we neared the dock. A press conference would follow.

'Everyone will want to smother us at the moment,' I told them. 'They'll want to take us under their wings and protect us. We are going to hate that, but we have to let them. We have had time to get over what happened out there, but they are just starting. Seeing us is the first step towards them dealing with their disappointment.'

Despite these words, our fear of being overtaken and separated by events on land had become almost physical. Helena suggested turning back and was only half joking. We even contemplated whether we could sail back to England with the jury rig and our remaining supplies. Would they try to catch us and bring us back?

My sleep that night was full of strange dreams. I woke to find that Sam had put muesli out and made tea and coffee. The sun rose over the snow-capped peaks, putting on a staggering display. Slowly it leaked down into the hills, revealing the neat square fields and farmhouses surrounded by hedges. South America was nothing like I expected.

The dock was packed with people waving and cheering. Chilean dancers dipped and whirled as a band played. The tug had come alongside us. Its crew were all wearing T-shirts we'd given them.

Untying the ropes, we drifted the last few feet. I took a deep breath, pinned a smile on my face and turned towards the crowd. Could they see me crying inside?

One, two, three steps and I set foot ashore almost exactly sixty days after we crossed the starting line.

TWENTY-SIX

THE week in Chile was a strange time. I felt caught between the end of one chapter and the beginning of the next. I don't often have the time to contemplate the past. Normally my life rolls straight from one event to the next.

When we finally flew into Heathrow, I was glad the limbo had ended. Now I could begin rebuilding.

The thought of having to do it all again filled me with dread. For the first time in my life I didn't look forward to the challenge with excitement. Perhaps, in a small corner of my soul, I didn't want to go through it again. Deadlines, rejections and mountainous debt seem to go hand in hand with everything I chose to do.

After a press conference at a hotel near Heathrow, I drove home with Trevor. Only when I dumped my bags in the hall did I realise how much I wanted to be home and safe. I am the luckiest person in the world when it comes to family. I guess some people would find it bizarre for a thirty-six-year-old to have her mother and brother living with her, but to me it felt perfectly natural.

All the family was there to welcome me home – Trevor, Mum, Uncle Arthur and Aunty Edna, Graeme, Gregor, Kerry and little Kaia. There were also friends waiting for me like David Tudor, Damian and Claire, my wonderful PA.

After months at sea, adjusting to life on land can be quite difficult. For weeks afterwards, I used to wake in the middle of the night and start getting dressed to go on watch. Then I'd realise I was home and crawl back into bed. I also caught myself stowing things in the kitchen so they wouldn't move around if the house suddenly nose-dived. And every time I passed the toilet I wondered if I should 'go now just in case'.

When I looked back on the race, there weren't too many things I would have done differently. Perhaps gone a little easier and taken fewer risks. It's very easy to get addicted to high speeds and long daily runs; taking risks that you swore you would never take like dropping too far south in the Southern Ocean or nudging closer to a low pressure system looking for more breeze.

There are two great secrets to winning the Jules Verne Trophy and neither has anything to do with weathering the horrors of the raging fifties or having a boat with a top speed of 40 knots.

The first is to improve the lowest speed of the boat in light airs and therefore increase its overall average. The second is knowing how hard to push the boat without it breaking.

After a month of PR commitments, I began looking at how I'd raise the money to try again. Despite earlier suggestions, Royal & SunAlliance wasn't interested in sponsoring us again. The company had already taken offers to buy the 'big cat' as we were still limping towards Chile.

The girls soon spread across the world, each with her own sailing commitments or career. Once I'd raised the money, I'd get them back together again. Helena had volunteered to help me. Initially, we planned to put together an all-female entry for 'The Race' – a non-stop circumnavigation of the world in January 2001. Giant multihulls were being designed, some of them 150 feet long.

Raising the money wouldn't be easy, but then again, it never is. Most of the major companies had already allocated their Millennium budgets, but I refused to be disheartened.

To support myself during the search for sponsorship, I began giving motivational talks again. I didn't go back to Will Carling's company. I felt it was standing still and wasting opportunities because the speakers tended to be giving one-off talks rather than structuring them to an overall plan. The driving force behind Insights was Mike Noel-Smith, who had some great ideas for seminars and training weekends. Mike had become frustrated with not being able to put them into practice and finally resigned in July 1998. When I heard the news I quickly contacted him with a proposition. We'd set up a new company – TEAM (Tracy Edwards Associates Motivation).

Wonderful speakers such as Sebastian Coe, David Gower, Rebecca Stevens (the mountaineer) and Mary Peters were happy to come on board. I gave Mike the freedom to create projects and plan seminars around our motivational speakers. In particular he designed tasks and puzzles that illustrated the main points of each talk, such as teamwork, leadership and communication.

For example, he invented dozens of very clever and amusing practical and cerebral problems that could be used at seminars to teach people how to co-operate and listen to each other.

The beauty of using sports people is obvious. If a speaker is introduced as an expert on teamwork or communication, people usually turn off. But if they have the chance to hear Rebecca talking about climbing Mount Everest, or Sebastian Coe describing winning Olympic gold, they sit up and take notice. The message is brought to life and people remember it.

I loved the new challenge of running a company. All the planning and management skills that I'd discovered during *Maiden* and *Royal & SunAlliance* now helped me to forge a career on land.

The deadline for competing in 'The Race' passed in October 1998. It didn't worry me overly. I was more interested in the Jules Verne Trophy because it felt like unfinished business.

Early in the New Year I talked to the girls and we agreed to put the project aside until after the Millennium, when fewer events would be competing for attention. This also gave me more time to concentrate on the new company.

As always, I'd managed to find new challenges to replace those that I had fulfilled or put on hold. Even so, I still questioned whether my ambition was a comfort or a curse.

I cried when I finished reading Rowland Huntsford's account of Shackleton's death. The great explorer died of a heart attack in South Georgia, 8,000 miles from home. Partly my tears were because this frightened me. Shackleton always had the craving to go back and challenge himself in spite of the dangers and close calls. If he was at home for long he grew restless and organised new expeditions. He could never be satisfied and say, 'I've done enough. I'm happy now.'

Was that going to be me? I wondered. Would I ever be satisfied?

I kept thinking back to Suzy's mother and the tarot cards. Unless I changed the last card, I'd never be happy, she said. I'd always be striving for something else.

I didn't have an answer. I only knew that if I thought about the possibility of *not* going back sailing, it felt as though someone had grabbed my heart in a fist of iron. And if I let myself think, even for a minute, that I might not ride the waves in the Southern Ocean again, or smile as an albatross wheeled above me, I couldn't breathe properly.

Five years earlier, in Wales, I had learned to stop fighting the urge to go sailing. It was a part of me that I couldn't change. And in the Southern Ocean I'd learned that it was OK to fail because how you handle that failure makes you the person that you are.

That's why I made myself a promise in my diary. 'Next time we shall succeed. Defeat will only come if we cannot get out there again.'

M y life has changed beyond comprehension since I wrote those words. The main architect of that change will be three months old tomorrow.

Mackenna Lily Jean Foy Edwards (what a grand-sounding name for such a small human being) is now sitting in a high chair near the kitchen door experimenting with a new gurgling sound that she invented this morning.

Let me tell you how she arrived. I worked up until the day beforehand. There were talks to give and meetings to attend. At the new house I was still unpacking boxes and hanging pictures. I had tons of energy and Gregor and Trevor kept trying to slow me down. We decorated the nursery first, painting the walls a sexless apricot colour because I didn't want any of my friends guessing my secret and buying pink dresses and booties.

The rest of the house needs a lot of work, but that can wait. I'm just relieved to have found a bigger house, with a separate cottage for Mum and enough land for a pony.

Being pregnant felt strange and wonderful. Being so short, I'd always imagined that I'd look like a Weeble. Remember those adverts? 'Weebles wobble but they don't fall down!'

My other fear was that I'd lose jobs as the year wore on because companies didn't want to ask a heavily pregnant woman to come and give a talk. Thankfully, none of this happened. At eight months I was so tiny that I stood at a cocktail party having a conversation with someone who didn't realise I was pregnant. At that very moment, Mackenna was head-butting my bladder and seemed to be training for the synchronised swimming championships.

I loved being pregnant. I would cradle my stomach in my arms and wonder what my daughter would look like. Would she be like me?

Suzy came to visit and brought a bag of clothes.

'Now that is from Jo from *Maiden*, but previously it came from Claire from *Maiden*, who inherited it from Sally from *Maiden*.'

It was a complete *Maiden* hand-me-down.

I phoned Sally. 'Thanks for starting the chain of hand-me-downs.'

'Well, I certainly didn't think it would end up with you,' she said, laughing.

As always, I'd arranged Mackenna's arrival with military precision. Gregor had the task of getting me to the hospital. Meanwhile Kerry would come and keep an eye on Mum. Fi was to be my birth partner and also Mackenna's godmother, along with Suzy.

A week before Christmas I was at the house on my own. Trevor had left for his new life in Antigua the week before.

At about midnight, I woke with what seemed to be stomach cramps and then went back to sleep again. At three in the morning I woke again and realised that it wasn't stomach cramps. I didn't want to call Gregor if it was a false alarm so I waited until six. By then the contractions were ten minutes apart. I called the St Margaret's Hospital and the staff suggested I come in. I really couldn't believe it was finally happening. After months of longing for her arrival, what was about to happen to me stared me in the face and I was seized with an almost uncontrollable urge to cross my legs and stay pregnant. However, I called Gregor. He drove from Reading to the house in just over ten minutes – breaking all sorts of laws and records. I'd packed my bag only a day earlier.

As we reached the motorway the contractions were down to seven minutes and were a lot more intense. I phoned Fi and put her on standby.

'There's going to be a lot of hanging around,' I told her. 'I'll call you when I get to the hospital.'

We arrived at St Margaret's by 7.30 a.m. As I walked into my room the contractions began coming every five minutes and became painful.

By nine o'clock I was on my hands and knees, screaming blue murder every four minutes. Nobody could understand why I was in so much pain. Normally the last hour of the birth is the most distressing.

I could see Jan, the midwife, getting edgy. I was only a centimetre dilated and still had a long way to go. I have a very high pain threshold, yet I was climbing the walls.

Eventually Jan asked: 'Have you ever had a back injury, or broken your pelvis or hip?'

'A back injury,' I told her, through gritted teeth.

'That explains it.'

At this point Fi hadn't arrived and Gregor sat in the corner of my room wishing that he were somewhere completely different. I wouldn't let him leave.

At one point a nurse asked if I wanted any breakfast.

'Not for me, thanks,' I said.

From behind a newspaper, Gregor piped up, 'Oh, I'll have some toast and tea.'

Jan and the nursing staff looked at him as if he were the devil incarnate. They assumed that Gregor was my partner and expected him to be down on the floor next to me, rubbing my back and offering support.

As he munched a piece of toast, he set the record straight. 'I'm her cousin, not her partner.'

'Oh, I'm so sorry, dear,' said Jan. 'What a nice cousin you are.'

Suddenly, he was flavour of the month.

By midday, the contractions were every two or three minutes.

The gas and pethidine that I had sworn I wouldn't have, made no difference to the pain. I couldn't believe that I could live through so much agony. My senses were incredibly acute. I noticed every little facial expression and glance between the midwife and my doctor. They were concerned. A foetal monitor had been placed on the baby's head.

'Do you want an epidural?' asked my doctor.

'Yes. I'm not going to last much longer like this.'

Gregor opened the door. Although doubled up in pain, I managed to glance up. My entire family and Fi were waiting in the corridor. They'd been listening to me effing and blinding for three hours. Fi took one arm and Jan the other.

'You are going to have to sit perfectly still for five minutes so I can deliver the epidural,' said the anaesthetist.

'How can I possibly sit still? I'm going to have a contraction. It's impossible.'

'If you don't sit still, I won't be able to give you an epidural.'

'OK. OK. I'll sit still.'

At that point I would have handed over my house, my car, all my worldly possessions and my wages for the rest of my life to this man, as long as he took away the pain.

Jan held my right hand and Fi my left. I had to squeeze their hands but not move as the contractions came. Fi has an abiding memory of me growling at her and grinding her knuckles together.

The pain disappeared and life became wonderful. I lay back and chatted away. Unfortunately, the doctor checked me again and found I was only three centimetres dilated.

'Something isn't quite right,' he said. 'You're too far gone in the contraction stage.'

'I feel like I want to push.'

'Don't push.'

'But I really feel like I want to push.'

'Try not to.'

It was two in the afternoon and I'd been in labour for fourteen hours.

The monitor on the baby's head kept flashing up the heart rate. The doctor made the mistake of telling me what it shouldn't drop below. As I chatted to Fi my eyes kept watch on the monitor. Her heartbeat suddenly dropped from 140 to 90.

I panicked. The doctor arrived and checked me again.

'She's really trying to be born and you're not ready. I'd really like you to think about a Caesarean.'

He knew how much I wanted to have a natural birth. I always imagined that in such a situation I would argue. Instead, I agreed immediately. I didn't give a damn about anything else except making sure my baby was OK. I didn't care if they had to explode her out of the top of my head. Just get her out and make her safe.

Everything happened in a rush. I was taken to the operating theatre and the doctor explained exactly what was going to happen. The epidural had deadened everything from my waist down. I couldn't tell if my knees were down or up.

I found it amazing that I could be awake and conscious through the whole operation. Fi was down at the business end, giving me a running commentary.

'Oh, they have cut you open. Isn't that interesting? There isn't as much blood as I thought.'

'You're weird,' I told her.

I could feel them rummaging around inside me, but no pain. It was as though they were looking for something. Where is it? It has to be in here somewhere.

Suddenly the expression changed on Fi's face. She started crying and I felt myself start to go.

Suddenly in a rush, there she was. A tiny, perfect, wonderful little creature. They showed Mackenna to me before they cleaned her up and checked her out and I finally lost it. She was absolutely beautiful. Fi was crying and I was crying. I couldn't believe that anything could beat crossing the finish line first. I was wrong.

I'll never forget hearing her cry for the first time. From that moment I knew my life was never going to be the same again. People had told me, but I hadn't believed them. Now it became real. As they stitched me up, Fi took her up to the room for her first feed. Then I followed her up and they gently manoeuvred me into bed.

With my family looking on, Fi put Mackenna in my arms. She was so tiny at six and a half pounds, with a night-dress that was too big for her. She lay in the crook of my arm, gazing up at my face with absolute wonder. I could see her thinking, 'Oh, wow, so this is what you look like on the outside.'

I thought I was going to be scared of that first hour. I thought I'd be embarrassed because I wouldn't know what to do. Instead, somewhere deep inside me, all the maternal and nurturing instincts kicked in. It was so all-consuming that I wanted to explode with happiness.

Her names were chosen in advance. Mackenna after her great-great-great-great-grandmother from Co. Leitrim in Ireland. I chose Lily and Jean because of my grandmothers and Foy is an old family name, which had been passed down but had missed a couple of generations. I decided to revive the tradition.

And so we finished with Mackenna Lily Jean Foy Edwards. Now there's the sort of name that could belong to a rock star, a Prime Minister, a showjumper, a sailor, or a housewife. It doesn't matter as long as she's happy.

We left hospital in time for Christmas. On the big day we lay in bed together, snuggled up and staring into each other's eyes. I kept telling myself, 'I know someone who is only eight days old. How amazing is that!'

I took Mackenna into the nursery to get her changed. All her clothes were so big I had to roll up the sleeves. Holding her up at the nursery window, we looked out at the bare trees, shrouded in mist. There were puddles on the farm track and squirrels darting through the dead leaves. Suddenly, as if on cue, it began to snow. It was as though somebody up there had said, 'Here's a little scene for you to remember for the rest of your life.'

I started crying. My hormones have been playing havoc. Looking down at Mack's face I knew several things for certain. The first was that she would never love me as much as I love her. The second was that I have never before in my life loved someone as much as I love her. That's a scary thought.

So, will I ever sail the Southern Ocean again, or dodge icebergs in the North Atlantic? Will the phosphorous trails disappear behind other yachts and will the moon cast the sea silver for other eyes?

Nobody is forcing me to retire. For years I've watched male sailors hugging their children goodbye on the dock and disappearing for months on end. Now I have to decide whether what I do is too dangerous for me to continue.

When I first heard that the mountaineer Alison Hargreaves had died on K2, my first thoughts were for her two children. How could she have done that? How could she have put herself in that much danger when she had two little people relying on her? Now I have to make the same choice. To win the Jules Verne Trophy is like walking a tightrope between life and death. You must constantly juggle speed and safety, safety and speed.

Some of the conversations that Adrienne and I had during the challenge seem positively insane when I think back on them. But you can't really understand what it's like until you're out there. We reached a point where we asked each other, 'Do we really want to live without the record?' I look back on this and think, 'Was I mad? Had I completely lost the plot?'

Mountaineers and explorers must go through very similar moments. This is how boundaries are pushed back and records are broken. If we had won the Jules Verne Trophy it would have been because of this attitude.

Now that I have Mackenna, can I ever have the same belief again? I can't sail with a bunch of girls who I know can break the record unless I am willing to take the same risks as they are. Otherwise I might deny them their chance.

Managing is the logical next step for me anyway whatever I decide. Each generation moves up and new blood arrives. This could be a good thing. Without my influence on the boat, the dynamics would be different and a new chemistry would emerge.

Something amazing might happen. One of the girls who didn't shine before might suddenly move up and fill a place.

At the same time, I think I'll do a good job as shore manager. For one thing, I know the girls. I've also seen the pitfalls and mistakes that can be made. I hope that I'm big enough to be able to step back and give them the freedom they need if that's what I decide.

When I watch the videos of *Maiden* and *Royal & SunAlliance* I still get emotional. I haven't forgotten the bad times, although sometimes it's difficult to remember just how tough it was. I feel strangely removed; as if I'm watching somebody else battling the horrors of the Southern Ocean.

EPILOGUE

I HAVE a new challenge – as a single mother raising a daughter. I know that might sound hackneyed, but I truly believe it.

I still worry that there is not a father around for Mack – another person to indulge her life and love her as I do. Mum always told me how difficult it was after Dad died, raising her children alone. Now I see why.

I'd like to find someone nice, who wants both of us and will be our rock. I'm a lot more relaxed now about finding a partner. In the past I looked for someone who would fit in with *my* life. Now I know I'm looking for fifty-fifty. I'm also more patient and less judgmental. I don't have the obsession for sailing that has ruined past relationships and I'm more willing to compromise.

Perhaps, as Suzy's mother always told me, I've changed the last tarot card. Maybe I've reached the point where I can say, 'I have done enough. I have achieved as much as anyone could expect or desire.'

FURTHER INFORMATION

To find out more about Tracy's motivational, teambuilding and leadership interactive seminars, log on to the Tracy Edwards Associates Motivation (TEAM) website at www.tracyedwards.co.uk, and email through the site.

INDEX

Price, Megan 245
Price, Sally 245
Pritchard, Bev 249, 250, 253, 254, 255
Pritchard, Leighton 253
Puerto Banus 87
Puerto Montt 391, 395, 400, 402
Punch (T's dog) 143, 145
Punta Arenas 391
Punta del Este, Uruguay 168, 170, 172, 176, 207–10
Purley 2, 3, 7, 14, 17, 27, 110, 128, 131, 144
Purves, Libby 221

Quentin, Caroline 20

'Race, The' (a non-stop circumnavigation of the world, January 2001) 393, 406
Race Week 94
Race Committee, Punta del Este 208
Rachmaninov, Sergey 8
Radford, Arthur 86, 113–14
Reading 2, 6, 7, 49, 61, 63, 109, 110, 248, 292, 296, 297, 335
Reena (sail loft owner) 90
Rees, Edward 48
Rees, George 52, 60, 62
Rees, Jill 246, 255
Reilly, Dawn 159, 171, 177, 188, 194, 197, 205, 207, 208, 209, 211–12, 216, 260
Rhossili Down 246, 258, 310
Rice, Bob 285, 287, 288, 296, 297, 309
Rice, Caitlin 287
Richards, Emma 278, 279–80, 302, 305, 306, 312, 316, 318, 323–4, 331, 333, 334, 336, 338, 339, 340, 356, 358, 369, 370, 380, 383, 384, 385, 388, 389, 391, 397, 398, 401
Robert (Kovalam's engineer) 66, 67
Rocky (Annie's boyfriend) 98
Rothmans 165, 193
Round Britain and Ireland record 278
Round Isle of Wight record 278
Route of Discovery Race 160–63, 166
Royal & SunAlliance 416
    the crew 277–81, 283, 289, 293–4

Lady Endeavour renamed 282
attempt at the transatlantic speed record 284–7
the Jules Verne Trophy 301–3, 305–27, 329–54, 355–79
Australia to New Zealand speed sailing record broken 355–7
race abandoned after loss of mast 379–81
tea party on the crippled yacht 384–5
new mast made 385–6
RAF drops supplies 395–400
towed to Puerto Montt 400–403
Royal & SunAlliance (RSA) 274, 275, 276, 281, 291, 296, 314, 400, 406
Royal Air Force (RAF) 208, 395–400
Royal Bank of Scotland 271, 273
Royal Geographical Society 320
Royal Jordanian Airlines 155, 156, 163, 183, 193, 200–201, 214
Royal Navy 114, 166
Royal Southern Yacht Club, Hamble 152–3, 161, 228
Royal Yacht Squadron 155
Rucanor 168, 171, 172, 176–9, 182, 184, 186, 188, 195, 196, 197, 203, 211, 215, 217, 218
Rum Allipen (tugboat) 400
Russell, Claire 159, 179, 180, 188, 194, 204, 205, 206, 216, 280, 410

St Andrew's boys' school 14, 22
St Katharine's Dock, London 229–31
St Margaret's Hospital, Windsor xi, 410, 411
St Thomas 89
St Tropez 99
Salmon, Bob 102, 113
San Diego, California 265, 269
Sandy (Greek friend) 62–3
Santo Domingo, Dominican Republic 160, 162
Santos (Greek waiter) 59
Sarah (a school bully) 26, 27
Sarah, Duchess of York 141, 154–6, 163, 166, 167, 168, 172, 173, 231–2
Sardinia 98, 99